Distributed Storage in Practice

IEEE Press
445 Hoes Lane
Piscataway, NJ 08854

Endorsements

If data is the gold mine of the digital age, then this book serves as your comprehensive alchemy guide. It systematically elucidates the cutting-edge technical framework spanning from storage coding theory to system implementation, offering a cross-generational technical solution for the efficient storage and circulation of data. The technical system established in the book not only addresses current demands but also strategically envisions digital infrastructure development over the next 30–50 years, ensuring that your data gold mine remains efficiently exploitable and continues to deliver long-term value growth in the future.

— by Prof. Weimin Zheng

In the era of data deluge, storage coding serves as the most reliable "safe box" for data. This book, for the first time, deeply integrates the optimal storage coding theory based on network coding with binary encoding and decoding operations, innovatively proposing practical erasure codes that achieve the optimal boundary of encoding and decoding. Furthermore, it combines emerging blockchain and quantum technologies to construct a novel storage architecture that balances security and efficiency. It is anticipated that this book will serve as a benchmark in advancing China's storage technology to the forefront of the global stage while contributing Eastern wisdom to the development of global digital storage.

— by Prof. Shuo-Yen Robert Li

Distributed Storage Coding Theory and Applications offers a cutting-edge overview of three critical technologies shaping the future of secure data systems. Combining advanced storage coding, decentralized trust via blockchain, and the challenges of quantum computing, this book provides clear insights into building resilient, next-generation infrastructures. Ideal for researchers, engineers, and tech professionals, it bridges theory and practice to address the evolving landscape of cybersecurity, distributed systems, and quantum-resilient technologies.

— by Prof. Peter Chong

Distributed Storage in Practice

Hui Li
Shenzhen Graduate School
Peking University
Guangdong
China

Hanxu Hou
Dongguan University of Technology
Guangdong
China

Hong Tan
Shenzhen Graduate School
Peking University
Guangdong
China

IEEE Press
WILEY

Published by John Wiley & Sons, Inc., Hoboken, New Jersey.

Library of Congress Cataloging-in-Publication Data Applied for

Hardback ISBN: 9781394334759

Cover Design: Wiley
Cover Image: © zf L/Getty Images

Set in 9.5/12.5pt STIXTwoText by Straive, Chennai, India

Contents

Foreword by Prof. Shuo-Yen Robert Li

In the digital era characterized by an overwhelming surge of data, distributed storage coding technology serves as a critical and often unseen infrastructure that ensures the reliable storage and efficient transmission of vast amounts of information. Prof. Hui Li and his team have dedicated over two decades to advancing this field. Their latest publication "Distributed Storage Coding Theory and Applications" not only encapsulates the collective wisdom of academia but also leverages practical engineering insights to pioneer new directions in the global evolution of storage technologies.

As a pioneer in the field of distributed storage coding, Prof. Hui Li's academic contributions have consistently aligned with technological innovation. At the dawn of cloud computing, he astutely identified the critical challenges in storage coding and introduced maximum distance separable (MDS) codes into distributed storage systems. This patented technology has since become a globally recognized de facto standard in the industry. Subsequently, his team overcame the limitations of traditional erasure codes by pioneering binary Reed–Solomon codes and binary regenerating codes, achieving the theoretical bound of encoding and decoding efficiency and bridging the gap between theoretical coding and practicability. Prof. Hui Li is also a leading figure in international research on blockchain consensus algorithms and applications, having filed over 20 blockchain-related patents and systematically addressed the CAP trilemma—ensuring strong consistency, high availability, and partition tolerance—in large-scale, high-throughput consortium blockchain. Furthermore, his team has successfully integrated blockchain consensus algorithms with storage coding. The "Distributed Storage System Based on Blockchain and Mimic Security," which he leads, has achieved an unbroken record of zero breaches in top-tier global cybersecurity competitions, thereby exemplifying the seamless fusion of theory and practice.

The unique value of this book is embodied in three key dimensions.

First, the sophistication and breadth of the theoretical framework. The authors deconstruct the core principles of distributed storage coding from the perspective of an engineer, progressing from classic erasure codes to the team's original binary coding methods. It not only dissects the essence of algorithm design but also directly addresses the pain points in system implementation, making it a "map for storage engineers."

Second, the forward-looking cross-disciplinary vision. The book systematically explains the collaborative mechanism between blockchain and storage coding for the first time. Taking the "blockchain and mimetic security" model as an example, it reveals how decentralized architecture can empower reliable data storage. At the same time, it incorporates the forward-looking exploration of quantum technology, proposing a quantum multi-identifier network architecture, which sets the direction for the efficiency and security of future storage systems.

Third, technological breakthroughs in global practice. The storage technology based on MDS codes led by Prof. Hui Li's team has been adopted by top domestic and international enterprises. The book uses system cases such as Microsoft WAS and Facebook HDFS-RAID as examples, not only demonstrating the universality of the technology but also highlighting the influence of Chinese scholars in the formulation of global standards.

This book is not only another masterpiece by Prof. Hui Li following "Distributed Storage Coding and Systems" (Science Press, 2016), "Principles and Applications of Blockchain Consensus Algorithms: A Case Study of Multi-identifier Network Management Systems" (Science Press, 2019), and "Principle & Applications of Blockchain Systems: How to Overcome the CAP Trilemma in Consortium Blockchain" (IEEE & Wiley, January 2025), but also a milestone in the field of distributed storage as it moves toward a trinity of "storage coding – blockchain – quantum." Whether researchers dedicated to coding optimization, engineers building storage systems, or decision-makers concerned with digital infrastructure, all can draw inspiration from it. On the occasion of its publication, I sincerely recommend this book to both the academic and industrial communities with confidence—it is bound to inject strong momentum into the next leap in data storage technology.

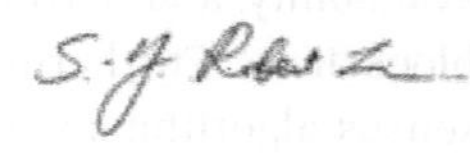

Prof. Shuo-Yen Robert Li
Emeritus Professor of the Chinese University of Hong Kong
IEEE Life Fellow

Foreword by Prof. Weimin Zheng

Data storage technology, as the cornerstone of the digital age, is experiencing a transformative shift from massive data storage to intelligent resource scheduling. In addition to requiring theoretical breakthroughs, storage systems must also deeply integrate with practical methodologies to construct a robust digital infrastructure that underpins the future intelligent society. This book by Prof. Hui Li and his team timely addresses this era's demands, establishing a bridge that connects the frontier of storage technology theory with its practical applications.

Looking back at the evolution of storage technology, from centralized architectures to distributed systems, and from single-protocol designs to multi-modal integration, each advancement has been driven by breakthroughs in foundational theories and innovations in engineering practices. Prof. Hui Li has dedicated over two decades to the field of distributed storage coding, with his accomplishments extensively featured in the IEEE Spectrum series. The advancements achieved by Prof. Hui Li's team in the core theory of storage coding have not only markedly improved data storage efficiency but also successfully bridged the gap between theoretical optimality and practical engineering through pioneering innovations in binary encoding and decoding technologies. This full-spectrum approach, which integrates theoretical algorithms with system-level practices, plays a critical role in ensuring data reliability while optimizing the utilization of storage resources. The book's comprehensive exploration of storage technologies based on MDS codes not only preserves the fundamental principles of traditional storage coding but also introduces innovative solutions for addressing the reliability challenges of large-scale data. This is the primary reason why leading global enterprises have adopted these technologies as integral components of their core infrastructures. Compared to the traditional three-replica redundancy method, distributed storage technology based on MDS codes requires only 1.5 times the redundancy. This approach can theoretically enable global data centers to save approximately 50% of storage space and associated energy consumption, thereby reducing a corresponding proportion of annual carbon emissions and yielding substantial environmental benefits.

The case studies of international benchmark systems, such as Facebook and Microsoft, presented in the book not only highlight the universality of Chinese technology but also underscore the paradigm shift of local innovation from a follower to a leader within the global technology ecosystem. Notably, the author transcends merely detailing technical aspects of storage coding by constructing a novel storage architecture that balances security and efficiency through the deep integration of storage coding, storage systems, blockchain, and quantum technologies. This cross-disciplinary integration approach serves as a model for the industry.

The rise of China's storage technology is closely tied to the in-depth research and breakthroughs in core technologies achieved by domestic scholars. From the classic Reed–Solomon code to regenerating codes grounded in network coding theory, and from distributed storage system based on blockchain and mimic security to the forward-looking exploration of quantum multi-identifier network, this closed-loop innovation pathway—characterized by "theoretical breakthrough – practical verification - technological leadership"—has positioned Prof. Hui Li's team at the forefront of technological advancement.

As a researcher in the storage field, I take great pleasure in recommending this book to both academia and industry. It not only offers a comprehensive knowledge framework spanning from principles to practice in distributed storage but also, through an interdisciplinary lens, establishes a technical pathway of "coding innovation – practical application." Whether for researchers in storage coding theory, engineers designing intelligent storage systems, or decision-makers strategizing digital infrastructure, this book serves as a source of valuable insight. I anticipate that this book will become a significant milestone in advancing China's storage technology to the forefront of the global stage while contributing the wisdom of the East to the evolution of global digital civilization.

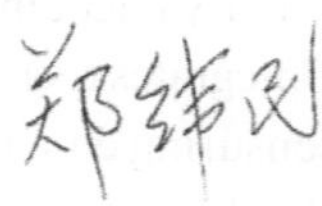

Prof. Weimin Zheng
Professor of Tsinghua University
Academician of Chinese Academy of Engineering
Former President of the China Computer Federation

About the Authors

Prof. Hui Li is Professor Emeritus of Peking University Shenzhen Graduate School. He received his B.Eng. and M.S. degrees from School of Information Engineering, Tsinghua University, Beijing, China, in 1986 and 1989, respectively, and Ph.D. degree from the Department of Information Engineering, The Chinese University of Hong Kong in 2000. He was Director of Shenzhen Key Lab of Information Theory & Future Internet Architecture, Director of PKU Lab of CENI (China Environment for Network Innovations), National Major Research Infrastructure. His research interests include network architecture, cyberspace security, distributed storage, and blockchain.

His research group is the first team to apply Maximum Distance Separable Codes (MDS) to network distributed storage, obtaining patent authorization in both the United States and China (US9961142B2, CN102624866B), which has now become the de facto standard in the global industry. He has optimized traditional Reed–Solomon (RS) codes and regenerating codes (RGC) based on network information theory coding, achieving the theoretically optimal encoding and decoding. He proposed Binary Reed–Solomon (BRS) code, which achieved optimal theoretical computational complexity in RS codes and received patents from both the United States and China (US20160285476A1, CN105518996B). To address the high computational complexity and practical challenges of RGC based on network information coding theory, his team introduced Binary RGC (BRGC) codes based on *GF*(2)—BMBR and BMSR. These advancements optimized encoding and decoding complexity while enabling practical applications of RGC in industry. Consequently, a series of patents were obtained from both the United States and China (US9722637B2, CN103688515B, US9647698B2, and CN103688514B). Additionally, he has authored the first monograph on topic of "Distributed Storage Coding and Systems," 2016.08, China Science

Press in the world, which combines storage coding and systems to explain the principles. In 2019, he published his first Chinese blockchain monograph ("Principles and Applications of Blockchain Consensus Algorithm - A Case Study of Multi-identifier Network Management System," China Science Press, 2019), filling the gap in the Chinese blockchain consensus algorithm monograph market. The Chinese monograph was expanded into an English monograph titled "Principle & Applications of Blockchain Systems: How to Overcome the CAP Trilemma in Consortium Blockchain," jointly published by IEEE & Wiley in January 2025.

Additionally, he proposed the first co-governing future networking "MIN" based on blockchain technology and implemented its prototype on Operators' Network in the world, and this project "MIN: Co-Governing Multi-Identifier Network Architecture and Its Prototype on Operators' Network" was awarded the World Leading Internet Scientific and Technological Achievements at the 6th World Internet Conference in 2019, Wuzhen, China. The first English monograph on the theme of "Cyberspace UN" has been published by Springer Publisher with the title "Co-governed Sovereignty Network: Legal Basis and Its Prototype & Applications with MIN Architecture." In April 2024, Prof. Li was invited to give a keynote speech at the 27th Session of the United Nations Commission on Science and Technology for Development and DWC Geneva Summit with the theme of "MIN: for Every Nation to jointly Build a Trust Cyberspace in the Digital World," advocating the establishment of the MIN Standards Working Group and inviting countries to participate in the research and application of the MIN network and jointly promote the construction of a global digital world with network and data security.

Prof. Hanxu Hou received the B.Eng. degree in Information Security from Xidian University, Xian, China, in 2010 and the Ph.D. degrees in the Department of Information Engineering from The Chinese University of Hong Kong in 2015 and in the School of Electronic and Computer Engineering from Peking University in 2016. He is currently a distinguished professor of Leading Talents at Dongguan Institute of Technology and a part-time senior researcher at Huawei Theory Research Department. His main research interests include information theory, distributed storage coding, etc. He has published more than 90 papers in international top journals and conferences in the field of information theory and coding and more than 30 authorized invention patents, some of the coding technologies and algorithms have been applied to a number of big data projects and have been widely used. He presided or co-presided over three projects of National Natural Science Foundation of China, one National Key Research and Development

Project of China, and participated in one National Basic Research Program of China as a technical backbone. He has won the Best Paper Award of the China Academic Annual Conference on Information Theory (2017 and 2019, the first author), Second Prize of Shenzhen Science and Technology in 2018, the Young Rising Star Awards of the 27th China Academic Annual Conference on Information Theory in 2020, Exemplary Reviewer 2020 in IEEE Transactions on Communications (less than 2% were rated as exemplary reviewers), 2020 Huawei Hong Kong Research Institute Director's Award, first prize of Spark Award, first prize of Innovation Pioneer of Huawei in 2023, etc. In addition, he has long been a reviewer of the top international journals IEEE TIT, IEEE TCOM, IEEE CL, and IEEE ISIT.

Hong Tan received the B.Eng. degree from the Department of Bigdata and Software, Chongqing University, Chongqing, China, in 2022. He is an R&D Engineer in the School of Electronic and Computer Engineering, Peking University. His research interests include distributed storage coding and systems, database, and log-structured merge-tree.

Preface

In the present data-driven era, distributed storage coding assumes a crucial role. It effectively copes with the rapid expansion of data storage demand by minimizing redundancy and enhancing data reliability. As the cornerstone of modern information technology, distributed storage coding plays a vital role in facilitating the sustainable development of the digital economy and society. Nevertheless, the extant literature on distributed storage coding in the market predominantly focuses on a single aspect, such as coding theory or system application, and fails to comprehensively encompass the extensive domain of storage coding. Specifically, with the emergence of emerging technologies like blockchain and quantum computing, their integration with distributed storage coding and systems has grown increasingly intense. However, there is currently a dearth of a comprehensive monograph for in-depth exploration of this interdisciplinary field. Consequently, the publication of this book is intended to bridge this academic void and furnish readers with comprehensive and profound knowledge of distributed storage coding theory and applications.

In this book, we not only undertake a detailed analysis and summary of the existing researches in distributed storage coding and systems but also broaden our research scope to innovative technologies such as blockchain and quantum computing.

First, this book provides a comprehensive analysis of the current distributed storage codes. Owing to the abstract notions, complex coding procedure, and the difficulty in understanding erasure coding, this book undertakes various attempts to enhance the understanding of distributed storage coding theory. We encompass a wide range of practical erasure codes that have found extensive application in numerous storage systems, such as LRC in Microsoft WAS, butterfly codes and Clay codes incorporated in HDFS and Ceph, binary RGCs proposed by our team, and applications of erasure codes by several domestic and international large enterprises. In terms of content, it centers on the specific operational procedures of data coding, rather than extensive theoretical analysis, with the objective of highlighting the design concepts and reinforcing the coding methods for actual distributed storage systems.

Meanwhile, blockchain technology, with its characteristics such as decentralization, immutability, and transparency, is gradually reshaping the future of storage systems, providing a secure and reliable way for data storage and verification. In the blockchain section of this book, we will focus on elaborating several important achievements of our team in the field of blockchain and storage. The most typical one is the "Distributed Storage System Based on Blockchain and Mimic Security," which perfectly integrates blockchain with the practical erasure codes (Binary RGCs) independently developed by our team and is a typical example of the combination of storage coding and blockchain.

In addition, quantum technology has broad development prospects in the field of storage. Although, as of now, technologies like quantum memory, quantum coding, quantum security, and quantum computer network have not yet reached the practical stage, we hope to explore the path of integrating quantum with storage systems and storage coding by introducing the progress of some quantum technologies and our research results. For example, the Quantum Multi-Identifier Network independently developed by our team can well ensure the efficiency and security of communication between distributed storage nodes, thereby improving the performance of storage systems and coding.

Our aim is to review the latest developments in the field, facilitate cross-disciplinary exchanges and integration by delving into key theoretical frameworks and practical cases, and establish a solid foundation for future research endeavors.

Owing to the author's limited capacity, inevitable omissions might exist. Readers are earnestly invited to offer their valuable comments and suggestions.

Hui Li
Professor Emeritus of Peking University
Director PKU Lab, China Major Sci. & Tech. Infrastructure for Future Network
Chair of Expert Committee of IEEE Blockchain Theoretical and Mathematical Modeling
Member of the National Academy of Artificial Intelligent (NAAI) USA
Foreign Academician of Russia Academy of Natural Science
Member of Expert Committee of World Digital Tech. Academy, UN, Geneva
Tech. Exe. Director of Sino-EU Intelligent Connected Vehicle & Autonomous Driving Industry Innovation Alliance (SASD)

Acknowledgments

This book stems from the work of Professor Hui Li's research group at Peking University. We are profoundly grateful to all the students, engineers, and teachers who have contributed to this book. Without their precious efforts, this book could not have been accomplished.

This book is altogether divided into seven chapters. The first author, Prof. Hui Li, was responsible for the overall planning and coordination, ensuring that the book's structure and content aligned with the intended objectives. Prof. Hui Li meticulously wrote Chapters 1, 3, 6, and 7, covering a wide range of topics with thorough research and insightful analysis. His dedication and expertise were instrumental in shaping the book's comprehensive and cohesive narrative. The second author, Prof. Hanxu Hou, oversaw the organization and language refinement of the book and contributed to the writing of Chapters 2 and 4. The third author, Hong Tan, was responsible for the writing of Chapter 5 and the coordination of the later manuscript.

Furthermore, we sincerely wish to convey our deepest gratitude to the students who provided writing materials and post-stage assistance, including, but not limited to, Rui Chen, Zhuoliang Xiao, Qiufan Wu, and Shiwei Zhang who participated in the drawing work of Chapters 1, 2, 3, 4, 5, and 6; Jianming Lin for the drawings, typography, and proofreading in Chapter 7; Zhixiong Luo for checking the format of the book.

We are truly grateful for the funding support for our research, including, but not limited to, The YinLing Teacher Program for Universities in Yunnan Province; Open Project of the Key Laboratory of Yunnan University of Finance and Economics YNUFE-2023-07; Key Lab. Development Project of Huanghe Science and Technology College HHSCU-2023-021; Kunlun Talent Program No.2024-03; Open Fund Project of Guangxi Key Laboratory of Multimedia Communication and Network Technology KLF-2021-01; China Mobile Internet Co., Ltd. Joint Laboratory for Sovereign and Trusted Internet (R2442101010147U), Guangdong Provincial Key Laboratory of Ultra High Definition Immersive Media Technology,

GuangDong Prov., R&D Key Program (No. 2019B010137001), Basic Research Enhancement Program of China under Grant (2021-JCJQ-JJ-0483), GuangDong Prov. Basic Research (No. 2022A1515010836), China Environment for Network Innovation (CENI) GJFGW (No. [2020]386, SZFGW No. [2019]261), Shenzhen Research Programs (JCYJ20220531093206015), Shenzhen Fundamental Research Program (No. GXWD20201231165807007-20200807164903001), National Keystone R&D Program of China (No. 2017YFB0803204), NSFC (No. 61671001), ZTE Funding (No. 2019ZTE03-01), and HuaWei Funding (No. TC20201222002).

Finally, we would like to express our sincere thanks to the dedicated staff at Wiley for their invaluable assistance and unwavering support throughout the publication process. Additionally, we extend our heartfelt thanks to each reader for engaging with this book and contributing to the ongoing discourse in this field.

On March 2025

Hui Li
Hanxu Hou
Hong Tan

1

Fundamentals of Distributed Storage

As the digital economy emerges as a new driver for economic and social development, accelerating the realization of data as a production factor has become an essential requirement to promote the digital economy and facilitate high-quality development. The advent of new technologies such as 5G, cloud computing, artificial intelligence (AI), high-performance computing (HPC), and big data has given rise to numerous emerging applications, leading to an explosive growth of data volume. The aggregation, circulation, and application of massive data have placed higher demands on data storage systems. Distributed storage, as a critical infrastructure, represents an optimal solution for substantial volumes of data. Therefore, it is imperative to expedite research and development efforts related to super-large-scale, highly reliable, highly available, and high-performance distributed storage in order to adapt to the expanding industrial spaces and evolving application scenarios.

This chapter first introduces the evolution and characteristics of distributed storage and then focuses on the concept of data reliability, as well as on the common fault-tolerant mechanisms. Finally, it discusses the future trends of distributed storage from a macro perspective.

1.1 Introduction to Distributed Storage

More than 60 years ago, the first-generation computer ENIAC (McCartney 1999, pp. 1–11) could execute over 5,000 additions or more than 400 multiplications per second with only 100 B of magnetic core storage capacity. However, a compressed digital photo with a resolution of 3,600 × 2,700 pixels is approximately 4 MB in size, while a photograph of the spectacular spiral galaxy *M*81 captured by the Hubble Space Telescope occupies 689 MB. The storage capacity required for high-definition movie playback is around 20 GB, and this necessitates an input/output (I/O) sustained data transfer rate of at least 3 MB/s. In addition

Distributed Storage in Practice, First Edition. Hui Li, Hanxu Hou, and Hong Tan.

to capacity requirements, many applications impose stringent demands on response time, throughput, transmission bandwidth, and so on. These escalating demands propel the evolution of storage systems from small to large, slow to fast, simple to complex, and single-machine to a distributed system; they also present higher-level requirements for robustness, availability, reliability, and performance.

1.1.1 Evolution of Storage Systems

Generalized storage devices include CPU registers, multi-level caches, memory, and the external storage system. The first three are also known as the memory system. In a narrow sense, storage systems usually refer to external storage systems. This book also mainly centers on the external storage systems.

The data units of a computer are byte (B), kilobyte (KB), megabyte (MB), gigabyte (GB), terabyte (TB), petabyte (PB), exabyte (EB), zettabyte (ZB), and so on. One byte represents one character of information and is composed of eight binary bits. The conversion relations between the units are as follows: 1 KB is equal to 1024 B, 1 MB is equal to 1024 KB, 1 GB is equal to 1024 MB, and 1 TB is equal to 1024 GB.

If users usually only create simple documents or spreadsheets, then most files may be a few hundred KBs or occasionally a few MBs in size. However, if the computer is used to store and process digital photos, then the average file size will be in the range of several MBs. When the computer is used to edit and store videos, the size of a single file may be tens of MB or even several GB. For example, one hour of DV format video footage consumes approximately 12 GB; one minute of uncompressed 1,920 × 1,080 high-definition video is approximately 9 GB. Therefore, adequate and scalable storage capacity is very important.

Apart from capacity, the update and access frequency of stored data is also a key factor to be considered in the selection of external storage devices. For example, digital photographers may have incremental storage capacity requirements. With each shoot, they will add several hundred MB or several GB of photos as backups to the storage system and require these photos to be stored permanently without being altered. In contrast, three-dimensional (3D) computer animation may require regularly repeated access to several GB of data and replace the previously stored data. In this case, not only rewritable storage media is needed, but higher requirements are also imposed on the response speed. It is these various requirements that have given rise to different storage systems. Next, the development of storage systems is introduced in chronological order.

1) **Hard Disk:**

   Most desktop computers and laptops nowadays still rely on rotational hard disks as high-capacity storage devices for storing the operating system kernel, applications, user data, and so on. Traditional rotational hard disk drives consist of one or more disks that are stacked together and covered with surface magnetic media that can be driven by write heads and read heads. Hard disk drives can transfer data directly to other computer hardware through three interface types: SATA, IDE/UDMA, or SCSI, and their speed ranges from 4,200 to 15,000 rpm.

2) **Redundant Array of Independent Disks:**
Redundant array of independent disks (RAID) (Perumal and Kritzinger 2004, pp. 1–9) refers to the use of multiple hard disks connected together in servers and high-end personal computer workstations and to the operation of storing data through multiple physical drives. There are many available RAID configurations, of which the three basic ones are explained as follows:
   a) **RAID 0** divides a data file into blocks and stores them on two or more hard disks, with each hard disk storing the data blocks evenly. Parallel read operations can be used to improve system performance without increasing capacity.
   b) **RAID 1** employs data mirroring to symmetrically distribute data blocks across two or more disks, effectively reducing the risk of disk faults. This redundancy ensures that in the event of a disk fault, the complete dataset can still be retrieved from other disks.
   c) **RAID 5** requires at least three disks. Similar to RAID 0, it not only spans multiple disks to store different data blocks but also simultaneously stores parity blocks for these data blocks. This configuration ensures that in the event of a single disk fault, the failed data can be recovered using the parity blocks stored on other disk drives.

Other RAID configurations are generally further optimized or combined from the basic configurations mentioned earlier, such as increasing the fault-tolerant level of the disks and expanding to disk arrays across different regions.

3) **Distributed Storage:**
The exponential growth in data volume has necessitated more rigorous storage requirements, including scalable storage capacity, enhanced reliability, increased throughput, and reduced cost. Traditional single-machine storage such as RAID is no longer suitable for large-scale data. Distributed storage systems have emerged as a viable solution. Generic distributed storage involves the dispersion of data across multiple servers in a cluster of storage nodes, and the synchronization or access of data through a distributed network between the nodes. Data is spread across multiple nodes, and reliability is maintained through specific redundant mechanisms. Specifically speaking, a distributed storage system typically comprises the following components:
   a) **Client:** Client encompasses the user interface and is responsible for engaging with users, receiving their requests, and delivering responses.

b) **Network Link:** The network link plays a crucial role in transmitting diverse data, including user requests, read and write operations, and responses.

c) **Storage Node:** Storage node, as a fundamental component of the distributed storage system, plays a pivotal role in both actual data storage and the processing of read and write operations.

d) **Metadata Management Node:** Metadata management node is tasked with overseeing metadata information of the distributed storage system, encompassing data file storage locations, copy counts, and access permissions. It also facilitates load balancing and data migration of storage nodes to optimize system performance.

4) **Cloud Storage:**

Cloud storage (Ghani et al. 2020, pp. 1–21) represents highly scalable distributed storage that disperses data across diverse geographical locations. It typically adopts a distributed storage architecture to cater to users' requirements for data storage. Unlike traditional distributed storage, which is limited by geography and network bandwidth, cloud storage is typically offered by global cloud service providers, allowing users to directly access data via the Internet. Therefore, cloud storage can be viewed as an extension of distributed storage on the Internet, delivering a more efficient, dependable, and adaptable solution.

1.1.2 Characteristics of Distributed Storage

A distributed storage system can provide storage services by interconnecting multiple storage nodes, which are composed of soft and hardware components. Compared with traditional centralized storage, distributed storage distributes data across multiple relatively independent storage nodes to achieve higher response speed and scales the capacity by increasing the number of storage nodes. It also maintains stable system performance by using specific system optimization such as load balancing and data migration. Distributed storage generally provides storage space at the exabyte level, which is suitable for storage scenarios with massive data, such as big data analysis and large-scale data backup archiving.

Based on the actual application scenarios, distributed storage can abstract the following significant advantages:

1) **High Scalability:** Achieving highly scalable distributed storage involves pooling storage resources across multiple nodes, enabling the system to exhibit horizontal scalability and dynamically expand the number of storage nodes. This represents a fundamental distinction from centralized storage, where a tightly coupled architecture is employed with the storage controller

undertaking all data management tasks. Though it also offers small-scale horizontal scalability, the performance of controller experiences a significant decline as the capacity reaches a certain threshold. In contrast, distributed storage adopts a loosely coupled architecture where each node shares responsibility for data management. Horizontal scaling of nodes results in an increase in linear performance as the capacity continues to expand.

2) **Multi-protocol Support:** Centralized storage often supports only block and file storage protocols, whereas distributed storage can accommodate block, file, object, and other storage protocols. This versatility caters to the diverse data storage needs of both traditional businesses such as sales and taxation and emerging enterprises involved in big data analysis and HPC.
3) **High Performance:** Large-scale distributed storage relies on a loosely coupled architecture and robust horizontal scalability of distributed storage, enabling throughput of millions of transactions and lower latency. This capability caters to diverse workloads, such as traditional databases and large-scale commercial storage.
4) **High Reliability:** Distributed storage can dynamically remove failed nodes and automatically rebuild invalid data through distributed cluster management. In practical scenarios, by deploying large-scale, practical erasure codes (ECs) in combination with replication strategies, distributed storage can achieve a higher fault tolerance level.

There exist numerous evaluation metrics for a storage system, with the typical ones being capacity, throughput, response time, and transmission bandwidth.

Capacity is typically compared in terms of the quantity of bytes. At present, the capacity of a randomized storage stands at the GB level, whereas that of a single disk is at the TB level; the capacity of a DVD disk amounts to approximately 5 GB; the capacity of a Blu-ray disk is 20 GB; the capacity of RAID is contingent upon the number and configuration of disk drives within it, but generally does not surpass the TB level; the capacity of large-scale distributed storage systems ranges from dozens of TB to dozens of PB, demonstrating a considerable capacity advantage.

Throughput is defined as the quantity of tasks that a system is capable of accomplishing within a unit of time. It constitutes a significant metric reflecting the task-processing capacity. Nevertheless, in practical applications, the magnitude of throughput frequently relies on diverse tasks. For instance, throughput is associated with the size of specific requests. Generally, the smaller the request, the higher the throughput. However, the relationship between throughput and the size of the request is not an absolute linear one. This is due to the fact that each request, irrespective of its size, demands a relatively fixed amount of time for analyzing the request packet. Hence, the overall performance of the system cannot be gauged solely by throughput.

Response time is a crucially significant metric for user experience, denoting the period from transmitting a request to obtaining a response. This metric is impacted by multiple facets. Systems with larger buffers typically have shorter response time than those with smaller buffers; the traits of requests also exert an influence on the response time, such as the physical location and size of the accessed data; moreover, when the system load is substantial, it necessitates a longer response time. These factors render the calculation and analysis of response time highly challenging.

Transmission bandwidth of a distributed storage network refers to the maximum data transmission rate between all nodes. High bandwidth can ensure that data is transmitted quickly between different storage nodes; improve data read and write speed; achieve efficient data repair, backup, and synchronization; reduce data access latency; and meet the needs for large-scale data storage and high-concurrent access.

1.2 Reliability of Distributed Storage

As the value of data gains escalating significance, the reliability of distributed storage systems is attracting heightened attention from users. This section centers on the reliability of distributed storage systems. First, it presents the related notions of reliability and availability with their distinctions and subsequently delves further into the methods and metrics of system reliability.

1.2.1 Availability and Reliability

Availability refers to the capability of a system to offer normal services when confronted with various faults. It reflects the feature that the system is accessible to users at all times, meaning that users can utilize the system to accurately execute their instructions at any moment. Availability can be gauged by the proportion of system downtime to normal service time. For instance, if the availability of a certain system is four 9s, namely, 99.99%, it is equivalent to that the system's downtime within a year must not exceed $365 \times 24 \times 60 \div 10{,}000 = 52.56$ minutes.

Reliability pertains to the capability of a system to furnish services during the event of faults. Reliability and availability are not the same concept. Reliability mirrors the attributes over a period of time, whereas availability reflects the characteristics at a specific moment. A system with high reliability can function continuously for an extended duration without disruption. If a system malfunctions for merely 1 ms/h, its availability can attain 99.9999%; yet, it remains a highly unreliable system due to the short period of continuous operation. Likewise, if a system never crashes but is shut down for two weeks annually, then this system has high reliability, but its availability amounts to only 96%.

With the rapid advancement, data, serving as the vehicle of information, has been escalating continuously in quantity, thereby giving rise to the continuous expansion of the storage system scale and the increasingly prominent issues regarding the system's reliability. Failed node problems in distributed storage have become the norm over the past decade. In November 2014, Tencent Cloud servers experienced access faults, causing difficulties for users to access. In September 2015, Alibaba Cloud encountered large-scale faults, and all the basic requests failed to operate normally. In February 2017, Baidu Cloud suffered a downtime incident, resulting in the inability of Baidu's mobile terminal to search for content. In June 2019, Google Cloud Storage had a severe network downtime incident, and the hosting services in the eastern and central regions of the United States could not operate normally. In December 2021, Amazon Cloud Computing witnessed three downtime incidents of varying degrees, causing severe impacts and substantial economic losses. In September 2023, Microsoft Azure services situated in Sydney, Australia, suddenly disrupted, and users were unable to access Azure, Microsoft 365, and Power Platform for 24 hours.

To achieve high reliability in large-scale distributed storage systems, several challenges will be faced, including:

1) The enhancement of system performance and reliability is not concurrent. Despite the considerable improvement in the capacity and performance of the storage system along with a significant price reduction, the advancement of reliability is comparatively sluggish. Additionally, maintaining reliability incurs system resources, thereby exerting an influence on system performance.
2) The augmentation in the quantity of system disks leads to more frequent faults. The average mean time between faults of a disk is one million hours. For a large-scale storage system constituted by 10,000 hard disks, the probability of a fault within one hour stands at 1%.
3) The growth of hard disk capacity and bandwidth is not concurrent. For a 400-GB Serial ATA hard disk, it takes four-and-a-half hours to accomplish the data reconstruction of the entire hard disk under the bandwidth condition of 25 MB/s. The disparity between capacity and bandwidth will protract the time for the data reconstruction and might result in further data loss during the repair process.

1.2.2 Fault Tolerance

The reliability of distributed storage systems primarily depends on fault tolerance data. Fault tolerance refers to saving data in a specific manner that enables the utilization of remaining valid data to restore lost data. Any fault tolerance method can merely handle a limited number of failed nodes. Once the number exceeds the threshold, the data will be permanently lost. Consequently, a crucial aspect of fault tolerance is how to effectively repair data to guarantee reliability. Currently, the majority of commonly utilized fault tolerance methods adopt data redundancy, the most typical ones being replication and ECs.

1) **Replication:**
   Replication refers to replicating a data file and distributing these copies across multiple storage nodes. The fault-tolerant capability enhances as the quantity of copies rises. For any data file, as long as there are still valid copies available, it can be restored, thereby enhancing the reliability of the system. Meanwhile, copies are disseminated in distinct storage nodes. When users access data, they can dynamically identify the copy that is closest to their geographical location, reducing the data transmission delay. Large files can even be read concurrently through multiple copies, enhancing the efficiency of access. This greatly reduces the probability of a large number of users accessing a single server at the same time and ensures the load balance of the entire system.

   However, replication possesses rather conspicuous flaws. Due to the necessity of storing additional copies, the time cost and network bandwidth for system write operations escalate significantly. Additionally, as new data is being written, the total amount of data within the system will increase linearly, thereby resulting in additional hardware resource expenditures.

   Replication is extensively utilized in contemporary distributed systems, with a typical illustration being Google File System (GFS) (Ghemawat, Gobioff and Leung 2003, pp. 29–43). Files housed within GFS are partitioned into fixed-sized chunks, and the management node (master) assigns a 64-bit unique ID to each chunk upon its creation. Generally, there exist three copies of the chunk in GFS, which are stored in different data nodes. For each chunk, the write operation writes all copies to the addresses specified by the master. During the read operation, the master selects the optimal address for all copies and reads the data. In the event of a node fault, the master automatically replicates a data copy from another node to a replacement node to uphold the reliability.

2) **Erasure Codes:**
   Compared with replication, ECs are increasingly utilized in large-scale distributed storage systems due to their lower redundancy and higher reliability. Briefly, ECs initially divide the file into k data blocks, encode them to generate m encoded blocks, and distribute and store these $n = k + m$ blocks to n distinct

storage nodes. Furthermore, it is fulfilled that by obtaining any k valid blocks from these nodes, the original file can be reconstructed.

Currently, numerous cloud storage systems employ ECs to enhance the availability and reliability of the system. Microsoft, in Windows Azure Storage (WAS), with the aim of reducing the network bandwidth during data recovery, adopts Locally Repairable Codes (LRCs) (Calder et al. 2011, pp. 143–157). This code classifies parity blocks into two categories: global parity blocks and local parity blocks. For example, the LRC(12,2,2) divides the original data into 12 blocks and further evenly distributes these blocks into 2 groups, each group consisting of 6 data blocks. Each group of data blocks is required to calculate a local parity block and then 2 global parity blocks are calculated for all 12 data blocks. In this manner, when any data block fails, the number of helper nodes necessary for recovery is decreased from 12 in the traditional RS(16,4) to 6, leading to the repair bandwidth being halved. Facebook also utilizes similar ECs instead of the traditional three-copy strategy in its cloud system framework (Sathiamoorthy et al. 2013, pp. 1–19), saving PB-level storage space while maintaining the reliability of the cluster.

According to the latest "Global DataSphere 2023" report released by the International Data Corporation (IDC), the global total volume of data is projected to increase from 103.66 ZB in 2022 to 284.3 ZB in 2027. If all data is stored in three copies, this would result in an astonishing 852.9 ZB of actual data stored in the global storage system by 2027, leading to a substantial consumption of global storage and power resources. In contrast, distributed storage based on ECs reduces storage overhead through coding and achieves enhanced reliability. For instance, with a parameter ratio of (10,5), this EC can significantly decrease the required storage volume and the actual data stored in the global storage system is estimated to be 426.45 ZB, demonstrating that distributed storage based on ECs has the potential to halve the required storage volume and reduce global storage resources as well as data center power consumption by 50%. In addition, in order to select an appropriate data replication strategy, it is essential to consider additional factors such as the consistency of copies and load balancing. These considerations may necessitate a substantial allocation of resources.

However, distributed storage based on ECs mitigates the need for excessive deliberation on these factors and allows for easy scalability, significantly enhancing storage efficiency, particularly in large-scale storage scenarios. Moreover, Weatherspoon and Kubiatowicz (2002, pp. 1–11) conducted a quantitative comparison between replication and ECs. The study indicated that when the average availability of nodes in the system is 0.5, maintaining a file retrieval probability greater than 0.999 at any given time requires at least 10 copies for replication; whereas utilizing ECs results in only 2.49 times the original file size as storage overhead.

1.2.3 Reliability Metrics

Constructing reliable storage has always posed a significant challenge in distributed storage. In large-scale storage systems, the inefficiency of reliability strategies can result in frequent hardware and software faults. Therefore, it is imperative to conduct a detailed analysis of the causes and probability distribution of faults for each node. This necessitates a series of reliability metrics for quantitative analysis.

At different stages of development, different metrics are generated due to the different focus on reliability, maintainability, availability, and executability, as well as some fault quantitative metrics. A detailed introduction to various metrics is defined as follows:

1) **Reliability:**
   Reliability $R(t) = 1 - \int_{t_0}^{t} f(u)du$ is the probability that a system will continue to function normally between time intervals $[t_0, t]$, given that it is functioning normally at time t_0 and $f(u)$ is the failure probability density function. This quantifies the system's reliability in terms of its operational duration. This metric is primarily limited to systems that are irreparable or pose significant challenges for repair, making it particularly suitable for the initial stages of reliability development.
2) **Maintainability:**
   With the advent and widespread implementation of repairable systems, the concept of maintainability emerged. Maintainability $M(t) = P\{X < = t\}$ is a metric that quantifies the ease or difficulty of repairing a system following fault, representing the probability that the system will be restored within a specified time interval t after a fault.
3) **Availability:**
   By integrating reliability and maintainability, availability $A(t)$ is defined as the probability of the system normally functioning at any given time t, as follows:

$$A(t_1, t_2) = \frac{1}{t_2 - t_1} \int_{t_1}^{t_2} A(t)dt. \tag{1.1}$$

   As illustrated in Eq. (1.1), the average availability $(A(t_1, t_2))$ serves as a metric for the system's mean uninterrupted operation during the interval $[t_1, t_2]$. When $t_1 = t_2$, the limit of the result obtained using Eq. (1.1) yields the instantaneous availability of the system, which is also considered the most effective measure of system availability.

4) **Executability:**
   The executability $P(L, t)$ is defined as the probability that the system maintains performance at level L or above at time t. It serves as a performance metric that integrates reliability and introduces the concept of partial fault. The system may encounter specific faults, which do not impact its function but cause a drop in performance to a certain level. Notably, with the introduction of quality-of-service, enhancing system executability has gained increasing significance. It is important to note that one key distinction between executability and reliability lies in their definitions: While reliability measures the system's ability to correctly execute all functions, executability assesses its capability to correctly perform the most basic functions.
5) **Fault Quantitative Metrics:**
   In industry, the reliability is often measured from the perspective of faults using three simplified metrics:
   a) Mean time between failures (MTBF): The mean time between two temporally adjacent failures. A higher MTBF indicates greater system reliability.
   b) Mean time to failure (MTTF): The average time that a system can operate without failure. A higher MTTF indicates greater system reliability.
   c) Mean time to repair (MTTR): The average time to repair a system, i.e., the time it takes from the occurrence of a fault to the system being fully restored. A shorter MTTR indicates better recoverability and higher system availability.

Figure 1.1 illustrates the relationship between MTBF, MTTF, and MTTR. For a simple maintainable system, $MTBF = MTTF + MTTR$. Since MTTR is typically

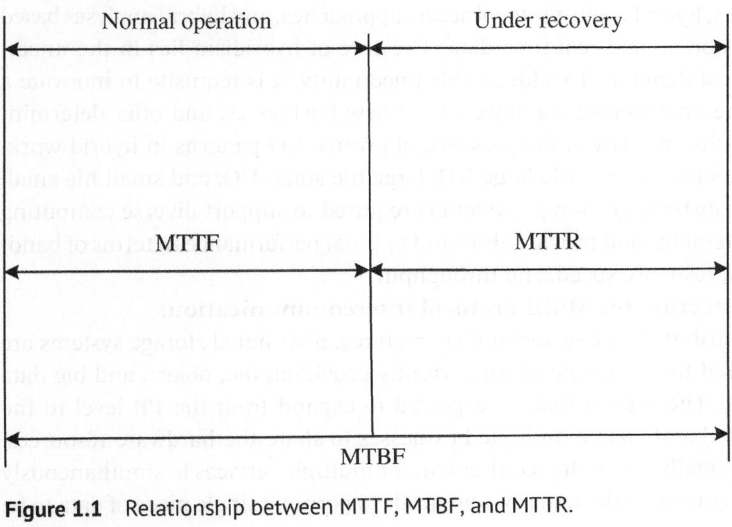

Figure 1.1 Relationship between MTTF, MTBF, and MTTR.

much smaller than MTTF, MTBF can be approximated by MTTF and is often replaced by it.

1.3 Trends in Future Development

Currently, with the continuous growth of data volume and the increasing complexity of user requirements, distributed storage has become one of the main solutions for storing large-scale data. This subsection explores the trends and prospects of distributed storage in future development from multiple dimensions, including architecture, infrastructure, data management, and green energy efficiency. Through analysis of the current technical background, market demands, and innovation dynamics, it aims to provide readers with a comprehensive and in-depth understanding to assist them in grasping and foreseeing the future development direction of distributed storage.

1) **Architecture:**
   To address the challenges posed by the voluminous and heterogeneous data applications, distributed storage is continuously evolving toward the architecture of catering to hybrid workloads, multi-protocol intercommunication, and the separation of storage and computing.
   a) **Architecture for Hybrid Workloads:**
      The advancement of HPC, big data analysis, and AI has stimulated the emergence of a multitude of novel applications and business flows. The typical characteristic of these flows is hybrid, encompassing hybrid performance models, hybrid multi-protocol access approaches, and hybrid analyses based on historical and real-time data. The core of hybridism lies in the uncertainty of demand. To address this uncertainty, it is requisite to innovate a storage architecture, embrace varied new businesses, and offer deterministic solutions. Given the presence of diverse I/O patterns in hybrid workloads, such as large file large I/O, large file small I/O, and small file small I/O, a distributed storage system is required to support diverse computing requirements and provide all-round optimal performance in terms of bandwidth, response speed, and throughput.
   b) **Architecture for Multi-protocol Intercommunication:**
      As distributed storage technology matures, distributed storage systems are required to be capable of concurrently providing file, object, and big data access. The system scale is expected to expand from the PB level to the EB level and enable multiple businesses to share the hardware resources. Additionally, given the requirement for multiple services to simultaneously access the same data, the system needs to permit a single piece of data to be

accessed by multiple protocols concurrently and natively support protocols such as files, objects, and HDFS, minimizing the performance loss caused by protocol conversion to the greatest extent possible.

c) **Separation of Storage and Computing:**
As the disparity between the computing resources of the storage system and the computing requirements continues to expand, distributed storage demands flexible planning or independent expansion of computing resources. For diverse data applications, such as containers, big data, and AI platforms, computing and storage resources can be independently expanded as necessary to prevent resource waste resulting from the integrated expansion of computing and storage and significantly enhance CPU utilization to achieve precise investment. Through decoupling storage services from storage media, distributed storage in the future will not only support general-purpose servers but also gradually evolve into a composable, uninstallable, and large-scale scalable separated computing and storage architecture (Geyer et al. 2023, pp. 1–8). This can be achieved by establishing storage media clusters to address the escalating data storage issues and utilizing storage service clusters to solve their own computing problems, such as storage characteristics and access rules.

2) **Hardware Acceleration:**
The acceleration of data processing, data encryption, and the popularization of flash memory media have posed severe challenges to the controller capabilities of storage systems. Functions such as erasure coding and compression consume a large amount of CPU resources and are more suitable for computing on specific processors. Therefore, the idea of hardware acceleration has been proposed in the industry, of which DPU is a dedicated processor for data centers (Burstein 2021, pp. 1–20). In the storage system, complex computations such as the encoding and decoding of ECs, data compression, and encryption are transplanted to the DPU, while the CPU only needs to be responsible for the system control functions.

3) **Software:**
Data storage serves as the impregnable "safe box" for information and represents the ultimate bulwark in safeguarding data security. In the contemporary era, nations are increasingly prioritizing the refinement of pertinent legislation to bolster data security measures. The robustness, reliability, and security of distributed storage systems have emerged as pivotal in mitigating the risks associated with data breaches. Looking ahead, distributed storage systems must offer high-performance encryption for data transmission between the host and storage disks and exhibit resilience through capabilities such as ransomware detection and disaster recovery protocols. Moreover, they should integrate support for data access control policies and security compliance

mechanisms within a multi-cloud framework, ensuring that the handling of sensitive personal information adheres to legal and regulatory stipulations. Concurrently, it is imperative to establish a comprehensive security and trustworthiness framework that encompasses the static integrity of storage system software and the behavior of software operations throughout its lifecycle.

Furthermore, the exponential growth of data, particularly in certain business sectors where the annual increase has reached PB level, necessitates a distributed storage architecture capable of scaling to thousands of nodes. This architecture must also be designed to accommodate future expansions to EB level of data storage. Consequently, this demands an elevated standard for data compression techniques, encompassing lossless performance, accelerated compression processes, and enhanced compression ratios. Beyond conventional data compression algorithms, there is a pressing need to explore innovative compression methodologies tailored to diverse scenarios.

In the cloud-native era, the automated operational capabilities of storage systems have become a focal point of interest. To align more closely with the demands of cloud-native applications, distributed storage systems are evolving along several key trajectories: maintenance personnel utilize standardized Kubernetes tools to uniformly manage containerized applications and the underlying storage infrastructure; they embrace declarative interfaces for the management of storage system operations and maintenance, enabling automated processes; they integrate with cloud-native maintenance systems to facilitate monitoring, alerting, and log processing; and they are designed to interoperate with cloud-native databases, thereby providing a seamless experience across both public and private cloud environments.

4) **Data Management:**

In the current information age, data management has become one of the increasingly severe challenges for enterprises and organizations. With the continuous growth of data volume and the increase in diversity, future distributed storage needs to adopt new strategies for further development in the field of data management, improve the efficiency of data management, and meet the growing data demands.

a) **Multi-data Center Disaster Recovery:**

Multi-data center disaster recovery has emerged as a crucial approach for effectively addressing and mitigating the risks associated with data concentration and ensuring business continuity. Enterprises typically establish multiple data centers to promptly restore data and applications in the event of a disaster, thereby minimizing the resultant losses. In addition, requirements such as concurrent reading and writing, cross-site consistency, no distance constraint, and scalability to multiple data centers will constitute the key to the advancement of distributed storage technology.

b) **Intelligent Operation and Maintenance:**
Intelligent operation and maintenance has emerged as a consensus within the industry and has been pragmatically implemented in the domain of AIOps (Dang, Lin and Huang 2019, pp. 4–5). However, in storage areas such as fault prediction, performance optimization, and capacity planning, there is still scope for improvement, encompassing the enhancement of accuracy and system auto-tuning based on business characteristics. In the future, distributed storage is required to achieve intelligent operation and maintenance, be capable of detecting and automatically resolving potential faults in advance, and possess abundant application programming interface (API) for seamless connection with multi-cloud environments.

c) **Data Inter-platform Mobility:**
Currently, enterprise data is frequently stored in numerous private clouds or distant public clouds. The distributed storage data under diverse CPU architectures fail to be interconnected, giving rise to an extremely prominent data island phenomenon (Carruthers 2022, pp. 29–50). To address these issues, future distributed storage must take into account data and application characteristics, enabling the free flow across clouds and architectures. This will allow users to obtain a consistent experience on any cloud platform and infrastructure, and they only need to pay attention to the data.

5) **Green Energy Efficiency:**
More than half of the cost incurred in a data center is attributed to electricity consumption. To attain carbon neutrality, the storage system, being one of the major elements of the data center, has made green energy efficiency a key and indispensable demand. Under the precondition of ensuring performance, data storage needs to comprehensively take into account factors such as scale, medium, architecture, and innovation to minimize energy consumption. Currently, several potential directions can be contemplated for attempts at green energy conservation, including:

a) **A Balance Between Storage and Computing:** Optimize the proportion of storage and computing in the data center and strive toward concurrent advancement in both storage and computing to enhance resource utilization and minimize energy consumption.

b) **Energy Conservation in Storage Efficiency:** Enhance data storage efficiency through the adoption of a separated computing and storage architecture, high-density data storage, and ECs.

c) **Algorithmic Energy Conservation:** Utilize data deduplication and compression technologies to enhance data utilization efficiency and employ multi-protocol access technologies to improve data access efficiency.

d) **Medium Energy Conservation:** Transform the conventional magnetic medium into flash memory medium (Pavan et al. 1997, pp. 1248–1271) and substitute mechanical hard disks with solid-state drives (Deng 2011, pp. 1–27). Given that solid-state drives lack a mechanical structure and feature higher density, they can cut energy consumption by approximately 50% compared to disk media of the same capacity. Meanwhile, cold Blu-ray media has supplanted tapes as the cold storage medium. Currently, the operating power consumption of a light disk library can be restricted within 200 W, and the static power consumption does not exceed 10 W.

1.4 Chapter Summary

Data is increasingly emerging as the core of social life, thereby drawing escalating attention to the research on data storage. Highly available and highly reliable distributed storage systems constitute the crucial guarantee for ensuring data integrity. This chapter commences by discussing the fundamental concepts and evolution of storage systems, subsequently elaborating in detail on the disparities between reliability and availability, and introducing two typical redundancy mechanisms, namely, replication and ECs. Additionally, it explores various metrics related to reliability that may be utilized in the subsequent chapters. Finally, the future development trend of distributed storage is elaborated comprehensively, with the aim of providing a guiding orientation for future research.

Discussion Questions

1 What is distributed storage? Explain briefly its definition and four main characteristics.

Distributed storage refers to a system consisting of a cluster of storage nodes formed by multiple interconnected servers. This system leverages network connectivity to perform data synchronization and read/write operations. Data is distributed across different nodes, and reliability is ensured through redundancy mechanisms. Key characteristics of distributed storage include high scalability (horizontal scaling of storage capacity and performance), multi-protocol support (support for block, file, object, and big data storage protocols), high performance (high throughput and data bandwidth), and high reliability (dynamic detection and isolation of faulty nodes with automatic data reconstruction).

Explain the principle of ECs and their application advantages in distributed storage.

2 Erasure coding is a data redundancy technology that splits the original data into k data blocks and generates m parity blocks, resulting in a total of $n = k + m$ blocks stored across different nodes. As long as any k valid blocks are available, the original data can be fully reconstructed. The key advantages of erasure coding include high storage efficiency (with lower redundancy compared to replication strategies), strong fault tolerance (capable of recovering from multiple node failures), and reduced network overhead (e.g., local repairable codes minimize the number of helper nodes, while regenerating codes optimize repair bandwidth).

3 Compare the advantages and disadvantages of the replication strategy and the EC strategy, and illustrate their respective applicable scenarios with examples.

The replication strategy ensures reliability by creating multiple replicas of data. Its advantages include simple implementation and high read efficiency (enabling parallel reads across replicas), while its disadvantages involve significant storage overhead (e.g., three replicas require three times the storage space) and higher write operation costs. This strategy is well suited for scenarios where high read performance and relatively small data volumes are required, such as in GFS. On the other hand, the erasure coding strategy generates redundant data through encoding. Its key advantages are higher storage efficiency (with lower redundancy compared to replication) and suitability for large-scale data storage. However, it also has disadvantages, including computationally complex encoding and decoding processes and longer recovery times. Erasure coding is particularly suitable for large-scale data storage scenarios, such as cloud storage or cold data backup. For example, Facebook has saved petabytes of storage space using erasure coding.

References

Burstein, I., 2021, August. Nvidia data center processing unit (dpu) architecture. In 2021 IEEE Hot Chips 33 Symposium (HCS) (pp. 1–20). IEEE.

Calder, B., Wang, J., Ogus, A., Nilakantan, N., Skjolsvold, A., McKelvie, S., Xu, Y., Srivastav, S., Wu, J., Simitci, H. and Haridas, J., 2011, October. Windows azure storage: a highly available cloud storage service with strong consistency. In Proceedings of the Twenty-Third ACM Symposium on Operating Systems Principles (pp. 143–157).

Carruthers, A., 2022. Breaking data silos. In: Building the snowflake data cloud: monetizing and democratizing your data (pp. 29–50). Berkeley, CA: Apress.

Dang, Y., Lin, Q. and Huang, P., 2019, May. Aiops: real-world challenges and research innovations. In 2019 IEEE/ACM 41st International Conference on Software Engineering: Companion Proceedings (ICSE-Companion) (pp. 4–5). IEEE.

Deng, Y., 2011. What is the future of disk drives, death or rebirth? ACM Computing Surveys (CSUR), 43(3), pp. 1–27.

Geyer, A., Ritter, D., Lee, D.H., Ahn, M., Pietrzyk, J., Krause, A., Habich, D. and Lehner, W., 2023. Working with disaggregated systems. What are the challenges and opportunities of RDMA and CXL? (pp. 1–8).

Ghani, A., Badshah, A., Jan, S., Alshdadi, A.A. and Daud, A., 2020. Issues and challenges in cloud storage architecture: a survey. arXiv preprint arXiv:2004.06809. (pp. 1–21).

Ghemawat, S., Gobioff, H. and Leung, S.T., 2003, October. The Google file system. In Proceedings of the nineteenth ACM symposium on Operating systems principles (pp. 29–43).

McCartney, S., 1999. ENIAC: the triumphs and tragedies of the world's first computer. Walker & Company. (pp. 1–11)

Pavan, P., Bez, R., Olivo, P. and Zanoni, E., 1997. Flash memory cells-an overview. Proceedings of the IEEE, 85(8), pp. 1248–1271.

Perumal, S. and Kritzinger, P., 2004. A tutorial on RAID storage systems. (pp. 1–9).

Sathiamoorthy, M., Asteris, M., Papailiopoulos, D., Dimakis, A.G., Vadali, R., Chen, S. and Borthakur, D., 2013. Xoring elephants: novel erasure codes for big data. arXiv preprint arXiv:1301.3791. (pp. 1–19).

Weatherspoon, H. and Kubiatowicz, J.D., 2002, March. Erasure coding vs. replication: a quantitative comparison. In International Workshop on Peer-to-Peer Systems (pp. 328–337). Berlin, Heidelberg: Springer Berlin Heidelberg. (pp. 1–11).

2
Codes for Distributed Storage

With the rapid proliferation of big data and cloud computing, the field of data storage technology has witnessed substantial advancements, underscoring the growing significance of distributed storage systems (DSSs). The deficiencies inherent in conventional data replication strategies, such as exorbitant storage costs, feeble fault tolerance, and substantial network bandwidth consumption when handling vast amounts of data, have garnered considerable attention. First, traditional replication strategies necessitate the storage of multiple copies of the original data on distinct storage nodes, resulting in significant wastage of storage space. Second, the prevalent three-replica strategy offers limited fault tolerance, rendering it incapable of accommodating failures or losses of more than two nodes. Moreover, the synchronization and transmission between replicas consume a substantial portion of network bandwidth, thereby adversely impacting the overall system performance.

To tackle these challenges, the domain of DSSs has witnessed the emergence of coding technology. This technology mitigates redundancy, enhances data fault tolerance, and improves storage efficiency through data coding. Unlike conventional replication mechanisms, storage coding initially partitions the original data into data blocks. Subsequently, these data blocks undergo coding processes to generate redundant blocks known as encoded blocks or parity chunks. Ultimately, all the data blocks and encoded blocks are dispersed and stored across diverse storage nodes, thereby accomplishing efficient data protection and recovery. EC stands as a pivotal storage coding technique that facilitates high-reliability storage with low redundancy. It attains superior reliability and availability in comparison to replication strategies while effectively curtailing storage costs.

Following the division and encoding of data, EC disperses the data blocks and encoded blocks across multiple distinct nodes. Leveraging specific characteristics, it achieves reliable data recovery even in the presence of multiple node failures. Moreover, EC effectively utilizes network transmission bandwidth

Distributed Storage in Practice, First Edition. Hui Li, Hanxu Hou, and Hong Tan.

resources. In comparison to traditional replication strategies, certain EC implementations facilitate the dispersed transmission of repair data, while others minimize the volume of repair data transmitted. This substantial reduction in network transmission load significantly enhances data transmission efficiency. This aspect assumes paramount importance in DSSs, where ensuring the reliability of vast amounts of data poses not only a challenge but also a bottleneck. EC emerges as a pivotal technology in surmounting this bottleneck.

This chapter commences by offering a comprehensive overview of maximum distance separable (MDS) codes and ECs. Subsequently, it provides a detailed introduction to several efficient ECs possessing MDS or near-MDS property.

2.1 Preliminaries

In this section, an elaboration on a significant property of ECs, namely, MDS, is presented initially. Furthermore, ECs are categorized in accordance with their MDS property.

2.1.1 MDS Codes and ECs

From the Singleton bound (Singleton 1964, pp. 116–118), it can be proven that in a linear code (n, k, d), where the redundancy level is defined as $r = n - k$, its minimum distance d satisfies $d \leq r + 1$. When $d = r + 1$, an $(n, n - r, r + 1)$ code is called an MDS code. In other words, MDS codes are linear codes with a redundancy level of r and a minimum distance $d = r + 1$. From the perspective of storage coding, a file is divided into k data blocks and then encoded to generate $n - k$ blocks with $n > k$, and these n blocks are subsequently stored on different nodes based on specific placement rules. In the event of a storage node failure, selecting any k nodes from the remaining nodes enables the recovery of the original data. Codes possessing this property are commonly referred to as MDS codes. Unless explicitly specified, the ECs mentioned below pertain to codes possessing MDS property.

ECs originated in the field of communication transmission as a forward error correction technique. Initially, they were employed in network transmission to prevent data loss. Presently, ECs are widely used in large-scale DSSs for data maintenance. Notable examples include DiskReduce (Fan et al. 2009, pp. 6–10) developed by Carnegie Mellon University, HDFS-RAID (Sathiamoorthy et al. 2013, pp. 1–13) by Facebook, Colossus (Serenyi 2017, pp. 1–10) by Google, and Azure (Calder et al. 2011, pp. 143–157) by Microsoft. These systems leverage ECs to enhance reliability while minimizing costs. In the realm of ECs, the file is

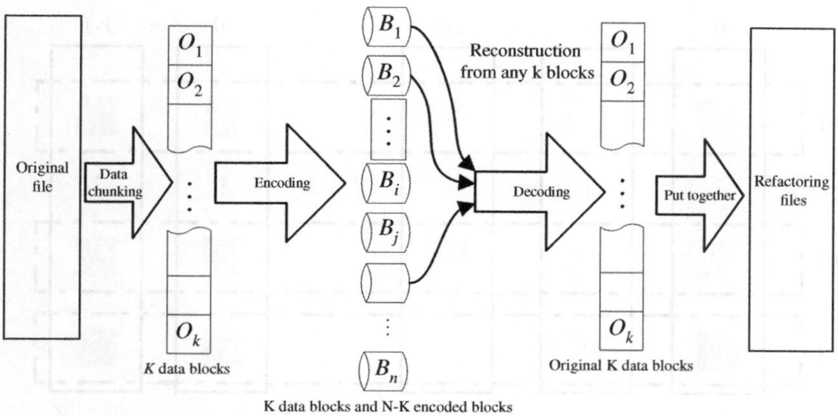

Figure 2.1 Coding process of erasure codes.

partitioned into k blocks, which are subsequently coded to generate n blocks for distributed storage. ECs, as opposed to replication strategies, minimize redundant storage while upholding a heightened level of reliability. By harnessing the MDS property of ECs, the original file can be reconstructed with just k valid blocks.

The fundamental principle of ECs is depicted in Figure 2.1. Initially, the original file O is partitioned into k data blocks, denoted as $O_1, O_2, \ldots, O_k$. Subsequently, encoding is performed to generate $n - k$ encoded blocks, where $n > k$. The data blocks and encoded blocks are represented as $B_1, B_2, \ldots, B_n$ at this stage. Lastly, following specific rules, these n blocks are stored on different nodes in a DSS. In the event of node failures within this system, as long as there are no fewer than k blocks remaining, any k blocks of which can be utilized to recover the lost data and maintain the reliability of the DSS.

In a DSS, data is distributed among multiple interconnected storage nodes. Figure 2.2 presents a distributed storage model based on MDS codes. Assume that the system consists of n storage nodes, where k nodes are data nodes, and r nodes are coding nodes, satisfying $n = k + r$. The k data nodes store data blocks labeled as $D_0, D_1, \ldots, D_{k-1}$, while the r coding nodes store encoded blocks labeled as $C_0, C_1, \cdots, C_{r-1}$. The MDS code divides the original file O into k equal parts, which are then stored in the k data nodes sequentially. The r encoded blocks generated by the encoding process are placed in the r coding nodes. In scenarios involving large files, the original file needs to be further divided into smaller segments, and each segment is encoded separately. The original data and encoded data involved in one encoding process are regarded as a stripe. Each stripe independently constitutes a set of data and encoded blocks, and different stripes are unrelated to each other. Notably, the mapping between logical stripes and

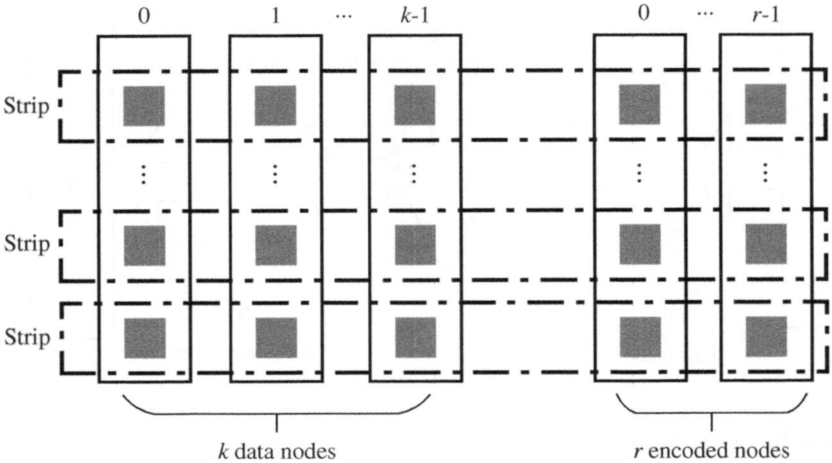

Figure 2.2 Distributed storage model based on erasure codes.

physical storage nodes is not fixed and can be achieved through stripe rotation. This dynamic mapping strategy facilitates load balancing within DSSs, ensuring optimal utilization of storage resources.

Compared to replication strategies, ECs offer a compelling solution to reduce storage overhead while ensuring reliability and storage efficiency. However, it is important to acknowledge the limitations of ECs in DSSs. First, in a DSS based on ECs, the failure of a node necessitates the download of data from k nodes to recover the original file and then regenerate the missing data. This process incurs a significant amount of data transmission, which is k times the size of the failed data. Particularly in scenarios where nodes are distributed widely across the network, node repair consumes substantial network bandwidth, impacting overall system performance. This effect is particularly pronounced in big data environments where both data volume and the number of storage nodes grow exponentially. Second, the extensive data downloads required for repair operations inevitably slow down the node repair process. For a DSS that experiences frequent failures, the repair rate of nodes directly affects its reliability. If the repair rate fails to keep pace with the rate of node failures, the system will be unable to maintain effective reliability. Furthermore, the high computational complexity involved in the encoding and decoding of ECs poses challenges for large-scale industrial applications. In conclusion, the aforementioned limitations associated with ECs have emerged as bottlenecks that hinder further advancements in the field.

2.1.2 Classification of ECs

The current mainstream ECs can be classified based on the completeness of the MDS property, as depicted in Figure 2.3. Several ECs have been extensively investigated in DSSs, including Reed–Solomon (RS) codes (Wicker and Bhargava 1999, pp. 1–19), regenerating codes (RGCs) (Dimakis et al. 2010, pp. 4539–4551), array codes (Blaum et al. 1998, pp. 1855–1909), and LRCs (Papailiopoulos and Dimakis 2014, pp. 5843–5855). The following is a brief introduction to each of them:

1) **RS Codes:** RS code, being the earliest form of MDS codes, originated in 1960 and has since undergone extensive development, resulting in a well-established theoretical foundation. RS codes can be categorized into two types based on their generator matrices: Vandermonde Reed–Solomon (VRS) codes and Cauchy Reed–Solomon (CRS) codes. VRS employs Vandermonde matrices as their generator matrices, while CRS utilizes Cauchy matrices for the same purpose.
2) **Regenerating Code:** RGCs possess the MDS property and can be regarded as a branch derived from RS codes, thereby incorporating linear network coding principles and leveraging the max-flow min-cut property to significantly enhance repair efficiency for node failures. From a network information theory perspective, it can be mathematically demonstrated that an equivalent amount of network bandwidth as the lost data is sufficient for repairing the loss. Consequently, RGCs enable node repair by retrieving only a fraction of the entire data, eliminating the need for complete file reconstruction. The underlying principle of RGCs remains rooted in their MDS property, where helper nodes transmit information to recover lost data when certain storage nodes encounter failures within the network.
3) **Array Codes:** Array codes are designed to store both original and redundant data in a 2D or multidimensional array, employing only XOR operations for encoding, decoding, updating, and reconstruction processes. In comparison with RS codes, the simplicity of these operations renders array codes highly

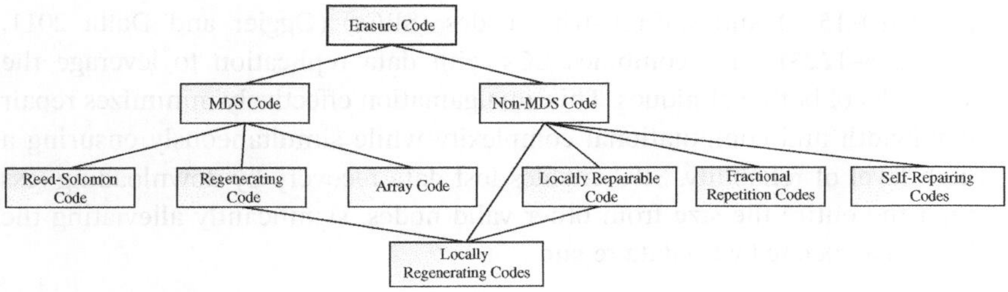

Figure 2.3 Classification of erasure codes.

versatile and applicable across various domains. Array codes can be classified into two categories: horizontal array codes and vertical array codes.

Horizontal array codes pertain to an array coding methodology wherein redundancy is stored in separate redundant columns, distinct from the data columns. The distinguishing characteristic of this structure lies in the allocation of dedicated disks, referred to as redundant disks, exclusively for storing redundancy, while the remaining disks are devoted to data storage. This configuration offers exceptional scalability for the entire disk array.

Vertical array codes are a coding method that integrates redundancy within data columns. In this approach, certain disks store both original and redundant data, resulting in simpler structures that evenly distribute computational complexity across disks. Unlike horizontal array codes, which can lead to concentrated hotspots on disks due to continuous write operations and frequent access to redundant data disks, vertical array codes naturally address this bottleneck through its structural balance. However, the uniformity of vertical array codes also creates significant inter-disk dependencies that may hinder scalability.

4) **Locally Repairable Code:** LRCs, although not fully possessing MDS property, are classified as non-MDS codes. However, the locally repairable capability of LRCs enables faster repair speeds in comparison to RS codes, thus positioning LRCs as one of the most popular choices for ECs in recent years. Because of remarkable performance and practicality, LRCs have gained widespread adoption by influential industry players, such as Microsoft and Facebook. Furthermore, LRCs exhibit strong scalability and can be effectively combined with various other ECs. For example, the combination of LRCs and RGCs results in locally regenerating codes (LRGCs) (Kamath et al. 2014, pp. 4637–4660), which harnesses the collective advantages of RGCs and LRCs. This amalgamation holds considerable research value and presents exciting opportunities for further exploration.

Additionally, there are other notable codes within the realm of DSSs, such as fractional repetition codes (FRCs) (El Rouayheb and Ramchandran 2010, pp. 1510–1517) and self-repairing codes (SRCs) (Oggier and Datta 2011, pp. 1215–1223). FRC combines ECs with data replication to leverage the strengths of both techniques. This amalgamation effectively minimizes repair bandwidth and computational complexity while simultaneously ensuring a high level of reliability. SRC enables lost data recovery by downloading less than the entire file size from other valid nodes, significantly alleviating the burden associated with data repair.

2.2 RS Codes

This section mainly centers on the RS codes, which are extensively utilized in storage systems, along with the prominent variant derived therefrom—CRS code.

2.2.1 Original RS Code

Original RS code (Reed and Solomon 1960, pp. 300–304) is a type of channel code proposed by I.S. Reed and G.S. Solomon in 1960. Owing to its remarkable error correction capabilities, the RS code has found extensive application across large-scale industrial storage systems. Here is a theoretical elaboration of an RS code(n, k). Let $a_i \in GF(q)$ stand for the k message symbols, where $i = 0, 1, \dots, k-1$. $(x_0, x_1, \dots, x_{n-1})$ constitute any n distinct elements from $GF(q)$, and the polynomial f be defined as

$$f(x) = \sum_{i=0}^{k-1} a_i \prod_{\substack{j=0 \\ (j \neq i)}}^{k-1} \frac{(x - x_j)}{(x_i - x_j)} := \sum_{i=0}^{k-1} b_i x^i. \tag{2.1}$$

It follows that f is the $(k-1)$-degree interpolation polynomial that complies with

$$f(x_i) = a_i, \quad 0 \leq i \leq (k-1). \tag{2.2}$$

The k message symbols in an RS codeword are precisely encoded to n ordered symbols $(f(x_0), f(x_1), \dots, f(x_{n-1}))$. The initial k symbols denote message symbols, while the rest form redundant symbols.

The MDS property of RS codes arises from the fact that the polynomial f can be calculated using any set of k evaluations, by solving a nonsingular system of k equations involving the unknown coefficients $\{b_i\}_{i=0}^{k-1}$, as follows:

$$\begin{bmatrix} f(x_{i_1}) \\ f(x_{i_2}) \\ \vdots \\ f(x_{i_k}) \end{bmatrix} = \begin{bmatrix} 1 & x_{i_1} & \cdots & x_{i_1}^{k-1} \\ 1 & x_{i_2} & \cdots & x_{i_2}^{k-1} \\ \vdots & \vdots & \vdots & \vdots \\ 1 & x_{i_k} & \cdots & x_{i_k}^{k-1} \end{bmatrix} \begin{bmatrix} b_0 \\ b_1 \\ \vdots \\ b_{k-1} \end{bmatrix}, \tag{2.3}$$

where $i_1, \dots, i_k$ represent any set of k distinct indices selected from $\{0, \dots, n-1\}$. It can be discerned from this that RS codes are capable of achieving recovery from the loss of any $n-k$ symbols. However, in the case of the loss of a single symbol, RS codes are required to reconstruct the entire data first and then restore the lost symbol.

Currently, RS code is a crucial coding technology widely utilized in the domain of DSSs. It attains high reliability with low redundancy and can withstand multiple failed storage nodes, consequently ensuring data integrity amidst various failure scenarios. Nevertheless, the RS code also exhibits certain drawbacks. First, its encoding and decoding computational complexity is high, particularly in large-scale storage systems that may result in performance bottlenecks. Second, due to the slow repair speed of the RS code, when multiple nodes fail, data repair processes may take an extended period. Therefore, it is essential to weigh the pros and cons of RS code while making specific improvements based on practical scenarios.

2.2.2 CRS Code

The CRS code (Blomer 1995, pp. 2–11), derived from the Cauchy matrix, is a kind of RS code. Unlike the original RS code, which involves high computational complexity due to n-dimensional dot product and multiplication operations on a finite field during encoding, CRS code achieves improved encoding and decoding speed by exclusively utilizing *XOR* operations while avoiding complex multiplications.

2.2.2.1 Encoding Process of CRS Code

Select the desired values for r and k, and utilize them to construct a Cauchy matrix. For instance, if $r = 2$ and $k = 4$, assign $x_1 = 1, x_2 = 2, y_1 = 3, y_2 = 4, y_3 = 5$, and $y_4 = 6$ as variables. Note that $x_1, x_2, y_1 \sim y_4$ should not be repeated. The aforementioned parameters are randomly chosen. The Cauchy matrix C can be constructed using

$$C = \begin{bmatrix} \frac{1}{x_1+y_1} & \frac{1}{x_1+y_2} & \cdots & \frac{1}{x_1+y_k} \\ \frac{1}{x_2+y_1} & \frac{1}{x_2+y_2} & \cdots & \frac{1}{x_2+y_k} \\ \vdots & \vdots & \ddots & \vdots \\ \frac{1}{x_r+y_1} & \frac{1}{x_r+y_2} & \cdots & \frac{1}{x_r+y_k} \end{bmatrix} = \begin{pmatrix} \frac{1}{1+3} & \frac{1}{1+4} & \frac{1}{1+5} & \frac{1}{1+6} \\ \frac{1}{2+3} & \frac{1}{2+4} & \frac{1}{2+5} & \frac{1}{2+6} \end{pmatrix} = \begin{pmatrix} 2^{-1}5^{-1}4^{-1}7^{-1} \\ 1^{-1}6^{-1}7^{-1}4^{-1} \end{pmatrix}, \tag{2.4}$$

where the addition is an *XOR* operation.

According to the values of k and r, a specific value for w is chosen such that $2^w \geq k + r$. In this case, $w = 3$ is selected, which corresponds to setting the finite field as $GF(2^3)$. The selection of the primitive polynomial depends on the value of w. For $w = 3$, the primitive polynomial p chosen is x^3+x+1. Table 2.1 presents

Table 2.1 Primitive polynomials.

w	**Primitive polynomial *P***	**Octal form**
$w = 3$	$x^3 + x + 1$	013
$w = 4$	$x^4 + x + 1$	023
$w = 5$	$x^5 + x^2 + 1$	045
$w = 6$	$x^6 + x + 1$	0103
$w = 7$	$x^7 + x^3 + 1$	0211
$w = 8$	$x^8 + x^4 + x^3 + x^2 + 1$	0435

Table 2.2 Binary matrix corresponding to element 7.

Rows	***R***	**Matrix**		
Row_1	$Row_1R_1 = 7 = x^2 + x + 1$	1	1	1
Row_2	$Row_2R_1 = 7 = (xRow_1)\, mod\, pR_1 = 7R_{i+1} = xR_i mod$ $P = (x^3x^3 + x + 1 + x^2 + x)\, mod\, p = x^2 + 1$	1	0	1
Row_3	$Row_3R_1 = 7 = (xRow_2)\, mod\, pR_1 = 7R_{i+1} = xR_i mod$ $P = (x^3x^3 + x + 1 + x)\, mod\, p = 1$	0	0	1

several alternative primitive polynomials that can be utilized to generate corresponding binary matrices for each element.

For example, when $w = 3$, the binary matrix corresponding to element 7 is shown in Table 2.2. Take 7 at the first row, that is, $Row_1 R_1 = 7$, and then follow the recursive formula $Row_{i+1}R_1 = 7 = (xRow_i)\ mod\ p$ to get the value of Row_{i+1} and then a total of w rows are obtained, where p is the primitive polynomial of $w = 3$. Then convert the *row* value back to binary form. Finally, combine the binary form of each row's value into a square matrix in order, and invert the square matrix to get the final matrix:

$$7 = \begin{pmatrix} 001 \\ 101 \\ 111 \end{pmatrix}.$$

The addition and subtraction operations on binary matrices follow the same rules as those for ordinary matrices, with the exception that all additions and subtractions are performed using *XOR*. The multiplication of binary matrices is carried out using the standard algorithm for multiplication of ordinary matrices. Similarly, obtaining the inverse matrix of a binary matrix can be achieved through

Gaussian elimination, which is identical to the approach used for ordinary matrices.

The inverse matrix of the binary matrix corresponding to 7, denoted as

$$7^{-1} = \begin{pmatrix} 110 \\ 011 \\ 100 \end{pmatrix},$$

which is the binary matrix corresponding to 7^{-1}. Consequently, these binary matrix elements are subsequently integrated back into the preceding Cauchy matrix C. Ultimately, the resultant $6 * 12$ matrix represents the binary representation of the Cauchy matrix B in accordance with the following:

$$B = \begin{pmatrix} 010011001110 \\ 001100101011 \\ 101010111100 \\ 100111110001 \\ 010110011101 \\ 001011100111 \end{pmatrix}.$$

According to the binary form of the Cauchy matrix, encoding is performed. First, the original data is evenly divided into k data blocks and named $s_1, s_2, \dots, s_k$. Then each data block is further divided into w parts on average. For instance, S_1 can be partitioned as $s_{1,1}, s_{1,2}, \dots, s_{1,w}$. In relation to the aforementioned Cauchy matrix B, it needs to be segmented into 4 original data blocks and 12 smaller data blocks on average. Finally, these divided data blocks are arranged in a sequential manner to obtain a vector denoted as S with $k * w$ elements. Each element represents a small unit of data. Subsequently, matrix multiplication $P = B * S$ is conducted.

After matrix multiplication, the encoding data $P_1, P_2, P_3, \cdots$ of the above example is as follows:

$$P_1 = s_{1,2} + s_{2,2} + s_{2,3} + s_{3,3} + s_{4,1} + s_{4,2},$$
$$P_2 = s_{1,3} + s_{2,1} + s_{3,1} + s_{3,3} + s_{4,2} + s_{4,3},$$
$$P_3 = s_{1,1} + s_{1,3} + s_{2,2} + s_{3,1} + s_{3,2} + s_{3,3} + s_{4,1},$$
$$\vdots .$$

Considering that matrix B comprises only 0 and 1, the product is zero when the element is 0, while it retains the original value when the element is 1. Furthermore, all aforementioned addition operations are performed using *XOR*.

In the process of CRS code encoding, the number of *XOR* operations becomes a crucial factor influencing performance. Hence, minimizing the number of 1 in B

will result in fewer *XOR* operations and reduced computation time. Subsequently, the obtained P are merged to form m parity check blocks. For instance, in the aforementioned example, P_1, P_2, and P_3 are combined into R_1 while P_4, P_5, and P_6 are combined into R_2. The k original data blocks, along with r parity check blocks, are distributed across distinct storage nodes for encoding completion.

2.2.2.2 Decoding Process of CRS Code

Collect any valid k data blocks from $k + r$ blocks. The obtained k blocks are merged into D, and the relationship between D and the original data block S can be easily determined as $D = C_{code}S$, where C_{code} represents the residual matrix associated with the selected k blocks. Calculate the inverse matrix of C_{ccde}, C^{-1}_{code}, and finally calculate $S = C^{-1}_{code}$D.

The CRS code has significant advantages in distributed storage coding, especially in terms of computational performance. By using the Cauchy matrix, the encoding and decoding process becomes more efficient, reducing processing latency and improving overall system performance. CRS code is adaptable and scalable, making them suitable for different sizes and types of data blocks in large-scale DSSs. However, it also faces limitations due to complex operations based on finite fields, resulting in high computational complexity.

2.3 Regenerating Codes

In a DSS, data of size M is encoded and then partitioned across $n = k + r$ storage nodes, with each node holding a M/k block of the original or redundant data. The failure of a storage node necessitates a repair process to maintain system reliability and redundancy, involving the recovery and transfer of lost data to a replacement node. This repair process incurs bandwidth consumption known as repair bandwidth. Traditional ECs, such as RS codes, require downloading data from k nodes and reconstructing the entire original data for encoding and recovering data of the failed node. Consequently, RS codes result in inefficient repair bandwidth utilization equal to M multiplied by k times the repaired data size. This inefficiency becomes more pronounced when k is large or when multiple node failures occur in larger scale storage systems, requiring substantial downloads from other nodes for repairs. Therefore, minimizing repair bandwidth is crucial for enhancing repair speed and improving storage efficiency.

This section primarily concentrates on RGCs that can diminish the repair bandwidth. First, a concise introduction to RGC is presented, succeeded by a summary of diverse constructions of RGC. Eventually, rack-aware regenerating codes (RRCs) are introduced, a kind of RGC tailored for rack scenarios.

2.3.1 Introduction to RGCs

In order to maintain the reliability of a DSS, data regeneration is necessary when a node fails. A study (Dimakis et al. 2010, pp. 4539–4551) conducted in 2007 focused on minimizing transmission bandwidth during the repair process for distributed storage with a single failed node and referred to symbols as the basic encoding and decoding elements, where file size represents the number of symbols. A data file of size M on $GF(2^w)$ was encoded into n blocks of size α and distributed among n nodes, each storing one block, which still adheres to the MDS property, enabling recovery of the original data from any k nodes. Although k nodes are sufficient for data recovery after a node failure, it is possible to regenerate the data in a new node by downloading β symbols from d valid nodes, where $k < d < = n - 1$. These helper nodes involved in the repair process are responsible for providing storage assistance. The total downloaded data from helper nodes is $\gamma = d * \beta$, also known as repair bandwidth.

Drawing upon network coding theory, an information flow graph (IFG) (Dimakis et al. 2010, pp. 4539–4551) is employed to model the data flow encompassing storage coding, fault repair, and other processes within DSS. The depiction of the IFG incorporates parameters $(n, k, d, \alpha, \gamma)$, while introducing the concept of RGC. RGC must satisfy two essential requirements: (1) enabling reconstruction of original data using any k nodes out of n nodes to tolerate up to $n - k$ node failures and (2) facilitating repair of data stored on any failed node by utilizing data from any d helper nodes. The parameter d denotes the repair degree, α represents the size of data stored per node, and γ represents the cumulative size of downloaded data required from a set of d selected available nodes for the purpose of repairing a failed node. The size of downloaded data from each node is $\beta = \gamma / d$. A balanced relationship exists between parameter α and parameter γ that adheres to the following equation (2.5):

$$M \leq \sum_{i=1}^{k} min\{(d - i + 1)\beta, \alpha\}. \tag{2.5}$$

The different values of the function corresponding to this relationship give rise to a curve in the 2D coordinate system, known as the trade-off curve of repair bandwidth and storage. As depicted in Figure 2.4, the RGCs associated with the two optimal points on this curve are referred to as minimum-storage regenerating (MSR) codes and minimum-bandwidth regenerating (MBR) codes.

The objective of MSR codes is to minimize repair bandwidth while minimizing storage overhead, ensuring that each node only stores M/k bits of data. Consequently, MSR codes can be derived using

$$(\alpha_{MSR}, \gamma_{MSR}) = \left(\frac{M}{k}, \frac{Md}{k(d - k + 1)}\right). \tag{2.6}$$

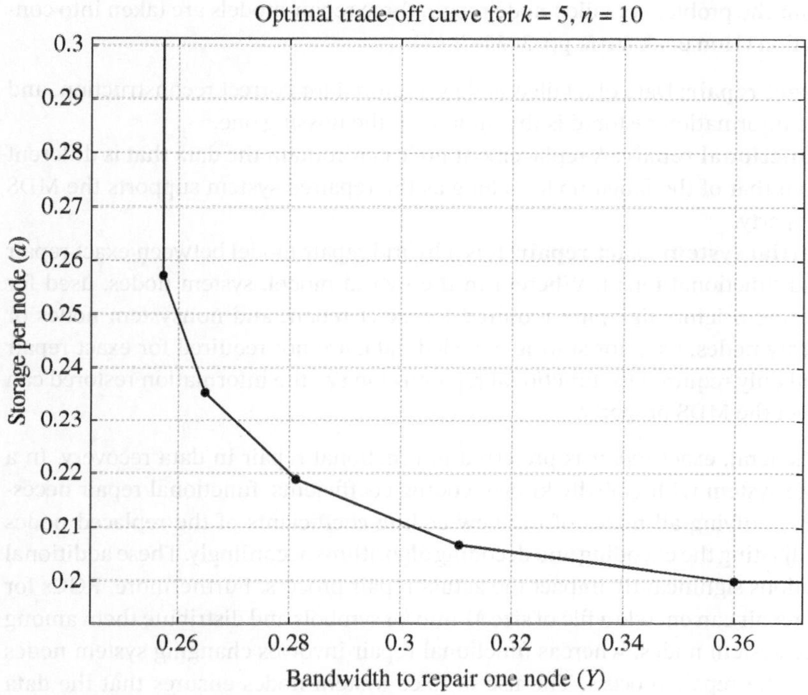

Figure 2.4 Trade-off curve of repair bandwidth and storage.

when $d = n - 1$, the repair bandwidth and storage are minimized to

$$\left(\alpha_{MSR}^{min}, \gamma_{MSR}^{min}\right) = \left(\frac{M}{k}, \frac{M}{k} \cdot \frac{n-1}{n-k}\right). \tag{2.7}$$

The MBR codes achieve the lowest repair bandwidth compared to MSR codes, albeit with a slight increase in storage overhead. MBR codes can be derived using

$$(\alpha_{MBR}, \gamma_{MBR}) = \left(\frac{2Md}{k(2d-k+1)}, \frac{2Md}{k(2d-k+1)}\right). \tag{2.8}$$

when $d = n - 1$, the minimum repair bandwidth and storage are attained, and the corresponding parameters satisfy

$$\left(\alpha_{\text{MBR}}^{min}, \gamma_{MBR}^{min}\right) = \left(\frac{M}{k} \cdot \frac{2n-2}{2n-k-1}, \frac{M}{k} \cdot \frac{2n-2}{2n-k-1}\right). \tag{2.9}$$

Furthermore, Dimakis et al. (2010, pp. 4539–4551) suggest that the utilization of linear network coding (Li et al. 2003, pp. 371–381) enables the construction of RGCs corresponding to any point on the trade-off curve of repair bandwidth and storage. Simulation experiments have demonstrated that RGCs can effectively reduce network bandwidth overhead during fault repair processes.

As for the problem of failed node repair, three repair models are taken into consideration (Hou et al. 2016, pp. 3053–3069):

1) **Exact repair:** Data of a failed node is required for correct reconstruction, and the information restored is the same with the missing one.
2) **Functional repair:** A replacement node can contain the data that is different from that of the failed node as long as the repaired system supports the MDS property.
3) **Partial system exact repair:** It is a hybrid repair model between exact repair and functional repair. Wherein in the hybrid model, system nodes, used for storing original data, are required for exact repair, and nonsystem nodes or parity nodes, used for storing encoded data, are not required for exact repair and only required for functional repair as long as the information restored can meet the MDS property.

In general, exact repair is preferred to functional repair in data recovery. In a storage system with globally known coding coefficients, functional repair necessitates notifying all nodes of the new coding coefficients of the replaced nodes and adjusting the encoding and decoding algorithms accordingly. These additional operations significantly impact the actual repair process. Furthermore, RGCs for exact repair can encode a file of size M into $k\alpha$ symbols and distribute them among k fixed system nodes, whereas functional repair involves changing system nodes during the repair process. The use of fixed system nodes ensures that the data collector (DC) can obtain original data symbols to accelerate the repair speed. Therefore, in data recovery scenarios, exact repair is often faster than functional repair and has broader application prospects.

The optimization of RGCs on failed node repair bandwidth is significant, making them a popular research topic in the field of ECs. In recent years, there have been numerous studies focusing on optimizing RGCs, including modifications to construction methods, reduction of computational complexity, and enhancement of practicality. The next section provides a detailed introduction to some typical strategies for optimizing RGCs.

2.3.2 Constructions of RGCs

RGCs, as a class of efficient ECs that combine network linear codes, are designed to achieve high efficiency in data repair processes. In particular, when dealing with single-node failures, RGCs can minimize data transmitted compared to other types of ECs. However, in practical DSSs, constructing RGCs requires consideration of factors such as bandwidth limitations, repair speed, and computing resources. Therefore, since the introduction of RGCs, there have been many construction methods with distinctive features. This subsection focuses on several typical constructions for RGCs, including interference alignment (IA), repair by transfer (RT), and product-matrix (PM).

2.3.2.1 Interference Alignment

In the field of communication, IA (Cadambe and Jafar 2008, pp. 3425–3441) refers to the deliberate design of signals emitted by multiple transmitters to project "overlapping shadows" onto receivers that do not require them, ensuring that each receiver can effectively distinguish the desired signal from other interfering signals. Building on IA technology for interference channels, a regenerating coding method (Wu and Dimakis 2009, pp. 2276–2280) based on IA was proposed, which effectively reduces network bandwidth required for repairing single-node failures. The following example illustrates RGCs based on IA.

As illustrated in Figure 2.5, four equally sized original information blocks A_1, A_2, B_1, and B_2 are encoded to produce a total of eight blocks. These blocks are distributed across four storage nodes, each containing two blocks. It is evident that the MDS(4, 2) code possesses the capability to rectify any two node failures. For instance, in the failed event of node 1, conventional methods necessitate downloading four blocks from other nodes for recovering lost A_1 and A_2. However, IA only requires downloading three blocks for completing the repair process. Specifically, $B_1 + B_2$ can be retrieved from node 2, while $(A_1 + B_1) + (2A_2 + B_2)$ can be computed through linear operations on the two blocks in node 3; finally, $2A_1 + B_1 + (A_2 + B_2)$ will be obtained from node 4. Notably, $B_1 + B_2$ can be eliminated from both $(A_1 + B_1) + (2A_2 + B_2)$ and $2A_1 + B_1 + (A_2 + B_2)$, leaving behind two linearly independent equations involving only A_1 and A_2, Therefore,

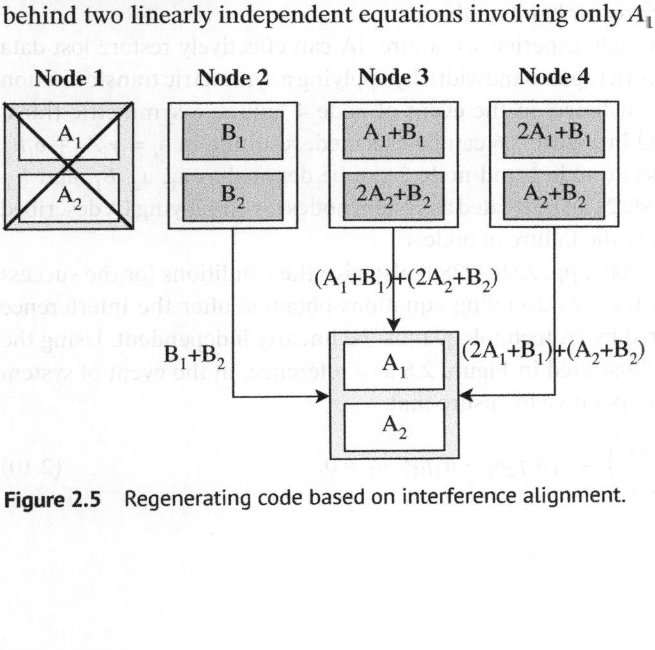

Figure 2.5 Regenerating code based on interference alignment.

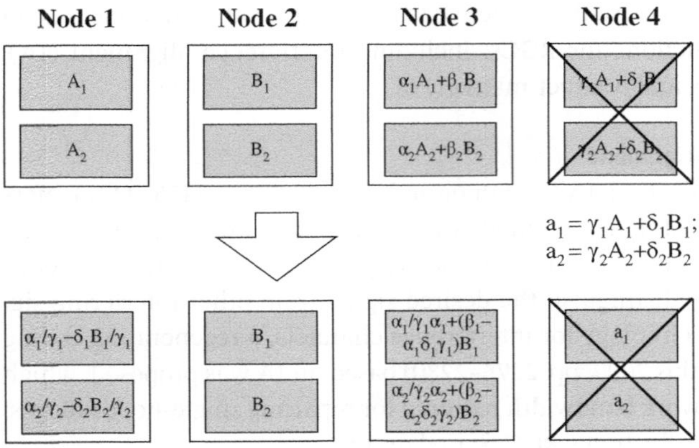

Figure 2.6 Regenerating code repair nonsystem node fault.

A_1 and A_2 can be derived, culminating in the completion of the restoration process.

From the aforementioned process, it is evident that upon recovery of A_1 and A_2, all other nodes generate linear combinations involving A_1, A_2, and $B_1 + B_2$. Consequently, despite the presence of four unknown blocks, $B_1 + B_2$ can be treated as a unified entity; therefore, DC effectively observes only three unknown blocks. As the objective of DC is to recover A_1 and A_2 exclusively, B_1 and B_2 are regarded as "interference signals." In Figure 2.5, these interference signals are aligned in parallel $B_1 + B_2$ to reduce the dimensionality of the interference signals, consequently minimizing network repair bandwidth.

When nonsystem node experiences failure, IA can effectively restore lost data and reduce the network repair bandwidth by applying a symmetric transformation to valid blocks. For instance, in the event of node 4 failure, a symmetric transformation illustrated in Figure 2.6 can be executed, resulting in $\mathrm{a}_i = \gamma_i A_i + \delta_i B_i$. Subsequently, blocks at node 1 and node 3 can be denoted as a_1, a_2, B_1, and B_2. Then, node 4 and node 2 can be treated as system nodes for employing IA described in Figure 2.5 to rectify the failure of node 4.

Wu and Dimakis (2009, pp. 2276–2280) also give the conditions for the success of IA, namely, that the two decoding equations obtained after the interference information is cleared by IA technology must be linearly independent. Using the parameter settings illustrated in Figure 2.6 as a reference, in the event of system node 1 failure, it is imperative to ensure that

$$det\begin{pmatrix} \alpha_1\beta_2 & \alpha_2\beta_1 \\ \gamma_1\delta_2 & \gamma_2\delta_1 \end{pmatrix} = \alpha_1\beta_2\gamma_2\delta_1 - \alpha_2\beta_1\gamma_1\delta_2 \neq 0. \tag{2.10}$$

When nonsystem node 4 fails, the parameters set need to meet the following requirements:

$$det\begin{pmatrix} \dfrac{\delta_2}{\gamma_1\gamma_2} & \dfrac{\delta_1}{\gamma_1\gamma_2} \\ \left(\beta_2 - \dfrac{\alpha_2\delta_2}{\gamma_2}\right)\dfrac{\alpha_1}{\gamma_1} & \left(\beta_1 - \dfrac{\alpha_1\delta_1}{\gamma_1}\right)\dfrac{\alpha_2}{\gamma_2} \end{pmatrix} \neq 0. \tag{2.11}$$

Expanding on this, Shah et al. (2011b, pp. 2134–2158) demonstrate the crucial role of IA in constructing exact repair MSR codes and validate the creation of an MSR code with a repair degree $d = n - 1 \geq 2k - 1$, which satisfies the lower bound for system node repair bandwidth, as well as a high-rate MSR code with a repair degree $d = k + 1$. As one of the earliest construction methods for RGCs, IA has exhibited outstanding performance in reducing repair bandwidth. Furthermore, the concept of aligning and clearing interfering information in the same direction for different decoding equations holds significant implications for practical RGCs.

2.3.2.2 Repair by Transfer

While RGCs can effectively reduce the amount of network bandwidth for repair, they also lead to an increase in computational workload, resulting in higher consumption of computing resources and potential impact on repair speed. Shah et al. (2011a, pp. 1837–1852) introduce a class of exact repair MBR codes with a repair degree $d = n - 1$. Their most significant characteristic, known as repair by transfer (RT), enables failed node repair through simple data transmission without the need for any computational operations. These codes are referred to as RT-MBR codes in this book.

First, utilizing the properties of MBR codes and equation (2.8), the following equation can be derived:

$$\begin{aligned} &\alpha = d\beta, \\ &M = \left(kd - \frac{k(k-1)}{2}\right)\beta. \end{aligned} \tag{2.12}$$

According to the principle of data striping, Shah et al. (2011a, pp. 1837–1852) demonstrated that the value of β in equation (2.12) does not affect the properties of codes. For ease of explaining the principle of RT-MBR codes, let $\beta = 1$, yielding

$$\begin{aligned} &\alpha = d, \\ &M = kd - \binom{k}{2}. \end{aligned} \tag{2.13}$$

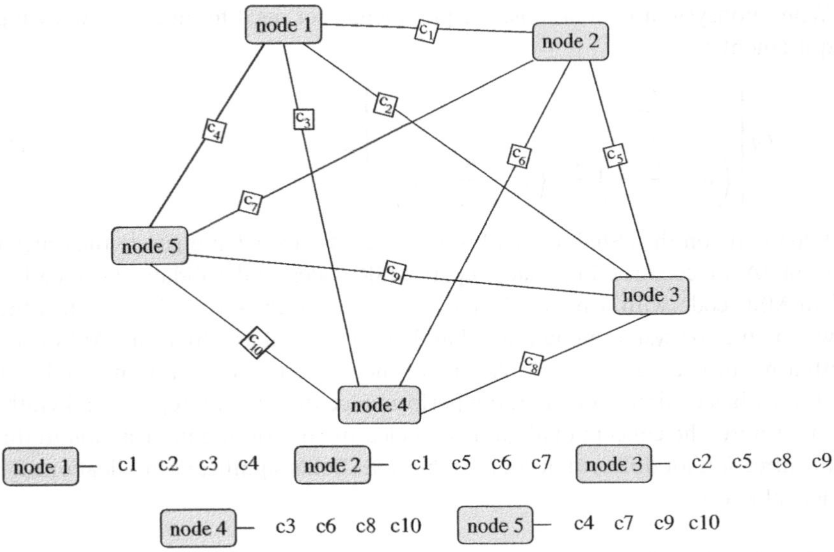

Figure 2.7 Construction of RT-MBR(**5**, **3**, **4**) code.

For an RT-MBR($n = 5$, $k = 3$, $d = 4$) code with $\beta = 1$, the values of α and M can be determined from equation (2.13) as $\alpha = 4$ and $M = 9$, respectively. The set $\{m_i \mid 1 \leq i \leq 9\}$ is utilized to denote nine original information symbols.

As depicted in Figure 2.7, the construction of the RT-MBR(5, 3, 4) code can be visualized on five fully connected graph nodes. Each of these nodes represents an independent storage node, designated as N_i, where $1 \leq i \leq 5$. First, nine information symbols are encoded through MDS(10, 9) code to attain an encoded symbol set $\{c_i \mid 1 \leq i \leq 10\}$. Subsequently, 10 symbols in $\{c_i \mid 1 \leq i \leq 10\}$ are, respectively, allocated to the ten edges of the fully connected graph. Every storage node is accountable for storing the encoded symbols corresponding to the four edges connected to it.

Now assume that node 3 fails. Each of the remaining nodes transfers an information symbol necessary for node 3 to the replacement node for the purpose of completing the repair. It can also be discerned from the fully connected graph depicted in Figure 2.7 that the remaining nodes all possess a common edge with node 3, that is, they encompass the same information symbol. Consequently, this code is capable of conducting the exact repair on node 3 completely, and the repair process is accomplished merely through data transmission. No computation operation is required to be performed on the helper nodes or DC. Furthermore, when β adopts other positive figures, only the number of nodes and the MDS code rate need to be modified for constructing the RT-MBR code corresponding to β.

RT-MBR precludes the execution of any computational procedures throughout repair, thereby maximizing consumption of computing resources. Furthermore, even if a particular node is under repair, users can still access the data stored in this node at any moment since the same data is also stored in other nodes.

Since the proposition of RT, numerous studies have been committed to establishing more efficient RT-RGCs. In a study by Shum and Hu (2012, pp. 1192–1196), a class of linear RT-RGCs aiming at realizing functional repair were put forward, which can minimize disk I/O and repair bandwidth. Nevertheless, Lin and Chung (2014, pp. 3232–3241) presented an exact repair RT-MBR code with superior performance. Compared with the RT-MBR described earlier, under the same circumstances, the necessary field size of this code is reduced from $\binom{k}{2}$ to k, and the encoding computational complexity is also lowered from $O(n^4)$ to $O(n^3)$. Additionally, Chen and Wang (2015, pp. 2070–2073) proved that the requisites for constructing RT-MSR codes are more demanding, and when $k \geq 3$ and $\beta < d - k + 1$, there exists no RT-MSR codes. Moreover, through designing a more complicated two-layer coding framework, high-speed coding of RT-RGCs was accomplished (Zeng et al. 2022, pp. 1099–1104).

2.3.2.3 Product-Matrix

Among diverse construction methods of RGCs (Shah et al. 2010, pp. 1–5; Wu 2011, pp. 3738–3741), the key construction parameters of exact repair RGCs are (n, k, d, α, β), which are subject to the restrictive condition that $n = d + 1$. Nevertheless, Rashmi, Shah and Kumar (2011, pp. 5227–5239) put forward a novel coding framework based on PM, enabling the construction of MBR(n, k, d) codes. These codes merely need to satisfy $k < d < n - 1$ and no longer require to take into account the quantitative relationship between n and d.

Assuming there are n storage nodes, with each node storing α symbols, all the symbols can be organized into a $n * \alpha$ matrix C. In this matrix, the vector $\underline{c}_i^t$ in the i-th row represents the α symbols stored on the i-th node. The matrix C can be expressed as a product of matrices, as shown in the following equation:

$$C = \Psi M. \tag{2.14}$$

This comprises an $n * d$ encoding matrix Ψ and a $d * \alpha$ message matrix M. Ψ is a fixed-value matrix that is independent of M, while M contains all the original symbols and may include repeated symbols. The i-th row of Ψ, denoted as $\underline{\psi}_i^t$, is regarded as the encoding vector for node i, and its relationship with $\underline{c}_i^t$ is described by

$$\underline{c}_i^t = \underline{\psi}_i^t M, \tag{2.15}$$

where t represents the transpose operation.

Data reconstruction requires the recovery of M from $k\alpha$ symbols at any k nodes. First, let us define the set of k nodes connected to DC as $\{i_1, \dots, i_k\}$, where the j-th node transmits the vector $\underline{\psi}_{i_j}^t M$ to DC. Therefore, DC is able to construct a PM as shown in the following equation:

$$\Psi_{DC}M, \tag{2.16}$$

where Ψ_{DC} is a known matrix composed of elements from the set $\{\underline{\psi}_{i_1}, \dots, \underline{\psi}_{i_k}\}$. The inverse of Ψ_{DC} can be utilized for the computation of M.

In the event of storage node f failure, DC must establish connections with d valid storage nodes for repair, denoted as the set $\{h_1, \dots, h_d\}$. Subsequently, during the repair process, a length α vector $\underline{\mu}_i$ is initially established to serve as a subset of the encoding vector $\underline{\psi}_i^t$. Each helper node transmits α symbols to DC for repair. For instance, helper node h_j will transmit $\underline{\psi}_{h_j}^t M\underline{\mu}_f$. Consequently, DC will receive the following matrix product:

$$\Psi_{repair}M\underline{\mu}_f,$$

where Ψ_{repair} is a $d * d$ matrix composed of elements from the set $\{\underline{\psi}_{h_1}, \dots, \underline{\psi}_{h_d}\}$. The dimensionality of the product determines that $\Psi_{repair}M\underline{\mu}_f$ fully satisfies the required number of symbols for recovery. However, the specific procedure relies on the selection of Ψ and $\underline{\mu}_f$, given that different codes exhibit distinct structures.

Next, this framework will be utilized to construct MBR(n, k, d) codes, where the parameters of the MBR code need only satisfy $k < d < n - 1$. According to the principle of data striping, during the construction process, we will set $\beta = 1$ for the MBR code. The specific composition of the encoding matrix Ψ and message matrix M for the MBR(n, k, d) code will be detailed.

First, according to equation (2.8), the parameter set of the MBR(n, k, d) code can be represented as

$$\left(\alpha = d, \quad \beta = 1, \quad B = \binom{k+1}{2} + k(d-k)\right). \tag{2.17}$$

Here B represents the quantity of symbols in the original data.

Let S be a $k * k$ matrix, where the upper triangular part is filled with $\binom{k+1}{2}$ distinct symbols from set B. The remaining lower triangular part of S is derived by reflecting the upper triangular part, resulting in S being a symmetric matrix. The remaining $k(d-k)$ symbols from set B form a $k * (d-k)$ matrix T. The message matrix M is defined as

$$M = \begin{bmatrix} S & T \\ T^t & 0 \end{bmatrix}, \tag{2.18}$$

which is a $d * d$ symmetric matrix and plays a crucial role in achieving node repair.

The encoding matrix Ψ is defined as an $n * d$ matrix, where any set of d rows is linearly independent, as follows:

$$\Psi = [\Phi \ \Delta], \tag{2.19}$$

where Φ and Δ are $n * k$ and $n * (d - k)$ matrices, respectively, and any k rows of Φ are linearly independent. The requirement of Ψ can be met by selecting either the Cauchy matrix or the Vandermonde matrix. Additionally, based on the aforementioned coding framework, the code matrix C can be expressed as equation (2.14).

During the data reconstruction of this MBR code, it is demonstrated that by connecting any k nodes, B original message symbols can be recovered. Let $\Psi_{DC} = [\Phi_{DC} \ \Delta_{DC}]$ be a $k * d$ submatrix of Ψ. The rows of Ψ_{DC} are composed of the corresponding rows in Ψ for the k helper nodes connected by DC. Therefore, the symbols obtained by DC are as shown in the following equation:

$$\Psi_{DC}M = [\Phi_{DC}S + \Delta_{DC}T^t \ \ \Phi_{DC}T]. \tag{2.20}$$

Based on the previous construction, it is known that Φ_{DC} is a nonsingular matrix. Therefore, by left-multiplying Φ_{DC}^{-1} to $\Psi_{DC}M$, we can first obtain T and then calculate S.

During the repair process of the failed node in the MBR code, it can be demonstrated that connecting any d nodes out of the remaining $n - 1$ nodes will suffice to complete the repair. The proof is explained as follows:

Let $\underline{\psi}_f^t$ denotes the row in Ψ that corresponds to the failed node f, indicating the symbols of α stored in f as follows:

$$\underline{\psi}_f^t M.$$

DC is connected to any d helper nodes, denoted as the set $\{h_j \mid j = 1, \dots, d\}$. As $\underline{\psi}_f^t$ for the helper nodes is known, each helper node h_j sends $\underline{\psi}_{h_j}^t M \underline{\mu}_f$ to DC, where $\underline{\mu}_f = \underline{\psi}_f$. DC obtains symbols $\Psi_{\text{repair}} M \underline{\psi}_f$ from d helper nodes, where Ψ_{repair} satisfies

$$\Psi_{repair} = \begin{bmatrix} \underline{\psi}_{h_1}^t \\ \underline{\psi}_{h_2}^t \\ \vdots \\ \underline{\psi}_{h_d}^t \end{bmatrix}$$

Since Ψ_{repair} is known and invertible, DC can calculate $M\underline{\psi}_f$ by multiplying it with Ψ_{repair}^{-1}. Since M is a symmetric matrix, $(M\underline{\psi}_f)^t = \underline{\psi}_f^t M$ can be obtained, which is the exact data stored in faulty node f earlier.

Since the introduction of construction methods for RGCs based on PM (PM-RGCs), it has garnered extensive attention and undergone significant refinement. Lin et al. (2014, pp. 873–886) proposed a novel PM framework that enables the construction of all feasible exact MSR codes with $d \geq 2k - 2$. Furthermore, Scouarnec (2014, pp. 3–25) explored a specific storage structure aimed at accelerating the encoding and decoding process of PM-RGCs. Building upon this work, Zhang (2019, pp. 289–294) extended the node repair capability of PM-RGCs from a single node to multiple nodes, thereby enhancing its reliability and robustness. Furthermore, Mahdaviani Mohajer and Khisti (2017, pp. 41–45) achieved an optimization of repair cost through an analysis of how different numbers of helper nodes influence repair cost within the PM coding framework.

Furthermore, Hou et al. (2016, pp. 3053–3069) transformed the PM-RGCs based on $GF(2^w)$ to $GF(2)$ for encoding and decoding, termed as BASIC-PM-RGCs. BASIC-PM-RGCs involve only XOR and circular shift operations during coding, significantly reducing complexity. The BASIC-PM-RGCs utilize the Vandermonde matrix as the encoding matrix Ψ. Through LU decomposition of the Vandermonde matrix (Oruç 2007, pp. 982–987), the intricate encoding matrix is decomposed into a series of sparse matrices, further diminishing the complexity. Furthermore, Hou et al. (2016, pp. 3053–3069) provided an example solely for converting PM-RGCs to BASIC codes; in fact, the BASIC coding framework exhibits high scalability, enabling conversion of most exact repair RGCs to BASIC codes.

2.3.3 Rack-aware Regenerating Codes

In real scenarios, storage nodes are typically arranged on racks, and the communication cost among racks is frequently higher than that within a rack. Hence, in the realm of ECs, reducing the cross-rack repair bandwidth is highly significant, that is, minimizing the total amount of data symbols transferred across different racks during the repair process. Nevertheless, RGCs did not take into account the optimization of cross-rack repair bandwidth, thereby giving rise to numerous studies on rack repair in data centers.

Wang et al. (2014, pp. 1878–1886), Tebbi, Chan and Sung (2014, pp. 55–59). and Ernvall et al. (2013, pp. 2701–2709) focus on the capacity constraints of heterogeneous models and on the ECs deployed in heterogeneous storage. Li and Li (2016, pp. 1257–1270) consider the problem of bandwidth balance between two racks. Tebbi, Chan and Sung (2014, pp. 55–59) present a class of LRCs applicable to multirack storage. Shen, Shu and Lee (2016, pp. 323–334) put forward a rack-aware repair algorithm specially designed for RS codes. Hu, Lee and Zhang (2016, pp. 245–249) introduce double regenerating codes (DRCs), which effectively minimize cross-rack repair bandwidth by integrating previously repaired symbols across racks to facilitate the local repair of invalid symbols within each rack. The results indicate that, under certain coding parameter selections, DRC can obtain a smaller cross-rack repair bandwidth than RGCs. Nevertheless, DRC fails to consider the optimal trade-off between storage redundancy and cross-rack repair bandwidth. Pernas et al. (2013, pp. 1237–1241) propose a cross-rack repair model and provide the optimal trade-off curve among storage redundancy, cross-rack repair bandwidth, and intra-rack repair bandwidth. However, in order to repair a failed node, the DC is required to establish connections with all other racks.

Hou et al. (2019b, pp. 4730–4745) proposed RRCs and elaborated the trade-off between the storage overhead and the cross-rack repair bandwidth. Similar to RGCs, the optimal trade-off curve of RRCs also possesses two extreme points, referred to as the minimum storage rack-aware regenerating (MSRR) point and the minimum bandwidth rack-aware regenerating (MBRR) point, corresponding to the minimum storage and the minimum cross-rack repair bandwidth. Compared with the various studies mentioned earlier, RRCs exhibit superior performance in terms of storage overhead and repair bandwidth. Later, RRCs are introduced in details in terms of the repair model, the trade-off curve, and construction methods.

2.3.3.1 Cross-rack Repair Model

Compared with the general RGC repair model, the cross-rack repair model attaches greater importance to the network bandwidth between racks. As depicted in Figure 2.8, assume that a data center is composed of n nodes, which are evenly distributed among r racks, and each rack contains n/r nodes, where n is a multiple of r. The nodes are labeled from 1 to n, and let $h = 1, 2 \ldots r$ and $I = 1, 2 \ldots n/r$. Let $X_{h,i}$ represent the i-th node of the h-th rack. A data file is regarded as a sequence containing M symbols and is encoded and transformed into $n\alpha$ symbols and stored on the corresponding n nodes, with each node storing α symbols.

In each rack, one of n/r nodes is designated as the relayer node of a specific data file. Such a node has the capability to access data stored in other nodes within this rack. Supposing that the intra-rack bandwidth is adequate, the cost among nodes within the rack is disregarded. Furthermore, when a storage node fails, a new node can be introduced as a substitute and placed in the same rack. The new node ought to randomly select d racks from the other racks, with the condition that $d < r$, and establish connections with the relayer nodes within the selected racks. These relayer nodes or racks participating in the repair process are termed helper nodes or helper racks, and d represents the repair degree of RRCs. After carrying out specific operations on $(n/r)\alpha$ symbols stored in a certain helper rack, the corresponding helper node transmits β symbols to the new node, obtaining the cross-rack repair bandwidth as $\gamma = d\beta$.

Subsequently, based on the received $d\beta$ symbols and the $(n/r - 1)\alpha$ symbols stored in the host rack, the data of the new node is regenerated. A relayer node can be any valid node within the rack, and different data files are associated

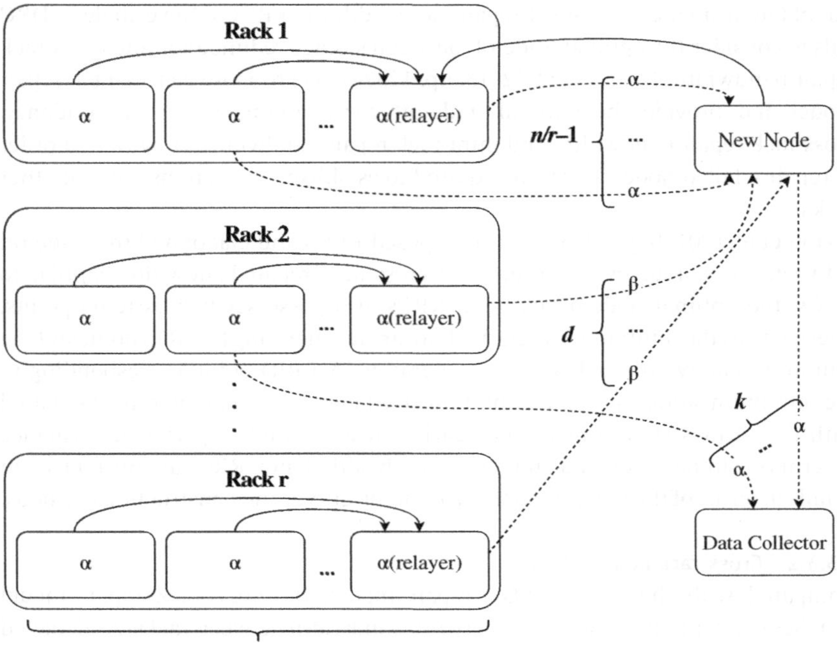

Figure 2.8 System model.

with different relayer nodes to achieve workload balancing in the repair process. Furthermore, when connecting to a relayer, it is tantamount to establishing connections with all the n/r nodes in this rack.

For ease of elaboration, it is always assumed hereafter that $X_{h,1}$ is the relayer of rack h during the repair process. Additionally, if a DSS implements the aforementioned cross-rack repair model and meets the relevant parameter requirements, it can be dubbed a rack storage system (RSS) $(n, k, r, d, \alpha, \beta)$.

2.3.3.2 Optimal Trade-off in RRCs

In this section, we utilize an IFG to depict the aforementioned cross-rack repair model. For a given system parameter set $(n, k, r, d, \alpha, \beta)$, the IFG can be regarded as a directed acyclic graph (DAG) constructed according to specific rules.

In the DAG, there exists a vertex S representing the data file and a vertex T representing the DC. The i-th storage node $X_{h,i}$ in rack h, where $h = 1, 2, \ldots, r$ and $i = 1, 2, \ldots, n/r$, is denoted by a pair of vertices $In_{h,i}$ and $Out_{h,i}$. Here, α represents the capacity of the edge from $In_{h,i}$ to $Out_{h,i}$, signifying the storage overhead of each storage node. Additionally, the edge from S to $In_{h,i}$ has infinite capacity. Similarly, the edge from $Out_{h,i}$ to $Out_{h,1}$ also possesses infinite capacity. This indicates that relayer node $X_{h,1}$ can access all symbols stored in rack h at no cost.

Assuming the f-th node in rack h fails, where $h = 1, 2, \ldots, r$ and $f \in \{1, 2, \ldots, n/r\}$. Place n/r pairs of vertices in the IFG such as $In'_{h,i}$ and $Out'_{h,i}$ to represent the repaired rack h, where $i = 1, 2, \ldots, n/r$. For $j \in \{1, 2, \ldots, n/r\}\backslash\{f\}$, set the edges from $Out_{h,j}$ to $In'_{h,j}$ and from $In'_{h,j}$ to $Out'_{h,j}$ with infinite capacity to indicate that the stored data of j-th node remains unchanged after repair. For the vertex representing the new node $In'_{h,f}$, set the edge capacity from $Out_{h,j}$ to $In'_{h,f}$ as infinite to allow unrestricted access for the new node to all symbols stored in other valid nodes within the same rack at no cost. Additionally, similar to a valid rack, set α as the capacity of edge from $In'_{h,f}$ to $Out'_{h,f}$, and set edges from $Out'_{h,j}$ to $Out'_{h,1}$ with infinite capacity for $j = 2, \ldots, n/r$.

Assuming the new node establishes d connections with relayers in racks $h_1, h_2, \ldots, h_d$, where racks $h_1, h_2, \ldots, h_d$ are different from rack h. Let β be the capacity of the edge from $Out_{h_\ell,1}$ to $In'_{h,f}$, where $\ell = 1, 2, \ldots, d$. Therefore, the new node $In'_{h,f}$ has $(n/r - 1) + d$ incoming arcs, where d edges have a capacity of β and $(n/r - 1)$ edges have an infinite capacity. Through the transfer of this network flow, $X_{h,f}$ can be repaired.

Furthermore, by drawing k edges from k valid vertices to T, it is possible to utilize T for data reconstruction. If T is connected to the vertex $X_{h,1}$ corresponding to the relayers in rack h, then T effectively connects to all vertices in rack h. The resulting IFG can be denoted by the parameters $(n, k, r, d, \alpha, \beta)$. Figure 2.9 provides an example of an IFG with parameters $(9, 5, 3, 2, \alpha, \beta)$, in which the failure of a node can be repaired by connecting two nodes from other racks and one node from the internal rack.

In accordance with the Mx-flow Mn-cut property in Network Coding Theory (Yeung et al. 2006, pp. 241–329), for given parameters $(n, k, r, d \geq m, \alpha, \beta)$, where $m = \lfloor kr/n \rfloor$, if there exists an RSS$(n, k, r, d, \alpha, \beta)$ with data file of size M, and its repair model employs a coding scheme satisfying

$$k\alpha + \sum_{\ell=1}^{m} min\{(d - \ell + 1)\beta - \alpha, 0\} \geq M, \tag{2.21}$$

then this scheme can be denoted as an RRC$(n, k, r, d, \alpha, \beta)$.

The curve corresponding to equation (2.21) represents the optimal trade-off between storage overhead and cross-rack repair bandwidth. This curve has two extreme points, resulting in MSRR code and MBRR code. The MSRR code is obtained by first minimizing α and then minimizing β, while the MBRR code is obtained by first minimizing β and then minimizing α.

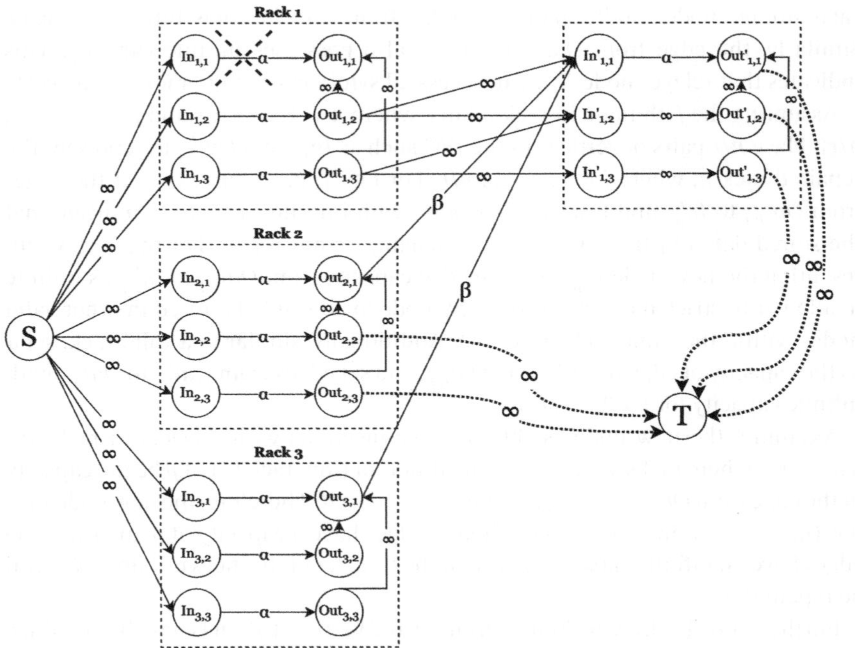

Figure 2.9 The information flow graph for (9, 5, 3, 2, α, β).

Upon reaching the MSRR point, the following condition is satisfied:

$$(\alpha_{MSRR}, \gamma_{MSRR}) = \left(\frac{M}{k}, \frac{Md}{k(d-m+1)}\right). \tag{2.22}$$

Upon reaching the MBRR point, the following condition is satisfied:

$$(\alpha_{MBRR}, \gamma_{MBRR}) = \left(\frac{Md}{(k-m)d + m\left(d - \frac{m-1}{2}\right)}, \frac{Md}{(k-m)d + m\left(d - \frac{m-1}{2}\right)}\right). \tag{2.23}$$

According to equations (2.22) and (2.23) and the calculations for MSR and MBR in the study by Dimakis et al. (2010, pp. 4539–4551), it is evident that when $r = n$, indicating the absence of multiple racks, the MSRR code reduces to the MSR code and the MBRR code to the MBR code. Additionally, within the MBRR code, the cross-rack repair bandwidth γ equals storage α, signifying that the amount of data downloaded from other racks is equivalent to the size of failed data.

If a RGC(n, k, d') is directly used in RSS, i.e., by downloading β symbols from $d' = dn/r + n/r - 1$ helper nodes to repair failed nodes, including $n/r - 1$ nodes in the host rack and dn/r nodes in other racks, then the cross-rack repair bandwidth of RGC(n, k, d') in terms of MSR and MBR are

$$\gamma'_{\text{MSR}} = \frac{Md(n/r)}{k(dn/r + n/r - k)}, \tag{2.24}$$

$$\gamma'_{\text{MBR}} = \frac{2Md(n/r)}{k(2dn/r + 2n/r - k - 1)}. \tag{2.25}$$

Due to $m = \left\lfloor \frac{kr}{n} \right\rfloor$, when kr/n is an integer, it satisfies the condition $kr/n = m$ and

$$\gamma'_{\text{MSR}} = \frac{Mdn/r}{k(dn/r + n/r - k)} = \frac{Md}{k(d - m + 1)},$$

which is equivalent to the cross-rack repair bandwidth of the MSRR code in equation (2.22). However, if kr/n is not an integer, then $kr/n > m$. In this case, the cross-rack repair bandwidth of MSR will exceed that of MSRR.

If kr/n is an integer, then $m = kr/n$. The MBRR code has a smaller cross-rack repair bandwidth than the MBR code only when satisfying

$$\begin{aligned}
&\gamma'_{\text{MBR}} - \gamma_{\text{MBRR}} \\
&= \frac{2Mdn/r}{k(2dn/r + 2n/r - k - 1)} - \frac{Md}{(k-m)d + m\left(d - \frac{m-1}{2}\right)} \\
&= \frac{2Mdn}{k(2dn + 2n - kr - r)} - \frac{2Md}{2kd - m(m-1)} \\
&= \frac{2Md(2nkd - nm(m-1) - k(2dn + 2n - kr - r))}{k(2dn + 2n - kr - r)(2kd - m(m-1))} \\
&= \frac{2Md(k^2 r + kr - 2kn - m^2 n + mn)}{k(2dn + 2n - kr - r)(2kd - m(m-1))} \\
&= \frac{2Md\left(k^2 r + kr - 2kn - \frac{k^2 r^2}{n} + kr\right)}{k(2dn + 2n - kr - r)(2kd - m(m-1))} \text{ by } m = \frac{kr}{n} \\
&= \frac{2Md\left(k^2 r + 2kr - 2kn - \frac{k^2 r^2}{n}\right)}{k(2dn + 2n - kr - r)(2kd - m(m-1))} \\
&= \frac{2Md\left(\frac{1}{n} - \frac{2}{kr}\right)}{k(2dn + 2n - kr - r)(2kd - m(m-1))} k^2 r(n - r) > 0.
\end{aligned} \tag{2.26}$$

From equation (2.26), it can be derived that as long as $k/n > 2/r$, the MBRR code has smaller cross-rack repair bandwidth than the MBR code. In other words, if the code rate is not too low, the cross-rack repair bandwidth of the MBRR code is strictly less than that of the MBR code.

2.3.3.3 Construction of Cross-rack RGCs

Considering the trade-off curve between storage overhead and cross-rack repair bandwidth, Hou et al. (2019b, pp. 4730–4745) introduce a class of hybrid MSRR codes and present a design for exact repair hybrid MSRR codes. When kr is a multiple of n, the first $m = kr/n$ racks containing k data nodes are referred to as data racks, while the remaining $r - m$ racks serve as encoded racks, in which it is known as homogeneous MSRR codes. In cases where kr is not a multiple of n, the first m racks still function as data racks, followed by $r - m - 1$ encoded racks. However, the $(m + 1)$-th rack is designated as a hybrid rack. This hybrid rack contains $t = k \bmod (n/r)$ data nodes and $n/r - t$ encoded nodes. In this scenario, it is termed a hybrid MSRR code.

When kr/n is an integer, the MSR code and the homogeneous MSRR code have the same cross-rack repair bandwidth. This means that all existing methods for constructing MSR codes can be directly applied to MSRR codes. Since the existing MSR codes already support all parameters (Goparaju, Fazeli and Vardy 2017, pp. 6318–6328), there is no need to develop a special structure for homogeneous MSRR codes. In hybrid MSRR codes, it is easy to extend the construction from $\beta = 1$ to cases where $\beta \neq 1$. For ease of calculation Hou et al. (2019b, pp. 4730–4745) assume $\beta = 1$ in the construction process of hybrid MSRR codes, and according to equation (2.22), it can be derived that

$$\alpha = d - m + 1, \quad M = k(d - m + 1).$$

The first $k - t$ data nodes are placed in m data racks, and the last $t = k\, mod\, (n/r)$ data nodes are placed in a hybrid rack. Since $\beta = 1$, each node stores $\alpha = d - m + 1$ symbols. During the repair process of data nodes in the data racks, the DC accesses all other $(n/r - 1) * (d - m + 1)$ symbols in the host rack. The number of downloaded symbols from other racks by DC is composed as follows:

a) $(m - 1)$ symbols, respectively, from $(m - 1)$ data racks;
b) an encoded symbol from the hybrid rack;
c) $(d - m)$ encoded symbols, respectively, from $(d - m)$ encoded racks.

In order to successfully complete the repair, it is essential to ensure that the decoding equation formed by the downloaded symbols has a unique solution after eliminating the interference information. To satisfy this requirement and effectively eliminate interference, Hou et al. (2019b, pp. 4730–4745) employ the concept of IA (Cadambe and Jafar 2008, pp. 3425–3441), select a suitable coding matrix, and introduce orthogonal vectors for matrix construction. This code is the first exact repair MSRR code; however, it is necessary for the parameters to satisfy $\alpha n/r \geq m + \alpha t$ and for data nodes to be recovered through specific d helper racks rather than any d racks. Therefore, there remains significant room for optimization.

After the proposal of RRCs, there was a surge in research. Hou, Lee and Han (2020, pp. 554–559) proposed a coding framework to convert any MSR code into an MSRR code that meets the minimum storage redundancy requirement while minimizing cross-rack repair bandwidth. Zhang and Zhou (2023, pp. 2874–2885) constructed an RRC by introducing a vertical–horizontal architecture and achieved low subpacketization, which is significant in reducing I/O overhead during repair. Single-node repair in RRCs requires the inclusion of all remaining nodes in the failed rack and a large number of valid helper racks. Therefore, multiple nodes may fail and become unrepairable. To address this issue, methods such as reducing the repair degree and cooperative repair are used to repair multiple node faults (Zhou and Zhang 2022, pp. 4316–4326; Wang et al. 2023, pp. 1–26; Gupta and Lalitha 2020, pp. 264–268). Many studies on RRCs focus on repairing node-level faults; however, due to continuous storage scale expansion, rack-level faults also occur occasionally. Hou and Lee (2021, pp. 2191–2196) achieved optimal balance between storage overhead and cross-rack repair bandwidth for single-rack fault scenarios and proposed generalized GRRCs, including minimum storage generalized rack-aware regenerating (MSGRR) codes and minimum bandwidth generalized rack-aware regenerating (MBGRR) codes that, respectively, realize minimum storage overhead and minimum repair bandwidth in single-rack fault.

2.4 Array Codes

In recent years, the computational efficiency of ECs has garnered significant attention and emerged as a pivotal metric for evaluating their efficacy. Array codes, characterized by their low complexity in encoding and decoding operations, have assumed a prominent position as a focal point of research within the domain of distributed storage coding.

The initial section provides an introduction to the fundamental concepts, current research trends, and commonly used array codes. Subsequently, a comprehensive coding framework for efficient binary array codes is presented in detail, followed by a discussion on binary Vandermonde array codes (BVACs) and binary Cauchy array codes (BCACs) constructed based on this framework. Lastly, this section offers a concise overview of optimization techniques for array codes concerning repair bandwidth and computational complexity.

2.4.1 Introduction to Array Codes

The study of array codes holds significant importance in the field of ECs. During the encoding and decoding process, array codes exclusively employ simple binary *XOR* operations, thereby efficiently accomplishing data repair functionalities. In order to fully leverage redundant data for enhanced reliability, it becomes particularly crucial to adhere to the MDS property when selecting array codes.

Array code can be represented by an $l * n$ matrix, where each element in the matrix represents one bit. This matrix consists of n columns, with the first k columns referred to as information columns that store l information bits each, and the remaining r columns known as redundant columns that store l redundant bits each, where $n = k + r$. In a storage system, there are n storage nodes responsible for storing these columns individually, with each node assigned to store l bits within a complete column. In case of a failure in any node within the storage system, it results in the loss of data represented by the corresponding entire column. Hence, it is evident that array codes represent linear block codes, organizing data in a 2D format.

In terms of computational complexity and redundancy overhead, MDS array codes offer distinct advantages over other non-MDS array codes. Theoretically, MDS array codes can tolerate more than three failed columns, striking an optimal balance between storage efficiency and reliability. Consequently, this section exclusively focuses on introducing MDS array codes. For alternative array codes that do not possess the MDS property, such as HDD2, WEAVER, HoVer, and T-code, refer to Hafner (2005, p. 16), Cassuto and Shokrollahi (2014, pp. 3279–3291), Hafner (2006, pp. 217–226), and Tang et al. (2008, pp. 578–581). Unless specifically stated otherwise, the subsequent array codes discussed herein pertain exclusively to MDS array codes. Moreover, the array codes in this section correspond to system array codes consisting of k information columns and r redundant columns. Additionally, in cases where an information column or a redundant column is absent, it signifies the loss of all bits contained within the column.

The restoration of lost information columns with optimal repair bandwidth is a highly significant problem in current research on array codes. Blaum, Bruck and Vardy (1996, pp. 529–542) conducted an extensive investigation into the repair bandwidth of BBV array codes, and the experimental results demonstrate that there exists a ratio $\gamma_{BBV} = 3(k+1)/4k$ between the repair bandwidth of BBV array codes and the number of original information bits when $r = 2$. However, the value presented in γ_{BBV} significantly deviates from the theoretically optimal value provided by Dimakis et al. (2010, pp. 4539–4551), indicating that γ_{BBV} has not yet achieved the theoretically optimal repair bandwidth. An array code based on vector transpose is proposed by Tamo, Wang and Bruck (2011, pp. 1240–1244), where binary bits in the array codes are replaced by elements on $GF(q)$, achieving the optimal repair bandwidth. However, due to its higher computational complexity compared to existing binary array codes, its practicality is limited. Furthermore, although Xu and Bruck (1999, pp. 272–276), Corbett et al. (2004, pp. 1–14), and

Blaum (et al. 1995, pp. 192–202) provide insights into repair bandwidth and load balancing for $r = 2$ array codes such as X-code, EVENODD codes, and RDP codes, their investigations have yet to achieve the theoretical optimum.

The computational complexity of array codes is a crucial performance evaluation metric, encompassing both coding and update. When the number of redundant columns is not less than 3, Subedi and He (2013, pp. 1528–1537) investigate the complexity of encoding and decoding for MDS array codes, revealing that Triple-Star array codes (Wang, Li and Zhong 2012, pp. 1731–1472) exhibit the lowest complexity in cases where there are exactly three redundant columns. Furthermore, Farrell (1992, pp. 441–454) proposes reducing the complexity of encoding and decoding as a primary research focus for array codes. Update complexity refers to the average number of calculation operations required to update a single information bit. Blaum and Roth (1999, pp. 46–59) pioneer the concept of update complexity for array codes and provide its theoretical optimal value. Subsequently, different construction methods are presented to achieve optimal update complexity for array codes (Cassuto and Bruck 2009, pp. 1721–1729; Sandell and Tosato 2015, pp. 1251–1264; Louidor and Roth 2006, pp. 3186–3197). Sandell and Tosato (2013, pp. 645–652) employ incomplete graph construction, while Li and Shu (2010, pp. 1315–1319) and Li and Shu (2011, pp. 1–9) utilize graph theory to offer construction approaches that attain the lowest update complexity.

Most research on MDS array codes primarily focuses on constructing codes that can handle failures of two columns simultaneously, such as X-code, RDP code, and EVENODD code. The two redundant columns of EVENODD code are coded separately by the information columns, while the RDP code generates a diagonal redundant column by encoding both the information column and the row redundant column. Another MDS array code that addresses two failed columns is X-code, which exhibits optimal update complexity. Notably, X-code introduces an innovative approach where each storage node stores a row of data instead of a column. Additionally, most other MDS array codes (Katti and Ruan 2005, pp. 348–351; Huang et al. 2015, pp. 1670–1673) capable of handling two failed columns are derived from modifications to RDP, EVODD, or X-code.

Ongoing research is conducted on MDS array codes with $r > 2$, resulting in significant advancements. Notably, Extented EVENODD (EEOD) codes (Blaum et al. 1995, pp. 192–202), Extended RDP (ERDP) codes (Blaum 2006, pp. 2784–2788), STAR (Huang and Xu 2008, pp. 889–901) codes, Triple-Star (Wang, Li and Zhong 2012, pp. 1731–1472) codes, Reed–Solomon-Like (RS-Like) codes (Feng et al. 2005a, pp. 1071–1080), and TIP codes (Zhang et al. 2015a pp. 136–147) have been expanded to accommodate simultaneous failures of three columns. Specifically, among these array codes, the Triple-Star code exhibits the lowest decoding complexity, while the TIP code demonstrates the lowest update complexity. However, given the escalating frequency of node failures in DSSs and the exponential growth of global data volume, there is an urgent need to investigate MDS array codes with enhanced fault tolerance.

Based on distinct construction matrices, MDS array codes can be categorized into Vandermonde array codes and Cauchy array codes. Currently, three primary types of MDS array codes constructed using Vandermonde matrix offer fault tolerance greater than 3: ERDP, BBV code, and BVAC (Hou et al. 2014, pp. 2369–2374). Furthermore, the construction process of other array codes such as X-code, S-code, RDP code, EVENODD code, STAR, Triple-Star, TIP code, and RS-Like code, despite limited fault tolerance ability, are represented by Vandermonde matrices. Henceforth, they also fall under the category of Vandermonde array codes.

According to Table 2.3, some conclusions can be inferred: for $r = 2$, X-code exhibits the lowest decoding complexity; for $r = 3$, Triple-Star demonstrates the lowest decoding complexity; and for $r > 3$, BVAC possesses the lowest decoding complexity.

Cauchy array codes are another type of MDS array codes, constructed using Cauchy matrices. There exist various types of Cauchy array codes, such as optimized CRS codes (Plank and Xu 2006, pp. 173–180; Zhang et al. 2015b, pp. 435–447), Rabin-Like codes (Feng et al. 2005b, pp. 1473–1483), circulant Cauchy array codes (Schindelhauer and Ortolf 2013, pp. 334–345), and BCAC. The earliest proposed code based on the Cauchy matrix is CRS code, where operations are performed over $GF(q)$. Feng et al. (2005b, pp. 1473–1483) introduced a method to convert the Cauchy matrix into a sparse matrix based on transpose and proposed RS-Like and Rabin-Like codes with lower computational complexity than CRS codes. To further reduce computational complexity, Schindelhauer and Ortolf (2013, pp. 334–345) consider a special type of CRS code that effectively reduces calculation operations by utilizing a binary circulant matrix during encoding and decoding.

When $r > 3$, Table 2.4 provides a comprehensive overview of encoding and decoding complexity for Cauchy array codes. It can be inferred that BCAC exhibits the lowest complexity, irrespective of the information column parameter k.

Table 2.3 Decoding complexity of Vandermonde array codes.

Redundant columns	Array codes	Lowest decoding complexity
$r = 2$	X-code, RDP, EVENODD	X-code
$r = 3$	STAR, Triple-Star, TIP	Triple-Star
$r > 3$	ERDP, BBV, BVAC	BVAC

Table 2.4 Coding complexity of Cauchy array codes.

Array codes	Complexity of encoding and decoding (when k is small)	Complexity of encoding and decoding (when k is large)
Optimized CRS codes	Lower	Highest
Rabin-Like codes	Higher	Higher
Circulant Cauchy array codes	Highest	Lower
BCAC	Lowest	Lowest

2.4.2 A Coding Framework for Binary Array Codes

The construction of BVAC and BCAC can be facilitated by employing an efficient coding framework for binary array codes (Hou et al. 2014, pp. 2369–2374). The coding framework of binary array codes is a linear code derived from binary cyclic codes. In the polynomial ring $F_2[x]/(1 + x^p)$, where p is a positive odd number, the vector $(a_0, a_1, \dots, a_{p-1}) \in F_2^p$ corresponds to the polynomial $a(x) = \sum_{i=0}^{p-1} a_i x^i$ in the ring $F_2[x]/(1 + x^p)$, and the variable x represents the cyclic right shift operation of $F_2[x]/(1 + x^p)$.

A binary parity code is defined as a polynomial consisting of an even number of nonzero coefficients in $F_2[x]/(1 + x^p)$, which can be expressed as

$$C_p = \{a(x)(1 + x) : a(x) \in F_2[x]/(1 + x^p)\}. \tag{2.27}$$

The parity polynomial of C_p is shown as

$$h(x) = 1 + x + \cdots + x^{p-1}. \tag{2.28}$$

The coding framework consists of k data polynomials and $v - k$ encoded polynomials. Among the v polynomials, any k polynomials are decodable, indicating that k data polynomials can be reconstructed from them. The encoding process is determined by the generator matrix G, which needs to ensure solvability of any k polynomials.

Specifically, the encoding process of this framework involves partitioning $(p - 1)k$ bits into k groups, with each group containing $p - 1$ bits. For each group, a parity bit is added to generate a polynomial in C_p. These generated polynomials are then combined into a k-tuple $w = (s_1(x), s_2(x), \dots, s_k(x)) \in C_p^k$. These k polynomials are referred to as data polynomials. Subsequently, the encoding of the $(p - 1)k$ bits can be obtained through wG, resulting in a set of encoding polynomials. Each encoding polynomial is a linear combination of k data polynomials based on C_p, which is also represented by the polynomial in $F_2[x]/(1 + x^p)$.

Table 2.5 A concise example of the coding framework for binary array codes.

Column 1	Column 2	Column 3	Column 4
$s_{1,0}$	$s_{2,0}$	$s_{3,0} = s_{1,0} + s_{2,0}$	$s_{4,0} = s_{1,0} + s_{2,1}$
$s_{1,1}$	$s_{2,1}$	$s_{3,1} = s_{1,1} + s_{2,1}$	$s_{4,1} = s_{1,1} + s_{2,2}$
$s_{1,2}$	$s_{2,2}$	$s_{3,2} = s_{1,2} + s_{2,2}$	$s_{4,2} = s_{1,2} + s_{2,3}$
$s_{1,3}$	$s_{2,3}$	$s_{3,3} = s_{1,3} + s_{2,3}$	$s_{4,3} = s_{1,3} + s_{2,4}$
$s_{1,4}$	$s_{2,4}$	$s_{3,4} = s_{1,4} + s_{2,4}$	$s_{4,4} = s_{1,4} + s_{2,5}$
$s_{1,5}$	$s_{2,5}$	$s_{3,5} = s_{1,5} + s_{2,5}$	$s_{4,5} = s_{1,5} + s_{2,6}$
$s_{1,6} = \sum_{j=0}^{5} s_{1,j}$	$s_{2,6} = \sum_{j=0}^{5} s_{2,j}$	$s_{3,6} = s_{1,6} + s_{2,6}$	$s_{4,6} = s_{1,6} + s_{2,0}$

Table 2.5 serves to illustrate the encoding process of the framework, wherein $2(p-1)$ information bits are stored across four columns, with p representing an odd positive integer. Each column accommodates p bits. Columns 1 and 2 are referred to as information columns, housing $p-1$ information bits and one parity bit, respectively. Columns 3 and 4 are designated as redundant columns or parity columns, each storing p redundant bits.

The $2(p-1)$ information bits are divided into two parts. The bits in the first part are represented as $s_{1,0}, s_{1,1}, \dots, s_{1,p-2}$, and the bits in the second part are represented as $s_{2,0}, s_{2,1}, \dots, s_{2,p-2}$. For $i = 1, 2$, column i stores bit $s_{i,0}, s_{i,1} \dots, s_{i,p-2}$. For convenience, the parity bit of $s_{i,0}, s_{i,1} \dots, s_{i,p-2}$ is shown in equation (2.29) that

$$s_{i,p-1} = \sum_{j=0}^{p-2} s_{i,j}. \tag{2.29}$$

The redundant bits stored in column 3 are illustrated in equation (2.30) that

$$s_{3,j} = s_{1,j} + s_{2,j}, \tag{2.30}$$

where $j = 0, 1, \dots, p-1$. The redundant bits stored by column 4 are shown in equation (2.31) that

$$s_{4,j} = s_{1,j} + s_{2,j \oplus_p 1}, \tag{2.31}$$

where $j = 0, 1, \dots, p-1$ and $\oplus_p$ denotes modular addition with respect to p. Unless otherwise specified, calculations involving subscripts represent modular operations with respect to p. When $p = 7$, Table 2.5 provides an example of the coding framework for binary array codes. It should be noted that the redundant bits stored in column 3 are obtained by summing the bits stored in columns 1 and 2, while the redundant bits stored in column 4 are derived from cyclic bit transformations and additions stored in columns 1 and 2.

The original information bits can be restored from any two columns. In columns 1 and 2, the information bits can be directly retrieved. To decode the information bits from columns 1 and 3, one can subtract $s_{1,j}$ from $s_{3,j} = s_{1,j} + s_{2,j}$ to obtain $s_{2,j}$. Similarly, the information bits can be restored from any one information column and any one redundant column. Finally, to decode the information bits from columns 3 and 4, equation (2.32) should first be calculated by

$$C_j = s_{3,j} + s_{4,j} = s_{2,j} + s_{2,j+1}, \tag{2.32}$$

where $j = 1, 3, 5, \ldots p - 2$. Next, $s_{2,0}$ can be calculated by

$$\sum_{l=1}^{(p-1)/2} c_{2l-1} = s_{2,1} + s_{2,2} + \cdots + s_{2,p-1} = s_{2,0}. \tag{2.33}$$

After calculating the value of $s_{2,0}$, $s_{1,0}$ can be obtained by $s_{3,0} + s_{2,0} = s_{1,0}$, and $s_{2,1}$ can be obtained by $s_{4,0} + s_{1,0} = s_{2,1}$. The remaining information bits can be iteratively decoded.

The parameters of coding framework mentioned above are $p = 7$, $k = 2$, and $v = 4$. The two data polynomials can be represented as $s_i(x) = \sum_{j=0}^{6} s_{i,j} x^j$ for $i = 1, 2$. Additionally, the generator matrix G is illustrated in equation (2.34) that

$$G = \begin{bmatrix} 1 & 0 & 1 & 1 \\ 0 & 1 & 1 & x^6 \end{bmatrix}. \tag{2.34}$$

The encoding polynomial, as a linear combination of data polynomials, can be obtained through various methods. For instance, equation (2.35) presents a suitable generator matrix for this example:

$$G = \begin{bmatrix} 1 & 0 & 1 & 1 \\ 0 & 1 & 1 & 1 + x + \cdots + x^5 \end{bmatrix}. \tag{2.35}$$

The performance of this coding framework is intricately linked to the generator matrix. When the generator matrix consists of a unit matrix and a Vandermonde matrix, the resulting binary array code is referred to as a binary Vandermonde array code. Due to its regular mathematical structure, the linear equation possesses an efficient solution method that satisfies solvability of any k polynomials. On the other hand, when the generator matrix comprises a unit matrix and a Cauchy matrix, a binary Cauchy array code is obtained. Similar to the Vandermonde matrix, the Cauchy matrix also exhibits a distinctive mathematical structure, thereby enabling an efficient decoding approach. Subsequent subsections delve into these two codes in detail.

2.4.3 Binary Vandermonde Array Codes

This subsection provides a comprehensive exposition on BVAC, encompassing the construction and two decoding methods.

2.4.3.1 Construction of BVACs

The size of BVAC is equal to $(p-1)*(k+r)$, where p represents a prime number and $p \leq min\{k, r\}$, k denotes the number of information columns, and r refers to the number of redundant columns. The initial k columns are designated as information columns, whereas the final r columns are referred to as redundant columns. This representation can be concisely denoted as $V(k, r, p)$. The information column $(p-1)*k$ corresponds to row $0, 1, \dots, p-2$ and column $1, 2, \dots, k$; similarly, the redundant column $(p-1)*r$ corresponds to row $0, 1, \dots, p-2$ and column $1, 2, \dots, r$. The indices $i = 0, 1, \dots, p-2$ and $j = 1, 2, \dots, k$ are defined such that $s_{i,j}$ represents the i-th bit of the j-th information column. Similarly, the indices $i = 0, 1, \dots, p-2$ and $l = 1, 2, \dots, r$ are defined such that $c_{i,l}$ denotes the i-th bit of the l-th redundant column.

In order to illustrate the encoding and decoding process of $V(k, r, p)$, for $j = 1, 2, \dots, k$, we defined as equation (2.36) that

$$s_{p-1,j} = s_{0,j} + s_{1,j} + \cdots + s_{p-2,j}. \tag{2.36}$$

Let $s_{p-1,j}$ denote the parity bit of the j-th information column, which is solely introduced for facilitating the representation of encoding and decoding process of $V(k, r, p)$, without actually storing this bit.

Let $i = 0, 1, \dots, p-2$, and $l = 1, 2, \dots, r$. The redundancy bit $c_{i,l}$ is shown in equation (2.37) that

$$c_{i,l} = \sum_{j=1}^{k} s_{i-(j-1)*(l-1),j}. \tag{2.37}$$

The operations involving the subscript in equation (2.37) exclusively entail calculations of the modulus p. The initial superfluous column is referred to as the row redundant column, while the remaining redundant columns are denoted as diagonal redundant columns. The redundant columns of $V(4, 3, 5)$ are presented in Table 2.6, with the brackets indicating the calculation process for each parity bit.

To further clarify the construction principle of BVAC, the following algebraic description of $V(k, r, p)$ is provided.

Let $l = 1, 2, \dots, r$ and define the parity bit of the l-th redundant column as

$$c_{p-1,l} = c_{0,l} + c_{1,l} + \cdots + c_{p-2,l}. \tag{2.38}$$

The information bits, redundant bits, and parity bits can be arranged in an array $A_{p*(k+r)}$ of $p*(k+r)$, as illustrated in equation (2.39):

$$A_{p*(k+r)} = \begin{bmatrix} s_{0,1} & \cdots & s_{0,k} & c_{0,1} & \cdots & c_{0,r} \\ s_{1,1} & \cdots & s_{1,k} & c_{1,1} & \cdots & c_{1,r} \\ \vdots & \vdots & \vdots & \vdots & \ddots & \vdots \\ s_{p-2,1} & \cdots & s_{p-2,k} & c_{p-2,1} & \cdots & c_{p-2,r} \\ s_{p-1,1} & \cdots & s_{p-1,k} & c_{p-1,1} & \cdots & c_{p-1,r} \end{bmatrix}. \tag{2.39}$$

Table 2.6 Redundant columns of *V*(4, 3, 5).

Redundant column 1	Redundant column 2	Redundant column 3
$s_{0,1} + s_{0,2} + s_{0,3} + s_{0,4}$	$s_{0,1} + (s_{0,2} + s_{1,2} + s_{2,2} + s_{3,2}) + s_{3,3} + s_{2,4}$	$s_{0,1} + s_{3,2} + s_{1,3} + (s_{0,4} + s_{1,4} + s_{2,4} + s_{3,4})$
$s_{1,1} + s_{1,2} + s_{1,3} + s_{1,4}$	$s_{1,1} + s_{0,2} + (s_{0,3} + s_{1,3} + s_{2,3} + s_{3,3}) + s_{3,4}$	$s_{1,1} + (s_{0,2} + s_{1,2} + s_{2,2} + s_{3,2}) + s_{2,3} + s_{0,4}$
$s_{2,1} + s_{2,2} + s_{2,3} + s_{2,4}$	$s_{2,1} + s_{1,2} + s_{0,3} + (s_{0,4} + s_{1,4} + s_{2,4} + s_{3,4})$	$s_{2,1} + s_{0,2} + s_{3,3} + s_{1,4}$
$s_{3,1} + s_{3,2} + s_{3,3} + s_{3,4}$	$s_{3,1} + s_{2,2} + s_{1,3} + s_{0,4}$	$s_{3,1} + s_{1,2} + (s_{0,3} + s_{1,3} + s_{2,3} + s_{3,3}) + s_{2,4}$

In the polynomial ring $F_2[x]/(1 + x^p)$, the $p * (k + r)$ array is analyzed using equation (2.39). Let $j = 1, 2, \dots, k$ and express the polynomial representation of the $(p - 1)$ information bit stored in the j-th information column along with its parity bit as presented in equation (2.40):

$$s_j(x) = s_{0,j} + s_{1,j}x + \cdots + s_{p-2,j}x^{p-2} + s_{p-1,j}x^{p-1}. \tag{2.40}$$

Similarly, let $l = 1, 2, \dots, r$, and represent the $p - 1$ redundant bits stored in the l-th redundant column along with their parity bits as a polynomial depicted by

$$c_l(x) = c_{0,l} + c_{1,l}x + \cdots + c_{p-2,l}x^{p-2} + c_{p-1,l}x^{p-1}. \tag{2.41}$$

$A_{p*(k+r)}$ can be represented as the vector $\mathfrak{R}_{k+r}$ in the polynomial ring $F_2[x]/(1 + x^p)$ of length $k + r$, as shown in equation (2.42):

$$\mathfrak{R}_{k+r} = (s_1(x), \dots, s_k(x), c_1(x), \dots, c_r(x)). \tag{2.42}$$

The encoding process of $V(k, r, p)$ can be represented as the multiplication operation depicted in equation (2.43) within the polynomial ring $F_2[x]/(1 + x^p)$, as follows:

$$\mathfrak{R}_{k+r} = (s_1(x), s_2(x), \dots, s_k(x)) \cdot V. \tag{2.43}$$

The matrix V is given by

$$V = [I\ P]. \tag{2.44}$$

Matrix V is the $k * (k + r)$ generator matrix of $V(k, r, p)$. In V, the first k columns form the unit matrix I, while the remaining r columns compose the Vandermonde matrix P:

$$P = \begin{bmatrix} 1 & 1 & \cdots & 1 \\ 1 & x & \cdots & x^{r-1} \\ \vdots & \vdots & \ddots & \vdots \\ 1 & x^{k-1} & \cdots & x^{(r-1)(k-1)} \end{bmatrix}. \tag{2.45}$$

In summary, the encoding process of $V(k, r, p)$ can be described as follows: given $k(p-1)$ information bits, k parity bits are calculated and added to obtain k polynomials according to equation (2.40). Subsequently, the polynomials are evaluated using equation (2.41), where terms with a degree of $p-1$ are disregarded and the coefficients of the polynomials from 0 to $p-2$ are stored.

2.4.3.2 Decoding Methods of BVACs

Decoding refers to the process of recovering data columns from binary array codes by retrieving information from other surviving columns. Two decoding methods for BVAC include the general decoding method, known as Cramer's rule (Chen 1993, pp. 177–186), as well as an efficient technique—LU factorization of Vandermonde matrix—which is applicable in cases where only information columns are missing (Hou et al. 2014, pp. 2369–2374).

Cramer's Rule For $V(k, r, p)$, assume that the γ information columns F_s and the δ redundant columns F_p, as illustrated in equation (2.47), are absent, as follows:

$$F_s = \{f_{i_1}, f_{i_2}, \cdots, f_{i_\gamma}\}, \tag{2.46}$$

$$F_p = \{f_{j_1}, f_{j_2}, \cdots, f_{j_\delta}\}. \tag{2.47}$$

These parameters fulfill the equation (2.48):

$$1 \leq f_{i_1} < f_{i_2} < \ldots < f_{i_\gamma} \leq k, 1 \leq f_{j_1} < f_{j_2} < \ldots < f_{j_\delta} \leq r, \tag{2.48}$$

where $k \geq \gamma \geq 0$, $r \geq \delta \geq 0$, $\gamma + \delta \leq r$. The expressions for the surviving information and redundant columns are given by equation (2.49) and equation (2.50) as follows:

$$\mathrm{A} = \{1, 2, \ldots, k\} \backslash \{f_{i_1}, f_{i_2}, \cdots, f_{i_\gamma}\}, \tag{2.49}$$

$$\mathrm{B} = \{1, 2, \ldots, r\} \backslash \{f_{j_1}, f_{j_2}, \cdots, f_{j_\delta}\}. \tag{2.50}$$

The lost γ information columns can be reconstructed by extracting the information bits from $k-\gamma$ information columns $i_1, i_2, \ldots, i_{k-\gamma} \in A$ and the redundant bits from γ redundant columns $l_1, l_2, \ldots, l_\gamma \in B$. Subsequently, the corresponding encoded vectors and k data polynomials can be cormputed to recover the redundant columns.

Let P_γ denote the set of polynomials comprising solely the missing data polynomials $\{s_{f_{i_1}}(x), \ldots, s_{f_{i_\gamma}}(x)\}$, obtained by subtracting the selected $k-\gamma$ data polynomials from the chosen γ redundant polynomials, as depicted in equations (2.51) and (2.52):

$$P_\gamma = \{p_{l_1}(x), p_{l_2}(x), \ldots, p_{l_\gamma}(x)\}, \tag{2.51}$$

$$\begin{aligned} p_{l_h}(x) = {} & c_{l_h}(x) + x^{(i_1-1)(l_h-1)} s_{i_1}(x) \\ & + \cdots + x^{(i_{k-\gamma}-1)(l_h-1)} s_{i_{k-\gamma}}(x). \end{aligned} \tag{2.52}$$

The missing γ information columns can be retrieved by solving the linear system of equations presented in

$$\begin{bmatrix} x^{(l_1-1)(f_{i_1}-1)} & x^{(l_1-1)(f_{i_2}-1)} & \dots & x^{(l_1-1)(f_{i_\gamma}-1)} \\ x^{(l_2-1)(f_{i_1}-1)} & x^{(l_2-1)(f_{i_2}-1)} & \dots & x^{(l_2-1)(f_{i_\gamma}-1)} \\ \vdots & \vdots & \ddots & \vdots \\ x^{(l_\gamma-1)(f_{i_1}-1)} & x^{(l_\gamma-1)(f_{i_2}-1)} & \dots & x^{(l_\gamma-1)(f_{i_\gamma}-1)} \end{bmatrix} * \begin{bmatrix} s_{f_{i_1}}(x) \\ s_{f_{i_2}}(x) \\ \vdots \\ s_{f_{i_\gamma}}(x) \end{bmatrix} = \begin{bmatrix} p_{l_1}(x) \\ p_{l_2}(x) \\ \vdots \\ p_{l_\gamma}(x) \end{bmatrix}. \tag{2.53}$$

The determinant of the leftmost square matrix in equation (2.53) can be regarded as polynomials in the polynomial ring $F_2[x]/(1 + x^p)$, and their inverse elements can be obtained in $F_2[x]/(1 + x^p)$. Consequently, the utilization of Cramer's rule allows for the computation of the missing γ information columns.

The Cramer's rule evidently exhibits a high level of computational complexity. The key to mitigating this complexity lies in efficiently solving the linear equations presented in the form of Vandermonde matrices. One viable approach involves employing the factorization technique for the generalized Vandermonde matrix (Li and Tan 2008, pp. 1651–1666).

LU Factorization of Vandermonde Matrices When only the information columns are missing, a more efficient LU factorization technique can be employed for Vandermonde matrices. The LU factorization refers to the factorization of a matrix into the product of a lower triangular matrix and an upper triangular matrix. This decoding method enables the restoration of any $min\{r, k\}$ missing information columns. In comparison to Cramer's rule, the LU factorization offers computational advantages by transforming complex linear equation solving into multiple operations with reduced computational complexity.

The Vandermonde matrix $V_v(a)$, denoted as equation (2.54), is constructed from a vector $a = (a_0, a_1, \dots, a_v)$, as follows:

$$V_v(a) = \begin{bmatrix} 1 & a_0 & \cdots & a_0^v \\ 1 & a_1 & \cdots & a_1^v \\ \vdots & \vdots & \ddots & \vdots \\ 1 & a_v & \cdots & a_v^v \end{bmatrix}. \tag{2.54}$$

The second column of $V_v(a)$ represents vector a. By employing symmetric functions and linear algebra, the LU factorization of the Vandermonde matrix was established (Yang 2005, pp. 102–105), which further demonstrated that both the L and U matrices can be expressed as products of multiple sparse matrices.

The Vandermonde matrix $V_v(a)$ can be decomposed into v lower triangular matrices $L_v^{(1)}, L_v^{(2)}, \dots, L_v^{(v)}$ and v upper triangular matrices $U_v^{(1)}, U_v^{(2)}, \dots, U_v^{(v)}$ that satisfies

$$V_v(a) = L_v^{(1)} L_v^{(2)} \cdots L_v^{(v)} U_v^{(v)} U_v^{(v-1)} \cdots U_v^{(1)}. \tag{2.55}$$

The elements of the matrices $L_v^{(l)}$ and $U_v^{(l)}$, corresponding to the i-th row and j-th column, are presented in equation (2.56) and equation (2.57), as follows:

$$L_v^{(l)}(i,j) = \begin{cases} 1 & \begin{array}{c} j = i, i \leq v - l \\ i = j+1, i \geq v - l + 1 \end{array} \\ a_j - a_{v-l} & i = j, i > v - l \\ 0 & otherwise \end{cases}, \tag{2.56}$$

$$U_v^{(l)}(i,j) = \begin{cases} 1 & j = i \\ a_{i-v+l} & j = i+1, j \geq v - l + 1 \\ 0 & otherwise \end{cases}, \tag{2.57}$$

where $0 \leq i, j \leq v$ and $1 \leq l \leq v$.

For example, the Vandermonde matrix $V_3(a)$ can be factorized into three lower triangular matrices, equations (2.58), (2.59), and (2.60), and three upper triangular matrices, equations (2.61), (2.62), and (2.63), as follows:

$$L_3^{(1)} = \begin{bmatrix} 1 & 0 & 0 & 0 \\ 0 & 1 & 0 & 0 \\ 0 & 0 & 1 & 0 \\ 0 & 0 & 1 & a_3 - a_2 \end{bmatrix}, \tag{2.58}$$

$$L_3^{(2)} = \begin{bmatrix} 1 & 0 & 0 & 0 \\ 0 & 1 & 0 & 0 \\ 0 & 1 & a_2 - a_1 & 0 \\ 0 & 0 & 1 & a_3 - a_1 \end{bmatrix}, \tag{2.59}$$

$$L_3^{(2)} = \begin{bmatrix} 1 & 0 & 0 & 0 \\ 1 & a_1 - a_0 & 0 & 0 \\ 0 & 1 & a_2 - a_0 & 0 \\ 0 & 0 & 1 & a_3 - a_0 \end{bmatrix}, \tag{2.60}$$

$$U_3^{(3)} = \begin{bmatrix} 1 & a_0 & 0 & 0 \\ 0 & 1 & a_1 & 0 \\ 0 & 0 & 1 & a_2 \\ 0 & 0 & 0 & 1 \end{bmatrix}, \tag{2.61}$$

$$U_3^{(2)} = \begin{bmatrix} 1 & 0 & 0 & 0 \\ 0 & 1 & a_0 & 0 \\ 0 & 0 & 1 & a_1 \\ 0 & 0 & 0 & 1 \end{bmatrix}, \tag{2.62}$$

$$U_3^{(1)} = \begin{bmatrix} 1 & 0 & 0 & 0 \\ 0 & 1 & 0 & 0 \\ 0 & 0 & 1 & a_0 \\ 0 & 0 & 0 & 1 \end{bmatrix}. \tag{2.63}$$

Given a $(v + 1) * (v + 1)$ Vandermonde matrix, the linear equation system $V_v(a)x = b$ is defined, where $x = (x_0, x_1, \dots, x_v)^t$ and $b = (b_0, b_1, \dots, b_v)^t$ represent column vectors of length $v + 1$. The vector x can be efficiently computed by solving the linear system of equations using the LU factorization of the Vandermonde matrix, given vector b and $V_v(a)$. The core principle of this method lies in the simplification of the intricate generator matrix into a product of multiple elementary matrices, thereby reducing the computational complexity.

In general, among the decoding methods of BVAC, Cramer's rule exhibits universality. When there are $min\{r, k\}$ lost information columns, the LU factorization of Vandermonde matrix can be employed to enhance the decoding performance. However, in cases where both information and redundant columns fail, the applicability of the LU factorization is usually limited.

2.4.4 Binary Cauchy Array Codes

This subsection first presents the construction of BCAC based on the coding framework for binary array codes, followed by an introduction to the efficient decoding approach utilizing LU factorization of Cauchy matrices.

2.4.4.1 Construction of BCACs

The BCAC arrays, similar to BVAC, also possess dimensions of $(p - 1)(k + r)$. However, the redundant columns in BCAC are derived from a Cauchy matrix denoted as $C(k, r, p)$.

The i-th bit of the j-th information column of $C(k, r, p)$ is denoted as $s_{i,j}$, where $i = 0, 1, \dots, p - 2$ and $j = 1, 2, \dots, k$. Similarly, the i-th bit of the l-th redundant column is denoted as $c_{i,l}$, where $i = 0, 1, \dots, p - 2$ and $l = 1, 2, \dots, r$. The parity bit $s_{p-1,j}$ for the p-th information bits $s_{0,j}, s_{1,j}, \dots, s_{p-2,j}$ stored in the j-th information column is defined as

$$s_{p-1,j} = s_{0,j} + s_{1,j} + \cdots + s_{p-2,j}. \tag{2.64}$$

The $(p-1)$ information bits, stored in the j-th information column along with its corresponding parity bit, is represented as a data polynomial denoted by

$$s_j(x) = s_{0,j} + s_{1,j}x + \cdots + s_{p-2,j}x^{p-2} + s_{p-1,j}x^{p-1}. \tag{2.65}$$

Similarly, let $l = 1, 2, \ldots, r$, and define the parity bit $c_{p-1,l}$ for redundant column l according to equation (2.66):

$$c_{p-1,l} = c_{0,l} + c_{1,l} + \cdots + c_{p-2,l}. \tag{2.66}$$

The $p-1$ redundant bits stored in the l-th redundant column and their parity bits are represented as

$$c_l(x) = c_{0,l} + c_{1,l}x + \cdots + c_{p-2,l}x^{p-2} + c_{p-1,l}x^{p-1}. \tag{2.67}$$

Therefore, there are k data polynomials and r encoded polynomials in the polynomial ring $F_2[x]/(1+x^p)$. The r encoded polynomials are calculated by the following equation:

$$\begin{bmatrix} c_1(x) \\ c_2(x) \\ \vdots \\ c_r(x) \end{bmatrix} = \begin{bmatrix} \frac{1}{1-x^r} & \frac{1}{1-x^{r+1}} & \cdots & \frac{1}{1-x^{k+r-1}} \\ \frac{1}{x-x^r} & \frac{1}{x-x^{r+1}} & \cdots & \frac{1}{x-x^{k+r-1}} \\ \vdots & \vdots & \ddots & \vdots \\ \frac{1}{x^{r-1}-x^r} & \frac{1}{x^{r-1}-x^{r+1}} & \cdots & \frac{1}{x^{r-1}-x^{k+r-1}} \end{bmatrix} * \begin{bmatrix} s_1(x) \\ s_2(x) \\ \vdots \\ s_k(x) \end{bmatrix}. \tag{2.68}$$

The generator matrix of $C(k, r, p)$ is presented in equation (2.69):

$$G = \begin{bmatrix} I & C \end{bmatrix}, \tag{2.69}$$

where the matrix I represents the $k * k$ identity matrix, and matrix C is the $k * r$ Cauchy matrix, as shown in the following equation:

$$C = \begin{bmatrix} \frac{1}{1-x^r} & \frac{1}{1-x^{r+1}} & \cdots & \frac{1}{1-x^{k+r-1}} \\ \frac{1}{x-x^r} & \frac{1}{x-x^{r+1}} & \cdots & \frac{1}{x-x^{k+r-1}} \\ \vdots & \vdots & \ddots & \vdots \\ \frac{1}{x^{r-1}-x^r} & \frac{1}{x^{r-1}-x^{r+1}} & \cdots & \frac{1}{x^{r-1}-x^{k+r-1}} \end{bmatrix}, \tag{2.70}$$

where the values of k, r, and p need to be selected rationally, such that an invertible Cauchy matrix C exists. Blomer (1995, pp. 2–11) explored the means to construct an appropriate nonsingular Cauchy matrix and attain optimization in storage coding.

The encoding process of $C(k, r, p)$ is analogous to BVAC. First, k parity bits are computed and appended to the given $k(p-1)$ information bits, resulting in k data polynomials as depicted in equation (2.65). Subsequently, the encoded

Table 2.7 Information and redundant columns of **C(2, 2, 5)**.

Information column 1	Information column 2	Redundant column 1	Redundant column 2
$s_{0,1}$	$s_{0,2}$	$(s_{0,1}+s_{1,1}+s_{3,1})+(s_{0,2}+s_{2,2})$	$(s_{0,1}+s_{1,1}+s_{3,1})+(s_{0,2}+s_{3,2})$
$s_{1,1}$	$s_{1,2}$	$s_{1,1}+(s_{0,2}+s_{1,2}+s_{2,2}+s_{3,2})$	$s_{1,1}+s_{2,2}$
$s_{2,1}$	$s_{2,2}$	$(s_{0,1}+s_{1,1}+s_{2,1}+s_{3,1})+s_{2,2}$	$(s_{0,1}+s_{1,1}+s_{2,1}+s_{3,1})+s_{0,2}$
$s_{3,1}$	$s_{3,2}$	$(s_{1,1}+s_{3,1})+(s_{0,2}+s_{2,2}+s_{3,2})$	$(s_{1,1}+s_{3,1})+(s_{0,2}+s_{1,2}+s_{3,2})$

polynomials are calculated according to equation (2.67), wherein terms with a degree of $p-1$ are disregarded. Finally, the coefficients of polynomials with polynomial degrees from 0 to $p-2$ are stored.

Taking $k=2$, $r=2$, and $p=5$ as an illustrative example, the encoding process of $C(2, 2, 5)$ is introduced. In this particular instance, two data polynomials are involved as depicted in equations (2.71) and (2.72), and the encoded polynomials $c_1(x)$ and $c_2(x)$ can be computed by equation (2.73) as follows:

$$\begin{aligned} s_1(x) = {} & s_{0,1}+s_{1,1}x+s_{2,1}x^2+s_{3,1}x^3 \\ & +(s_{0,1}+s_{1,1}+s_{2,1}+s_{3,1})x^4, \end{aligned} \tag{2.71}$$

$$\begin{aligned} s_2(x) = {} & s_{0,2}+s_{1,2}x+s_{2,2}x^2+s_{3,2}x^3 \\ & +(s_{0,2}+s_{1,2}+s_{2,2}+s_{3,2})x^4, \end{aligned} \tag{2.72}$$

$$\begin{aligned} c_1(x) &= \frac{1}{1-x^2}s_1(x)+\frac{1}{1-x^3}s_2(x), \\ c_2(x) &= \frac{1}{x-x^2}s_1(x)+\frac{1}{x-x^3}s_2(x). \end{aligned} \tag{2.73}$$

The information and redundant bits of this example are listed in Table 2.7. In the calculation of an encoded polynomial, a division operation based on $F_2[x]/(1+x^p)$ needs to be performed for each data polynomial. Subsequently, the results of the corresponding data polynomial division operations are added together. Consequently, the encoding process of BCAC is more intricate compared to BVAC, resulting in higher computational complexity. However, BCAC offers the advantage of greater flexibility and scalability in parameter selection.

2.4.4.2 Decoding Methods of BCACs

The subsequent section provides a comprehensive exposition of a rapid decoding method for BCAC, which is meticulously based on the LU factorization of Cauchy matrices. In contrast to the limited applicability of LU factorization for BVAC, exclusively suitable for information columns loss, the proposed LU factorization for BCAC accommodates any data column loss.

First, the LU factorization of Cauchy matrix is briefly introduced. Given $2k$ nonidentical variables $x_1, x_2, \ldots, x_k, y_1, y_2, \ldots, y_k$, the Cauchy square matrix is defined as

$$C(x_{1:k}, y_{1:k}) = \begin{bmatrix} \frac{1}{x_1 - y_1} & \frac{1}{x_1 - y_2} & \cdots & \frac{1}{x_1 - y_k} \\ \frac{1}{x_2 - y_1} & \frac{1}{x_2 - y_2} & \cdots & \frac{1}{x_2 - y_k} \\ \vdots & \vdots & \ddots & \vdots \\ \frac{1}{x_k - y_1} & \frac{1}{x_k - y_2} & \cdots & \frac{1}{x_k - y_k} \end{bmatrix}. \tag{2.74}$$

Boros, Kailath and Olshevsky (1999, pp. 265–293) find the inverse matrix of Cauchy matrix and propose the LU factorization of the inverse matrix. First, the inverse matrix of $C(x_{1:k}, y_{1:k})$ can be factorized as

$$C(x_{1:k}, y_{1:k})^{-1} = U_k^1 U_k^2 \cdots U_k^{k-1} D_k L_k^{k-1} L_k^{k-2} \cdots L_k^1. \tag{2.75}$$

According to equation (2.75), the factorized simple matrices consist of L_k^i, U_k^i, and D_k, where $i = 1, 2, \ldots, k-1$. These matrices are represented by equations (2.76), (2.77), and (2.78) correspondingly:

$$L_k^i = \begin{bmatrix} I_i & 0 & 0 & 0 & 0 \\ 0 & \frac{1}{x_{i+1} - x_1} & 0 & 0 & 0 \\ 0 & 0 & \frac{1}{x_{i+2} - x_2} & 0 & 0 \\ 0 & 0 & 0 & \ddots & 0 \\ 0 & 0 & 0 & 0 & \frac{1}{x_k - x_{k-i}} \end{bmatrix}$$

$$* \begin{bmatrix} I_{i-1} & 0 & 0 & 0 & 0 \\ 0 & 1 & 0 & 0 & 0 \\ 0 & -(x_1 - y_1) & (x_{i+1} - y_i) & 0 & 0 \\ 0 & 0 & \ddots & \ddots & 0 \\ 0 & 0 & 0 & -(x_{k-i} - y_i) & (x_k - y_i) \end{bmatrix}, \tag{2.76}$$

$$U_k^i = \begin{bmatrix} I_{i-1} & 0 & 0 & 0 & 0 \\ 0 & 1 & -(x_i - y_1) & 0 & 0 \\ 0 & 0 & (x_i - y_{i+1}) & \ddots & 0 \\ 0 & 0 & 0 & \ddots & -(x_i - y_{k-i}) \\ 0 & 0 & 0 & 0 & (x_i - y_k) \end{bmatrix}$$

$$* \begin{bmatrix} I_i & 0 & 0 & 0 & 0 \\ 0 & \frac{1}{y_1 - y_{i+1}} & 0 & 0 & 0 \\ 0 & 0 & \frac{1}{y_2 - y_{i+2}} & 0 & 0 \\ 0 & 0 & 0 & \ddots & 0 \\ 0 & 0 & 0 & 0 & \frac{1}{y_{k-i} - y_k} \end{bmatrix}, \tag{2.77}$$

$$D_k = diag\left\{ (x_1 - y_1)\ (x_2 - y_2)\ \cdots\ (x_k - y_k) \right\}. \tag{2.78}$$

For example, when $k = 2$, the Cauchy inverse matrix $C(x_{1:2}, y_{1:2})^{-1}$ can be factorized as

$$U_2^1 \cdot D_2 \cdot L_2^1 = \begin{bmatrix} 1 & -(x_1 - y_1) \\ 0 & x_1 - y_2 \end{bmatrix} * \begin{bmatrix} 1 & 0 \\ 0 & \frac{1}{y_1 - y_2} \end{bmatrix}$$
$$* \begin{bmatrix} x_1 - y_1 & 0 \\ 0 & x_2 - y_2 \end{bmatrix} * \begin{bmatrix} 1 & 0 \\ 0 & \frac{1}{x_2 - x_1} \end{bmatrix} * \begin{bmatrix} 1 & 0 \\ -(x_1 - y_1) & x_2 - y_1 \end{bmatrix}. \tag{2.79}$$

Considering a linear equation system $C(x_{1:k}, y_{1:k})z = b$, where $z = (z_1, z_2, \ldots, z_k)^t$ and $b = (b_1, b_2, \ldots, b_k)^t$ represent k-dimensional column vectors in the context of a $k * k$ Cauchy matrix, it is feasible to compute the value of vector $z = (z_1, z_2, \ldots, z_k)^t$ by leveraging the provided values of vector $b = (b_1, b_2, \ldots, b_k)^t$ and matrix $C(x_{1:k}, y_{1:k})z = b$, as demonstrated in the following equation:

$$z = U_k^1 U_k^2 \cdots U_k^{k-1} D_k L_k^{k-1} L_k^{k-2} \cdots L_k^1 b. \tag{2.80}$$

Given the loss of γ information columns $a_1, a_2, \ldots, a_\gamma$ and δ redundant columns $b_1, b_2, \ldots, b_\delta$, where $1 \le a_1 < a_2 < \ldots < a_\gamma \le k, 1 \le b_1 < b_2 < \ldots < b_\gamma \le r, k \ge \gamma \ge 0$, $r \ge \delta \ge 0$ and $\gamma + \delta = \rho \le r$, the remaining intact information and redundant columns can be represented by

$$M = \{1, 2, \ldots, k\} \backslash \{a_1, a_2, \ldots, a_\gamma\}, \tag{2.81}$$

$$P = \{1, 2, \ldots, r\} \backslash \{b_1, b_2, \ldots, b_\delta\}. \tag{2.82}$$

First, download $k - \gamma$ surviving information columns $i_1, i_2, \ldots, i_{k-\gamma} \in M$ and γ redundant columns $l_1, l_2, \ldots, l_\gamma \in P$. Next, recover the missing γ information columns and subsequently calculate the lost redundant polynomials by multiplying the encoding vector of the missing redundant columns with k data polynomials. The detailed process is as follows:

For $\tau = 1, 2, \ldots, k - \gamma$, a parity bit should be added to the information column i_τ and a data polynomial should be formed as follows:

$$s_{i_\tau}(x) = s_{0,i_\tau} + s_{1,i_\tau}x + \cdots + s_{p-2,i_\tau}x^{p-2} + \left(\sum_{j=0}^{p-2} s_{j,i_\tau}\right)x^{p-1}. \tag{2.83}$$

For $h = 1, 2, \ldots, \gamma$, append a zero bit to the redundant column l_h and construct the encoded polynomial as depicted in equation (2.84):

$$c_{l_h}(x) = c_{0,l_h} + c_{1,l_h}x + \cdots + c_{p-2,l_h}x^{p-2} + 0x^{p-1}. \tag{2.84}$$

Similar to Cramer's rule in BVAC, a set of polynomials are obtained by subtracting $k - \gamma$ data polynomials from γ encoded polynomials, then equation (2.86) is obtained, as follows:

$$P_\gamma = \{p_{l_1}(x), p_{l_2}(x), \ldots, p_{l_\gamma}(x)\}, \tag{2.85}$$

$$\begin{aligned} p_{l_h}(x) = c_{l_h}(h) &+ \frac{1}{x^{l_h-k-1} - x^{l_h-k+i_1+r-1}}s_{i_1}(x) \\ &+ \cdots + \frac{1}{x^{l_h-k-1} - x^{l_h-k+i_\gamma+r-1}}s_{i_{k-\gamma}}(x), \end{aligned} \tag{2.86}$$

where $h = 1, 2, \ldots, \gamma$.

Then, the missing γ data polynomials can be obtained by solving the linear equations presented in equation (2.87):

$$\begin{bmatrix} \frac{1}{x^{l_1-1} - x^{a_1-1+r}} & \frac{1}{x^{l_1-1} - x^{a_2-1+r}} & \cdots & \frac{1}{x^{l_1-1} - x^{a_\gamma-1+r}} \\ \frac{1}{x^{l_2-1} - x^{a_1-1+r}} & \frac{1}{x^{l_2-1} - x^{a_2-1+r}} & \cdots & \frac{1}{x^{l_2-1} - x^{a_\gamma-1+r}} \\ \vdots & \vdots & \ddots & \vdots \\ \frac{1}{x^{l_\gamma-1} - x^{a_1-1+r}} & \frac{1}{x^{l_\gamma-1} - x^{a_2-1+r}} & \cdots & \frac{1}{x^{l_\gamma-1} - x^{a_\gamma-1+r}} \end{bmatrix} * \begin{bmatrix} s_{a_1}(x) \\ s_{a_2}(x) \\ \vdots \\ s_{a_\gamma}(x) \end{bmatrix} = \begin{bmatrix} p_{l_1}(x) \\ p_{l_2}(x) \\ \vdots \\ p_{l_\gamma}(x) \end{bmatrix}. \tag{2.87}$$

Subsequently, the corresponding encoded vectors are multiplied with k information polynomials to obtain the missing δ redundant columns. Use the LU factorization of the Cauchy matrix in equation (2.87) and then obtain the result quickly.

The LU factorization of the Cauchy matrix offers two distinct advantages. First, it exhibits superior computational complexity compared to existing optimization algorithms for Cauchy array codes. Second, when dealing with relatively large parameters, certain decoding optimization algorithms such as CaCo (Zhang et al. 2015b, pp. 435–447), CCRS (Yin et al. 2015, pp. 360–363), and parallel optimization (Chu et al. 2015, pp. 436–441; Sobe and Schumann 2014, pp. 1–6) suffer from significant performance degradation due to their exponential increase in complexity with parameter size. In contrast, the computational complexity of LU factorization remains unaffected by parameter growth.

2.4.5 Optimization of MDS Array Codes

This subsection is dedicated to the optimization of MDS array codes, with a primary focus on repair bandwidth, locally repairable property, and computational complexity. One difference between array codes and RGCs is that the former stores a column of its array in each storage node. So, in an array code, a column failure can be equivalent to a storage node failure in RGCs.

2.4.5.1 Repair Bandwidth

It is crucial to understand that the repair bandwidth of array codes aligns with that of the aforementioned RGCs. In a DSS, when a node fails, it becomes imperative to download bits from d helper nodes, where $k \leq d \leq k + r - 1$, in order to repair the failed node. The repair bandwidth represents the number of downloaded bits during this process. Reducing repair bandwidth not only accelerates the repair operation but also stabilizes system performance, which holds paramount importance where network transmission bandwidth acts as a bottleneck.

Dimakis et al. (2010, pp. 4539–4551) suggest that the minimum repair bandwidth of an array code with minimal storage redundancy is given by $dL/(d-k+1)$, where L is the number of bits stored in each column. If the minimum repair bandwidth can be achieved by accessing any d helper columns, then the array code attains optimal repair. However, if achieving the minimum repair bandwidth requires accessing only specific d helper columns, then the array code exhibits weak-optimal repair. Additionally, it is important to emphasize that the aforementioned repair is the exact repair, meaning that the data restored by the new column remains entirely identical to the original failed column. Although numerous RGCs achieve optimal repair on sufficiently large finite fields, the number of array codes that attain optimal repair is limited. To minimize the repair bandwidth of a single failed column in binary MDS array codes, conventional approaches attempt to reduce disk reads for RDP codes, EVENODD codes, and X-codes. However, these methods only achieve suboptimal repair bandwidth that is 50% higher than the theoretically optimal repair bandwidth.

Binary MDS array code with asymptotically weak-optimal repair (Hou et al. 2019a, pp. 7095–7113) ensures that repair bandwidth achieves the minimum value asymptotically in d. Different from the array codes with weak optimal repair (Gad et al. 2013, pp. 887–891; Hou et al. 2017, pp. 839–843; Wang, Yin and Wang 2016, pp. 1293–1296), the array code is constructed by using a quotient ring with a cyclic structure, and the fault tolerance is no less than 3. Through a well-designed encoding matrix, the bits accessed in the repair process are intersected as much as possible, thereby reducing the repair bandwidth. Hou et al. (2019a, pp. 7095–7113) provide two construction methods. The first method has an odd number of redundant columns and asymptotically weak-optimal repair for any information column. Conversely, the code in the second structure features an even number of redundant columns and showcases asymptotically weak-optimal repair for any column failure. When the value of d is sufficiently large, the first construction method exhibits a weak-optimal repair of $d = k + (r - 1)/2$, while the second construction method has a weak-optimal repair of $d = k + r/2 - 1$. Binary MDS codes (Sasidharan, Vajha and Kumar 2016, pp. 1–18) exist that are weak-optimal repair for any (n, k, d). However, the techniques used to construct these MDS codes by Sasidharan, Vajha and Kumar (2016, pp. 1–18) differ from those employed by Hou et al. (2019a, pp. 7095–7113). The construction used in the study by Sasidharan, Vajha and Kumar (2016, pp. 1–18) involves coupling transformation over binary vectors to ensure codes possess a weak-optimal repair property. A generic transformation, proposed by Li, Tang and Tian (2017, pp. 1623–1627), can be applied to nonbinary MDS codes to generate new binary MDS codes with information columns possessing weak-optimal repair bandwidth. A potential future direction involves modifying the transformation method proposed by Li, Tang and Tian (2017, pp. 1623–1627) to enable weak-optimal repair bandwidth for parity columns while maintaining asymptotically weak-optimal repair bandwidth for information columns.

In the realm of array codes, attaining optimal repair presents a greater challenge than achieving weak-optimal repair due to the increased number of constraints that must be taken into account. A nonbinary MDS code transformation (Li, Tang and Tian 2018a, pp. 6257–6267) aimed to achieve optimal repair. However, the complexity was high, and its practicality was limited due to the field element being considered the minimum operation unit of this code. A binary MDS array code (Pamies-Juarez et al. 2016, pp. 81–94) is capable of achieving optimal repair for information column faults, albeit with a limited fault tolerance performance due to the presence of only two redundant columns.

Hou and Lee (2019, pp. 1405–1422) proposed a comprehensive transformation framework for binary MDS array codes, aiming to achieve optimal repair bandwidth when $k + 1 \leq d \leq k + r - 1$. The calculation process of this framework solely involves *XOR* operations, thereby exhibiting low complexity and high practicality. Hou and Lee (2019, pp. 1405–1422) employ the EVENODD code as an illustrative example to showcase this transformation framework. First, it presents a generic transformation for an $m \times (k + r)$ EVENODD code. The transformed EVENODD code is of size $m(d - k + 1) \times (k + r)$ and has three properties:

a) The transformed EVENODD code achieves optimal repair for the selected $d - k + 1$ columns.

b) The property of optimal repair for the selected $d - k + 1$ columns of the transformed EVENODD code remains intact upon applying the transformation once again to the transformed EVENODD code.
c) The transformed EVENODD code is an MDS code.

The construction of an EVENODD code family with $r \geq 2$ and $m(d-k+1)^{\left\lceil \frac{k}{d-k+1} \right\rceil + \left\lceil \frac{r}{d-k+1} \right\rceil} \times (k+r)$ multilayer transform is achieved. In scenarios where $k+1 \leq d \leq k+r-1$, the transformed EVENODD achieves optimal repair for all columns. The efficient decoding method of the original EVENODD code is also applicable to the multilevel transformed EVENODD code family. The transformation framework can be applied not only to EVENODD codes but also to other binary array codes, such as those mentioned in the studies by Hou and Han (2017, pp. 521–533) and Hou and Han (2018, pp. 1–11).

Currently, the majority of MDS array codes are designed to achieve optimal repair in the event of a single-column failure. However, in practical storage systems, the occurrence of simultaneous failures involving multiple columns is becoming increasingly common. Li, Tang and Tian (2018b, pp. 1894–1898) were the first to propose an MDS array code that can attain optimal repair bandwidth even when faced with simultaneous column failures. The subpacketization level (Li, Tang and Tian 2018b, pp. 1894–1898) is further optimized (Liu, Li and Tang 2023, pp. 4407–4428), resulting in a significant enhancement of the repair efficiency.

2.4.5.2 Locally Repairable Property

The data files in modern DSSs are typically spread across different nodes, racks, or even data centers. Users require uninterrupted access to the data, even if certain nodes, racks, or data centers experience downtime. This has led to the development of distributed storage coding that aims to minimize transmission bandwidth by busy helper nodes or enable local recovery of data failures during periods of high helper node activity. Currently, extensive research focuses on LRCs with locally repairable property; however, there is a relative lack of studies on locally repairable array codes (LRACs) (Blaum and Hetzler 2019, pp. 3675–3690).

The Expanded-Blaum-Roth (EBR) codes and Expanded-Independent-Parity (EIP) codes (Blaum, Deenadhayalan and Hetzler 2019, pp. 954–957), respectively, extending the BR codes (Blaum and Roth 1993, pp. 66–77) and Independent-Parity codes (Blaum, Bruck and Vardy 1996, pp. 529–542), allow any r columns to fail in all columns and enable local repair of lost columns by adding parity information bits to each column. This approach enhances the performance of repairing invalid columns as it can be accomplished locally without accessing other columns. Based on further research on EBR and EIP, two more efficient array codes (Hou et al. 2022b, pp. 107–125), namely, generalized EBR (GEBR) codes and generalized EIP (GEIP) codes, were proposed. These codes enable local recovery of failed columns, with the number of symbols in each column being either a prime number or a power of an odd prime number. GEBR and GEIP codes offer a greater number of parameters compared to EBR codes and EIP codes, respectively. When m is a power of an odd prime number, the MDS property holds for $m * \mathrm{n}$ $(n = k + r)$ GEBR codes, ensuring that all information can be reconstructed by any k in the n columns. An efficient decoding method for GEBR and GEIP codes was also proposed by Hou et al. (2022b, pp. 107–125), which is based on the LU factorization of the Vandermonde matrix and has a lower complexity compared to existing decoding methods.

Furthermore, during the repair process, when one or more helper columns are occupied and unable to transmit information, a novel class of MDS array codes (Hou et al. 2022a, pp. 3132–3137) is proposed, which exhibits reduced repair bandwidth and lower coding complexity through a well-designed binary cyclic ring and small subpacketization. It is noteworthy that this code incorporates a specialized repair method for busy columns, thereby minimizing the transmission of required repair bandwidth by such columns. The binary MDS array codes serve as the foundation for designing a novel LRAC (Lv et al. 2022, pp. 2184–2189), which enables efficient local single-column repair and multicolumn repair across distinct groups. The concept of combined locality was first proposed by Hu et al. (2021, pp. 233–248), which integrates parity locality and topology locality to address the issue of high repair caused by wide stripes of array codes. Additionally, a novel coding method is introduced to further enhance the efficiency of combined locality.

2.4.5.3 Computational Complexity

In DSSs, the computational complexity of array codes plays a pivotal role as a performance metric encompassing update and coding complexities. Array codes fundamentally aim to enhance original information reliability and fault tolerance by incorporating redundant bit data. As information symbols frequently require updates, it becomes imperative to update the associated redundant symbols correspondingly in order to maintain consistency and integrity. High update complexity implies that substantial computing and network resources are required for modifying redundant symbols with each update. Consequently, this leads to increased latency, thereby impacting overall system performance and response time. Particularly in large-scale DSSs, frequent data updates significantly burden network load and servers, potentially causing performance bottlenecks. Henceforth, designing array codes with low update complexity assumes paramount importance.

The update complexity is determined by the maximum row weight of the generator matrix, which is determined by the maximum number of nonzero elements

Table 2.8 A 2 ∗ 6 low-density MDS array code.

a_0	a_1	a_2	a_3	a_4	a_5
$a_2 + a_3 + a_4$	$a_3 + a_4 + a_5$	$a_4 + a_5 + a_0$	$a_5 + a_0 + a_1$	$a_0 + a_1 + a_2$	$a_1 + a_2 + a_3$

in each row of the matrix. This means that in the worst case, a change in a single information symbol will result in an update of redundant symbols equal to the number of maximum row weight. The reduction of the maximum row weight in the array code generator matrix is observed to have a positive impact on the complexity of updates. The lower bound on the number of nonzero elements in the generator matrix of linear MDS codes over $GF(q)$ was initially proposed by Blaum and Roth (1999, pp. 46–59), along with the introduction of a low-density MDS code that satisfies this lower bound. Huang, Jiang and Xiao (2017, pp. 834–838) proposed the construction of a cyclically symmetric low-density MDS array code. To illustrate its principle, a special 2 ∗ 6 low-density MDS array code was defined as shown in Table 2.8, where + represents the binary XOR operation.

The array code consists of six columns, comprising six information symbols $a_0, \dots, a_5$ and six encoded symbols $a_2 + a_3 + a_4, a_3 + a_4 + a_5, \dots, a_1 + a_2 + a_3$. It is evident that all six information symbols can be retrieved from any combination of three columns. For instance, to retrieve a_3, a_4, and a_5 from the leftmost three columns:

$$a_3 = (a_3 + a_4 + a_5) + (a_4 + a_5 + a_0) + a_0,$$
$$a_4 = a_2 + (a_2 + a_3 + a_4) + a_3,$$
$$a_5 = (a_3 + a_4 + a_5) + a_3 + a_4.$$

It is evident that the update of an information symbol necessitates solely updating three encoded symbols, thereby achieving the lower bound of update complexity for MDS array codes. Additionally, the construction of the array code takes into account cyclicity, ensuring that all indexes in each column can be calculated by incrementing the index to the left by 1. The aforementioned coding examples pertain to a subclass of cyclic array codes (Peterson and Brown 1961, pp. 228–235), specifically called systematically cyclic array codes. In comparison to conventional cyclic array codes, systematically cyclic array codes offer distinct advantages in updating and coding computation. By combining the advantages of cyclic array codes and low-density array codes, Cassuto and Bruck (2006, pp. 2794–2798) initially construct a noncyclic low-density MDS code. Subsequently, it explicitly transforms the parity matrix to obtain a novel and nonequivalent systematically cyclic MDS array code with identical density.

The problem of high update complexity of Extended EVENODD codes was optimized (Hou 2023, pp. 2563–2575), and a new EEOD+ code was proposed, resulting in a significant reduction in the update complexity of EEOD codes. Moreover, this reduction effect became more pronounced with increasing redundancy. These findings offer valuable insights for optimizing common array codes such as RDP and X-code. Fu, Hou and Zhang (2021, pp. 1–6) proposed an extended STAR code, known as STAR+ code, which effectively reduces the update complexity while preserving the exceptional performance of STAR codes.

The coding complexity, which refers to the computational requirements for data storage and repair, plays a crucial role in the optimization of MDS array codes. Minimizing this complexity can significantly enhance the practicality of the code.

A general decoding method for MDS array codes is proposed (Lv et al. 2023, pp. 1–11), which includes a scheduled algorithm for syndrome computation with asymptotically optimal computational complexity. This algorithm can be directly applied to MDS array codes under the condition of no more than three failed columns, leading to comprehensive improvements in decoding efficiency. The decoding algorithm is implemented based on a cyclic matrix. In comparison to the general method of calculating the $\rho(m - \tau)$ order inverse matrix of an array code, the decoding algorithm only requires computation of the $(m - \tau)$ order inverse matrix, resulting in a reduced decoding complexity from $O(\rho^3(m - 1)^3)$ to $O((m - 1)^3)$. Additionally, Louidor and Roth (2006, pp. 3186–3197) actively investigated the potential for establishing a novel relationship between MDS array codes and LDPC, leveraging the respective advantages of both techniques to further enhance optimization of coding complexity.

In order to reduce the coding complexity, many studies (Cassuto and Bruck 2012, pp. 146–158; Fu, Hou and Zhang 2021, pp. 1–6) on MDS array codes have used cyclic shifts and XOR operations to replace expensive operations over $GF(q)$ or reduce operations over $GF(q)$ with efficient scheduling algorithms. Lin (2017, pp. 3235–3244) designed a scheduling algorithm for RS codes, which reduced the decoding complexity by reusing some common intermediate results. When $r = 3$, the minimum coding complexity was achieved in the existing results. Hou, et al. (2017, pp. 839–843) reduced the coding complexity by constructing MDS array codes on cyclic polynomials that only involve cyclic shifts and XOR operations. At the same time, to further improve the encoding efficiency, it also proposed an efficient scheduling algorithm to minimize the number of additions or multiplications in the encoding process.

2.5 Codes with Locality

RGCs and array codes are designed to minimize repair bandwidth and storage overhead, but often require a higher repair degree, i.e., an increase in the number of helper nodes in the repair process. In contrast, LRCs reduce the repair degree by enhancing coding locality, thereby improving repair efficiency. This section commences with a concise overview of the fundamental concepts of LRCs and their classification, followed by an introduction to a novel type of LRGC that integrates LRCs and RGCs. Finally, it presents another coding scheme that emphasizes locality, referred to as integrated interleaved (II) codes.

2.5.1 Introduction to LRCs

LRCs leverage the inherent locality of coding to reduce repair degree, thereby decreasing repair bandwidth and enhancing repair speed. However, LRCs require additional redundancy to achieve locality, resulting in lower storage efficiency compared to MDS codes. Ramkumar et al. 2021, (pp. 735–762) categorize LRCs into two primary types: LRCs with information symbol locality (ISL-LRCs) and LRCs with all-symbol locality (ASL-LRCs). ISL-LRCs are systematic linear codes that specifically reduce the repair degree for failed system nodes storing information symbols; ASL-LRCs reduce the repair degree for all failed nodes, regardless of whether the failed node stores information symbols or encoded symbols.

2.5.1.1 Information Symbol Locality Locally Repairable Codes

In the codeword of a linear code, if k information symbols are explicitly present in n coding symbols, then this linear code is considered a systematic linear code. The LRC(n, k, r) over $GF(q)$ represents a (n, k) systematic linear block code, where each information symbol c_t for $t \in [k]$ can be retrieved by computing the following linear combination:

$$c_t = \sum_{i \in S_t} a_i c_i, a_i \in GF(q),$$

where the size of S_t in the above equation is at most r. The lower bound on the minimum distance d that LRCs must satisfy

$$d_{min} \leq (n - k + 1) - \left(\left\lceil \frac{k}{r} \right\rceil - 1 \right). \tag{2.88}$$

Under the same parameters (n, k), the minimum distance of LRCs is smaller than that of MDS codes by $\lceil k/r \rceil - 1$. This represents the cost paid by LRCs to maintain its locality. Similar to RGCs, a class of LRCs for which equal sign in equation (2.88) holds is referred to as optimal LRCs.

A typical example of optimal LRCs is the pyramid codes (Huang, Chen and Li 2013, pp. 1–28), which are classic linear LRCs. Meanwhile, there has been relatively less research on nonlinear LRCs (further details can be found in Papailiopoulos and Dimakis 2014, pp. 5843–5855 and Forbes and Yekhanin 2014, pp. 78–84). Next, the construction of optimal ISL-LRCs and pyramid codes with parameters $(n = 9, k = 6, r = 3)$ is briefly introduced.

First, construct a generator matrix C_R for a RS(8, 6) code as follows:

$$G_R = \begin{bmatrix} 1\ 0\ 0\ 0\ 0\ 0\ a_{11}\ a_{12} \\ 0\ 1\ 0\ 0\ 0\ 0\ a_{21}\ a_{22} \\ 0\ 0\ 1\ 0\ 0\ 0\ a_{31}\ a_{32} \\ 0\ 0\ 0\ 1\ 0\ 0\ a_{41}\ a_{42} \\ 0\ 0\ 0\ 0\ 1\ 0\ a_{51}\ a_{52} \\ 0\ 0\ 0\ 0\ 0\ 1\ a_{61}\ a_{62} \end{bmatrix}.$$

The generator matrix G_{pyr} of pyramid codes is constructed by splitting individual parity column from G_R, as illustrated below:

$$G_{\text{pyr}} = \begin{bmatrix} 1\ 0\ 0\ a_{11}\ 0\ 0\ 0\ \ 0\ \ a_{12} \\ 0\ 1\ 0\ a_{21}\ 0\ 0\ 0\ \ 0\ \ a_{22} \\ 0\ 0\ 1\ a_{31}\ 0\ 0\ 0\ \ 0\ \ a_{32} \\ 0\ 0\ 0\ \ 0\ \ 1\ 0\ 0\ a_{41}\ a_{42} \\ 0\ 0\ 0\ \ 0\ \ 0\ 1\ 0\ a_{51}\ a_{52} \\ 0\ 0\ 0\ \ 0\ \ 0\ 0\ 1\ a_{61}\ a_{62} \end{bmatrix}.$$

The locality of G_{pyr} is reflected in the fact that the first four columns and the subsequent four columns of the matrix locally form two RS(4, 1) codes, enabling local repair. Furthermore, based on the MDS property of RS codes, we know that the minimum distance of G_R is 3; therefore, the minimum distance of G_{pyr} is at least $d_{min} \geq 3$. Additionally, according to equation (2.88), the minimum distance d_{min} of G_{pyr} should satisfy

$$d_{min} \leq (n - k + 1) - \left(\left\lceil \frac{k}{r} \right\rceil - 1 \right) = 3.$$

If this equality is satisfied, it implies that G_{pyr} represents an optimal LRC. From generator matrices of RS(n, k) codes, the LRCs formed by partitioning a parity column are all optimal and can be regarded as pyramid codes with parameters ($n_{\text{pyr}} = n + \lceil k/r \rceil - 1, k_{\text{pyr}} = k, r$).

2.5.1.2 All-symbol Locality Locally Repairable Codes

All symbols can be recovered from the linear combination of at most r other symbols; these LRCs are called ASL-LRCs. Tamo and Barg (2014, pp. 4661–4676) propose a class of classical optimal ASL-LRCs, which is briefly referred to as OA-LRCs. Each symbol in an OA-LRC codeword over GF(q) can be interpreted as the result of evaluating a polynomial associated with the information symbols. Specifically, the codeword can be represented as a set $F = (f(P_1), \cdots f(P_n))$, where $f(x) = \sum_{i=0}^{k-1} m_i x^i$ and $P_1, \ldots, P_n$ are different elements in $GF(q)$. The codeword is associated with the set of information symbols $\{m_i\}_{i=0}^{k-1}$. The lost symbols can be repaired using a subset of F. As shown in Figure 2.10, when $r = 2$, through explicit construction, for any $f(P_a)$ in the OA-LRC, a suitable subset $(f(P_b), f(P_c))$ can always be found

Figure 2.10 An OA-LRC with $r = 2$.

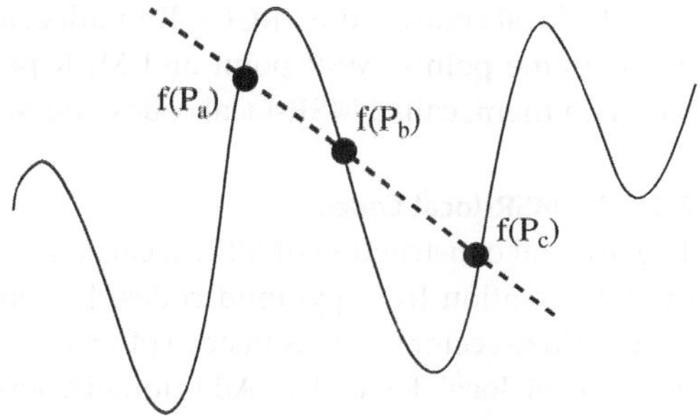

in F such that $(f(P_a), f(P_b), f(P_c))$ lies on a straight line and satisfies

$$u_a f(P_a) + u_b f(P_b) + u_c f(P_c) = 0. \tag{2.89}$$

Specifically, u_a, u_b, $u_c \subseteq GF(q)$. Consequently, $f(P_a)$ can be restored using $f(P_b)$ and $f(P_c)$. Tamo and Barg 2014, pp. 4661–4676 also proposed a general construction method capable of generating any (n, k, r) OA-LRCs and demonstrated that any ASL-LRC satisfying the parameter $(r + 1) \nmid n$ cannot satisfy equation (2.88). Several studies (Wang and Zhang 2015, pp. 5280–5294; Mehrabi and Ardakani 2017, pp. 1–5) also concentrated on adjusting the boundary in equation (2.88) to optimize ASL-LRCs. Tamo et al. (2016, pp. 345–364) focused on the construction of optimal ASL-LRCs using cyclic codes in $GF(n)$. Silberstein, Rawat and Vishwanath (2012, pp. 1150–1157) presented a construction method for ASL-LRCs via rank-metric codes.

However, the aforementioned optimal LRCs, whether ISL-LRCs or ASL-LRCs, are all built on large finite fields $GF(q)$. The operations related to $GF(q)$ often have higher computational complexity, which in turn affects the actual encoding and decoding speed. Some studies (Cadambe and Mazumdar 2015, pp. 5787–5794; Goparaju and Calderbank 2014, pp. 676–680; Agarwal et al. 2018, pp. 3481–3492; Barg, Tamo and Vlăduţ 2017, pp. 4928–4939) also focused on researching LRCs over smaller finite fields and even binary fields to reduce computational complexity.

2.5.2 Locally Regenerating Codes

RGCs and LRCs are capable of effectively repairing nodes to ensure data reliability. During the repair process, RGCs focus on minimizing repair bandwidth, while LRCs are dedicated to minimizing repair degree. The pursuit of developing a novel class of codes that integrates the strengths of RGCs and LRCs holds significant research value. LRGCs (Kamath et al. 2014, pp. 4637–4660) are a category of vector codes that optimize repair bandwidth and repair degree simultaneously, with local codes being RGCs.

In the local codes of the LRGCs, Kamath et al. (2014, pp. 4637–4660) considered two extreme points, MSR point and MBR point, and built two types of LRGCs based on them, called MSR-local codes and MBR-local codes.

2.5.2.1 MSR-local Codes

The original construction of MSR-local codes (Kamath et al. 2014, pp. 4637–4660) drew inspiration from pyramid codes. In contrast to pyramid codes, MSR-local codes utilize vector symbols instead of scalar symbols and employ local MSR codes in place of local RS codes. Additionally, leveraging the principles of pyramid codes enables support for extensions in larger finite fields and a broader range of coding parameters. Another construction method for MSR-local codes, known as Sum-Parity MSR-local codes (Kamath et al. 2013, pp. 1–5), achieves optimality for any number of local codes as long as the global minimum distance d_{min} does not exceed twice the local minimum distance δ. As depicted in Figure 2.11, m^t denotes the transpose matrix of the original data, I represents the identity matrix, and P_1 and P_2 are the parity matrices. The Sum-Parity MSR-local codes start with a parent MSR code represented by a generator matrix in the form $[I \mid P_1 \mid P_2]$ and further ensure that both local code 1 and local code 2, constructed from the submatrix $[I \mid P_1]$, also adhere to the requirements of MSR codes. The resulting codeword is depicted as

$$\left[m_a^t \mid m_a^t P_1 \mid m_b^t \mid m_b^t P_1 \mid (m_a + m_b)^t P_2\right], \tag{2.90}$$

where m_a and m_b are message vectors associated with two local codes.

2.5.2.2 MBR-local Codes

The construction of MBR-local codes (Kamath et al. 2014, pp. 4637–4660) primarily relies on the RT. As depicted in Figure 2.12, the LRGC, comprising a set of 30 scalar symbols, initially constructs an ASL-LRC at the lower level.

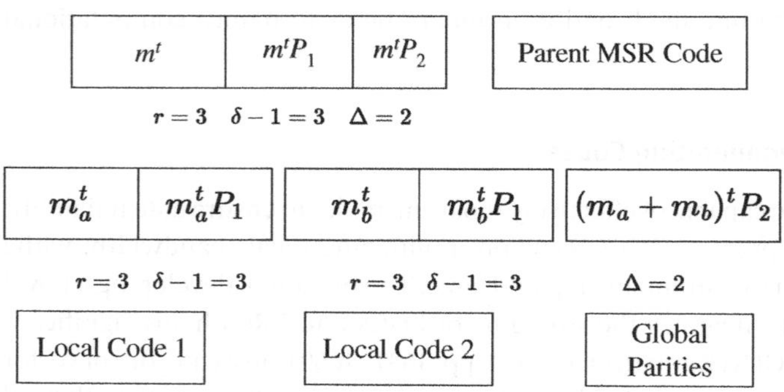

Figure 2.11 Sum-parity MSR-local codes.

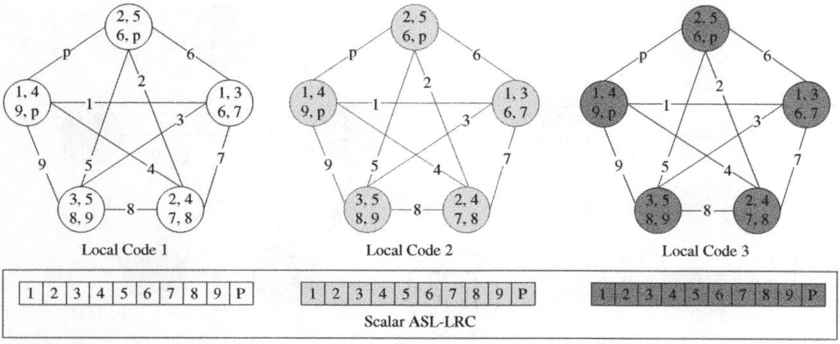

Figure 2.12 The MBR-local codes consist of three local codes, each of which is a pentagon MBR code.

This ASL-LRC encompasses three mutually independent local codes, with each local code consisting of nine data symbols and one parity symbol. Subsequently, at the upper level, the RT is employed to construct a pentagon MBR code for each local code.

Furthermore, it is possible to substitute different LRCs for the lower level scalar code in the MBR-local codes. For example, as shown in Figure 2.13, when using a scalar pyramid code, the lower layers contain only two local codes and one global parity code. Therefore, during the upper layer transformation, there are also only two corresponding pentagonal MBR codes, while the global parity code remains unchanged.

Rawat et al. (2013, pp. 212–236) also investigate vector codes with properties of local regeneration. In comparison to LRGCs employed by Kamath et al. (2013, pp. 1–5), those used by Rawat et al. (2013, pp. 212–236) place greater emphasis on the combination of communication security and local repair, while allowing for nonlinear local codes. Furthermore, Rawat et al. (2013, pp. 212–236) present a specific construction for MSR-local codes, which is based on an ASL-LRC from Gabidulin maximum rank-distance codes. These codes can achieve optimal performance through specific parameter settings. Gligoroski et al. (2017, pp. 979–984) utilize HashTable to construct LRGCs, and Krishnan, Lalitha and Didugu (2020, pp. 2669–2673) propose integrating cooperative RGCs into LRCs as a strategy to enhance fault tolerance in LRGCs.

LRGCs, as a coding technique that integrates the advantages of RGCs and LRCs, have the potential to decrease local repair bandwidth and reduce repair degree during data restoration. Nevertheless, akin to LRCs, most LRGCs are designed based on large finite fields, resulting in heightened coding complexity and substantial requirements for computational resources and energy consumption. Moreover, the intricate structure of LRGCs leads to suboptimal practical

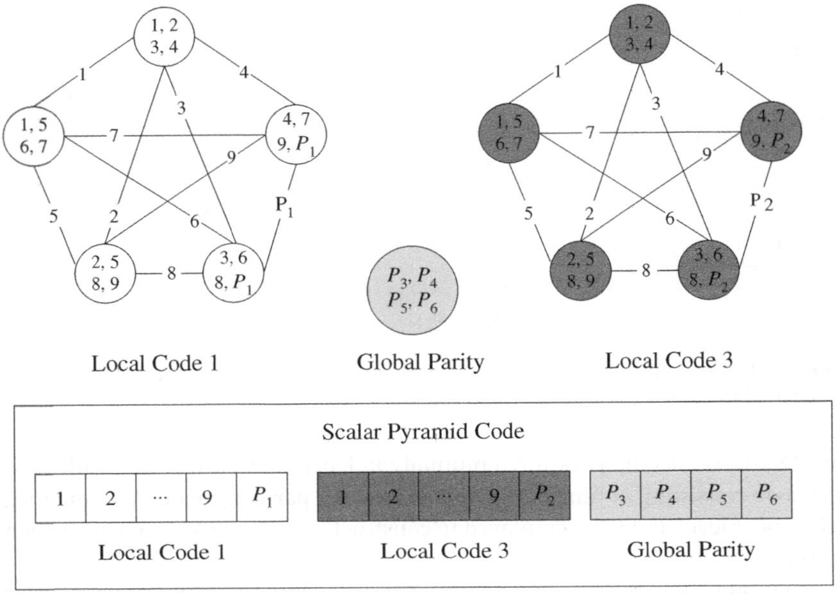

Figure 2.13 The MBR-local codes consist of three local codes, which compose a scalar pyramid code.

performance. Henceforth, optimizing the structures and coding algorithms of existing LRGCs represents a pivotal direction for future research.

2.5.3 Integrated Interleaved codes

II codes represent a category of rate-adaptive, multilevel coding schemes that facilitate the utilization of redundancy in a nonuniform manner to effectively address varying degrees of faults. In a storage system, codewords are frequently regarded as distinct interleaves between data sectors. The objective of II codes is to develop redundant data that can be shared across all interleaves, enabling the repair of those interleaves that experience faults exceeding the first-level error-correcting capacity.

Prior to the introduction of II codes, a two-layer coding scheme was examined (Patel 1989, pp. 470–484; Abdel-Ghaffar and Hassner 1991, pp. 735–741), which utilized parity symbols shared among all interleaves to address certain severely faulty interleaves. However, this construction fails to provide adequate protection for the shared parity symbols, necessitating additional coding measures to ensure their reliability.

In 2001, II RS codes (Hassner et al. 2001, pp. 773–775) were introduced for the first time. II RS codes initially generate m interleaves using RS codes in the first

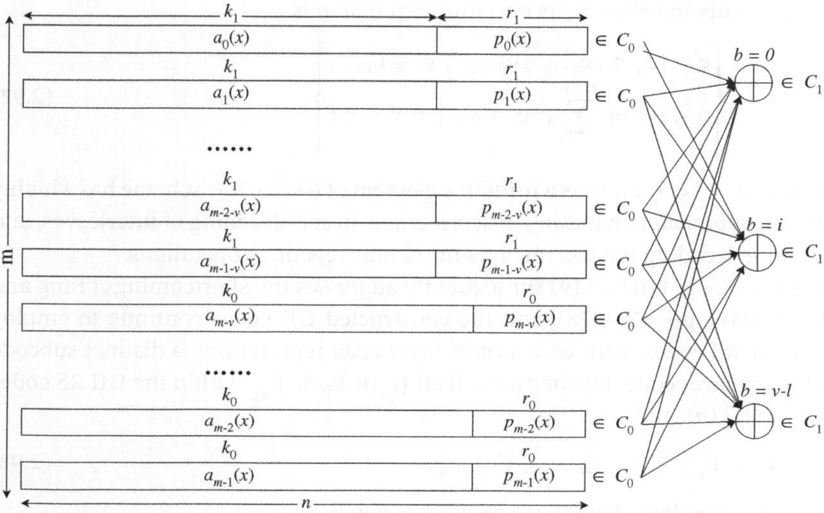

Figure 2.14 Graphical representation of an II RS code.

layer and subsequently produce v codewords with enhanced error tolerance based on these m interleaves in the second layer. The second layer is also referred to as the nested layer, and these codewords can be regarded as subcodes of the first layer coding. Let $\{C_i(n, k_i, d_i)\}_{i=0}^{1}$ be two RS codes over the Galois field $GF(q)$, such that $C_1 \subset C_0$. The definition of an II RS code is as follows:

$$C \triangleq \begin{Bmatrix} \mathbf{c} = [\mathbf{c}_0, \mathbf{c}_1, \mathbf{c}_2, \dots, \mathbf{c}_{m-1}] : \mathbf{c}_i \in C_0, \\ \forall i, \sum_{i=0}^{m-1} \alpha^{bi}\mathbf{c}_i \in C_1, 0 \le b < v \end{Bmatrix}, \tag{2.91}$$

where it satisfies $v < m < q$ and α is a primitive element of $GF(q)$. The graphical representation of II RS code is shown in Figure 2.14, where an interleave refers to a specific $\mathbf{c}_i$ such that $\mathbf{c}_i \in C_0$ and $0 \le i < m$. For an interleaved M_i, self-decoding refers to the independent decoding of $\mathbf{c}_i$ in the first layer, while nested decoding involves executing a decoding algorithm in the second layer to recover the entire data M and subsequently retrieve M_i.

It is important to note that the quantity of nested codes utilized within an II code is designated as the level. For instance, II codes employing t nested codes are referred to as t-level II codes, while those with $t \ge 2$ are classified as generalized integrated interleaved (GII) codes. A GII coding scheme (Tang and Koetter 2006, pp. 474–478) featuring unequal protection has been proposed, based on the principle of employing nested codes with enhanced fault tolerance to address severely faulty interleaves, while utilizing nested codes with reduced fault tolerance for less severely faulty interleaves. Its encoding expression is

$$C \triangleq \left\{ \begin{array}{l} \mathbf{c} = [\mathbf{c}_0, \mathbf{c}_1, \mathbf{c}_2, \dots, \mathbf{c}_{m-1}] : \mathbf{c}_i \in C_0, \\ 0 \le i < m, \sum_{i=0}^{m-1} \alpha^{bi} \mathbf{c}_i \in C_{b+1}, 0 \le b < v \end{array} \right\}, \tag{2.92}$$

where $v < m < q$ and α is a primitive element of $GF(q)$. The scheme has a highly complex approach to handling miscorrections in self-decoding of interleaves, and the entire decoding process involves numerous repetitive operations.

Wu (2016, pp. 1102–1119) subsequently addresses the shortcomings (Tang and Koetter 2006, pp. 474–478), and the constructed GII codes continue to employ two-layer RS codes, with each nested layer code representing a distinct subcode of the first layer code. Furthermore, if all $\{C_i(n, k_i, d_i)\}_{i=0}^{v}$ within the GII RS codes reside in $GF(q)$, and

$$C_v \subseteq C_{v-1} \subseteq C_{v-2} \subseteq \dots \subseteq C_1 \subset C_0. \tag{2.93}$$

Its corresponding algebraic expression is denoted as

$$C \triangleq \left\{ \begin{array}{l} \mathrm{c} = [\mathrm{c}_0, \mathrm{c}_1, \mathrm{c}_2, \dots, \mathrm{c}_{m-1}] : \mathrm{c}_i \in C_0, \\ 0 \le i < m, \tilde{\mathrm{c}}_b = \sum_{i=0}^{m-1} \alpha^{bi} \mathrm{c}_i \in C_{v-b}, 0 \le b < v \end{array} \right\}, \tag{2.94}$$

where $v < m < q$ and α is a primitive element of $GF(q)$. Moreover, the nested encoding matrix of the GII RS code may be represented as a simple Vandermonde matrix, thereby reducing the complexity associated with the encoding design. The encoding expression for the nested layer of GII RS codes is

$$\begin{bmatrix} \tilde{\mathrm{c}}_0 \\ \tilde{\mathrm{c}}_1 \\ \vdots \\ \tilde{\mathrm{c}}_{v-1} \end{bmatrix} = \begin{bmatrix} 1 & 1 & 1 & \cdots & 1 \\ 1 & \alpha & \alpha^2 & \cdots & \alpha^{m-1} \\ \vdots & \vdots & \vdots & \ddots & \vdots \\ 1 & \alpha^{(v-1)} & \alpha^{2(v-1)} & \cdots & \alpha^{(m-1)(v-1)} \end{bmatrix} \begin{bmatrix} \mathbf{c}_0 \\ \mathbf{c}_1 \\ \vdots \\ \mathbf{c}_{m-1} \end{bmatrix}. \tag{2.95}$$

It is clear that the distinction between equations (2.92) and (2.94) lies in the parameter b, which corresponds to different subcodes. The subcodes constructed according to the order specified by equation (2.94) present opportunities for optimization during the iterative decoding process. For instance, Wu (2016, pp. 1102–1119) integrated the Berlekamp–Massey (Imamura and Yoshida 1987, pp. 146–150) update algorithm into an efficient iterative decoding framework, typically disregarding miscorrection from the first layer and intelligently reusing prior results throughout each iteration of the decoding attempts, thereby mitigating a significant number of redundant operations. Furthermore, Wu (2016, pp. 1102–1119) also explored the practical value of GII codes in redundant arrays of independent disks systems and extended the GII codes to binary Bose-Chaudhuri-Hocquenghem (BCH) codes, deriving encoding and decoding algorithms similar to those of RS codes.

Considering that self-decoding can effectively rectify most faults under normal operating conditions, GII codes are also applicable in scenarios where interleaves are distributed across different physical units within a distributed environment. Moreover, GII codes typically assume equal lengths for interleaves. However, this assumption can be relaxed without compromising the encoding and decoding algorithms, which is particularly advantageous for applications necessitating uniform original data lengths.

II codes possess numerous extensions. The extended integrated interleaved (EII) codes (Blaum and Hetzler 2018, pp. 1497–1513) integrate the concepts of II codes and product codes (Kschischang 2003, pp. 1–19), thereby expanding the scope of II codes by constructing them from the perspective of product codes. EII codes conceptualize II codes as an $m * n$ array, where each row corresponds to a codeword C_0, and specific linear combinations of these rows yield codewords C_i for nested layers, which also serve as subcodes of C_0. Although EII codes typically do not satisfy the minimum distance requirement, their construction necessitates only a smaller finite field and accommodates various parameter options, significantly reducing the computational complexity associated with encoding and decoding processes, thus rendering them appealing alternatives in practical applications. Moreover, EII codes exhibit superior code distance compared to II codes with equivalent code rates, and they facilitate simultaneous decoding across both rows and columns, thereby enhancing their correction capabilities.

Building upon the results of Blaum and Hetzler (2018, pp. 1497–1513), Blaum (2019, pp. 936–956) introduced a more comprehensive definition of EII codes, referred to as new EII codes in this section. The original definitions of II codes and EII codes can be considered special cases of the new EII codes. These new EII codes extend code construction to any field $GF(q)$, particularly the binary field $GF(2)$, by conceptualizing a t-level EII code as a direct sum of 1-level EII codes. In most instances, the new EII codes exhibit superior minimum distances compared to other LRCs with equivalent parameters while retaining the advantages inherent in the original EII codes.

The first layer of the II codes comprises the base code, while the second layer consists of all interleaved codewords derived from the base code and nested within one another. If any of the interleaves contains excessive errors, it must be repaired by accessing shared parity data, which necessitates access to all interleaves. To enhance locality, shared parity data can be allocated to different subgroups containing partial interleaves in a multilevel hierarchical structure. Provided that the errors within the subgroup do not exceed a specified threshold, it is sufficient to utilize the interleaves and shared parity data within that subgroup for repair.

Asano et al. (2005, pp. 1–11) developed a multilayer II coding scheme, wherein shared parity data provides effective protection for only one interleave within the subgroups. By analyzing the nested matrix properties that facilitate multi-interleaves repair capability, a generalized three-layer GII code is proposed by Zhang (2017, pp. 442–445). In comparison to the approach adopted by Asano et al. (2005, pp. 1–11), this coding approach permits the utilization of t-level codes in both the second and third layers, significantly enhancing error correction capabilities; additionally, the shared parity data in the third layer offers protection for multiple covered interleaves. The construction presented in Zhang (2017, pp. 442–445) focuses on nested matrices and posits that the key to constructing GII codes lies in identifying an invertible nested encoding matrix that satisfies all encoding and decoding constraints. Furthermore, by subdividing the interleaves into several higher layer groups, additional layers of GII codes can be achieved.

However, the complexity of the corresponding constraints for GII codes with an increased number of layers escalates exponentially, making it exceedingly challenging to identify an effective nested encoding matrix. This difficulty arises from the fact that the nested encoding matrices for GII codes with fewer layers differ significantly from those associated with multiple layers, and they cannot be readily transformed into one another through straightforward derivations. For example, as shown in equation (2.95), the nested encoding matrix for a simple two-layer GII code can be implemented using a Vandermonde matrix, while the nested encoding matrix for a three-layer GII code (Zhang 2017, pp. 442–445) must be a non-Vandermonde transform matrix.

A complex recursive extension algorithm was developed (Li, Lin and Wang 2020, pp. 1880–1884) to identify nested encoding matrices, thereby extending the three-layer GII codes (Zhang 2017, pp. 442–445) to multilayer GII codes. Subsequently, Blaum (2022, pp. 5098–5111) provides a theoretical foundation for the constructions presented by Zhang (2017, pp. 442–445) and Li, Lin and Wang (2020, pp. 1880–1884), broadening the scope of multilayer GII code construction to encompass a wider range of multilayer EII codes, where the constructions in Zhang (2017, pp. 442–445) and Li, Lin and Wang (2020, pp. 1880–1884) can be considered special cases of those outlined in Blaum (2022, pp. 5098–5111).

Furthermore, prior research on t-level EII codes has typically assumed that the nested codes are either RS codes or shortened RS codes, or at a minimum required that the minimum distance of the nested codes decreases. In contrast, Blaum (2022, pp. 5098–5111) redefined the concept of EII codes without any prerequisites or assumptions, significantly simplifying the recursive construction of multilayer EII codes and minimizing additional factors to consider. However, the constructed multilayer EII codes (Blaum 2022, pp. 5098–5111) are limited to specific-sized fields; thus, extending them to any field $GF(q)$, particularly binary fields, presents an intriguing avenue for future research.

2.6 Chapter Summary

This chapter underscores the significance of storage coding technology, particularly ECs such as RS codes, RGCs, array codes, and LRCs. By segmenting data into blocks, incorporating redundancy, and distributing these blocks across multiple nodes, ECs facilitate data recovery even in the event of multiple node faults. This approach not only minimizes storage redundancy but also optimizes network bandwidth compared to traditional replication. ECs are essential for contemporary storage systems, ensuring reliability, scalability, and high performance in managing vast volumes of information while optimizing resource allocation and energy efficiency.

Discussion Questions

1 What is an MDS code? Explain its significance in ECs.

MDS codes are a type of linear block codes that satisfy the Singleton bound, with their minimum distance reaching the theoretical maximum. Specifically, for an MDS code with parameters (n, k, d), its minimum distance d satisfies $d = r + 1$ (where the redundancy $r = n - k$). In ECs, the MDS property means that when the original data is divided into k data blocks and encoded to generate n blocks, as long as there are any k valid blocks in the system, the original data can be recovered. The significance of MDS codes lies in their ability to achieve the highest fault tolerance with the minimum redundancy. For example, RS codes, CRS codes, and RGCs all belong to MDS codes and are widely used in DSS to balance storage efficiency and reliability.

2 What is erasure coding? Explain its basic principle and describe its main advantages over traditional replication strategies.

Erasure coding is a technology that achieves highly reliable storage through data block division and redundant encoding. Its basic principle is to divide the original data into k data blocks and generate m redundant blocks through encoding, totaling $n = k + m$ blocks, which are then distributed and stored in different nodes. As long as any k valid blocks are obtained, the original data can be restored. Compared with replication strategies (such as three replicas), the advantages of erasure coding lie in higher storage efficiency (the redundancy is only $1 + m/k$ instead of the multiple growth in replication strategies), stronger fault tolerance (allowing m nodes to fail simultaneously), and lower network overhead (for example, LRCs reduce the amount of data transmission during repair). For instance, Facebook adopted erasure coding to replace the three-replica strategy, saving petabytes of storage space.

3 What are the differences between the MSR codes and the MBR codes in regenerating codes? Explain their design goals and applicable scenarios, respectively.

MSR codes aim to minimize storage overhead, with each node storing a data volume of M/k (where M is the file size), and the repair bandwidth is $M * d/(k(d-k+1))$. They are suitable for scenarios where storage resources are limited but the requirements for repair bandwidth are not strict. MBR codes, on the other hand, aim to minimize repair bandwidth, with both storage and repair bandwidth being $2Md/(k(2d-k+1))$. They are appropriate for situations where network resources are constrained but higher storage redundancy is acceptable. For instance, in cross-data center disaster recovery, MBR can reduce data transmission costs, while MSR is more suitable for cold data archiving to lower storage costs.

4 What are the design goals of RRC? What are its advantages in cross-rack repair?

RRC aims to optimize the relatively high cost of rack-to-rack communication during the repair process in a data center environment. By reducing the amount of cross-rack data transmission, it enhances repair efficiency. Its design goals include minimizing cross-rack repair bandwidth, maintaining MDS property, and supporting efficient node recovery in multirack environments. In cross-rack repairs, RRC groups storage nodes by rack and prioritizes the use of intra-rack redundant data for partial repairs, only downloading a small amount of necessary data from other racks. For instance, RRC's MSRR and MBRR significantly reduce the network workload generated by traditional RGCs during cross-rack repairs by adjusting the balance between storage redundancy and repair bandwidth. Compared to ordinary RGCs, RRC can reduce cross-rack bandwidth consumption by approximately 30% during rack-level failures or node failures, making it suitable for large-scale data center scenarios.

5 How is the BVAC constructed? What are its advantages in DSSs?

BVAC is constructed based on Vandermonde matrices. It divides data into k information columns and generates r redundant columns through polynomial ring operations. The encoding process utilizes the linear combination characteristics of Vandermonde matrices, where each redundant column is generated by the linear *XOR* operation of information columns. The advantages of BVAC lie in its low decoding complexity (fast solution through LU decomposition of Vandermonde matrices), high storage efficiency (satisfying the MDS property and tolerating multiple node failures), and computational efficiency (requiring only binary operations).

References

Abdel-Ghaffar, K.A. and Hassner, M., 1991. Multilevel error-control codes for data storage channels. IEEE transactions on information theory, 37(3), pp. 735–741.

Agarwal, A., Barg, A., Hu, S., Mazumdar, A. and Tamo, I., 2018. Combinatorial alphabet-dependent bounds for locally recoverable codes. IEEE Transactions on Information Theory, 64(5), pp. 3481–3492.

Asano, H., Hassner, M.A., Heise, N.N. and Tamura, T., International Business Machines Corp, 2005. Multiple level (ML), integrated sector format (ISF), error correction code (ECC) encoding and decoding processes for data storage or communication devices and systems. U.S. Patent 6,903,887, pp. 1–11.

Barg, A., Tamo, I. and Vlăduţ, S., 2017. Locally recoverable codes on algebraic curves. IEEE Transactions on Information Theory, 63(8), pp. 4928–4939.

Blaum, M., 2006, July. A family of MDS array codes with minimal number of encoding operations. In 2006 IEEE International Symposium on Information Theory (pp. 2784–2788). IEEE.

Blaum, M., 2019. Extended integrated interleaved codes over any field with applications to locally recoverable codes. IEEE Transactions on Information Theory, 66(2), pp. 936–956.

Blaum, M., 2022. Multiple-layer integrated interleaved codes: A class of hierarchical locally recoverable codes. IEEE Transactions on Information Theory, 68(8), pp. 5098–5111.

Blaum, M., Brady, J., Bruck, J. and Menon, J., 1995. EVENODD: An efficient scheme for tolerating double disk failures in RAID architectures. IEEE Transactions on computers, 44(2), pp. 192–202.

Blaum, M., Bruck, J. and Vardy, A., 1996. MDS array codes with independent parity symbols. IEEE Transactions on Information Theory, 42(2), pp. 529–542.

Blaum, M., Deenadhayalan, V. and Hetzler, S., 2019. Expanded Blaum–Roth codes with efficient encoding and decoding algorithms. IEEE Communications Letters, 23(6), pp. 954–957.

Blaum, M., Farrell, P.G., van Tilborg, H.C., Pless, V.S. and Huffman, W.C., 1998. Array codes. Handbook of coding theory, 2, pp. 1855–1909.

Blaum, M. and Hetzler, S.R., 2018. Extended product and integrated interleaved codes. IEEE Transactions on Information Theory, 64(3), pp. 1497–1513.

Blaum, M. and Hetzler, S.R., 2019. Array codes with local properties. IEEE Transactions on Information Theory, 66(6), pp. 3675–3690.

Blaum, M. and Roth, R.M., 1993. New array codes for multiple phased burst correction. IEEE Transactions on Information Theory, 39(1), pp. 66–77.

Blaum, M. and Roth, R.M., 1999. On lowest density MDS codes. IEEE Transactions on Information Theory, 45(1), pp. 46–59.

Blomer, J., 1995. An XOR-based erasure-resilient coding scheme. Technical report at ICSI (pp. 2–11).

Boros, T., Kailath, T. and Olshevsky, V., 1999. A fast parallel Björck–Pereyra-type algorithm for solving Cauchy linear equations. Linear Algebra and its Applications, 302, pp. 265–293.

Cadambe, V.R. and Jafar, S.A., 2008. Interference alignment and degrees of freedom of the $ K $-user interference channel. IEEE transactions on information theory, 54(8), pp. 3425–3441.

Cadambe, V.R. and Mazumdar, A., 2015. Bounds on the size of locally recoverable codes. IEEE transactions on information theory, 61(11), pp. 5787–5794.

Calder, B., Wang, J., Ogus, A., Nilakantan, N., Skjolsvold, A., McKelvie, S., Xu, Y., Srivastav, S., Wu, J., Simitci, H. and Haridas, J., 2011, October. Windows azure storage: a highly available cloud storage service with strong consistency. In Proceedings of the Twenty-Third ACM Symposium on Operating Systems Principles (pp. 143–157).

Cassuto, Y. and Bruck, J., 2006, July. Cyclic low-density MDS array codes. In 2006 IEEE International Symposium on Information Theory (pp. 2794–2798). IEEE.

Cassuto, Y. and Bruck, J., 2009. Cyclic lowest density MDS array codes. IEEE Transactions on Information Theory, 55(4), pp. 1721–1729.

Cassuto, Y. and Bruck, J., 2012. Low-complexity array codes for random and clustered 4-erasures. IEEE Transactions on Information Theory, 58(1), pp. 146–158.

Cassuto, Y. and Shokrollahi, A., 2014. LDPC codes for 2D arrays. IEEE transactions on information theory, 60(6), pp. 3279–3291.

Chen, Y., 1993. A Cramer rule for solution of the general restricted linear equation. Linear and Multilinear Algebra, 34(2), pp. 177–186.

Chen, Y. and Wang, Y., 2015. On the non-existence of minimum storage regenerating codes with repair-by-transfer property. IEEE Communications Letters, 19(12), pp. 2070–2073.

Chu, X., Liu, C., Ouyang, K., Yung, L.S., Liu, H. and Leung, Y.W., 2015, June. Perasure: a parallel cauchy Reed–Solomon coding library for gpus. In 2015 IEEE international conference on communications (ICC) (pp. 436–441). IEEE.

Corbett, P., English, B., Goel, A., Grcanac, T., Kleiman, S., Leong, J. and Sankar, S., 2004, March. Row-diagonal parity for double disk failure correction. In Proceedings of the 3rd USENIX Conference on File and Storage Technologies (pp. 1–14).

Dimakis, A.G., Godfrey, P.B., Wu, Y., Wainwright, M.J. and Ramchandran, K., 2010. Network coding for distributed storage systems. IEEE transactions on information theory, 56(9), pp. 4539–4551.

El Rouayheb, S. and Ramchandran, K., 2010, September. Fractional repetition codes for repair in distributed storage systems. In 2010 48th Annual Allerton Conference on Communication, Control, and Computing (Allerton) (pp. 1510–1517). IEEE.

Ernvall, T., El Rouayheb, S., Hollanti, C. and Poor, H.V., 2013. Capacity and security of heterogeneous distributed storage systems. IEEE Journal on Selected Areas in Communications, 31(12), pp. 2701–2709.

Fan, B., Tantisiriroj, W., Xiao, L. and Gibson, G., 2009, November. DiskReduce: RAID for data-intensive scalable computing. In Proceedings of the 4th annual workshop on petascale data storage (pp. 6–10).

Farrell, P.G., 1992. A survey of array error control codes. European Transactions on Telecommunications, 3(5), pp. 441–454.

Feng, G.L., Deng, R.H., Bao, F. and Shen, J.C., 2005a. New efficient MDS array codes for RAID. Part I. Reed–Solomon-like codes for tolerating three disk failures. IEEE Transactions on Computers, 54(9), pp. 1071–1080.

Feng, G.L., Deng, R.H., Bao, F. and Shen, J.C., 2005b. New efficient MDS array codes for RAID. Part II. Rabin-like codes for tolerating multiple (/spl ges/4) disk failures. IEEE Transactions on Computers, 54(12), pp. 1473–1483.

Forbes, M. and Yekhanin, S., 2014. On the locality of codeword symbols in non-linear codes. Discrete mathematics, 324, pp. 78–84.

Fu, H., Hou, H. and Zhang, L., 2021, October. Extended EVENODD+ codes with asymptotically optimal updates and efficient encoding/decoding. In 2021 XVII International Symposium "Probleems of Redundancy in Information and Control Systems" (REDUNDANCY) (pp. 1–6). IEEE.

Gad, E.E., Mateescu, R., Blagojevic, F., Guyot, C. and Bandic, Z., 2013, July. Repair-optimal MDS array codes over GF (2). In 2013 IEEE International Symposium on Information Theory (pp. 887–891). IEEE.

Gligoroski, D., Kralevska, K., Jensen, R.E. and Simonsen, P., 2017, November. Repair duality with locally repairable and locally regenerating codes. In 2017 IEEE 15th Intl Conf on Dependable, Autonomic and Secure Computing, 15th Intl Conf on Pervasive Intelligence and Computing, 3rd Intl Conf on Big Data Intelligence and Computing and Cyber Science and Technology Congress (DASC/PiCom/DataCom/CyberSciTech) (pp. 979–984). IEEE.

Gopalan, S. and Calderbank, R., 2014, June. Binary cyclic codes that are locally repairable. In 2014 IEEE international symposium on information theory (pp. 676–680). IEEE.

Goparaju, S., Fazeli, A. and Vardy, A., 2017. Minimum storage regenerating codes for all parameters. IEEE Transactions on Information Theory, 63(10), pp. 6318–6328.

Gupta, S. and Lalitha, V., 2020, October. Rack-aware cooperative regenerating codes. In 2020 International Symposium on Information Theory and Its Applications (ISITA) (pp. 264–268). IEEE.

Hafner, J.L., 2005, December. WEAVER Codes: Highly Fault Tolerant Erasure Codes for Storage Systems. In Fast (Vol. 5, pp. 16–16).

Hafner, J.L., 2006, June. HoVer erasure codes for disk arrays. In International Conference on Dependable Systems and Networks (DSN'06) (pp. 217–226). IEEE.

Hassner, M., Abdel-Ghaffar, K., Patel, A., Koetter, R. and Trager, B., 2001. Integrated interleaving-a novel ECC architecture. IEEE Transactions on Magnetics, 37(2), pp. 773–775.

Hou, H., 2023. Extended evenodd+ and star+ with asymptotic optimal update and efficient decoding. IEEE Transactions on Communications, 71(5), pp. 2563–2575.

Hou, H. and Han, Y.S., 2017. A new construction and an efficient decoding method for Rabin-like codes. IEEE Transactions on Communications, 66(2), pp. 521–533.

Hou, H. and Han, Y.S., 2018. A class of binary MDS array codes with asymptotically weak-optimal repair. Science China Information Sciences, 61, pp. 1–11.

Hou, H., Han, Y.S., Bai, B. and Zhang, G., 2022a, June. Towards efficient repair and coding of binary MDS array codes with small sub-packetization. In 2022 IEEE International Symposium on Information Theory (ISIT) (pp. 3132–3137). IEEE.

Hou, H., Han, Y.S., Lee, P.P., Hu, Y. and Li, H., 2019a. A new design of binary MDS array codes with asymptotically weak-optimal repair. IEEE transactions on information theory, 65(11), pp. 7095–7113.

Hou, H., Han, Y.S., Lee, P.P., et al., 2022b. A generalization of array codes with local properties and efficient encoding/decoding. IEEE Transactions on Information Theory, 69(1), pp. 107–125.

Hou, H. and Lee, P.P., 2019. Binary MDS array codes with optimal repair. IEEE Transactions on Information Theory, 66(3), pp. 1405–1422.

Hou, H. and Lee, P.P., 2021, July. Generalized rack-aware regenerating codes for jointly optimal node and rack repairs. In 2021 IEEE International Symposium on Information Theory (ISIT) (pp. 2191–2196). IEEE.

Hou, H., Lee, P.P. and Han, Y.S., 2020, June. Minimum storage rack-aware regenerating codes with exact repair and small sub-packetization. In 2020 IEEE International Symposium on Information Theory (ISIT) (pp. 554–559). IEEE.

Hou, H., Lee, P.P., Han, Y.S. and Hu, Y., 2017, June. Triple-fault-tolerant binary MDS array codes with asymptotically optimal repair. In 2017 IEEE International Symposium on Information Theory (ISIT) (pp. 839–843). IEEE.

Hou, H., Lee, P.P., Shum, K.W. and Hu, Y., 2019b. Rack-aware regenerating codes for data centers. IEEE Transactions on Information Theory, 65(8), pp. 4730–4745.

Hou, H., Shum, K.W., Chen, M. and Li, H., 2014, December. New MDS array code correcting multiple disk failures. In 2014 IEEE Global Communications Conference (pp. 2369–2374). IEEE.

Hou, H., Shum, K.W., Chen, M. and Li, H., 2016. BASIC codes: Low-complexity regenerating codes for distributed storage systems. IEEE Transactions on Information Theory, 62(6), pp. 3053–3069.

Hu, Y., Cheng, L., Yao, Q., Lee, P.P., Wang, W. and Chen, W., 2021. Exploiting combined locality for {Wide-Stripe} erasure coding in distributed storage. In 19th USENIX Conference on File and Storage Technologies (FAST 21) (pp. 233–248).

Hu, Y., Lee, P.P. and Zhang, X., 2016, July. Double regenerating codes for hierarchical data centers. In 2016 IEEE International Symposium on Information Theory (ISIT) (pp. 245–249). IEEE.

Huang, C., Chen, M. and Li, J., 2013. Pyramid codes: Flexible schemes to trade space for access efficiency in reliable data storage systems. ACM Transactions on Storage (TOS), 9(1), pp. 1–28.

Huang, C. and Xu, L., 2008. STAR: An efficient coding scheme for correcting triple storage node failures. IEEE Transactions on Computers, 57(7), pp. 889–901.

Huang, Z., Jiang, H. and Xiao, N., 2017, June. Efficient lowest density MDS array codes of column distance 4. In 2017 IEEE International Symposium on Information Theory (ISIT) (pp. 834–838). IEEE.

Huang, Z., Jiang, H., Zhou, K., Zhao, Y. and Wang, C., 2015. Lowest density MDS array codes of distance 3. IEEE Communications Letters, 19(10), pp. 1670–1673.

Imamura, K. and Yoshida, W., 1987. A simple derivation of the Berlekamp-Massey algorithm and some applications (Corresp.). IEEE transactions on Information Theory, 33(1), pp. 146–150.

Kamath, G.M., Prakash, N., Lalitha, V. and Kumar, P.V., 2013, February. Codes with local regeneration. In 2013 Information Theory and Applications Workshop (ITA) (pp. 1–5). IEEE.

Kamath, G.M., Prakash, N., Lalitha, V. and Kumar, P.V., 2014. Codes with local regeneration and erasure correction. IEEE Transactions on information theory, 60(8), pp. 4637–4660.

Katti, R. and Ruan, X., 2005, May. S-code: new distance-3 MDS array codes. In 2005 IEEE International Symposium on Circuits and Systems (ISCAS) (pp. 348–351). IEEE.

Krishnan, M.N., Lalitha, V. and Didugu, S., 2020. Codes with minimum bandwidth cooperative local regeneration. IEEE Communications Letters, 24(12), pp. 2669–2673.

Kschischang, F.R., 2003. Product codes. Wiley encyclopedia of telecommunications, 3(1), pp. 1–19.

Li, H.C. and Tan, E.T., 2008. On a special generalized Vandermonde matrix and its LU factorization. Taiwanese Journal of Mathematics, 12(7), pp. 1651–1666.

Li, J. and Li, B., 2016. Beehive: erasure codes for fixing multiple failures in distributed storage systems. IEEE Transactions on Parallel and Distributed Systems, 28(5), pp. 1257–1270.

Li, J., Tang, X. and Tian, C., 2017, June. A generic transformation for optimal repair bandwidth and rebuilding access in MDS codes. In 2017 IEEE International Symposium on Information Theory (ISIT) (pp. 1623–1627). IEEE.

Li, J., Tang, X. and Tian, C., 2018a. A generic transformation to enable optimal repair in MDS codes for distributed storage systems. IEEE Transactions on Information Theory, 64(9), pp. 6257–6267.

Li, J., Tang, X. and Tian, C., 2018b, June. An alternative generic transformation for optimal repair bandwidth and rebuilding access in MDS codes. In 2018 IEEE International Symposium on Information Theory (ISIT) (pp. 1894–1898). IEEE.

Li, M. and Shu, J., 2010, June. On cyclic lowest density MDS array codes constructed using starters. In 2010 IEEE International Symposium on Information Theory (pp. 1315–1319). IEEE.

Li, M. and Shu, J., 2011. C-Codes: Cyclic lowest-density MDS array codes constructed using starters for RAID 6. arXiv preprint arXiv:1104.2547(pp. 1–9).

Li, S.Y., Yeung, R.W. and Cai, N., 2003. Linear network coding. IEEE transactions on information theory, 49(2), pp. 371–381.

Li, W., Lin, J. and Wang, Z., 2020. Multi-layer generalized integrated interleaved codes. IEEE Communications Letters, 24(9), pp. 1880–1884.

Lin, S.J., 2017. An encoding algorithm of triply extended Reed–Solomon codes with asymptotically optimal complexities. IEEE Transactions on Communications, 66(8), pp. 3235–3244.

Lin, S.J. and Chung, W.H., 2014. Novel repair-by-transfer codes and systematic exact-MBR codes with lower complexities and smaller field sizes. IEEE Transactions on Parallel and Distributed Systems, 25(12), pp. 3232–3241.

Lin, S.J., Chung, W.H., Han, Y.S. and Al-Naffouri, T.Y., 2014. A unified form of exact-MSR codes via product-matrix frameworks. IEEE Transactions on Information Theory, 61(2), pp. 873–886.

Liu, Y., Li, J. and Tang, X., 2023. A generic transformation to enable optimal repair/access MDS array codes with multiple repair degrees. IEEE Transactions on Information Theory, 69(7), pp. 4407–4428.

Louidor, E. and Roth, R.M., 2006. Lowest density MDS codes over extension alphabets. IEEE Transactions on Information Theory, 52(7), pp. 3186–3197.

Lv, J., Fang, W., Chen, B., Xia, S.T. and Chen, X., 2022, June. New constructions of binary MDS array codes and locally repairable array codes. In 2022 IEEE International Symposium on Information Theory (ISIT) (pp. 2184–2189). IEEE.

Lv, J., Fang, W., Chen, X., Yang, J. and Xia, S.T., 2023. New Constructions of q-ary MDS Array Codes with Multiple Parities and Their Effective Decoding. In: IEEE Transactions on Information Theory (pp. 7082–7098). IEEE.

Mahdaviani, K., Mohajer, S. and Khisti, A., 2017, November. Product matrix minimum storage regenerating codes with flexible number of helpers. In 2017 IEEE information theory workshop (ITW) (pp. 41–45). IEEE.

Mehrabi, M. and Ardakani, M., 2017, June. On minimum distance of locally repairable codes. In 2017 15th Canadian Workshop on Information Theory (CWIT) (pp. 1–5). IEEE.

Oggier, F. and Datta, A., 2011, April. Self-repairing homomorphic codes for distributed storage systems. In 2011 Proceedings IEEE INFOCOM (pp. 1215–1223). IEEE.

Oruç, H., 2007. LU factorization of the Vandermonde matrix and its applications. Applied mathematics letters, 20(9), pp. 982–987.

Pamies-Juarez, L., Blagojevic, F., Mateescu, R., Gyuot, C., Gad, E.E. and Bandic, Z., 2016. Opening the chrysalis: On the real repair performance of {MSR} codes. In 14th USENIX conference on file and storage technologies (FAST 16) (pp. 81–94).

Papailiopoulos, D.S. and Dimakis, A.G., 2014. Locally repairable codes. IEEE Transactions on Information Theory, 60(10), pp. 5843–5855.

Patel, A.M., 1989. Two-level coding for error control in magnetic disk storage products. IBM Journal of Research and Development, 33(4), pp. 470–484.

Pernas, J., Yuen, C., Gastón, B. and Pujol, J., 2013, July. Non-homogeneous two-rack model for distributed storage systems. In 2013 IEEE International Symposium on Information Theory (pp. 1237–1241). IEEE.

Peterson, W.W. and Brown, D.T., 1961. Cyclic codes for error detection. Proceedings of the IRE, 49(1), pp. 228–235.

Plank, J.S. and Xu, L., 2006, July. Optimizing Cauchy Reed–Solomon codes for fault-tolerant network storage applications. In Fifth IEEE International Symeposium on Network Computing and Applications (NCA'06) (pp. 173–180). IEEE.

Ramkumar, V., Vajha, M., Balaji, S.B., et al., 2021. Codes for distributed storage. In: W.C. Huffman, J.-L. Kim and P. Solé (eds.), Concise Encyclopedia of Coding Theory (pp. 735–762). Chapman and Hall/CRC.

Rashmi, K.V., Shah, N.B. and Kumar, P.V., 2011. Optimal exact-regenerating codes for distributed storage at the MSR and MBR points via a product-matrix construction. IEEE Transactions on Information Theory, 57(8), pp. 5227–5239.

Rawat, A.S., Koyluoglu, O.O., Silberstein, N. and Vishwanath, S., 2013. Optimal locally repairable and secure codes for distributed storage systems. IEEE Transactions on Information Theory, 60(1), pp. 212–236.

Reed, I.S. and Solomon, G., 1960. Polynomial codes over certain finite fields. Journal of the society for industrial and applied mathematics, 8(2), pp. 300–304.

Sandell, M. and Tosato, F., 2013, October. Lowest density MDS array codes on incomplete graphs. In 2013 51st Annual Allerton Conference on Communication, Control, and Computing (Allerton) (pp. 645–652). IEEE.

Sandell, M. and Tosato, F., 2015. Lowest-density MDS array codes for reliable Smart Meter networks. Transactions on Emerging Telecommunications Technologies, 26(11), pp. 1251–1264.

Sasidharan, B., Vajha, M. and Kumar, P.V., 2016. An explicit, coupled-layer construction of a high-rate MSR code with low sub-packetization level, small field size and all-node repair. arXiv preprint arXiv:1607.07335 (pp. 1–18).

Sathiamoorthy, M., Asteris, M., Papailiopoulos, D., Dimakis, A.G., Vadali, R., Chen, S. and Borthakur, D., 2013. Xoring elephants: Novel erasure codes for big data. arXiv preprint arXiv:1301.3791 (pp. 1–13).

Schindelhauer, C. and Ortolf, C., 2013, July. Maximum distance separable codes based on circulant cauchy matrices. In: T. Moscibroda and A.A. Rescigno (eds.), International Colloquium on Structural Information and Communication Complexity (pp. 334–345). Cham: Springer International Publishing.

Scouarnec, N.L., 2014. Fast product-matrix regenerating codes. arXiv preprint arXiv:1412.3022 (pp. 3–25).

Serenyi, D., 2017, November. Cluster-Level Storage@ Google. In Keynote at the 2nd Joint International Workshop on Parallel Data Storage and Data Intensive Scalable Intensive Computing Systems (pp. 1–10).

Shah, N.B., Rashmi, K.V., Kumar, P.V. and Ramchandran, K., 2010, January. Explicit codes minimizing repair bandwidth for distributed storage. In 2010 IEEE Information Theory Workshop on Information Theory (ITW 2010, Cairo) (pp. 1–5). IEEE.

Shah, N.B., Rashmi, K.V., Kumar, P.V. and Ramchandran, K., 2011a. Distributed storage codes with repair-by-transfer and nonachievability of interior points on the storage-bandwidth tradeoff. IEEE Transactions on Information Theory, 58(3), pp. 1837–1852.

Shah, N.B., Rashmi, K.V., Kumar, P.V. and Ramchandran, K., 2011b. Interference alignment in regenerating codes for distributed storage: Necessity and code constructions. IEEE Transactions on Information Theory, 58(4), pp. 2134–2158.

Shen, Z., Shu, J. and Lee, P.P., 2016, June. Reconsidering single failure recovery in clustered file systems. In 2016 46th Annual IEEE/IFIP International Conference on Dependable Systems and Networks (DSN) (pp. 323–334). IEEE.

Shum, K.W. and Hu, Y., 2012, July. Functional-repair-by-transfer regenerating codes. In 2012 IEEE International Symposium on Information Theory Proceedings (pp. 1192–1196). IEEE.

Silberstein, N., Rawat, A.S. and Vishwanath, S., 2012, OctoberError resilience in distributed storage via rank-metric codes. In 2012 50th Annual Allerton Conference on Communication, Control, and Computing (Allerton) (pp. 1150–1157). IEEE.

Singleton, R., 1964. Maximum distance q-nary codes. IEEE Transactions on Information Theory, 10(2), pp. 116–118.

Sobe, P. and Schumann, P., 2014, February. A Perfomance Study of Parallel Cauchy Reed/Solomon Coding. In ARCS 2014; 2014 Workshop Proceedings on Architecture of Computing Systems (pp. 1–6). VDE.

Subedi, P. and He, X., 2013, May. A comprehensive analysis of XOR-based erasure codes tolerating 3 or more concurrent failures. In 2013 IEEE International Symposium on Parallel & Distributed Processing, Workshops and Phd Forum (pp. 1528–1537). IEEE.

Tamo, I. and Barg, A., 2014. A family of optimal locally recoverable codes. IEEE Transactions on Information Theory, 60(8), pp. 4661–4676.

Tamo, I., Barg, A., Goparaju, S. and Calderbank, R., 2016. Cyclic LRC codes, binary LRC codes, and upper bounds on the distance of cyclic codes. International Journal of Information and Coding Theory, 3(4), pp. 345–364.

Tamo, I., Wang, Z. and Bruck, J., 2011, July. MDS array codes with optimal rebuilding. In 2011 IEEE International Symposium on Information Theory Proceedings (pp. 1240–1244). IEEE.

Tang, D., Wang, X., Cao, S. and Chen, Z., 2008, August. A new class of highly fault tolerant erasure code for the disk array. In 2008 Workshop on Power Electronics and Intelligent Transportation System (pp. 578–581). IEEE.

Tang, X. and Koetter, R., 2006, July. A novel method for combining algebraic decoding and iterative processing. In 2006 IEEE International Symposium on Information Theory (pp. 474–478). IEEE.

Tebbi, M.A., Chan, T.H. and Sung, C.W., 2014, November. A code design framework for multi-rack distributed storage. In 2014 IEEE Information Theory Workshop (ITW 2014) (pp. 55–59). IEEE.

Wang, A. and Zhang, Z., 2015. An integer programming-based bound for locally repairable codes. IEEE Transactions on Information Theory, 61(10), pp. 5280–5294.

Wang, J., Zheng, D., Li, S. and Tang, X., 2023. Rack-aware MSR codes with error correction capability for multiple erasure tolerance. IEEE Transactions on Information Theory, pp. 1–26.

Wang, Y., Li, G. and Zhong, X., 2012. Triple-Star: A coding scheme with optimal encoding complexity for tolerating triple disk failures in RAID. International Journal of Innovative Computing, Information and Control, 8(3), pp. 1731–1472.

Wang, Y., Wei, D., Yin, X. and Wang, X., 2014, April. Heterogeneity-aware data regeneration in distributed storage systems. In IEEE INFOCOM 2014-IEEE Conference on Computer Communications (pp. 1878–1886). IEEE.

Wang, Y., Yin, X. and Wang, X., 2016. Two new classes of two-parity MDS array codes with optimal repair. IEEE Communications Letters, 20(7), pp. 1293–1296.

Wicker, S.B. and Bhargava, V.K. eds., 1999. Reed–Solomon codes and their applications (pp. 1–19). John Wiley & Sons.

Wu, Y., 2011. A construction of systematic MDS codes with minimum repair bandwidth. IEEE Transactions on Information Theory, 57(6), pp. 3738–3741.

Wu, Y., 2016. Generalized integrated interleaved codes. IEEE Transactions on Information Theory, 63(2), pp. 1102–1119.

Wu, Y. and Dimakis, A.G., 2009, June. Reducing repair traffic for erasure coding-based storage via interference alignment. In 2009 IEEE International Symposium on Information Theory (pp. 2276–2280). IEEE.

Xu, L. and Bruck, J., 1999. X-code: MDS array codes with optimal encoding. IEEE Transactions on Information Theory, 45(1), pp. 272–276.

Yang, S.L., 2005. On the LU factorization of the Vandermonde matrix. Discrete applied mathematics, 146(1), pp. 102–105.

Yeung, R.W., Li, S.Y.R., Cai, N. and Zhang, Z., 2006. Network coding theory part I: single source. Foundations and Trends® in Communications and Information Theory, 2(4), pp. 241–329.

Yin, C., Lv, H., Cui, Z., Li, T., Yuan, S. and Zhou, H., 2015, August. CCRS: An Optimized Algorithm Based on CRS in Distributed Storage System. In 2015 Ninth International Conference on Frontier of Computer Science and Technology (pp. 360–363). IEEE.

Zeng, Z., Zhu, B., Zhao, X. and Wang, W., 2022, April. High-Rate Constructions of Exact-Repair Regenerating Codes. In 2022 IEEE Wireless Communications and Networking Conference (WCNC) (pp. 1099–1104). IEEE.

Zhang, G., Wu, G., Wang, S., et al., 2015b. CaCo: An efficient cauchy coding approach for cloud storage systems. IEEE Transactions on Computers, 65(2), pp. 435–447.

Zhang, J., 2019, December. Concurrent Failure Recovery for Product Matrix Regenerating Code. In 2019 20th International Conference on Parallel and Distributed Computing, Applications and Technologies (PDCAT) (pp. 289–294). IEEE.

Zhang, X., 2017. Generalized three-layer integrated interleaved codes. IEEE Communications Letters, 22(3), pp. 442–445.

Zhang, Y., Wu, C., Li, J. and Guo, M., 2015a, June. Tip-code: A three independent parity code to tolerate triple disk failures with optimal update complextiy. In 2015 45th Annual IEEE/IFIP International Conference on Dependable Systems and Networks (pp. 136–147). IEEE.

Zhang, Z. and Zhou, L., 2023. A vertical-horizontal framework for building rack-aware regenerating codes. IEEE Transactions on Information Theory, 69(5), pp. 2874–2885.

Zhou, L. and Zhang, Z., 2022. Rack-aware regenerating codes with multiple erasure tolerance. IEEE Transactions on Communications, 70(7), pp. 4316–4326.

3
Optimization for Practicality

Storage coding serves as a pivotal mechanism for enhancing the reliability and efficiency of storage systems. Its intrinsic value is realized through the integration of coding technology into practical storage architectures, thereby unlocking its full potential. To fulfill its intended role in real-world applications, storage coding must exhibit exceptional practicality. This chapter investigates the optimization of storage coding's practicality from both system and coding perspectives. On the system level, it will concentrate on patented technologies for implementing ECs within storage frameworks, encompassing distributed storage solutions based on MDS codes, trade-offs between ECs and replication strategies, configuration of coding parameters, and distribution schemes for coding blocks. On the coding level, this chapter presents several exemplary practical ECs that serve as superior alternatives to widely utilized traditional RS codes.

3.1 Practicality in System Level

The theories and techniques of storage coding discussed in the preceding chapters often overlook real-world applications, leading to limited practical efficacy. This is particularly true for industrial-grade storage systems developed by major vendors, where the intricate architecture and stringent performance requirements necessitate a more cautious approach to the use of erasure coding. This section provides an in-depth analysis of the technical patents and recent advancements by prominent storage vendors in the practical application of erasure coding from a system-level perspective.

3.1.1 Distributed Storage Based on MDS Codes

With the exponential growth of data volume, the probability of node failures in distributed storage systems has significantly increased. Consequently, there is

Distributed Storage in Practice, First Edition. Hui Li, Hanxu Hou, and Hong Tan.

a pressing need for storage systems with enhanced fault tolerance to effectively tackle this challenge. In this regard, existing technologies predominantly rely on ECs to attain the desired level of reliability in DSSs.

ECs leverage well-established coding theory to encode the original data into multiple blocks. Specifically, it partitions the data into k data blocks and generates $n - k$ encoded blocks, allowing for the recovery of the original data from any combination of k out of the n blocks. In a DSS, the nodes are responsible for storing either the original data blocks or the encoded blocks, with distinct roles and functions. It is important to note that the encoding process in a distributed storage environment may involve a central node, which can potentially impede coding efficiency. Furthermore, early proposed distributed storage random linear coding schemes also achieved distributed data storage by dividing the entire file into several blocks. The encoded block combines all blocks through random linear combinations, and the loss of a file can be recovered by collecting coding vectors and obtaining encoded blocks from other storage nodes. However, this approach increases the storage capacity and data processing load of nodes, as well as the communication bandwidth during the recovery process. In summary, early distributed storage coding techniques were unable to efficiently ensure the reliability of DSSs.

The granted patent (Li et al. 2018, pp. 1–10) (US 9961142, Data storage method, device and distributed network storage system) proposed by authors of this book introduces a distributed storage technology based on MDS codes and proposes a system prototype aimed at addressing the issue of existing data storage technologies failing to guarantee the reliability of DSSs efficiently. In brief, it can be succinctly divided into two key aspects:

3.1.1.1 Storage Coding Based on MDS Codes

The original file of size M is divided into k data blocks, each with a size of M/k. Then, utilizing these k data blocks, $n - k$ mutually independent encoded blocks are constructed using linear coding. These k data blocks and $n - k$ encoded blocks are distributed to n different storage nodes in the DSS. If the linear coding scheme allows any k out of the n nodes to recover the original file, then the linear coding is referred to as an MDS code.

3.1.1.2 Data Storage Device

The data storage device consists of a data partitioning unit, a data block distribution unit, a coding unit, and an encoded block distribution unit. The data partitioning unit evenly divides the original file of size M into k data blocks. The data block distribution unit is responsible for distributing these k data blocks to k different nodes in the DSS. The encoding unit utilizes the k data blocks to construct $n - k$ mutually independent encoded blocks by linear coding with

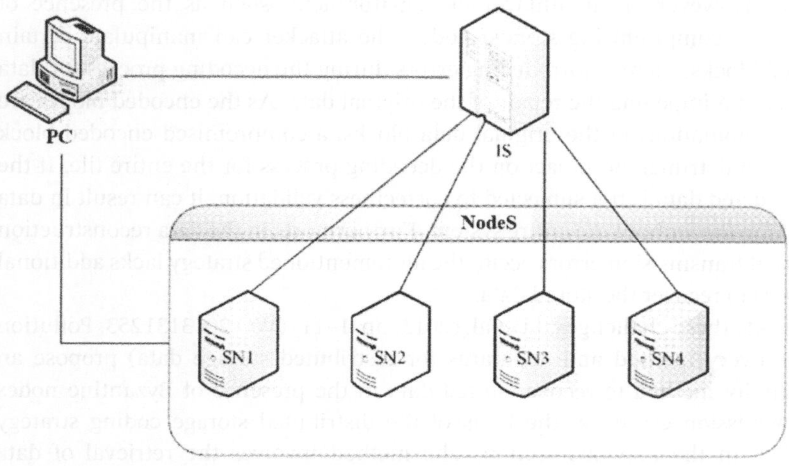

Figure 3.1 Prototype of distributed storage system based on MDS code.

the MDS property. The encoded block distribution unit distributes these $n - k$ encoded blocks to $n - k$ nodes in the DSS that have not yet stored data blocks.

Based on the aforementioned aspects, a comprehensive system prototype of distributed storage based on MDS codes can be constructed, as depicted in Figure 3.1. The server side of this system prototype comprises four storage nodes, namely, SN1, SN2, SN3, SN4, and an Index Server (IS). On the client side, a PC is responsible for initiating a series of storage commands. The IS plays a crucial role by storing essential information such as the naming and routing details of each storage node, the directory structure of the entire system, the mapping of file names to storage nodes, and the storage locations of each file block. Its function is analogous to the file partition table in traditional distributed file systems. When the PC intends to upload or download a file, it initially contacts the IS to locate the designated storage nodes, subsequently engaging with the respective storage nodes accordingly.

The system utilizes MDS codes to guarantee reliability, enabling the recovery of the original data from any k out of n storage nodes. Consequently, it can withstand the concurrent failure of $n - k$ storage nodes without experiencing data loss. Traditional replication strategies, such as three-replica, possess a redundancy of third the original data but can only accommodate the failure of up to two storage nodes. In contrast, distributed storage based on MDS codes, with a redundancy of n/k, can withstand the failure of $n - k$ storage nodes simultaneously.

However, the aforementioned strategy solely focuses on data regeneration following node failures and does not account for Byzantine nodes. In a favorable environment, ECs can significantly enhance the reliability of distributed storage systems. However, in an unfavorable environment, such as the presence of an attacker compromising storage nodes, the attacker can manipulate certain encoded blocks, thereby introducing errors during the decoding process for data recovery and impeding the repair of the original data. As the encoded blocks are linear combinations of the original data blocks, a compromised encoded block can have a detrimental impact on the decoding process for the entire file. If the reconstructed data is not subjected to correctness validation, it can result in data corruption throughout the entire system. Furthermore, in the data reconstruction process, if transmission errors occur, the aforementioned strategy lacks additional measures to recover the stored data.

To tackle these challenges, Li et al. (2013, pp. 1–11) (WO 2013131253, Pollution data recovery method and apparatus for distributed storage data) propose an extensibility method to recover stored data in the presence of Byzantine nodes or transmission errors on the basis of the distributed storage coding strategy described in the previous section. The method involves the retrieval of data or encoded blocks and checksums from k storage nodes to form the matrix Y, followed by the calculation of the CRC checksum. Subsequently, matrix Y undergoes decoding, yielding codeword C'. From C', the information sequence m' is derived, and its integrity is verified through CRC validation. If the validation is successful, the data recovery process concludes. If not, indicating data corruption or transmission errors, then when the remaining number of valid nodes is greater than 1, encoded data and checksums of two additional nodes are downloaded to replace two previous nodes and the above process is repeated until a valid information sequence m' is obtained, otherwise decoding will fail. Despite the additional computational resources and time required for validating the integrity of reconstructed data, this scheme effectively enhances the reliability of DSSs by mitigating attacks from malicious nodes and transmission errors. Moreover, the core idea and operation flow of it are relatively straightforward, rendering it highly practical in real-world scenarios.

In summary, given the escalating demand for data storage in contemporary times, distributed storage based on MDS codes emerges as a low-redundancy and highly reliable technology capable of supplanting relatively inefficient replication strategies across various application scenarios. However, it is important to note that different MDS codes possess distinct properties and advantages. Subsequently, this chapter comprehensively analyzes several classic and efficient MDS codes.

3.1.2 Trade-off of Replication and ECs

Data replication and ECs are two widely employed redundancy strategies for ensuring data reliability in distributed storage systems. Data replication improves data reliability and availability by maintaining multiple copies of data across different nodes or data centers; conversely, ECs store redundant encoded information on multiple nodes, enabling the recovery of original data through decoding operations when some portions are lost. While data replication offers advantages such as simplicity, ease of implementation, and high read performance, excessive redundancy can lead to heavy storage overhead. In contrast, ECs provide lower redundancy levels, enhanced storage efficiency, and superior fault tolerance; however, its repair process often demands substantial network bandwidth resources and incurs non-negligible computational delays.

Both technologies possess distinct advantages and disadvantages. Consequently, when selecting the appropriate technology for maintaining system reliability in an industrial-grade distributed storage system, it is essential to consider factors such as availability, reliability, storage capacity, and cost while conducting a comprehensive evaluation based on data access patterns.

Microsoft has implemented a strategy for balancing ECs and data replication that considers the hotness of data (Ozzie et al. 2014, pp. 1–21). This is achieved by monitoring the access frequency of various data files and assessing the data's hotness through comparisons between access frequencies and predetermined thresholds, thereby determining whether to employ ECs or data replication as the storage solution. Similarly, Amazon's trade-off strategy (He and Sorenson III 2013, pp. 1–18) incorporates not only access frequency but also the size of the data object. Specifically, if the size of the data object exceeds a specified threshold and the access frequency is lower than another threshold, the redundancy mechanism selects ECs, otherwise, the redundancy mechanism selects data replication.

Alibaba's Pangu storage system (Li et al. 2023, pp. 331–346) represents a quintessential distributed storage solution that has recently implemented erasure coding, significantly reducing network traffic amplification while simultaneously achieving robust fault tolerance performance. Assuming the size of the written data is x, the write traffic amounts to $1x$. The client employs EC(4,2) for online processing of the written data and utilizes the LZ4 algorithm (Bartík, Ubik and Kubalik 2015, pp. 179–182) to compress the encoded files, thereby decreasing the network traffic amplification ratio from $3x$ to $2.25x$ within the Pangu system. Nevertheless, this process encounters two primary challenges. First, applying ECs to small files incurs elevated costs due to its requirement for fixed-length operations; consequently, small files necessitate substantial zero padding. To mitigate this issue, Pangu optimizes resource consumption through a batching mechanism for small file write requests. Second, coding calculations introduce significant latency that cannot be overlooked. In response to this challenge, Pangu leverages Intel ISA-L (Center 2016, pp. 1–11) to expedite computation processes. In comparison to Jerasure (Plank and Greenan 2014, pp. 1–11), the calculation latency was reduced by a factor of 2.5–3.

Data replication and ECs can be synergistically integrated to fully leverage the advantages of both mechanisms. For instance, in addition to creating data center-level replicas, ECs can be employed to enhance reliability within each individual data center. Furthermore, the coded blocks may be replicated across multiple data centers to mitigate the impact of geographic faults. Amazon has proposed a hybrid approach that combines data replication with erasure coding technology (Lazier 2014, pp. 1–12), effectively reducing the high redundancy associated with traditional replication while maintaining rapid response times and robust reliability. Specifically, two data replicas are first generated through replication and stored in distinct nodes. Subsequently, one of these replicas is encoded using ECs, with the resulting coded blocks being distributed across different nodes. Read and write operation requests can then be directed to the replica nodes for prompt responses. In scenarios where all replicas become unavailable, erasure coding can facilitate decoding and reconstruction of the original data.

3.1.3 Coding Optimization for Realistic Scenarios

In practical applications, ECs must consider complex factors such as the operating environment, network latency, fault frequency, and data access hotness. Therefore, to fully harness the advantages of ECs, it is essential to optimize and refine them based on specific application scenarios. Currently, in order to enhance the practical performance of ECs, leading storage providers such as Microsoft, Amazon, and Alibaba have introduced a series of optimization techniques tailored to their unique contexts. These optimization strategies can be categorized into several key aspects.

3.1.3.1 Optimization for Heterogeneous Systems

An industrial-grade distributed storage system typically comprises various types of hardware and software components, representing a quintessential heterogeneous system. Due to the inherent differences among these devices, no single EC can be universally applicable for all data storage scenarios. For instance, certain devices possess limited storage resources and necessitate ECs with minimal storage overhead, while others are constrained by network bandwidth limitations and require ECs that minimize repair bandwidth. Consequently, it is essential to adopt appropriate ECs tailored to the specific characteristics of different devices.

Amazon adjusts its strategy for employing ECs based on factors such as system throughput, data storage costs, and user access hotness. For instance, Amazon has proposed a hierarchical erasure coding scheme that is predicated on storage duration for systems exhibiting time-locality access characteristics (Lazier 2020, pp. 1–20). In this scheme, newly created data objects are initially written to the first group of data storage devices, allowing read and write operations to directly access the stored data. Once the storage duration reaches a predetermined threshold, the data object undergoes encoding via ECs, with the resulting coded blocks subsequently distributed to a second group of data storage devices. This second group offers lower storage costs compared to the first group; however, it entails slower read and write operations. During the initial phase, newly written data requires frequent read and write interactions; thus, it is not subjected to ECs. Conversely, as its access popularity diminishes over time, implementing ECs can effectively reduce storage costs while enhancing data reliability.

Microsoft integrates multiple ECs within its cloud storage system to effectively ensure data reliability (Fetterly et al. 2013, pp. 1–11). Specifically, it employs its proprietary maximally recoverable (MR) cloud codes, resilient cloud codes, and robust product codes to enhance reliability for various types of data through the application of these three distinct erasure coding methodologies. Electron Machine Corporation (EMC) has developed a hierarchical erasure coding strategy (Danilov and Altaye 2021, pp. 1–23) tailored for large data object storage. Initially, large data objects are encoded using first-level ECs, and the resulting coded blocks are distributed across various data centers. Within each data center, these first-level coded blocks undergo further encoding with second-level ECs and are subsequently stored on distinct nodes within the same centers.

3.1.3.2 Optimization for Block Distribution

The fundamental principle of ECs involves partitioning the original data into blocks and encoding them to produce a series of redundant blocks. However, careful consideration must be given to the distribution of these blocks. Distributing all data blocks within a local data center ensures rapid reconstruction and efficient data extraction; however, it does not address faults at the entire data center level. Conversely, distributing blocks across geographically diverse multiple data centers can accommodate high-level faults but may adversely impact repair latency. Consequently, various storage vendors have developed distinct block distribution schemes according to their specific requirements.

Amazon has implemented a multiregion distribution strategy (Franklin, Donlan and Theimer 2019, pp. 1–16), wherein all blocks generated from the original data are distributed across various regions to enhance reliability. Furthermore, this strategy incorporates encryption technology for the data blocks, with the encryption keys being granted only to clients possessing legitimate access rights. This approach effectively controls access and facilitates data isolation, thereby bolstering security.

Microsoft has undertaken comprehensive research on block distribution and locality in ECs (Jenkins et al. 2018, pp. 1–13). A notable approach is an erasure coding scheme that operates across multiple zones and subzones (Yekhanin et al. 2016, pp. 1–12). This scheme has been effectively implemented in Microsoft's WAS by distributing blocks into zones, where a zone refers to a data center or geographical region providing storage services. Leveraging the LRCs) developed by Microsoft, this solution ensures efficient data reconstruction while minimizing cross-zone repair traffic, which involves organizing blocks from the same file in a zone into one or more local repair groups, with the size, location, and coding parameters of groups determined by factors such as coding requirements, repair time, and I/O throughput capacity.

Intel has proposed an adaptive block distribution strategy that leverages the network latency between storage network nodes (Zhang, DAI and Liu 2015, pp. 1–17). In this strategy, the first node to receive the data partitions the original dataset into N blocks and encodes them. Subsequently, this node notifies other nodes to accept $N - 1$ blocks, with the fastest responding $N - 1$ nodes designated as storage nodes for data retention. This strategy effectively capitalizes on the heterogeneity of network connections among nodes and employs broadcast response delays to adaptively identify storage nodes, thereby enhancing communication efficiency during the node repair process.

3.1.3.3 Optimization for System-level Coding

The theoretical calculations for ECs necessitate optimization and enhancement tailored to specific application scenarios, as theoretically simple operations such as multiplication and division can be quite time-consuming in hardware implementation. Furthermore, the theoretical coding scheme may not achieve the anticipated performance at the system level due to various complex factors, including user access frequency and preference, fault probability, and operating environments, which can lead to a significant decline in performance or even counterproductive outcomes. Consequently, storage vendors have refined the coding process of ECs based on their unique storage systems.

Microsoft has integrated the characteristics of its own research on LRCs and WAS to propose an efficient vertical local reconstruction code (VLRC) (Calder et al. 2019, pp. 1–11). VLRC leverages LRCs to facilitate high-efficiency local repair in cross-region deployments. Furthermore, given the variations in bandwidth and stability within each region, an inter-region adaptive EC, known as uber code, is employed to enhance the performance of inter-region repairs.

EMC focuses on optimizing the coding process of ECs to accommodate the expansion of storage systems. It has introduced a specialized EC (Danilov and Buinov 2020, pp. 1–14) designed to minimize the overhead of coding updates during both horizontal and vertical scaling of distributed storage systems. In the data coding phase, a submatrix of the encoding matrix is utilized to generate redundant encoded blocks, which are then distributed across various domains; when a new region is integrated into the system, a larger submatrix of the encoding matrix is employed to produce the encoded blocks required for that region, treating both previously generated and newly created blocks as a whole.

Alibaba has proposed a differential erasure coding method (Li 2018, pp. 1–16) aimed at reducing the computational overhead associated with coding in large-scale distributed storage systems. Upon receiving new data, the system identifies the differences between the original and new data. Subsequently, it applies erasure coding to these differences to generate parity blocks for them. Finally, the system utilizes these different parity blocks to update the parity blocks of the original data. Additionally, Alibaba proposes a cross-encoding method, which is suitable for large file storage. This approach first partitions the data associated with the same data node into K equal-sized blocks. Subsequently, the first erasure coding algorithm is applied to encode these K data blocks, resulting in the generation of the first set of parity blocks. Following this, one data block is selected from each data node, and these blocks are encoded by a second erasure coding algorithm to produce the second set of parity blocks. This procedure is iteratively conducted until all data blocks from every data node are encoded in the second round. This approach enhances the overall reliability of the data while ensuring both local fault tolerance and cross-node fault tolerance.

Furthermore, numerous research initiatives from various institutions are focused on enhancing the practical application of ECs. Hussain and Narayanamurthy (2019, pp. 1–14) propose the use of high rate minimum storage RGCs, which can achieve multinode repair. Zhang, Zhu and Hao (2021, pp. 1–13) further optimize the multinode repair bandwidth (Hussain and Narayanamurthy 2019, pp. 1–14) and enhance the flexibility of the minimum storage RGC, with its parameters dynamically configurable according to specific strategies. Arslan and Goker (2018, pp. 1–11) propose a strategy and storage system for selecting an appropriate EC based on data size, statistical fault data from storage devices, wear cycles of these devices, as well as limitations related to storage capacity or cost constraints, wherein MDS codes are employed. Yanovsky and Miloslavskaya (2021, pp. 1–9) introduce a reliable and secure framework that integrates ECs, information dispersion, secret sharing, and slope schemes while utilizing MDS codes. Wang, Li and Jafarkhani (2023, pp. 1–17) present a method and apparatus for determining an appropriate erasure coding strategy in the event of storage node failures, encompassing RS codes, MSR codes, and MBR codes, among others. Similar to the method used by Li (2018, pp. 1–16); Sipos et al. (2019, pp. 1–13) employ a coding technique that calculates data differences within distributed storage systems to minimize update bandwidth.

3.2 Practical ECs

In addition to optimizing the trade-off and deployment of ECs at the system level, it is essential to design practical erasure coding algorithms that are tailored for computing environments and specific application scenarios. This section provides a comprehensive overview of typical examples of practical ECs, including BRS codes, BRGCs, butterfly codes, clay codes, and practical LRCs.

3.2.1 BRS Codes

The most significant advantage of BRS code (Zhang et al. 2017, pp. 2676–2681) proposed by authors of this book, compared to the original RS code, lies in its ability to reduce the complexity associated with encoding and decoding operations. Specifically, BRS code employs the Vandermonde matrix as the generator matrix for encoding and utilizes the ZigZag method as a reference for decoding. Moreover, in order to minimize computational complexity, only shift and *XOR* operations on the $GF(2)$ are employed. Consequently, BRS code optimizes the computational performance of the original RS code while significantly enhancing both encoding and decoding speed.

3.2.1.1 Encoding Process of BRS Code

During the encoding process of BRS code, the original data is evenly divided into k blocks, with each block containing L bits of data on average. The resulting encoded data R consists of $n - k$ blocks, where each node stores one block, e.g., node 1 stores S_0 and node 2 stores S_1. In order to achieve repair in the decoding process of BRS code, it is necessary for the number of valid nodes to be greater than or equal to k. Hereafter follows a concise example illustrating the encoding process.

Considering the given values of $n = 6$ and $k = 3$, where each original data block is denoted as $s_i = s_{i,0}s_{i,1}\ldots s_{i,L-1}, i = 0, 1, 2, \ldots, k - 1$ and each encoded block is represented by $r_i = r_{i,0}, r_{i,1}\ldots r_{i,L+i*(k-1)-1}, i = 0, 1, 2, \ldots, n - k - 1$, the computation process for obtaining the encoded block is summarized in Tables 3.1–3.3. In the tables, the symbol $\oplus$ signifies *XOR* operation, while round brackets indicate shift operation.

Table 3.1 Calculate r_0, $r_0 = s_0(0) \oplus s_1(0) \oplus s_2(0)$.

$s_0(0)$	$s_{0,0}$	$s_{0,1}$	$s_{0,2}$	$s_{0,3}$	$s_{0,4}$	$s_{0,5}$
$s_1(0)$	$s_{1,0}$	$s_{1,1}$	$s_{1,2}$	$s_{1,3}$	$s_{1,4}$	$s_{1,5}$
$s_2(0)$	$s_{2,0}$	$s_{2,1}$	$s_{2,2}$	$s_{2,3}$	$s_{2,4}$	$s_{2,5}$
r_0	$r_{0,0}$	$r_{0,1}$	$r_{0,2}$	$r_{0,3}$	$r_{0,4}$	$r_{0,5}$

Table 3.2 Calculate r_1, $r_1 = s_0(0) \oplus s_1(1) \oplus s_2(2)$.

$s_0(0)$	$s_{0,0}$	$s_{0,1}$	$s_{0,2}$	$s_{0,3}$	$s_{0,4}$	$s_{0,5}$	0	0
$s_1(1)$	0	$s_{1,0}$	$s_{1,1}$	$s_{1,2}$	$s_{1,3}$	$s_{1,4}$	$s_{1,5}$	0
$s_2(2)$	0	0	$s_{2,0}$	$s_{2,1}$	$s_{2,2}$	$s_{2,3}$	$s_{2,4}$	$s_{2,5}$
r_1	$r_{1,0}$	$r_{1,1}$	$r_{1,2}$	$r_{1,3}$	$r_{1,4}$	$r_{1,5}$	$r_{1,6}$	$r_{1,7}$

Table 3.3 Calculate r_2, $r_2 = s_0(0) \oplus s_1(2) \oplus s_2(4)$.

$s_0(0)$	$s_{0,0}$	$s_{0,1}$	$s_{0,2}$	$s_{0,3}$	$s_{0,4}$	$s_{0,5}$	0	0	0	0
$s_1(2)$	0	0	$s_{1,0}$	$s_{1,1}$	$s_{1,2}$	$s_{1,3}$	$s_{1,4}$	$s_{1,5}$	0	0
$s_2(4)$	0	0	0	0	$s_{2,0}$	$s_{2,1}$	$s_{2,2}$	$s_{2,3}$	$s_{2,4}$	$s_{2,5}$
r_2	$r_{2,0}$	$r_{2,1}$	$r_{2,2}$	$r_{2,3}$	$r_{2,4}$	$r_{2,5}$	$r_{2,6}$	$r_{2,7}$	$r_{2,8}$	$r_{2,9}$

3.2.1.2 Decoding Process of BRS Code

The decoding of BRS code is based on the ZigZag decoding algorithm, which follows a sequential restoration process to recover lost bytes. This method resembles an intricate puzzle being unraveled layer by layer, as the required data is meticulously restored using available clues.

The BRS code encoding process involves dividing the original data into k data blocks, denoted as $s_0, s_1, \ldots, s_{k-1}$, and encoding them into $r = n - k$ encoded blocks, represented as $r_0, r_1, \ldots, r_{n-k-1}$, r_i is expressed as follows:

$$r_i = s_0 + x^i s_1 + \cdots + x^{i(k-1)} s_{k-1}, i = 0, 1, \ldots, n-k-1, \tag{3.1}$$

where $x^{i*(k-1)}$ represents the insertion of $i * (k-1)$ zeros at the beginning or shifting $i * (k-1)$ bits to the right. Here is a concise example illustrating the decoding process.

Let $n = 6$ and $k = 3$, where $+$ denotes the *XOR* operation. It can be deduced that

$$r_0 = s_0 + s_1 + s_2, \tag{3.2}$$

$$r_1 = s_0 + xs_1 + x^2 s_2, \tag{3.3}$$

$$r_2 = s_0 + x^2 s_1 + x^4 s_2. \tag{3.4}$$

Assuming that s_0 remains intact, while s_1 and s_2 are missing, we select r_1 and r_2 for repair. Let $r_1' = r_1 + s_0$ and $r_2' = r_2 + s_0$. Now r_1, r_2, and s_0 are valid and known. Therefore, $r_2' = x^2 s_1 + x^4 s_2$ and $r_1' = xs_1 + x^2 s_2$. By performing these operations, the following relationships are obtained:

$$s_{2,i-1} = r'_{1,i+1} + s_{1,i}, \tag{3.5}$$

$$s_{1,i+1} = r'_{2,i+3} + s_{2,i-1}. \tag{3.6}$$

Table 3.4 The bit-by-bit *XOR* representation of r'_1.

xs_1	0	$s_{1,0}$	$s_{1,1}$	$s_{1,2}$	$s_{1,3}$	$s_{1,4}$	$s_{1,5}$	0
x^2s_2	0	0	$s_{2,0}$	$s_{2,1}$	$s_{2,2}$	$s_{2,3}$	$s_{2,4}$	$s_{2,5}$
r'_1	$r'_{1,0}$	$r'_{1,1}$	$r'_{1,2}$	$r'_{1,3}$	$r'_{1,4}$	$r'_{1,5}$	$r'_{1,6}$	$r'_{1,7}$

Table 3.5 The bit-by-bit *XOR* representation of r'_2.

x^2s_1	0	0	$s_{1,0}$	$s_{1,1}$	$s_{1,2}$	$s_{1,3}$	$s_{1,4}$	$s_{1,5}$	0	0
x^4s_2	0	0	0	0	$s_{2,0}$	$s_{2,1}$	$s_{2,2}$	$s_{2,3}$	$s_{2,4}$	$s_{2,5}$
r'_2	$r'_{2,0}$	$r'_{2,1}$	$r'_{2,2}$	$r'_{2,3}$	$r'_{2,4}$	$r'_{2,5}$	$r'_{2,6}$	$r'_{2,7}$	$r'_{2,8}$	$r'_{2,9}$

After each operation of the above two equations, execute $i = i + 1$ and ensure $i >= 1$ until all the lost bits are repaired. The above iterative equations are rather abstract and complex. The actual operation process described below can help understand them more clearly. If each original data block has six bits, then r'_1 and r'_2 are presented in Tables 3.4 and 3.5.

In both tables, since $s_{1,0}$, $s_{1,1}$, $s_{2,4}$, and $s_{2,5}$ all have cases where they are XORed with 0, their values for bit can be directly obtained. Taking $s_{1,1}$ as the starting point of the above iterative operation, and following the iterative process, perform the operation in ascending order of the subscripts. The sequence is as follows:

$$s_{2,0} = r'_{1,2} + s_{1,1},\ s_{1,2} = r'_{2,4} + s_{2,0}(i = 1);$$
$$s_{2,1} = r'_{1,3} + s_{1,2},\ s_{1,3} = r'_{2,5} + s_{2,1}(i = 2);$$
$$s_{2,2} = r'_{1,4} + s_{1,3},\ s_{1,4} = r'_{2,6} + s_{2,2}(i = 3);$$
$$s_{2,3} = r'_{1,5} + s_{1,4},\ s_{1,5} = r'_{2,7} + s_{2,3}(i = 4).$$

At this point, all bits in s_1 and s_2 have been repaired.

Based on the iterative process presented in the example, each iteration cycle computes the values of two bits, with s_1 and s_2 each acquiring one bit per cycle. Given that the length of each original data block is L bits, and considering that certain bits can be directly determined, no more than $(L - k + 1)$ iterative computational operations are necessary to resolve all lost bits within the original data blocks, thus achieving complete data decoding.

The use of BRS code in DSSs today can enhance fault tolerance. Compared to the three-replica strategy, BRS code significantly improves reliability while maintaining equivalent redundancy. Additionally, the similarities in performance advantages and encoding process between BRS code and CRS code make it a viable alternative. By simplifying the computational complexity introduced by

ECs, BRS code achieves substantial enhancements in both encoding and decoding speed, achieving simplicity and efficiency.

3.2.2 Binary Regenerating Codes

Although RGCs have demonstrated significant advantages in storage coding, particularly in reducing repair bandwidth, they ingeniously integrate network coding theory to optimize the failed nodes repair process. This integration enables the recovery of lost information with reduced data transmission, thereby significantly decreasing the transmission bandwidth between storage nodes. Such a feature is crucial for large-scale distributed storage systems as it not only enhances data recovery efficiency but also reduces overall operational costs. However, most RGCs exhibit high computational complexity primarily due to their intricate mathematical structure and algorithm design, such as operating on $GF(q)$. In practical applications, these complex encoding and decoding processes demand substantial computing resources, which can lead to processing delays and impact response speed. Particularly in scenarios involving frequent data encoding and decoding operations, this high complexity may become a key limiting factor for system performance. Moreover, high complexity encoding and decoding algorithms necessitate higher hardware configurations that may require specialized hardware acceleration or more powerful processors to improve efficiency. Therefore, addressing the challenge of reducing the computational complexity in encoding and decoding is crucial during the implementation of RGCs.

To address the aforementioned challenges, Hou et al. (2013, pp. 1621–1625) proposed BRGCs and constructed on $GF(2)$, which solely employs *XOR* and right-shift operations. By converting the base field from $GF(q)$ to $GF(2)$, employing elementary *XOR* instead of addition operation, and utilizing bit-wise right shift in place of multiplication on the finite field, BRGC effectively reduces the computational complexity of encoding and decoding. Building upon storage repair bandwidth curve of BRGC, Li, Hou and Zhu (2017, pp. 1–21) developed binary minimum-storage regenerating (BMSR) and binary minimum-bandwidth regenerating (BMBR) codes (pp. 1–11). These novel codes retain all the benefits of MSR and MBR while significantly reducing encoding and decoding complexities. Prior to delving into detailed explanations about BMSR and BMBR, a simple example is presented to briefly illustrate encoding and decoding principles of BRGC.

Assuming the presence of four source data packets, denoted as $s_1(x)$ to $s_4(x)$, the coefficients $(a_0, a_1, a_2, a_3, \dots)$ assigned to each bit in a packet are utilized as the coefficients of polynomial $s(x)$, as follows:

$$s(x) = (a_0, a_1, a_2, a_3, \dots) \Leftrightarrow a_0 + a_1x + a_2x^2 + a_3x^3 + \cdots. \tag{3.7}$$

Table 3.6 A brief example of BRGC.

Node	Packets
1	$s_1(x), s_2(x)$
2	$s_3(x), s_4(x)$
3	$s'_1(x) = s_1(x) + s_3(x), s'_2(x) = s_2(x) + xs_4(x)$
4	$s'_3(x) = s_1(x) + xs_3(x), s'_4(x) = s_2(x) + s_4(x)$

Node 1 and node 2 are system nodes, and node 3 and node 4 are parity nodes. The encoding process is shown in Table 3.6, where + is the *XOR* operation, and multiplying by a coefficient x can be regarded as a right-shift operation, such as

$$xs(x) = x(a_0 + a_1x + a_2x^2 + \cdots) = 0 + a_0x + a_1x^2 + \cdots. \tag{3.8}$$

The verification of the fulfillment of the close to MDS property is required as a first step. Assuming that a DC is connected to a system node and a parity node, such as node 2 and node 3, packets $s_3(x)$ and $s_4(x)$ can be directly obtained. Moreover, packets $s_1(x)$ and $s_2(x)$ can also be acquired by $s'_1(x) + s_3(x)$ and $s'_2(x) + xs_4(x)$. Furthermore, considering that a DC is connected to both node 3 and node 4, starting from data packets $s_1(x) + s_3(x)$ and $s_1(x) + xs_3(x)$, the DC proceeds with the following calculations:

$$x(s_1(x) + s_3(x)) + s_1(x) + xs_3(x) = (x + 1)s_1(x). \tag{3.9}$$

Similar to BRS code, the coefficients of $s_1(x)$ can be obtained by bit-wise *XOR* operation in $(x + 1)s_1(x)$, while a similar approach can also be applied to obtain the coefficients of other source packets, namely, $s_2(x)$, $s_3(x)$, and $s_4(x)$.

There is a symmetry in this code. The $s_1(x)$~$s_4(x)$ packets of node 1 and node 2 can be obtained by the $s'_1(x) \sim s'_4(x)$ packets of node 3 and node 4:

$$s_1(x) := (1 + x)^{-1} \left(xs'_1(x) + s'_3(x)\right), \tag{3.10}$$

$$s_2(x) := (1 + x)^{-1} \left(s'_2(x) + xs'_4(x)\right), \tag{3.11}$$

$$s_3(x) := (1 + x)^{-1} \left(s'_1(x) + s'_3(x)\right), \tag{3.12}$$

$$s_4(x) := (1 + x)^{-1} \left(s'_2(x) + s'_4(x)\right). \tag{3.13}$$

The symmetry exhibited allows for the alternate designation of node 3 and node 4 as system nodes, while node 1 and node 2 can be considered parity nodes.

Utilizing this inherent symmetry, in the event of node 1 failure, it can be recovered by retrieving a package from each surviving node. Node 2 transmits the sum $s_3(x) + s_4(x)$ to a DC. Node 3 shifts the package $s_1(x) + s_3(x)$ toward the right by one bit, adds up with $s_2(x) + xs_4(x)$, and subsequently sends out the resultant package

$xs_1(x) + s_2(x) + x(s_3(x) + s_4(x))$. Node 4 moves the package $s_2(x) + s_4(x)$ to the right by one bit, adds up with $s_1(x) + xs_3(x)$, and then dispatches the resulting package as $s_1(x) + xs_2(x) + x(s_3(x) + s_4(x))$. By employing *XOR* operations, the DC can effectively eliminate $s_3(x) + s_4(x)$, resulting in $xs_1(x) + s_2(x)$ and $s_1(x) + xs_2(x)$. Subsequent computations lead to

$$x(xs_1(x) + s_2(x)) + s_1(x) + xs_2(x) = (1 + x^2)s_1(x),$$
$$xs_1(x) + s_2(x) + x(s_1(x) + xs_2(x)) = (1 + x^2)s_2(x). \tag{3.14}$$

Similar to BRS code, the decoding of $s_1(x)$ and $s_2(x)$ can now be performed independently by bit-wise *XOR* operation.

According to the above principles, Hou et al. 2013, pp. (1621–1625) propose the construction of BRGC at MBR points using the PM method. Assuming that the original file consists of $(k(k + 1))/2 + k(d - k)$ source data packets, and each node stores $\alpha = d$ packets, a $d * d$ message matrix M can be created as follows:

$$M = \begin{bmatrix} S & T \\ T^{\mathsf{T}} & 0 \end{bmatrix}. \tag{3.15}$$

Matrix S is a symmetric matrix of size $k * k$, the upper triangle is filled with source data packet $s_j(x)$ and flipped along the diagonal to get the lower triangle, where $j = 1, 2, \dots, k(k + 1)/2$. The rectangular matrix T is of size $k * (d - k)$, the elements are also source packets $s_j(x), j = k(k + 1)/2, \dots ,(k(k + 1))/2 + k(d - k)$. Matrix T^{T} is the transpose of T, and matrix 0 is the zero matrix of $(d - k) * (d - k)$. For $i = 1, 2, \dots, n$, let the encoding vector of node i be defined as $\psi_i^{\mathsf{T}} = [1\ x^{i-1}\ x^{2(i-1)}\ \cdots\ x^{(d-1)(i-1)}]$, and node i stores d data packets in ψ_i^{T}M.

For the case of $n = 6$, $k = 3$, and $d = 4$, matrix M can be expressed as follows:

$$M = \begin{bmatrix} s_1(x) & s_2(x) & s_3(x) & s_7(x) \\ s_2(x) & s_4(x) & s_5(x) & s_8(x) \\ s_3(x) & s_5(x) & s_6(x) & s_9(x) \\ s_7(x) & s_8(x) & s_9(x) & 0 \end{bmatrix}, \tag{3.16}$$

where each element has an encoding vector taken from $GF(2)$. For $i = 1, 2, \dots, 6$, the encoding vector of node i is

$$\psi_i^{\mathsf{T}} = [1\ x^{i-1}\ x^{2(i-1)}\ x^{3(i-1)}].$$

For any four different node indices i_1, i_2, i_3, i_4, the corresponding encoding vectors $\psi_{i_1}^{\mathsf{T}}, \psi_{i_2}^{\mathsf{T}}, \psi_{i_3}^{\mathsf{T}}$, and $\psi_{i_4}^{\mathsf{T}}$ can form a nonsingular 4×4 Vandermonde matrix.

For $i = 1, 2, \dots, 6$, node i will store four packets of the i-th row of matrix ΨM as follows:

$$s_1(x) + x^{i-1}s_2(x) + x^{2(i-1)}s_3(x) + x^{3(i-1)}s_7(x),$$
$$s_2(x) + x^{i-1}s_4(x) + x^{2(i-1)}s_5(x) + x^{3(i-1)}s_8(x),$$

$$s_3(x) + x^{i-1}s_5(x) + x^{2(i-1)}s_6(x) + x^{3(i-1)}s_9(x),$$
$$s_7(x) + x^{i-1}s_8(x) + x^{2(i-1)}s_9(x). \tag{3.17}$$

Each encoded packet is obtained by specific bit-wise right shift and *XOR* of the source packets.

In the data reconstruction process, assume that the data collector is connected to node 1, node 2, and node 3. For $s_7(z)$, $s_8(z)$, and $s_9(x)$, the following matrix can be calculated as

$$\begin{bmatrix} s_7(x) + s_8(x) + s_9(x) \\ s_7(x) + xs_8(x) + z^2s_9(x) \\ s_7(x) + x^2s_8(x) + x^4s_9(x) \end{bmatrix} = \begin{bmatrix} 1 & 1 & 1 \\ 1 & x & x^2 \\ 1 & x^2 & x^4 \end{bmatrix} \begin{bmatrix} s_7(x) \\ s_8(x) \\ s_9(x) \end{bmatrix}. \tag{3.18}$$

Since $s_7(x)$, $s_8(x)$, and $s_9(x)$ are known, similarly $s_1(x) - s_6(x)$ can be calculated from

$$\begin{bmatrix} 1 & 1 & 1 \\ 1 & x & x^2 \\ 1 & x^2 & x^4 \end{bmatrix} \begin{bmatrix} s_1(x) & s_2(x) & s_3(x) \\ s_2(x) & s_4(x) & s_5(x) \\ s_3(x) & s_5(x) & s_6(x) \end{bmatrix}. \tag{3.19}$$

In the process of fault repair, suppose that node 5 fails, which can be regenerated from node 1, node 2, node 3, and node 4. Since the encoding vector of node 5 is known to all nodes, the data packet sent to DC by node i is $\psi_i^{\mathrm{T}} M\psi_5$. If the data packets received by DC are written as column vectors, they can be written as

$$\begin{bmatrix} 1 & 1 & 1 & 1 \\ 1 & x & x^2 & x^3 \\ 1 & x^2 & x^4 & x^6 \\ 1 & x^3 & x^6 & x^9 \end{bmatrix} M\psi_5. \tag{3.20}$$

Since the left-hand matrix is nonsingular, the inverse matrix can be used to compute $M\psi_5$ and then perform transpose operation on $M\psi_5$ as follows:

$$(M\psi_5)^T = \psi_5^{\mathrm{T}} M^T. \tag{3.21}$$

Since the matrix M is a symmetric matrix, the storage data $\psi_5^{\mathrm{T}} M$ of the failed node 5 can be obtained. The repair of other nodes can be completed similarly.

The BRGC encoding and decoding method exclusively employs elementary *XOR* and right-shift operations, thereby significantly reducing the computational complexity involved in both encoding and decoding processes. Subsequently, two practical BRGCs based on two aforementioned granted patents are introduced.

3.2.2.1 BMSR Codes

BMSR overcomes the limitations of existing coding methods, such as high computational complexity, overhead, and repair bandwidth. It ensures minimal storage capacity and minimizes repair bandwidth within a certain range, making it

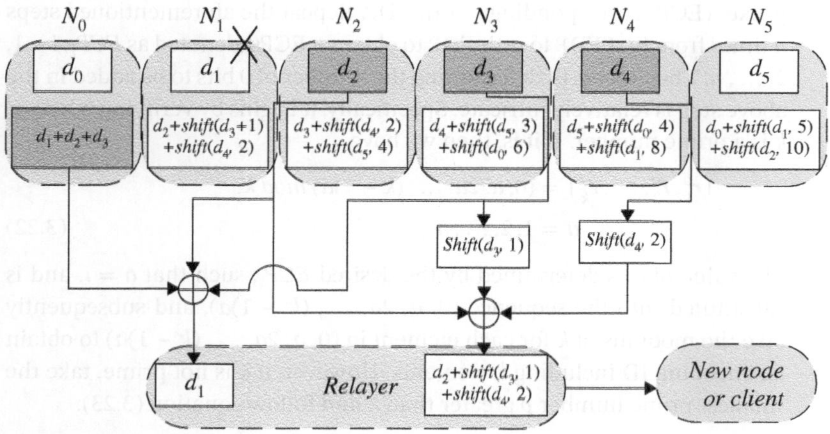

Figure 3.2 Brief example of coding and repair of binary minimum-storage regenerating.

particularly suitable for scenarios with limited storage capacity. Figure 3.2 presents a simplified example illustrating the encoding and repair process of BMSR using parameter settings of $n = 6$, $k = 3$, and $d = 4$. In BMSR(6,3,4), a failed node can be repaired by connecting to four helper nodes and downloading a packet from each helper node. Assume N_1 fails and requires reconstruction. The data stored by N_1 consists of d_1 and $d_2 + shift(d_3, 1) + shift(d_4, 2)$, where the *shift* represents a bit-wise right-shift operation whose essence is to add 0 bits to the header or tail of packets and the + denotes an *XOR* operation. A DC downloads d_2, d_3, d_4, and $d_1 + d_2 + d_3$ from N_0, N_2, N_3, and N_4, respectively, and then performs *XOR* and *shift* operations to recover the lost data. For example, d_1 can be obtained by $(d_1 + d_2 + d_3) + d_2 + d_3$. It is evident that BMSR offers similar storage capacity as RS codes but reduces the total size of data access and transmitted during the repair process compared to the original data.

In the following, the encoding and decoding of BMSR will be elaborated.

a) Encoding Process of BMSR
   i) The original data is evenly partitioned into n blocks, resulting in n first data packets (FDPs) denoted as FDP_i, $i = 1, 2, \ldots, n$. It should be noted that the value of n must be an even number.
   ii) Choose a set of n storage nodes for storing FDPs, where $n = 2k$ and the variable k is a positive integer.
   iii) Starting from the i-th FDP, add a specific number of 0 bits to the header or tail of each of the subsequent k consecutive FDPs to obtain k second data packets (SDPs), where the n-th FDP and the first FDP can be considered sequentially linked. Next, calculate these k SDPs to obtain an encoded data

packet (ECP) corresponding to i-th FDP. Repeat the aforementioned steps n times from first FDP to n-th FDP to obtain n ECPs, denoted as ECP_i, $i = 1, 2, \ldots, n$. The process of determining the number of 0 bits to be added in the above step is relatively intricate. Specifically, it begins by verifying whether k is a prime number. If it is, then we have

$$\left(r_1^a, r_2^a, \ldots, r_k^a\right) = (0, a, 2a, \ldots, (k-1)a) \; mod \; k,$$
$$a = 1, 2, \ldots, n. \tag{3.22}$$

The value of a is determined by the desired ECP_i, such that $a = i$, and is substituted into the sequence $(0, a, 2a, \ldots, (k-1)a)$, and subsequently take the modulus of k for each element in $(0, a, 2a, \ldots, (k-1)a)$ to obtain an encoding ID including k elements. However, if k is not prime, take the smallest prime number p greater than k and follow equation (3.23):

$$\left(r_1^a, r_2^a, \ldots, r_k^a\right) = (a-1, 2a-1, \ldots, ka-1) \; mod \; p,$$
$$a = 1, 2, \ldots, n. \tag{3.23}$$

The value of a is determined by the desired ECP_i, such that $a = i$, and is subsequently substituted into the sequence $(a-1, 2a-1, \ldots, ka-1)$, and subsequently takes the modulus of k for each element in $(a-1, 2a-1, \ldots, ka-1)$ to obtain an encoding ID including k elements. Subsequently, obtain the maximum value r_{max}^a in the encoding ID:

$$r_{max}^a = max\left(r_1^a, r_2^a, \ldots, r_k^a\right),$$
$$a = 1, 2, \ldots, n. \tag{3.24}$$

Let $a = i$, add r_t^i 0 bits to the data head of the $((i + t) \; mod \; n)$-th FDP, and add $r_{max}^i - r_t^i$ 0 bits to the data tail of the $((i + t) \; mod \; n)$-th FDP, where $t = 1, 2, \ldots, k$, obtaining an SDP corresponding to i-th FDP. Starting from this $((i+1) \; mod \; n)$-th FDP, repeat the above steps for successive $k - 1$ FDPs to obtain k SDPs, and perform *XOR* operations on these SDPs to obtain the i-th ECP:

$$ECP_i = \sum_{j=(i+1) \; mod \; n}^{(i+k) \; mod \; n} FDP_j\left(r_t^i\right),$$
$$i = 1, 2, \ldots, n, \quad t \in \{1, 2, \ldots, k\}, \tag{3.25}$$

where ECP_i represents the i-th ECP corresponding to i-th FDP, $FDP_j\left(r_t^i\right)$ represents the t-th SDP corresponding to i-th FDP in k consecutive FDPs, and j is a positive integer between $(i + 1) \; mod \; n$ and $(i + k) \; mod \; n$.

iv) The i-th FDP and i-th ECP are stored on the i-th storage node. The FDP and ECP should be stored separately, denoted as the set of packets stored by the i-th storage node as (FDP_i, ECP_i).

b) Decoding Process of BMSR
   i) Confirm the failure of the i-th storage node and obtain the corresponding encoding ID $(r_1^i, r_2^i, \ldots, r_k^i)$.
   ii) Sequentially download the FDPs from the $((i + 1)\, mod\, n)$-th to $((i + k)\, mod\, n)$-th consecutive available storage nodes; by encoding these k downloaded FDPs, obtain the ECP of the i-th storage node. For detailed procedures, refer to the encoding process of BMSR.
   iii) Download the ECP from the $((i - 1)\, mod\, n)$-th storage node, and retrieve the FDPs from the $((i + 1)\, mod\, n)$-th to the $((i + k - 1)\, mod\, n)$-th storage nodes. Obtain $k - 1$ SDPs based on the encoding process of BMSR. Perform an *XOR* operation between ECP from the $((i - 1)\, mod\, n)$-th storage node and the $k - 1$ SDPs to obtain the SDP of the i-th storage node as equation (3.26):

$$SDP_i = \sum_{j=(i+1)\, mod\, n}^{(i+k-1)\, mod\, n} FDP_j\left(r_t^{i-1}\right) + ECP_{((i-1)\, mod\, n)},$$
$$i = 1, 2, \ldots, n, \quad t \in \{2, \ldots, k\}. \tag{3.26}$$

   Finally, apply a *Shift* operation according to the encoding IDs $(r_1^{i-1}, r_2^{i-1}, \ldots, r_k^{i-1})$ to obtain the FDP of i-th storage node.
   iv) Combine the newly acquired FDP and ECP from the aforementioned steps to form a new set (FDP_i, ECP_i), which is then stored in the newly designated storage node.

3.2.2.2 BMBR Codes

Similar to BMSR, BMBR also overcomes the challenges of high computational complexity and large repair bandwidth associated with existing ECs. It provides a straightforward coding and storage node repair method with optimal repair bandwidth, making it particularly suitable for scenarios with limited bandwidth constraints. Figure 3.3 illustrates a simple and approximate example that describes the encoding and repair process of BMBR using parameters $n = 5$, $k = 3$, and $d = 3$. Assuming data node N_2 fails, the failed data can be regenerated through simple shift and *XOR* operations involving N_0, N_1, and N_3 to obtain d_2, d_4, and $d_2 + d_4 + d_5$ to repair the failed data packets. The repair process in BMBR involves adding helper nodes when a specific data node fails in order to recover the lost data. For repairing a single failed node, one data packet is obtained from three other nodes, which undergo encoding operations in DC to regenerate the lost data. Subsequently, the repaired node directly downloads the regenerated data from DC. Notably, it can be observed that BMBR achieves repair bandwidth equal to the size of stored data on each node, which is a significantly lower value compared to the total original data.

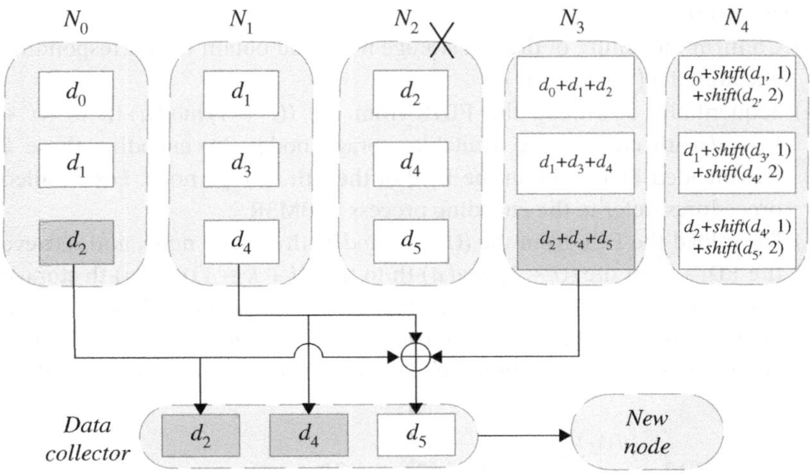

Figure 3.3 Brief example of encoding and repair of BMBR.

In the following, the encoding and decoding of BMBR will be elaborated.

a) Encoding Process of BMBR
   i) Assuming a total of n storage nodes, comprising k data nodes and $n - k$ redundant nodes. The original data of size B is partitioned into $k(k + 1)/2$ data blocks, called first data packets (FDPs). A FDP is denoted as c_i, $i = 1, 2, \ldots, k(k + 1)/2$.
   ii) The FDPs are utilized to construct a symmetric system matrix S of size $k * k$. To be specific, the FDP is acquired based on its assigned number and subsequently inserted into the upper triangular region of S row by row in accordance with the column element order. This process yields the upper triangular matrix of system matrix S as follows:

$$\begin{bmatrix} c_1 & c_2 & \cdots & c_k \\ 0 & c_{k+1} & \cdots & c_{2k-1} \\ 0 & 0 & \vdots & \vdots \\ 0 & 0 & 0 & c_{k(k+1)/2} \end{bmatrix}. \tag{3.27}$$

   iii) Subsequently, the upper triangular portion of S obtained in the aforementioned steps is folded along its diagonal to yield the lower triangular component of the system matrix. The resulting symmetric matrix S is ultimately generated and expressed as the following equation (3.28):

$$S = \begin{bmatrix} c_1 & c_2 & \cdots & c_k \\ c_2 & c_{k+1} & \cdots & c_{2k-1} \\ \vdots & \vdots & \vdots & \vdots \\ c_k & c_{2k-1} & \cdots & c_{k(k+1)/2} \end{bmatrix}. \tag{3.28}$$

iv) Construct k encoding IDs $\left(r_1^a, r_2^a, \ldots, r_k^a\right)$, each consisting of k elements, where $a = 1, 2, 3, \ldots, k$. The method for the construction of encoding IDs and setting the number of 0 bits is similar to that used in BMSR. For each FDP in a column j of S, append a specific number of 0 bits to the header or tail of the FDP based on element r_i^a ($i = 1, 2, 3, \ldots, k$) in an encoding ID, where i is the row number of this FDP. This process generates k SDPs, which are then operated upon to obtain an ECP by *XOR*. Repeat these steps using different k encoding IDs for the column j in S to obtain k ECPs.

v) Arrange these k ECPs sequentially to form a set $P_g = p_{g,1}, p_{g,2}, \cdots, p_{g,k}, g = 1, 2, \ldots, n - k$, where $p_{g,k}$ represents the ECP obtained by the k-th encoding ID and the g-th column of S. Repeat these steps for $n - k$ different columns of S to acquire $n - k$ sets of ECPs. The parameter needs to be set as $n = 2k$ in order to ensure the repairability of BMBR in the event of any single-node failure.

vi) Construct a parity matrix P of $(n - k) * k$, denoted as the following equation (3.29):

$$P = \begin{bmatrix} P_1 \\ P_2 \\ \vdots \\ P_{n-\dot{k}} \end{bmatrix} = \begin{bmatrix} p_{1,1} & p_{1,2} & \cdots & p_{1,\dot{k}} \\ p_{2,1} & p_{2,2} & \cdots & p_{2,\dot{k}} \\ \vdots & \vdots & \vdots & \vdots \\ p_{n-\dot{k},1} & p_{n-\dot{k},2} & \cdots & p_{n-\dot{k},\dot{k}} \end{bmatrix}, \tag{3.29}$$

where P_1 to P_{n-k} are the ECP sets obtained by the above steps, respectively. The S and P are arranged into a data matrix E, which is expressed as follows:

$$E = \begin{bmatrix} S \\ P \end{bmatrix}. \tag{3.30}$$

vii) Each row of E is stored in a storage node, respectively, where n storage nodes are required, including k system nodes and $n - k$ parity nodes.

b) Decoding Process of BMBR

i) Determine whether the failed node f is a system node, and f is the number of rows in S where the failed node is located, $f = 1, 2, \ldots, n$. If it is, enter ii), otherwise enter iii).

ii) Retrieve the f-th FDP stored by each remaining valid system node. As the matrix S is symmetric, this process allows for obtaining the $k - 1$ FDPs stored in the failed node. Select the corresponding parity node of the f-th column to retrieve its stored data. Utilize both a downloaded $p_{f,j}$ ($j = 1, 2, 3, \ldots, k$) from the parity node and the corresponding encoding ID, combining them with $(k - 1)$ SDPs corresponding to recovered $k - 1$ FDPs to obtain all information within the failed system node by *XOR* inverse operations, similar to equation (3.26). Store this acquired data in a new storage node as a replacement for the failed system node.

iii) Retrieve the column number c in S corresponding to the failed parity node f, download FDPs from all system nodes to construct the complete c-th column of S, and encode these FDPs using BMBR encoding method, and subsequently acquire all data pertaining to the failed parity node f. Store this acquired data in a new storage node as a replacement for the failed system node.

BMSR and BMBR offer significant advantages over traditional RGC codes and RS codes by greatly reducing computational complexity in the encoding and decoding process. They replace complex calculations based on finite fields with simple *XOR* and shift operations, resulting in improved node repair rates. Additionally, BMSR minimizes storage requirements for each node while reducing system complexity. In today's world where storage space and bandwidth resources are increasingly valuable, the benefits of BMSR are clear. Similarly, BMBR reduces computational complexity while minimizing bandwidth consumption during node repair processes. This makes it particularly useful for bandwidth-limited storage systems with high application value and development potential.

3.2.3 Butterfly Codes

Butterfly codes (Pamies-Juarez et al. 2016, pp. 81–94) are MSR codes characterized by a redundancy of $n - k = 2$. The repair of a single-node failure merely demands the transmission of half of the remaining data. Additionally, butterfly code is a binary vector code based on $GF(2)$, and the encoding and decoding are accomplished through *XOR* operations, thereby significantly enhancing the practicality of butterfly codes.

It is worth noting that the name "butterfly codes" first appeared in the research by Gad et al. (2013, pp. 887–891). Due to the recursive construction of one of the parity columns resembling a butterfly, it was called the butterfly parity column, and the code was named butterfly codes. However, in 2016, Pamies-Juarez et al. (2016, pp. 81–94) provided a new recursive construction for the butterfly parity column of this code. Compared with the original construction, although the new recursive construction no longer resembles a butterfly, it has a more simplified design, leading to a simpler implementation. Additionally, the new recursive construction supports the reuse of precomputed values and can achieve better cache locality.

Nevertheless, Gad et al. (2013, pp. 887–891) still retain the names "butterfly parity column" and "butterfly codes," so this book also uses these two names when introducing the corework of Gad et al. (2013, pp. 887–891).

Subsequently, the encoding and decoding process of butterfly codes are elaborated in detail.

3.2.3.1 Encoding Process of Butterfly Codes

Let D_k be a binary matrix of size $2^{k-1} * k$, where $k \geq 2$. D_k is employed to represent the original data that is required to be encoded and stored in the DSS. The internal structure of D_k is presented as

$$D_k = \begin{bmatrix} \boldsymbol{a} & E \\ \boldsymbol{b} & F \end{bmatrix}, \tag{3.31}$$

where both E and F are binary matrices of $2^{k-2} * (k-1)$ and both $\boldsymbol{a}$ and $\boldsymbol{b}$ are column vectors consisting of 2^{k-2} bits.

Let D_k^j denote the j-th column within D_k with $j \in \{0, \dots, k-1\}$. Then, D_k can be represented as a k-column vector $D_k = \left(D_k^{k-1}, \dots, D_k^0\right)$. After encoding, a systematic codeword $C_k = \left(D_k^{k-1}, \dots, D_k^0, H, B\right)$ is attained, where H and B are two vector columns respectively denoting the horizontal parity column and the butterfly parity column. Additionally, two functions, $H = \mathcal{H}(D_k)$ and $B = \mathcal{B}(D_k)$, are defined to delineate the generation procedures of H and B.

When $k = 2$, define

$$H = \mathcal{H}\left(\begin{bmatrix} d_0^1 & d_0^0 \\ d_1^1 & d_1^0 \end{bmatrix}\right) = \begin{bmatrix} d_0^1 \oplus d_0^0 \\ d_1^1 \oplus d_1^0 \end{bmatrix} \tag{3.32}$$

and

$$B = \mathcal{B}\left(\begin{bmatrix} d_0^1 & d_0^0 \\ d_1^1 & d_1^0 \end{bmatrix}\right) = \begin{bmatrix} d_1^1 \oplus d_0^0 \\ d_0^1 \oplus d_0^0 \oplus d_1^0 \end{bmatrix}. \tag{3.33}$$

When $k > 2$, define

$$H = \mathcal{H}(D_k) = \begin{bmatrix} \boldsymbol{a} \oplus \mathcal{H}(E) \\ P_{k-1}[P_{k-1}\boldsymbol{b} \oplus \mathcal{H}(P_{k-1}F)] \end{bmatrix} \tag{3.34}$$

and

$$B = \mathcal{B}(D_k) = \begin{bmatrix} P_{k-1}\boldsymbol{b} \oplus \mathcal{B}(E) \\ P_{k-1}[\boldsymbol{a} \oplus \mathcal{H}(E) \oplus \mathcal{B}(P_{k-1}F)] \end{bmatrix}, \tag{3.35}$$

where P_k is a $k * k$ matrix with 1 on the antidiagonal and 0 for the rest of bits. This leads to a vertical flip of a vector or matrix when multiplied by P_k on the left. Figures 3.4 and 3.5 show examples of recursive encoding operations for $\mathcal{H}(D_k)$ and $\mathcal{B}(D_k)$ when $k = 3$ and $k = 4$, respectively.

Figure 3.4 is relatively shallow and serves as a shallow parsing of Figure 3.5. Figure 3.5 presents an example of the recursive encoding operation of $\mathcal{H}(D_4)$ and $\mathcal{B}(D_4)$, where the part highlighted in red represents the submatrix E in D_4 and the redundant information related to E, and the part highlighted in yellow represents the submatrix F in D_4 and the redundant information related to F.

Note that in Figure 3.5, the data of column H and column B are divided into two parts, but in fact they represent only one column each. For instance, the first

C_3

	D_3^2	D_3^1	D_3^0	H	B
(a)	c_0	b_0	a_0	$c_0+b_0+a_0$	$c_3+b_1+a_0$
	c_1	b_1	a_1	$c_1+b_1+a_1$	$c_2+b_0+a_0+a_1$
(b)	c_2	b_2	a_2	$c_2+b_2+a_2$	$c_1+b_1+a_1+b_3+a_3+a_2$
	c_3	b_3	a_3	$c_3+b_3+a_3$	$c_0+b_0+a_0+b_2+a_3$

Figure 3.4 Butterfly codes C_3 for $k = 3$. (The color rendition of this image is available on the book's landing page on wiley.com).

C_4

	D_4^3	D_4^2	D_4^1	D_4^0	H (One column)		B (One column)	
(a)	d_0	c_0	b_0	a_0	d_0+	$c_0+b_0+a_0$	d_7+	$c_3+b_1+a_0$
	d_1	c_1	b_1	a_1	d_1+	$c_1+b_1+a_1$	d_6+	$c_2+b_0+a_0+a_1$
	d_2	c_2	b_2	a_2	d_2+	$c_2+b_2+a_2$	d_5+	$c_1+b_1+a_1+b_3+a_3+a_2$
	d_3	c_3	b_3	a_3	d_3+	$c_3+b_3+a_3$	d_4+	$c_0+b_0+a_0+b_2+a_3$
(b)	d_4	c_4	b_4	a_4	d_4+	$c_4+b_4+a_4$	$d_3+c_3+b_3+a_3+$	$c_7+b_7+a_7+b_5+a_4$
	d_5	c_5	b_5	a_5	d_5+	$c_5+b_5+a_5$	$d_2+c_2+b_2+a_2+$	$c_6+b_6+a_6+b_4+a_4+a_5$
	d_6	c_6	b_6	a_6	d_6+	$c_6+b_6+a_6$	$d_1+c_1+b_1+a_1+$	$c_5+b_7+a_7+a_6$
	d_7	c_7	b_7	a_7	d_7+	$c_7+b_7+a_7$	$d_0+c_0+b_0+a_0+$	$c_4+b_6+a_7$

Figure 3.5 Butterfly codes C_4 for $k = 4$. (The color rendition of this image is available on the book's landing page on wiley.com).

row element of column H should be $d_0 + c_0 + b_0 + a_0$, but in Figure 3.5, d_0+ is separated out, and $c_0 + b_0 + a_0$ is retained. The same applies to other elements in column H and column B. This is done to facilitate the clarification of the recursive relationship between Figure 3.4 and Figure 3.5. It can be observed that the red highlighted parts separated out in Figure 3.5 are exactly Figure 3.4, that is, the data of the butterfly code when $k = 3$. This indicates that the butterfly code when $k = 4$ can be derived from the basis of $k = 3$. As mentioned earlier, this will support precomputed values and can achieve better cache locality.

3.2.3.2 Decoding Process of Butterfly Codes

Given that butterfly codes are MDS codes with two redundant columns, the original data can be decoded successfully whenever any two columns are absent. This can be validated by induction.

Through undertaking a succession of straightforward *XOR* operations based on equation (3.32) and equation (3.33), it can be facilely demonstrated that when $k = 2$, butterfly codes are capable of decoding the original data in the context of any two column failures.

When $k > 2$, assume that C_{k-1} with $k - 1$ column vectors fulfill the MDS property. Hence, it is demonstrated that C_k with k column vectors also meets the MDS property. The proof is categorized into the following cases:

a) Two parity columns are invalid. They can be regenerated through encoding by employing the functions $H = \mathcal{H}(D_k)$ and $B = \mathcal{B}(D_k)$ based on the original data.
b) One parity column and one data column are invalid. Using the remaining data columns and a parity column and performing the inverse operation of the encoding process, the failed data column can be obtained and then the failed parity column can be repaired through encoding.
c) Two data columns are lost, and neither of them is the leftmost column. In such a case, the vectors $\mathcal{H}(E)$ and $\mathcal{B}(E)$ can be attained by separately conducting *XOR* on the upper halves of the two parity columns with $\boldsymbol{a}$ and $P_{k-1}\boldsymbol{b}$. The vectors $\mathcal{H}(E)$ and $\mathcal{B}(E)$ can be regarded as the two parity columns of the butterfly codes C_{k-1} possessing $k - 1$ column vectors. Through the utilization of the inductive hypothesis, the upper halves of two invalid columns, which form part of E, can be retrieved by the MDS property of C_{k-1}. Likewise, the values $\mathcal{H}(P_{k-1}F)$ and $\mathcal{B}(P_{k-1}F)$ can be generated by simple *XOR* operations. Based on the inductive hypothesis, the lower halves of the invalid columns, which form part of F, can be restored.
d) Two data columns are lost, among which one is the leftmost column and the other is the data column D_k^j, where $j \neq k - 1$. By combining the lower part of $\mathcal{B}(D_k)$, $P_{k-1}[\boldsymbol{a} \oplus \mathcal{H}(E) \oplus \mathcal{B}(P_{k-1}F)]$, and the upper part of $\mathcal{H}(D_k)$, $\boldsymbol{a} \oplus \mathcal{H}(E)$, $\mathcal{B}(P_{k-1}F)$ can be derived. The decoding process can acquire $P_{k-1}F$ and the lower part of D_k^j. Through the utilization of $P_{k-1}F$ and the lower part of $\mathcal{H}(D_k)$, $P_{k-1}[P_{k-1}\boldsymbol{b} \oplus \mathcal{H}(P_{k-1}F)]$, $\boldsymbol{b}$ can be computed. With $\boldsymbol{b}$ and the upper part of $\mathcal{B}(D_k)$, $P_{k-1}\boldsymbol{b} \oplus \mathcal{B}(E)$, $\mathcal{B}(E)$ can be calculated and subsequently E can be determined, thereby enabling the decoding of the upper part of D_k^j. Note that with E and the upper part of $\mathcal{H}(D_k)$, $\boldsymbol{a} \oplus \mathcal{H}(E)$, $\boldsymbol{a}$ can be computed. Ultimately, both the leftmost column $(\boldsymbol{a}^t, \boldsymbol{b}^t)^t$ and the lost data column D_k^j are restored.

Butterfly codes can accommodate the failure of up to two columns at most. The data reconstruction in various scenarios has been elaborated in detail above. Nevertheless, when only one column fails, butterfly codes possess a more efficient repair approach, which is presented in the following four cases:

a) $(D_k^{k-1}, \dots, D_k^1)$ undergoes the loss of one non-leftmost column. Denote the lost column as D_k^j, where $j \neq 0$. Each remaining column, encompassing both data columns and parity columns, is required to transmit the bit at position i, where i fulfills either $\left\lfloor \frac{i}{2^{j-1}} \right\rfloor \equiv 0 \, mod \, 4$ or $\left\lfloor \frac{i}{2^{j-1}} \right\rfloor \equiv 3 \, mod \, 4$. Let D_{k-1} be a matrix of size $(k - 1) * 2^{k-2}$ constituted by the transmitted data from the remaining data columns, and let H_{k-1} and B_{k-1} be vectors of length 2^{k-2} composed of the transmitted data from the parity columns, respectively. Let $h = \mathcal{H}(D_{k-1}) \oplus H_{k-1}$ and $b = \mathcal{B}(D_{k-1}) \oplus B_{k-1}$. At this juncture, the lost D_k^j is already encompassed within h and b. For $i \in \{0, \dots, 2^{k-2}\}$, let $p = \left\lfloor \frac{i+2^{j-1}}{2^j} \right\rfloor 2^j + i$, $r = p \bmod 2^j$, and thereby we can obtain $D_k^j(p) \leftarrow h(i)$ and $D_k^j(p - 2r + 2^j - 1) \leftarrow b(i)$.

b) The data column D_k^0 is lost. In this circumstance, $D_k^{k-1}, \dots, D_k^1$ and H transmit the elements whose index positions within their columns are even, while B transmits the elements whose index positions are odd. Acquire h and b by following precisely the same procedures as in i), where h can offer the elements with even indexes in D_k^0, and b can offer the elements with odd indexes in D_k^0.
c) The first parity column H is lost. All the remaining columns transmit their lower halves, specifically, the index $i \in \{2^{k-2}, \dots, 2^{k-1} - 1\}$. The data from data columns can recover the lower half of H, and the *XOR* operation of the data transmitted by $D_{k-1}^{k-2}, \dots, D_{k-1}^0$ along with the data from B can acquire the upper half of H.
d) The second parity column B is lost. D_k^{k-1} transmits the upper half, while H transmits the lower half. Moreover, $D_k^{k-2}, \dots, D_k^0$ will initially access their data to conduct *XOR* operations and subsequently transmit data whose size is equivalent to half of all stored data. Each D_k^j where $j \neq k - 1$ conducts *XOR* operations and the value transmitted is equal to their respective contributions within the lower half of column B. As a result, the lower half of B can be restored through simple *XOR* among the transmitted data from all data columns. Likewise, each D_k^j, where $j \neq k - 1$, refers to their respective contributions within the upper half of column B, then conducts *XOR* and finally transmits data. By performing *XOR* operations on this transmitted data with the lower half transmitted by column H, the upper half of column B can be restored.

Obviously, in any case of a single-column failure, the lost column can be restored with repair bandwidth equivalent to half of the remaining data volume. Furthermore, if the lost column is a data column, the repair bandwidth is precisely equal to the number of disk I/O, attaining the optimal disk I/O. For the repair of the parity column B, additional computation operations are demanded, causing a slight increase in the disk I/O, yet the repair bandwidth remains unaltered.

3.2.4 Clay Codes

Despite the fact that butterfly codes markedly curtail the repair bandwidth of MSR codes, the maximum fault-tolerant capability of these codes is merely two failed nodes and the disk I/O has not been fully optimized, leaving much room for improvement. Vajha et al. (2018, pp. 139–154) contends that in the application of MSR codes to practical systems, apart from fulfilling the demands of optimal repair bandwidth and low storage overhead, there are also certain additional desired requirements to be satisfied:

1) **Unified Repair Capacity:** It can repair data nodes and parity nodes under the same low repair bandwidth.
2) **Minimal Disk I/O:** Data accessed from the disk within helper nodes for repair is equivalent to data transmitted.
3) **Low Subpacketization:** Subpacketization is minimized as much as possible.
4) **Small Coding Space:** The finite field for coding is reduced to the smallest extent feasible.

Specifically, the concept of subpacketization is derived from array code. An array code $C(n, k, l)$ is denoted by an $l * n$ matrix $(C_1, \dots, C_n)$, where each column C_i represents a codeword component with dimension l. The parameter l is referred to as subpacketization, which constitutes a crucial constraint for achieving optimal repair coding. For an array code(n, k, l) to achieve optimal repair, it must satisfy the condition $l \geq r^{(k-1)r}$, where $r = n - k$. Subsequently, the concept of subpacketization was further expanded to encompass a broader spectrum of ECs, used to distinguish between scalar codes and vector codes:

1) **Scalar Codes:** Each data block comprises L bytes. During encoding, one byte is selected from each of the k data blocks, and m different linear combinations of the k bytes are used to generate m check bytes. The resulting set of $n = k + m$ bytes forms a codeword. This process is performed in parallel for all L bytes in the data block to produce L codewords. Additionally, this process results in the creation of m parity blocks, with each parity block consisting of L bytes.
2) **Vector Codes:** For each data block, $\alpha \geq 1$ bytes are selected to form a set, called superbytes, and k superbytes selected in the same way as scalar codes are encoded to form a codeword containing $(k + m)\alpha$ bytes. The operation of encoding k superbytes is performed in parallel for all $N = L/\alpha$ superbytes of a data block to obtain N codewords. In this case, the number of bytes α in a superbyte is called the subpacketization of the vector code.

For scalar codes, such as RS codes, the subpacketization α can be considered as 1. In other words, vector codes can be conceptualized as replacing α individual scalar codewords with a unified vector codeword. The MSR code represents a vector MDS code capable of achieving the minimal repair bandwidth possible. To recover a failed node containing α bytes, the coding process initially establishes communication with any d helper nodes, where $k < d < n - 1$. Subsequently, it retrieves $\beta = \alpha/((d - k + 1))$ bytes from each helper node and utilizes this data to restore the failed node. Typically, the total amount of downloaded data (i.e., repair bandwidth), $d\beta$ is significantly smaller than the total data $k\alpha$ stored in k nodes. Here, α denotes the subpacketization of the MSR code; maintaining a low value for α

helps obviate the necessity for designing additional interleaving block algorithms to optimize disk access. Ye and Barg (2017a, pp. 6307–6317; 2017b, pp. 2001–2014) introduced the initial MSR theoretical framework, known as the Ye-Barg code, which offers all of the aforementioned requirements from a parity matrix perspective. This coding approach minimizes storage overhead to closely approximate the theoretical optimal value, maintains a small subpacketization, limits the size of the finite field to not exceed n, and achieves optimal disk I/O and full-node repair. Coupled-layer (clay) codes have further refined and enhanced the practical aspects of Ye-Barg code. In addition to possessing all of the previously mentioned advantages, clay codes also offer additional benefits compared to Ye-Barg code. The following provides a detailed explanation of clay codes.

First, the basic performance characteristics of clay codes are briefly introduced by a simple example. The parameters of this clay code are ($n = 4, k = 2, d = 3, \alpha = 4, \beta = 2, M = 8$). The codewords are distributed across $n = 4$ nodes, comprising of $k = 2$ data nodes and $n - k = 2$ parity nodes. Each node stores a block of $\alpha = 4$ bytes. The storage overhead of the code is $n\alpha/k\alpha = n/k = 2$. During the repair process of failed nodes, each helper node transmits $\beta = 2$ bytes, resulting in a normalized repair bandwidth of $d\beta/k\alpha = d/(k(d - k + 1)) = 0.75$, representing a 25% reduction compared to the conventional MDS code.

The process of constructing a clay code can be delineated into the subsequent steps:

1) First, establish a straightforward distributed data storage topology comprising four nodes, where the nodes are indexed by coordinates (x, y): $\{(x, y) \mid (x, y) \in J\}$, $J = \{(0,0), (1,0), (0,1), (1,1)\}$. As depicted in Figure 3.6, employ a RS(4,2) code for encoding and storing data on the four nodes; with node (0,0), (1,0) responsible for data storage and node (0,1), (1,1) designated for parity check. Nodes sharing the same y-coordinate are referred to as being within the same y section.
2) In the same four nodes, four codewords from the same RS(4,2) code are stored, totaling 16 bytes. Consequently, each node now stores 4 bytes, with each byte being associated with a distinct codeword. By utilizing parameter $z \in \{0, 1, 2, 3\}$ to index the four codewords for constructing an uncoupled code U, denoted as $\{U(x, y, z) \mid (x, y) \in J, z \in \{0, 1, 2, 3\}\}$. As depicted in Figure 3.7, the stored 16 bytes can be visualized as residing within a data cube composed of four horizontal layers, and each layer contains 4 bytes. Additionally, the data cube can be perceived as comprising four vertical data columns; each column represents

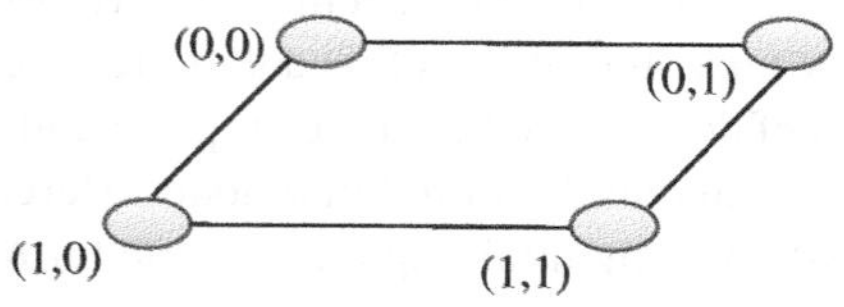

Figure 3.6 Storage topology of MDS codes (4,2).

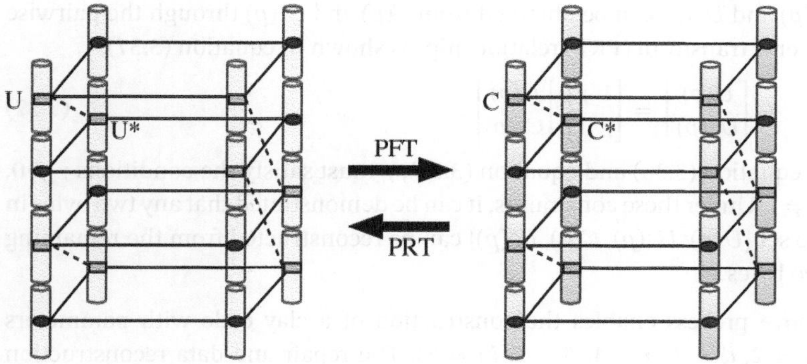

Figure 3.7 Conversion of uncoupled code U (left) and clay codes C (right). (The color rendition of this image is available on the book's landing page on wiley.com).

a storage node that stores a superbyte – amounting to four superbytes in total. It is straightforward to verify that U possesses the MDS property. However, due to every horizontal layer employing the same RS code, U cannot conserve repair bandwidth.

3) Next, utilize the notation $P(x, y, z)$ to denote the vertices (x, y, z) within the data cube and introduce the concept of vertex pairs (p, p^*). As illustrated in the left part of Figure 3.7, eight elliptic spherical vertices remain unpaired, while the remaining eight rectangular square vertices are paired. The paired vertices all pertain to the same y section and are interconnected by dashed lines. As previously mentioned, each vertex p in the data cube represents a byte of data in the U, denoted as $U(p) = U(x, y, z)$. We will employ $U^*(p)$ to represent the "partner" of $U(p)$.
4) Then the conversion from uncoupled code U to clay code C will be implemented. As shown in the right part of Figure 3.7, each codeword in C consists of 16 bytes, which are stored in an identical data cube composed of four horizontal layers and four vertical columns, with four nodes per layer and column. Each node corresponds to a column of this data cube and stores a superbyte consisting of 4 bytes. Likely, C associates each byte $C(p)$ with each vertex p of the data cube. The bytes $U(p)$ and $C(p)$ are related in a simple way:
   a) If p corresponds to an unpaired vertex, i.e., an elliptic spherical vertex, simply define $C(p) = U(p)$.
   b) If (p, p^*) is a pair of vertices with $p \neq p^*$, then $C(p)$ and $C^*(p)$ can be related to $U(p)$ and $U^*(p)$ through the pairwise forward transform (PFT), as shown in equation (3.36):

$$\begin{bmatrix} C(p) \\ C^*(p) \end{bmatrix} = \begin{bmatrix} 1 & \gamma \\ \gamma & 1 \end{bmatrix}^{-1} \begin{bmatrix} U(p) \\ U^*(p) \end{bmatrix}. \tag{3.36}$$

$U(p)$ and $U^*(p)$ can be obtained from $C(p)$ and $C^*(p)$ through the pairwise reverse transform (PRT) relationship, as shown in equation (3.37):

$$\begin{bmatrix} U(p) \\ U^*(p) \end{bmatrix} = \begin{bmatrix} 1 & \gamma \\ \gamma & 1 \end{bmatrix} \begin{bmatrix} C(p) \\ C^*(p) \end{bmatrix}. \tag{3.37}$$

In equation (3.36) and equation (3.37), γ must satisfy the conditions $\gamma \neq 0$, $\gamma^2 \neq 1$. Under these constraints, it can be demonstrated that any two bytes in the set $\{U(p), U^*(p), C(p), C^*(p)\}$ can be reconstructed from the remaining two bytes.

The above process enables the construction of a clay code with parameters ($n = 4$, $k = 2$, $d = 3$, $\alpha = 4$, $\beta = 2$, $M = 8$). The repair and data reconstruction process are as follows:

Clay codes enable unified repair, ensuring that each failed node can be restored at the same cost. For instance, in the event of a column failure at coordinates (1, 0), data from layers $z = 1$ and $z = 3$ can be utilized for repair. Initially, the PRT is applied to paired nodes $C(1,1,1)$ and $C(0,1,3)$ to derive $U(1,1,1)$ and $U(0,1,3)$. Subsequently employing the PRT transformation on unpaired nodes $C(0,1,1)$ and $C(1,1,3)$, we obtain $C(0,1,1) = U(0,1,1)$ and $C(1,1,3) = U(1,1,3)$. According to RS decoding principles, using $U(1,1,1)$ and $U(0,1,1)$, $U(0,0,1)$ and $U(1,0,1)$ can be obtained. By $U(1,1,3)$ and $U(0,1,3)$, we obtain $U(0,0,3)$ and $U(1,0,3)$. Then utilizing $C(0,0,1)$ and $U(0,0,1)$, we derive $C(1,0,0)$. Finally, employing $U(0,0,3)$ and $C(0,0,3)$, we arrive at $C(1,0,2)$. Thus, the restoration of the column with coordinates (1,0) is completed.

Throughout the process of repair, each of the remaining three valid columns transmits 2 bytes, precisely corresponding to the 6 remaining bytes in the horizontal layer $z = 1$ and $z = 3$. In contrast to conventional MDS codes that require a bandwidth equivalent to 8 bytes of the original data, the clay code saves 25% of the repair bandwidth.

The data reconstruction of clay codes is relatively more complicated. Vajha et al. (2018, pp. 139–154) put forward an Intersection Score (IScore) mechanism to make the repair process orderly. IScore represents the number of failures of each layer of unpaired nodes. Taking a clay code with parameters ($n = 4$, $k = 2$, $d = 3$, $\alpha = 4$, $\beta = 2$, $M = 8$) as an example, when the columns corresponding to the coordinates (0,0) and (0,1) fail, it can be observed from the right part of Figure 3.7 that there are two elliptic spherical vertexes failed at the $z = 0$ layer, thus $IScore = 2$. Similarly, the IScore corresponding to $z = 1$, $z = 2$, and $z = 3$ can be obtained as 1, 1, and 0, respectively.

The data reconstruction is conducted layer by layer in the ascending order of IScore. Initially, for the layer with $IScore = 0$, namely, $z = 3$, the two failed U nodes of this layer, $U(0,0,3)$ and $U(0,1,3)$, can be restored by employing the two remaining elliptic spherical vertexes of this layer. Subsequently, using the nodes $C(1,0,2)$

and $C(1,1,1)$ that are respectively paired with $U(0,0,3)$ and $U(0,1,3)$ in the two layers with $IScore = 1$, $C(0,0,3)$, $U(1,0,2)$, $C(0,1,3)$, and $U(1,1,1)$ can be decoded. In combination with $U(1,0,2)$ and $U(1,1,2)$, all the failed U nodes of the $z = 2$ layer can be decoded. By analogy, as long as decoding is performed layer by layer in the ascending order of IScore, all the data can be reconstructed. This is because the lower the IScore of the layer, the greater the number of valid nonpaired nodes, and the more feasible it is to decode the U node data of this layer. Moreover, only by utilizing the restored U node data in conjunction with the valid C node data of the higher IScore layer can the failed C node data of the higher IScore layer be decoded.

Vajha et al. (2018, pp. 139–154) further put forward that the generalized clay codes can be constructed in the following parameters:

$$(n = qt, k, d, \quad \alpha = q^t, \quad \beta = q^{t-1}),$$

where $q = (d - k + 1)$ and it satisfies that any positive integer $t \geq 1$ and the size of the finite field $Q > n$. Regarding the above parameter form, the encoding, decoding, and repair algorithms can all be generalized from the example ($n = 4$, $k = 2$, $d = 3$, $\alpha = 4$, $\beta = 2$, $M = 8$). However, in the case where $d < n - 1$, when selecting d helper nodes, all the nodes belonging to the y-section of the failed node must be encompassed. Additionally, the aforementioned parameters need to satisfy $q \bmod n = 0$, but it can be extended to the situation where q is not a factor of n through the shortening method (Liu, Ding and Tang 2021, pp. 5119–5132). For instance, for the parameters ($n = 14$, $k = 10$, $d = 13$), $q = d - k + 1 = 4$), when constructing the clay code, $n' = 16$ can be set, which is the smallest multiple of q greater than n, and set $k' = k + (n' - n) = 12$. During encoding, we set the bytes in $s = (n' - n) = 2$ system nodes to 0; thus, the generated code actually possesses the parameters ($n = 14$, $k = 10$, $d = 13$).

Clay codes extend the theoretical structure proposed by Ye and Barg from the perspective of coupled layer. Vajha et al. (2018, pp. 139–154) embed clay codes into the Ceph to evaluate the practical performance. Experiments demonstrate that with a storage overhead of 1.25 times, clay codes, respectively, reduce the repair bandwidth, disk I/O, and repair time of RS codes by 2.9, 3.4, and 3 times.

From a practical application perspective, both butterfly codes and clay codes can be embedded in renowned distributed storage systems like HDFS and Ceph, attaining remarkable performance. Nevertheless, to incorporate these two kinds of codes into the systems, certain adaptations and modifications to the codes and the systems are necessary, which will considerably augment the development cost. Moreover, clay codes conduct encoding and decoding computations based on multivariate fields, and there is still vast potential for optimizing the computational complexity. The BRGCs to be presented in the next section are a type of EC with lower computational complexity and higher practicability.

3.2.5 Practical LRCs

In large-scale distributed storage systems for extensive clusters, RS codes are commonly employed to ensure data reliability. Nevertheless, the substantial repair cost of RS codes is a necessary trade-off for achieving high storage efficiency and reliability. In contrast, LRCs can mitigate repair cost without compromising reliability. Many reputable vendors have integrated LRCs into their storage systems to enhance overall reliability. This section provides an overview of the LRCs utilized in the WAS system developed by Microsoft (Huang et al. 2012, pp. 15–26) and the LRCs implemented in the HDFS-RAID system developed by Facebook (Sathiamoorthy et al. 2013, pp. 1–16).

3.2.5.1 LRCs in WAS

The objective of WAS-LRCs is to minimize the reconstruction cost, defined as the minimum number of data blocks required for repairing a failed block. The fundamental concept behind WAS-LRCs is to enable local repair by adding additional local parity blocks for each subset of data blocks. Figure 3.8 illustrates the principles of WAS-LRCs using an example containing six data blocks, where four parity blocks are generated. This includes two global parity blocks, p_0 and p_1, computed from all data blocks. However, for the remaining two parity blocks, this WAS-LRC divides the six data blocks into two equally sized groups X and Y and computes a local parity block for each group. The six data blocks will be named as (x_0, x_1, x_2) and (y_0, y_1, y_2), respectively. Subsequently, the parity block p_x will be calculated from (x_0, x_1, x_2), while the local parity block p_y will be calculated from (y_0, y_1, y_2). Currently, if there is a need to restore x_0, the cost of using p_x and two data blocks (x_1, x_2) is lower compared to utilizing any six blocks from the other blocks, excluding the two local parity blocks. Similarly, the reconstruction

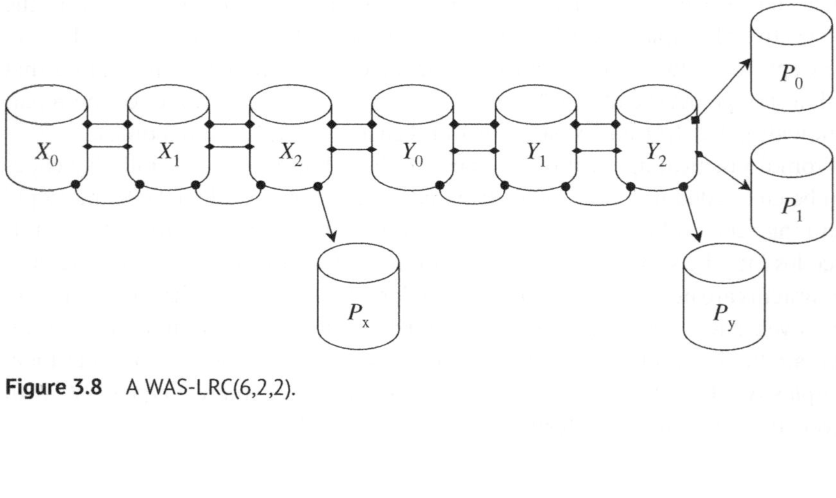

Figure 3.8 A WAS-LRC(6,2,2).

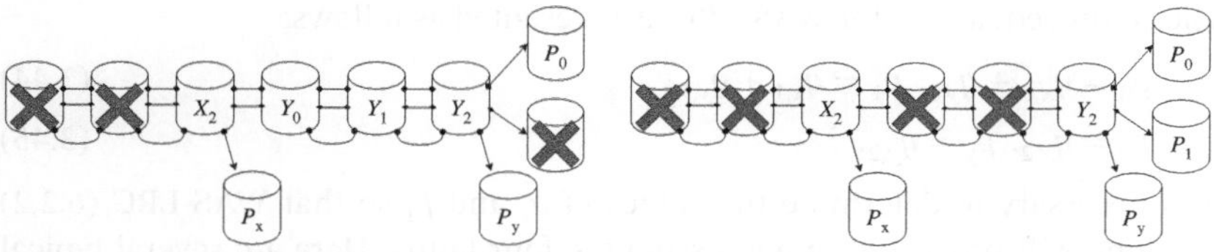

Figure 3.9 Information-theoretically decodable faults.

of any individual data block only requires three blocks, which is half the number required by an RS(8,6) code.

To expound the fault-tolerant principles of WAS-LRCs from an algebraic standpoint, it is essential to define appropriate coding equations, which articulate how to compute parity blocks from data blocks. The coding equations selected (Huang et al. 2012, pp. 15–26) enable WAS-LRCs to attain the property of MR (Gopalan et al. 2014, pp. 5245–5265) and ASL-LRCs to rectify any information-theoretically decodable faults (Huang et al. 2012, pp. 15–26).

In the example of WAS-LRC(6,2,2), it contains four parity blocks, so theoretically it can tolerate up to four faults. However, LRCs are not MDS codes and cannot repair any arbitrary four node failures. For instance, if (x_0, x_1, x_2) and p_x fail simultaneously, this fault is nondecodable. This is because there are only two global parity blocks and the local parity block p_y does not contribute to recovering from the failure of (x_0, x_1, x_2). These types of faults are known as information-theoretically nondecodable.

Faults that can be rectified are referred to as information-theoretically decodable. For instance, in Figure 3.9, the three faults on the left and the four faults on the right are all information-theoretically decodable. Consequently, coding equations can be devised to decode these aforementioned faults. While constructing coding equations capable of decoding specific fault is not challenging, creating coding equations that achieve MR properties – meaning it can decode all information-theoretically decodable fault modes – is indeed a formidable task.

To achieve the MR property, the WAS-LRC(6,2,2) needs to select two groups of coding coefficients (α_i, β_i) for encoding X and Y as follows:

$$q_{x,0} = \alpha_0 x_0 + \alpha_1 x_1 + \alpha_2 x_2, \tag{3.38}$$

$$q_{x,1} = \alpha_0^2 x_0 + \alpha_1^2 x_1 + \alpha_2^2 x_2, \tag{3.39}$$

$$q_{x,2} = x_0 + x_1 + x_2, \tag{3.40}$$

$$q_{y,0} = \beta_0 y_0 + \beta_1 y_1 + \beta_2 y_2, \tag{3.41}$$

$$q_{y,1} = \beta_0^2 y_0 + \beta_1^2 y_1 + \beta_2^2 y_2, \tag{3.42}$$

$$q_{y,2} = y_0 + y_1 + y_2. \tag{3.43}$$

The coding equations for WAS-LRC are presented as follows:

$$p_0 = q_{x,0} + q_{y,0},\ p_1 = q_{x,1} + q_{y,1}, \tag{3.44}$$

$$p_x = q_{x,2},\ p_y = q_{y,2}. \tag{3.45}$$

It is necessary to determine the values of α_i and β_i so that WAS-LRC (6,2,2) can exhibit MR properties in addressing the four faults. Here are several typical scenarios:

a) There is no case of a parity block fault. The four faults are evenly distributed between X and Y. As a result, we can derive four equations with coefficients provided by matrix G as follows:

$$G = \begin{pmatrix} 1 & 1 & 0 & 0 \\ 0 & 0 & 1 & 1 \\ \alpha_i & \alpha_j & \beta_s & \beta_t \\ \alpha_i^2 & \alpha_j^2 & \beta_s^2 & \beta_t^2 \end{pmatrix} \tag{3.46}$$

and

$$Det(G) = (\alpha_j - \alpha_i)(\beta_t - \beta_s)(\alpha_i + \alpha_j - \beta_s - \beta_t). \tag{3.47}$$

b) Only one of p_x and p_y faults. Assuming that p_y has failed, with the remaining three faults being two in group X and the third in group Y, we can obtain three equations with coefficients given by G', as follows:

$$G' = \begin{pmatrix} 1 & 1 & 0 \\ \alpha_i & \alpha_j & \beta_s \\ \alpha_i^2 & \alpha_j^2 & \beta_s^2 \end{pmatrix} \tag{3.48}$$

and

$$Det(G') = \beta_s(\alpha_j - \alpha_i)(\beta_s - \alpha_j - \alpha_i). \tag{3.49}$$

c) Both p_x and p_y have failed. Additionally, the remaining two faults are evenly distributed into X and Y groups, resulting in two equations with coefficients provided by the matrix G'', as shown below:

$$G'' = \begin{pmatrix} \alpha_i & \beta_s \\ \alpha_i^2 & \beta_s^2 \end{pmatrix} \tag{3.50}$$

and

$$Det(G'') = \alpha_i\beta_s(\beta_s - \alpha_i). \tag{3.51}$$

In order to ensure that all of the above cases are decodable, the matrices G, G', and G'' should all be nonsingular, from which the following conditions can be derived:

$$\alpha_i, \alpha_j, \beta_s, \beta_t \neq 0, \tag{3.52}$$

$$\alpha_i, \alpha_j \neq \beta_s, \beta_t, \tag{3.53}$$

$$\alpha_i + \alpha_j \neq \beta_s + \beta_t. \tag{3.54}$$

One approach to satisfy these conditions is to assign elements from the finite field $GF(2^4)$ to α and β, where each element in the field is represented by 4 bits. α is selected from the elements with lower order 2 bits equal to zero, while β is chosen from the elements with higher order 2 bits equal to zero. Consequently, they are never equal, and all of the aforementioned conditions are fulfilled. This method of constructing coding equations requires only a very small finite field, making implementation simple and highly practical. As demonstrated by Huang et al. (2012, pp. 15–26), the WAS-LRC(6,2,2) is capable of decoding any $r \leq 3$ faults and all information-theoretically decodable four faults, which accounts for 86% of all four fault types.

For a WAS-LRC (k, l, r), where there are k data blocks divided into l groups, with an average of (k/l) blocks per group, each group computes a local parity block. Additionally, r global parity blocks are computed from the k data blocks. Let n be the total number of blocks, such that $n = k + l + r$. The WAS-LRC possesses the following two properties:

a) Any $r + 1$ block faults can be repaired.
b) A single data block fault can be recovered from up to (k/l) blocks.

At present, WAS-LRC(12,2,2) has been employed in the Microsoft WAS system as an auxiliary mechanism for data replication strategy. In comparison with RS(12,4), both exhibit similar storage efficiency; however, under different workloads, WAS-LRC(12,2,2) demonstrates superior repair rate and repair bandwidth. Furthermore, when I/O access is frequent, WAS-LRC(12,2,2) also displays characteristics of lower latency (Huang et al. 2012, pp. 15–26).

3.2.5.2 LRCs in HDFS-RAID

In order to reduce the substantial repair bandwidth in RS codes, Facebook has implemented a class of specially designed LRCs, referred to as HR-LRCs, within its open-source storage system HDFS-RAID. These HR-LRCs are capable of saving PB-level storage overhead and significantly reducing cluster costs. In the following section, the coding principles are elucidated by the example of HR-LRC(10,6,5) that has been practically applied in HDFS-RAID.

As illustrated in Figure 3.10, the data X is uniformly divided into 10 blocks, denoted as $X_1, X_2, \ldots, X_{10}$. Using the RS(10,6) code, four parity blocks are generated and labeled as $P_1, P_2, \ldots, P_4$. Subsequently, additional local parity blocks need to be added to enhance repair efficiency. For instance, a local check block $S_1 = c_1X_1 + c_2X_2 + c_3X_3 + c_4X_4 + c_5X_5$ can be added so that when any one of the blocks $S_1, X_1, X_2, \ldots, X_5$ fails, repair can be carried out using the remaining five

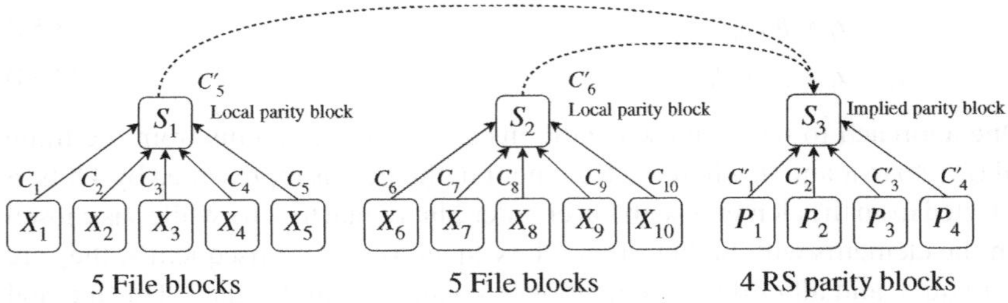

Figure 3.10 Encoding process of HR-LRC(10,6,5).

valid blocks. For example, if X_3 fails, repair can be performed using

$$X_3 = c_3^{-1}(S_1 - c_1X_1 - c_2X_2 - c_4X_4 - c_5X_5). \tag{3.55}$$

The above equation can be decoded as long as $c_3 \neq 0$, i.e., c_3^{-1} exists, then X_3 can be repaired.

HR-LRC(10,6,5) introduces three local parity blocks, theoretically increasing the storage overhead to 1.7 times. However, in order to reduce the additional storage, HR-LRC(10,6,5) utilizes a concept similar to interference alignment and establishes the equation $S_3 = c_5'S_1 + c_6'S_2$. By leveraging this simple linear relationship of the equation, S_3 can be treated as an implied parity block without actually storing it. In the event of a single block fault occurring in the global parity block, the implied parity block can be reconstructed and used for repairing the fault. For instance, if P_2 experiences a fault, it can be recovered by reading five blocks: P_1, P_3, P_4, S_1, S_2 and solving

$$P_2 = \left(c_2'\right)^{-1}\left(c_5'S_1 + c_6'S_2 - c_1'P_1 - c_3'P_3 - c_4'P_4\right). \tag{3.56}$$

The experimental results of Sathiamoorthy et al. (2013, pp. 1–16) show that, compared to RS, HR-LRCs can reduce repair bandwidth and disk I/O by half under the same conditions at the cost of a 14% increase in redundant storage. Therefore, they are more suitable for large-scale distributed storage systems with frequent failures.

The primary theoretical challenge faced by HR-LRCs is the selection of appropriate parameters c_i to ensure that all coding linear equations are linearly independent, thereby maximizing the fault tolerance of the coding. Unlike WAS-LRCs, in HR-LRCs(n, k, r), the parameters c_i depend not only on the nonsingularity of the decoding matrix but also on consideration of the global parity blocks P_i. The detailed method is demonstrated in Appendix of Sathiamoorthy et al. (2013, pp. 1–16), which includes a randomized algorithm and a deterministic algorithm for constructing c_i. However, both algorithms have exponential computational complexity in terms of parameters (n, k), making them suitable only for small size construction. Efficient construction methods for large coefficient cases are still subject to further research.

On the whole, LRCs have gradually found application in the field of distributed storage, effectively reducing repair cost and enhancing system reliability and availability. However, compared to RGCs, there is still room for optimization of the repair bandwidth for LRCs. Furthermore, LRCs constructed based on large finite fields often exhibit higher coding computational complexity, necessitating further research to address this limitation in the future.

3.3 Chapter Summary

Currently, most research studies in the field of storage coding predominantly emphasize theoretical aspects, while practical environments receive comparatively less attention, thereby limiting the applicability of many coding methods. Consequently, this chapter undertakes an in-depth exploration of the optimization of practicality in distributed storage coding from both system and coding levels. At the system level, this chapter offers a comprehensive introduction to distributed storage technologies based on MDS codes, block distribution schemes in actual scenarios, and trade-off strategies between replication and ECs. At the coding level, this chapter highlights practical ECs including BRS codes, RGCs, butterfly codes, clay codes, and practical LRCs.

Discussion Questions

1 In the context of system-level practicality optimization, what trade-off strategies between ECs and data replication have Microsoft and Amazon, respectively, proposed? Briefly explain their core ideas.

Microsoft adopts a data-tiering strategy based on data popularity: newly written and frequently accessed data is temporarily stored in the first group of devices (using data replication), and once its access frequency decreases, it is converted to erasure coding and stored in the second group of low-cost devices. Amazon, on the other hand, sets dual thresholds based on file size and access frequency: if the file size exceeds the threshold and the access frequency is below the threshold, erasure coding is used; otherwise, data replication is employed. The goal of both is to strike a balance between storage cost and access performance by dynamically adjusting the redundancy mechanism.

2 What are the advantages of BRS codes compared with traditional RS codes? How does the encoding and decoding process reduce the computational complexity?

BRS codes simplify computations by replacing finite field operations with binary *XOR* and right shift operations. Traditional RS codes rely on multiplication and division in finite fields, while BRS codes generate encoded blocks using Vandermonde matrices and recover data bit by bit during decoding using the ZigZag algorithm, which only requires *XOR* and shift operations, thus avoiding complex finite field operations and significantly improving the encoding and decoding speed.

3 How does butterfly codes optimize repair bandwidth through binary vector code structure? What is its core encoding and decoding mechanism?

Butterfly codes is a binary vector MSR code with redundancy $n - k = 2$, which generates horizontal parity columns and butterfly parity columns through iterative operations of symmetric binary matrices. During encoding, data is organized into a special iterative matrix, with the horizontal parity columns being the row *XOR* results and the butterfly parity columns being the cross-row iterative *XOR* results. When repairing a single node failure, only half of the data volume needs to be downloaded from the surviving nodes, and the lost data can be recovered using simple *XOR* operations.

References

Arslan, S. and Goker, T., Quantum Corp, 2018. Adaptive erasure codes. U.S. Patent 10,044,374.

Bartík, M., Ubik, S. and Kubalik, P., 2015. LZ4 compression algorithm on FPGA. In 2015 IEEE International Conference on Electronics, Circuits, and Systems (ICECS) (pp. 179–182). IEEE.

Calder, B.G., Gopalan, P.S., Huang, C., Ogus, A.W., Simitci, H. and Yekhanin, S.M., Microsoft Technology Licensing LLC, 2019. Flexible erasure coding with enhanced local protection group structures. U.S. Patent 10,187,083.

Center, I.O.S.T, 2016. Intel intelligent storage acceleration library [online].

Danilov, M. and Buinov, K., EMC IP Holding Co LLC, 2020. Scale-out distributed erasure coding. U.S. Patent 10,880,040.

Danilov, M. and Altaye, Y., EMC IP Holding Co LLC, 2021. Chunk segment recovery via hierarchical erasure coding in a geographically diverse data storage system. U.S. Patent 11,113,146.

Fetterly, D.C., Gopalan, S.P., Huang, C., et al. Microsoft Technology Licensing LLC, 2013. Local erasure codes for data storage. U.S. Patent 9,600,365.

Franklin, P.D., Donlan, B.J. and Theimer, M.M., Amazon Technologies Inc, 2019. Techniques and systems for data segregation in redundancy coded data storage systems. U.S. Patent 10,180,912.

Gad, E.E., Mateescu, R., Blagojevic, F., Guyot, C. and Bandic, Z., 2013. Repair-optimal MDS array codes over GF (2). In 2013 IEEE International Symposium on Information Theory (pp. 887–891). IEEE.

Gopalan, P., Huang, C., Jenkins, B. and Yekhanin, S., 2014. Explicit maximally recoverable codes with locality. IEEE Transactions on Information Theory, 60(9), pp. 5245–5256.

He, G. and Sorenson III, J.C., Amazon Technologies Inc, 2013. Erasure coding and redundant replication. U.S. Patent 8,504,535.

Hou, H., Shum, K.W., Chen, M. and Li, H., 2013. BASIC regenerating code: Binary addition and shift for exact repair. In 2013 IEEE International Symposium on Information Theory (pp. 1621–1625). IEEE.

Huang, C., Simitci, H., Xu, Y., Ogus, A., Calder, B., Gopalan, P., Li, J. and Yekhanin, S., 2012. Erasure coding in windows azure storage. In 2012 USENIX Annual Technical Conference (USENIX ATC 12) (pp. 15–26).

Hussain, S.A. and Narayanamurthy, S., NetApp Inc, 2019. Multiple node repair using high rate minimum storage regeneration erasure code. U.S. Patent 10,452,477.

Jenkins Jr, R.J., Gopalan, P.S., Huang, C., Nightingale, E.B., Shamis, A. and Yekhanin, S., Microsoft Technology Licensing LLC, 2018. Erasure coding of data within a group of storage units based on connection characteristics. U.S. Patent 9,983,959.

Lazier, C.L., Amazon Technologies Inc, 2014. Layered redundancy encoding schemes for data storage. U.S. Patent 8,869,001.

Lazier, C.L., Amazon Technologies Inc, 2020. Durability-based redundancy encoded data storage. U.S. Patent 10,649,845.

Li, H., Huang, X., Feng, J., et al. Peking University Shenzhen Graduate School, 2013. Pollution data recovery method and apparatus for distributed storage data. W.O. Patent 2013131253A1.

Li, H., Hou, H. and Zhu, B., Peking University Shenzhen Graduate School, 2017. Construction of MBR (minimum bandwidth regenerating) codes and a method to repair the storage nodes. U.S. Patent 9,722,637.

Li, H., Huang, X., Hou, H., Zhou, T., Zhu, B., Chen, C. and Zhou, J., SHENZHEN IPTV CO Ltd and Peking University Shenzhen Graduate School, 2018. Data storage method, device and distributed network storage system. U.S. Patent 9,961,142.

Li, Q., Xiang, Q., Wang, Y., Song, H., Wen, R., Yao, W., Dong, Y., Zhao, S., Huang, S., Zhu, Z. and Wang, H., 2023. More than capacity: Performance-oriented evolution of pangu in alibaba. In 21st USENIX Conference on File and Storage Technologies (FAST 23) (pp. 331–346).

Liu, Y., Ding, C. and Tang, C., 2021. Shortened linear codes over finite fields. IEEE Transactions on Information Theory, 67(8), pp. 5119–5132.

Ozzie, R.E., Mehr, J.D., Puri, S., McKelvie, S.J., Calder, B. and Pope, M., Microsoft Corp, 2014. Erasure coded storage aggregation in data centers. U.S. Patent 8,918,478.

Pamies-Juarez, L., Blagojevic, F., Mateescu, R., Gyuot, C., Gad, E.E. and Bandic, Z., 2016. Opening the chrysalis: On the real repair performance of {MSR} codes. In 14th USENIX conference on file and storage technologies (FAST 16) (pp. 81–94).

Plank, J.S. and Greenan, K., 2014. Jerasure: A library in C facilitating erasure coding for storage applications_version 2.0. technical report UT-EECS-14–721. University of Tennessee.

Sathiamoorthy, M., Asteris, M., Papailiopoulos, D., Dimakis, A.G., Vadali, R., Chen, S. and Borthakur, D., 2013. Xoring elephants: Novel erasure codes for big data. arXiv preprint arXiv:1301.3791 (pp. 1–16).

Sipos, M.A., Lucani, D.E., Heide, J., Pedersen, M.V. and Fitzek, F.H., Aalborg Universitet AAU, 2019. Method for file updating and version control for linear erasure coded and network coded storage. U.S. Patent 10,270,468.

Vajha, M., Ramkumar, V., Puranik, B., Kini, G., Lobo, E., Sasidharan, B., Kumar, P.V., Barg, A., Ye, M., Narayanamurthy, S. and Hussain, S., 2018. Clay codes: Moulding {MDS} codes to yield an {MSR} code. In 16th USENIX Conference on File and Storage Technologies (FAST 18) (pp. 139–154).

Wang, Z., Li, W. and Jafarkhani, H., 2023. Systems and methods for distributed storage using storage codes with flexible number of nodes. U.S. Patent Application 17/865,950.

Yanovsky, D. and Miloslavskaya, V.D., Cloud Storage Inc, 2021. Encoding and storage node repairing method for minimum storage regenerating codes for distributed storage systems. U.S. Patent 11,182,247.

Ye, M. and Barg, A., 2017a. Explicit constructions of optimal-access MDS codes with nearly optimal sub-packetization. IEEE Transactions on Information Theory, 63(10), pp. 6307–6317.

Ye, M. and Barg, A., 2017b. Explicit constructions of high-rate MDS array codes with optimal repair bandwidth. IEEE Transactions on Information Theory, 63(4), pp. 2001–2014.

Yekhanin, S., Simitci, H., Ogus, A.W., Li, J., Huang, C., Gopalan, P.S. and Calder, B.G., Microsoft Technology Licensing LLC, 2016. Erasure coding across multiple zones and sub-zones. U.S. Patent 9,244,761.

Zhang, H., DAI, Q., Liu, X., Intel Corporation, 2015. Technologies for adaptive erasure code. W.O. Patent 2017/107095.

Zhang, J., Hou, H., Li, K. and Li, H., 2017. On the implementation of BRS codes in Ceph. In 2017 IEEE International Conference on Big Data (Big Data) (pp. 2676–2681). IEEE.

Zhang, J., Zhu, J. and Hao, B., Shenzhen Huaer Data Technology Co Ltd, 2021. Methods of data concurrent recovery for a distributed storage system and storage medium thereof. U.S. Patent 11,188,404.

4
Optimization for Fault Recovery

In a DSS functioning within a heterogeneous network environment, a multitude of risks exist, encompassing hardware and software malfunctions, virus assaults, and natural calamities, which might induce storage node faults or even damage. To furnish storage solutions characterized by high reliability and availability within such an environment, data redundancy mechanisms are implemented. The mechanism primarily encompasses data replication and erasure codes (ECs): data replication attains rapid recovery by storing multiple copies of files on distinct nodes, yet it presents high storage redundancy and low disk space utilization; conversely, ECs achieve higher data reliability with lower redundancy by partitioning data into multiple data blocks and generating parity blocks, and it also demonstrates stronger robustness and lower maintenance cost when dynamically adjusting network nodes.

Despite the notable advantages that ECs offer in enhancing data reliability, their repair demands a considerable amount of network bandwidth and may consume a significant quantity of computing resources when multiple nodes fail concurrently, which imposes constraints on the system performance for users to access frequently large-scale DSSs. To tackle these issues, this chapter introduces some research on storage failed node repair optimization from the perspectives of ECs and network topology.

4.1 Optimization Based on ECs

ECs can attain high reliability under the circumstances of low redundancy. At present, a series of optimization techniques for ECs have facilitated the extensive application of ECs in DSSs (Li et al. 2023, pp. 331–346; Muralidhar et al. 2014, pp. 383–398; Tang et al. 2020, pp. 787–803), such as the construction optimization of RS codes, the optimization of repair bandwidth and storage overhead of RGCs,

Distributed Storage in Practice, First Edition. Hui Li, Hanxu Hou, and Hong Tan.

the optimization of repair bandwidth and update complexity of array codes, and the local repair optimization of LRCs. These optimization techniques have been elaborated in detail in the previous chapter.

Nevertheless, once the application scenarios extend to large-scale DSSs where multinode faults occur frequently and computing resources are severely limited, the performance of these optimization techniques will be significantly compromised. For instance, the coding process of RS codes is relatively intricate and demands a considerable amount of computing resources. Particularly when dealing with large-scale data, it will incur high computing costs and may cause substantial delays, affecting the real-time performance of the system.

Additionally, most studies on RGCs mainly focus on how to rapidly repair single-node failures. For the repair problem of simultaneous multinode faults, a delayed repair strategy is primarily adopted, that is, the system is repaired when the number of failed nodes reaches a certain threshold. However, how to select an appropriate repair threshold and code rate is related to the experience of system design, which can only achieve suboptimal repair bandwidth for multinode failures. To address the aforementioned issues, in this section, certain coding optimization techniques for multinode failures repair are emphasized and expounded.

4.1.1 Fractional Repetition Codes

In traditional RGCs, the node repair process typically involves a substantial number of linear operations. Helper nodes read specific data blocks from disk for these operations and then transmit the combined data block to the replacement node. This can potentially create a performance bottleneck during system failed node repair.

In order to reduce the complexity of node repair processes, a class of simple RGCs was proposed (Papailiopoulos et al. 2012, pp. 2801–2805). This type of code supports RT. The precise concept of RT was detailed in Chapter 2 and is not reiterated here. The core idea of the simple RGCs is to divide the original file into several equal-sized parts, encode each part by the same MDS code, and then extract one block from each part through *XOR* operations to obtain a parity block. These extracted blocks, along with the generated parity block, form a parity group. Following the encoding process, all blocks, including parity blocks, are uniformly stored in the file system, with blocks from the same parity group being distributed across different nodes.

According to Figure 4.1(a), a file is divided into two parts, each containing two original data blocks and being encoded using an MDS(4,2) code. The resulting

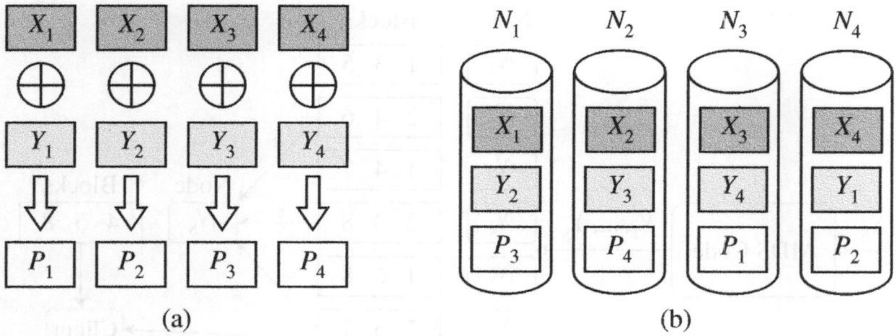

Figure 4.1 Simple regenerating codes.

blocks are labeled as $X_1, \ldots, X_4$ and $Y_1, \ldots, Y_4$, respectively. Subsequently, an *XOR* operation is conducted between X_i and Y_i with the same subscript to generate the corresponding parity block P_i. All blocks stored on the storage nodes are organized in a cyclic arrangement as illustrated in Figure 4.1(b).

Consider a scenario where node N_1 experiences a failure and the lost data can be reconstructed by retrieving the data directly from the remaining nodes. For instance, retrieving P_1 from node N_3 and Y_1 from node N_4, followed by performing an *XOR* operation to reconstruct data block X_1. Similarly, other lost data can be reconstructed using the same approach. It is important to note that while simple RGCs facilitate RT, their repair bandwidth may not be optimal.

There are numerous similar studies. Sung and Gong (2013, pp. 341–345) introduced a vector code construction method based on the ZigZag decoding algorithm (Tamo, Wang and Bruck 2011, pp. 1240–1244), which involves transmitting a portion of stored data and using XOR operations to recover lost data during the repair process. Designs (2014, pp. 1–13) developed RGCs that facilitate exact repair by integrating two ECs during encoding and arranging the resulting blocks according to specific rules. These RGCs support repair by transfer and exhibit favorable storage performance. Additionally, Shum and Hu (2012, pp. 1192–1196) and Rashmi et al. (2009, pp. 1243–1249) proposed RGCs that also support RT under the functional repair model, allowing replacement nodes to store different data from failed nodes. Furthermore, El Rouayheb and Ramchandran (2010, pp. 1510–1517) introduced FRCs, which present significant benefits in node repair. The encoding process of FRCs is divided into two stages:

1) After the original file is encoded using an MDS code, each resulting block is uniformly replicated multiple times before being stored in the file system.
2) The placement of all blocks is determined by a specific internal repetition code.

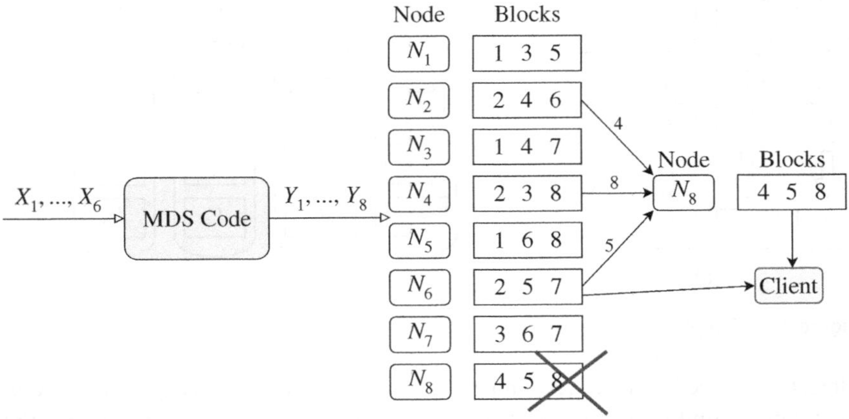

Figure 4.2 A simple example of fractional repetition codes.

For instance, consider an original file comprising six data blocks, denoted as $X_1, \dots, X_6$. Following encoding with an MDS(8,6) code, eight resulting blocks, $Y_1, Y_2, \dots, Y_8$ can be generated. Each block is triplicated and stored on $n = 8$ nodes, as depicted in Figure 4.2. The numbers in the figure denote the subscripts of blocks; for example, the three blocks stored on node N_1 are denoted as Y_1, Y_3, Y_5. In practice, a user connecting to three nodes will receive at least six distinct blocks. If data is downloaded from nodes N_1, N_2, and N_3, seven different blocks can be obtained. When the user connects to nodes N_1, N_3, and N_7, six distinct blocks can be obtained. According to the MDS property, the original file can be reconstructed from that stored on any three nodes. In case of a node failure, the system can retrieve data from other nodes and store it on a replacement node to complete repair.

The general structure of FRCs is illustrated in Figure 4.3. In this structure, an original data file comprises M data blocks, which are encoded using MDS(θ, M) code to produce θ blocks. Subsequently, each block is replicated ρ times and stored individually on n nodes ($N_1, N_2, \dots, N_n$), with the specific placement of all blocks being determined by FRCs. Thus, FRCs can be regarded as an allocation strategy of θ blocks, each replicated ρ times, across n storage nodes; it is essential that the allocation strategy ensures that copies of one block are stored on distinct nodes. In case of node failure, the system retrieves a copy of the lost block from another valid node and stores it on a new node.

FRCs clearly feature a two-layer coding design, with an external MDS code used for data reconstruction, while internal FRCs optimize the efficiency of node fault repair. Given a storage system with n nodes, where each node stores α data blocks. Let the FRC $C = (\Omega, \mathcal{W})$ for this storage system, with the replication multiple ρ,

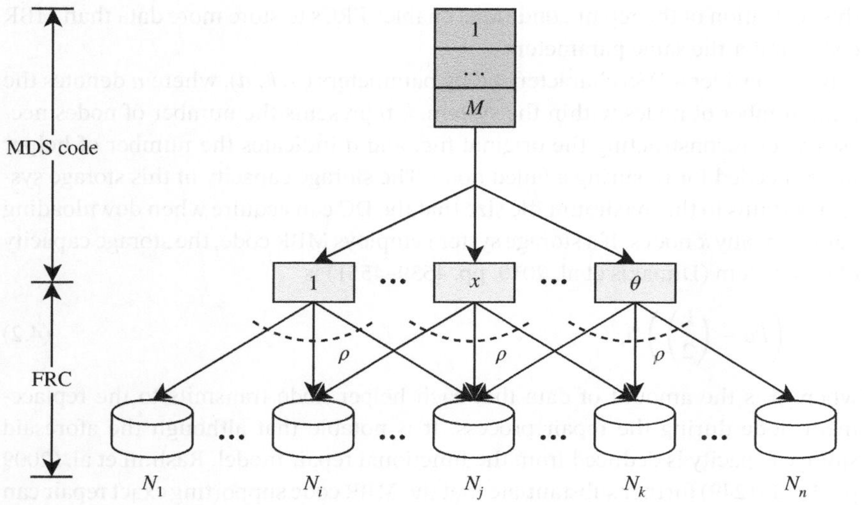

Figure 4.3 The encoding process of fractional repetition codes.

and $\mathcal{W}$ includes n specific sets $\{W_1, W_2, \ldots, W_n\}$, where each element of $\mathcal{W}$ is taken from the set $\Omega = \{1, 2, \ldots, \theta\}$, and simultaneously satisfy the following two conditions:

1) For all $1 \leq i \leq n$, we have $|W_i| = \alpha$.
2) Each block of Ω appears in ρ different W_i.

The elements within the Ω denote the block subscripts encoded by MDS(θ, M). Each W_i within $\mathcal{W}$ corresponds to a storage node, meaning that this node stores the blocks corresponding to the elements within W_i. Given that the cardinality of each W_i is α, each node stores α blocks. C that fulfills all the aforementioned conditions is an FRC with parameters (n, α, θ, ρ), and the parameters satisfy

$$n\alpha = \theta\rho. \tag{4.1}$$

For general RGCs, node repair can be achieved by randomly choosing a specific quantity of nodes from the valid nodes. Nevertheless, for FRCs, the node repair process is table based, and the repair table specifies the available repair alternatives for each failed node. As depicted in Figure 4.2, if node N_8 malfunctions, the system can be restored by downloading data from nodes N_2, N_4, and N_6, but nodes N_1, N_2, and N_3 are incapable of completing the repair. Regarding the reduction of the complexity of the repair process, the expense of establishing and maintaining a node repair table is justified. Although FRCs adopt a table-based repair approach, the repair bandwidth can reach the theoretical minimum and thus can also be regarded as a special category of MBR codes that supports exact repair. Moreover, this relaxation of the repair conditions enables FRCs to store more data than MBR codes under the same parameters.

Now consider a DSS characterized by parameters (n, k, d), where n denotes the total number of nodes within the system, k represents the number of nodes necessary for reconstructing the original file, and d indicates the number of helper nodes needed for repairing a failed node. The storage capacity of this storage system pertains to the maximum file size that the DC can acquire when downloading data from any k nodes. If a storage system employs MBR code, the storage capacity of this system (Dimakis et al. 2010, pp. 4539–4551) is

$$\left(kd - \binom{k}{2}\right)\beta, \tag{4.2}$$

where β is the amount of data that each helper node transmits to the replacement node during the repair process. It is notable that although the aforesaid storage capacity is deduced from the functional repair model, Rashmi et al. (2009 pp. 1243–1249) further substantiate that the MBR code supporting exact repair can also attain the storage capacity in eq. (4.2).

Although FRCs are regarded as a special class of MBR codes, due to the different requirements in the node repair process between the FRCs and MBR codes, the storage capacity in eq. (4.2) is not applicable to FRCs. The concept of supported file size can be used to describe the storage capacity of FRCs. Since the data reconstruction of FRCs is based on external MDS codes, the supported file size refers to the minimum number of different blocks that can be obtained through any k nodes. Given an FRC $C = (\Omega, \mathcal{W})$, denote its supported file size as $M_k(C)$, then there is

$$M_k(C) = \min_{\mathcal{K}} |\cup_{W \in \mathcal{K}} W| = min_{\mathcal{K}} |p \in \Omega : p \in W, W \in \mathcal{K}|, \tag{4.3}$$

where $\mathcal{K} \subset \mathcal{W}$, $|\mathcal{K}| = k$. Under specific circumstances, the supported file size of FRCs can surpass the storage capacity based on the MBR code. This increase in storage stems from the relaxation of repair conditions, such as the utilization of a table-based node repair method.

Since the concept of FRCs was put forward, it has received extensive attention both domestically and internationally due to its remarkable advantages in node repair. Currently, the proposed construction methods mainly include two types: graph theory (Silberstein and Etzion 2015, pp. 4164–4180) and combinatorial designs theory (Olmez and Ramamoorthy 2016, pp. 1565–1591; Park and Kim 2016, p. 441). Porter et al. (2018, pp. 1–10) investigated the design of FRCs that can achieve load balancing in the process of multinode repair, namely, each participating node transmits the same amount of data for repair. In combination with the actual data center environment, Itani et al. (2016, p. 10), based on the repair cost of the storage nodes of FRCs, respectively, considered the scenarios of single-node and multinode repair and designed a genetic algorithm that can reduce the system repair cost.

At present, the research on MDS codes has been relatively mature, and many specific constructions have been proposed. Therefore, the construction difficulty of FRCs lies in the design of internal repetition codes. Ernvall (2012, p. 1201) theoretically proves the necessary conditions satisfied by the parameters for constructing FRCs and indicates that the existing specific codeword construction methods are mainly based on graph theory and combinatorial design theory, which limits the extension of the parameter set of FRCs. Zhu, Li and Li (2017, pp. 26251–26256), Zhu et al. (2014, pp. 660–663), and Zhu, Shum and Li (2019, pp. 150–160) proposed a general fractional repetition (GFR) code. The GFR code is based on a combinatorial structure called a group divisible design, extending the parameter selection of FRCs to a larger range and optimizing the supported file size. In addition, Zhu and Li (2015, pp. 2078–2081) studied on the use of FRC codes in dynamic storage systems and introduce an adaptive FRC that can effectively adapt to system changes. Zhu and Li (2016, pp. 2350–2353) carried out research on the repair locality of nodes in FRCs and implement a class of FRCs with local repair property. These researches are of great significance for guiding the future development direction of FRCs.

4.1.2 Self-repairing Codes

SRCs also leverage the locality property to minimize the number of helper nodes needed, thereby reducing repair bandwidth. However, unlike LRCs, SRCs do not utilize block grouping or construct local parity blocks to maintain local reliability. In general, SRCs possess the following properties:

1) SRCs are capable of downloading partial blocks directly from a subset of all valid blocks, thereby repairing faults by downloading a smaller amount of data than the original data.
2) During the repair process, the number of required blocks is solely determined by the number of lost blocks and is independent of which specific blocks have been lost.

These properties enable SRCs to not only possess low repair bandwidth but also potentially achieve independent and parallel repairs for different faults.

Similar to SRCs, hierarchical codes (HCs) (Duminuco and Biersack 2008, pp. 89–98) possess similar properties. HCs utilize an iterative construction method, starting with small codes and gradually transitioning to larger codes, enabling the download of a smaller data volume for fault repair compared to the original data. However, the blocks in HCs are not homomorphic, meaning that the number of effective blocks required for fault repair in HCs depends not only on the quantity of failed blocks but also on their own characteristics and interconnections.

Oggier and Datta (2011a, pp. 1215–1223) first introduced a method for constructing SRCs based on linearized polynomials, known as homomorphic self-repairing codes (HSRCs).

In an HSRC, the original data M is first uniformly divided into k blocks, denoted as $M = (M_1, \dots, M_k)$, $M_i \in GF(2^{M/k})$. Let a linearized polynomial over $GF(2^{M/k})$ be defined as

$$p(X) = \sum_{i=0}^{k-1} p_i X^{2^i}, \tag{4.4}$$

where $p_i = M_{i+1}$, $i = 0, \dots, k-1$. Subsequently, substituting the n-dimensional vector $(\alpha_1, \dots, \alpha_n)$ from $GF(2^{M/k})$ into $p(X)$ yields a codeword as follows:

$$(p(\alpha_1), \dots, p(\alpha_n)), \tag{4.5}$$

which is necessary to satisfy the condition $k < n \le 2^{M/k} - 1$, and the values of $p(\alpha_i)$ should be stored in node i.

$GF(2^{M/k})$ can be considered as a basis of $GF(2)$, denoted as $B = \{b_1, \dots, b_{M/k}\}$, which contains M/k linearly independent elements. When $n = 2^{M/k} - 1$, α_i can be represented as a linear combination of elements in set B as follows:

$$\alpha_i = \sum_{j=1}^{M/k} \alpha_{ij} b_j, \alpha_{ij} \in GF(2) \Rightarrow p(\alpha_i) = \sum_{j=1}^{M/k} \alpha_{ij} p(b_j), \tag{4.6}$$

where $i = 1, \dots, n$. This implies that a $p(\alpha_i)$ can be expressed in terms of other $p(\alpha_j)$, where $j = 0, \dots, M/k$ and $j \neq i$. In other words, faults can be repaired by utilizing other valid blocks. As a result of the conversion from $GF(2^{M/k})$ to $GF(2)$, the computation operations exclusively involve binary *XOR*s, significantly optimizing the coding complexity of SRCs. In addition, a highly practical class of HSRCs is adopted (Li, Huang and Hou 2013, pp. 1–15), which can ensure that a node failure can be repaired by selecting $(n-1)/2$ pairs of nodes at random from the remaining nodes to serve as helper nodes.

Oggier and Datta (2011b, pp. 30–34) propose a novel type of SRCs based on projective geometry, PSRCs. The coding process of PSRCs only involves *XOR* operations and not polynomial calculations. Additionally, PSRCs no longer require helper nodes to transmit the entire storage data, and only utilizing part of their respective data can also complete repair. However, PSRCs face some practical challenges. They have very high redundancy, which will greatly waste storage resources; the repair degree is 2; repair bandwidth is twice the size of the failed data; and no optimal repair bandwidth is achieved. Hou and Li (2012, pp. 76–81) proposed a practical projective geometric SRC (PPSRC) with a lower repair bandwidth, lower redundancy, and higher performance to address the shortcomings of PSRCs.

4.1.3 RGCs for Multiple Failed Nodes

The optimization of RGCs predominantly centers on a single fault, yet for the repair of $t > 1$ faults, it still demands a considerable amount of bandwidth consumption. Nevertheless, even during the repair of multiple nodes, RGCs still hold substantial potential advantages.

As the first concurrent repair framework for multiple node faults in the DSS, CORE (Li, Lin and Lee 2013, pp. 1–6) not only retains the advantages of ECs but also can conveniently deploy various ECs to mainstream systems (You et al. 2014, pp. 325–338). However, CORE is not optimized for ECs themselves and cannot implement repair optimization for arbitrary multiple node faults. Considering and exploring ECs for multiple failed nodes repair will be more conducive to resolving the current problem of simultaneous faults of multiple nodes.

Compared with the method of repairing one node by one using RGCs, in multiple node faults recovery, Wang et al. (2010, pp. 1–5) propose a multiple-loss flexible repair (MFR) mechanism based on minimum storage, allowing replacement nodes to connect to helper nodes and nodes that have completed the repair to continue the repair, thereby significantly reducing the repair bandwidth consumption. Specifically, the replacement nodes are represented as the sequence $y_1, \dots, y_t$, where y_i can download data from all valid nodes, including those that have been repaired prior to y_i, such as y_j, where $j < i$. Assuming that there are a total of d_i available nodes for y_j, the total repair bandwidth satisfies

$$\sum_{i=1}^{t} \frac{Bd_i}{k(d_i - k + 1)}. \tag{4.7}$$

However, MFR does not efficiently use all replacement nodes, because the subsequently repaired replacement nodes do not contribute to the previously repaired nodes. For example, y_j cannot download data from y_i where $i > j$.

A more efficient approach is cooperative regenerating codes (CooRGCs) (Lee and Lee 2017, pp. 7267–7282; Shum and Hu 2013, pp. 7229–7258), which minimizes the repair traffic through the exchange of information among t repair nodes after downloading data from helper nodes. The repair bandwidth of CooRGCs can be categorized into two phases. In the first phase, each replacement node downloads β_1 symbols from d helper nodes. In the second phase, each replacement node exchanges β_2 symbols, respectively, with each of the other $t - 1$ nodes. Similar to RGCs, CooRGCs likewise possess two extreme points, which correspond to the minimum storage cooperative regenerating codes (MSCooRGCs) and the minimum bandwidth cooperative regenerating codes (MBCooRGCs), as follows:

$$(\alpha_{\mathrm{MSCooRGC}}, \gamma_{\mathrm{MSCooRGC}}) = \left(\frac{M}{k}, \frac{Mt(d+t-1)}{k(d-k+t)}\right), \tag{4.8}$$

$$(\alpha_{\mathrm{MBCooRGC}}, \gamma_{\mathrm{MBCooRGC}}) = \left(\frac{M(2d+t-1)}{k(2d+t-k)}, \frac{Mt(2d+t-1)}{k(2d+t-k)}\right). \tag{4.9}$$

By employing the classic constructions of RGCs, Li and Li (2014, pp. 316–324) put forward the exact-repair MBCooRGCs and exact-repair MSCooRGCs based on the PM. Chen and Shum (2013, pp. 1441–1445) presented the MSCooRGCs based on the IA technology. Nevertheless, CooRGCs also possess deficiencies:

1) Each node is required to communicate with d helper nodes and $t-1$ other replacement nodes. If the information channel between two nodes is regarded as a link, logically, the system is in need of maintaining a total of $td + t(t-1)/2$ links.
2) Before each replacement node acquires all symbols from d helper nodes, the data dispatched to other replacement nodes cannot be regenerated. Meanwhile, the data of a replacement node cannot be regenerated until it receives all the data from the other $t-1$ replacement nodes. This imposes extremely high requirements on synchronism and consistency.
3) A minor error during the repair of CooRGCs will result in the failure of the entire repair process.
4) Owing to the complex repair process of CooRGCs and their high sensitivity to parameters, only a few CooRGCs with a few specific parameters exist.

CooRGCs can be adopted in regular and robust distributed storage networks. However, these drawbacks complicate management and weaken its optimization of repair bandwidth in a realistic scenario. Therefore, more efficient and practical codes are required, and concurrent regenerating codes (ConRGCs) (Zhang et al. 2017, pp. 362–369) constitute a superior option. Similar to CooRGCs, ConRGCs also possess two extreme points, namely, minimum bandwidth concurrent regenerating codes (MBConRGCs) and minimum storage concurrent regenerating codes (MSConRGCs). The storage overhead and repair bandwidth of these two extreme points, respectively, satisfy

$$(\alpha_{\mathrm{MBConRGC}}, \gamma_{\mathrm{MBConRGC}}) = \left(\frac{2Md}{k(2d-k+t)}, \frac{2Mtd}{k(2d-k+t)}\right) \tag{4.10}$$

and

$$(\alpha_{\mathrm{MSConRGC}}, \gamma_{\mathrm{MSConRGC}}) = \left(\frac{M}{k}, \frac{Mtd}{k(d-k+t)}\right), \tag{4.11}$$

where the parameters M, k, d, and t, respectively, represent the size of the original data, the number of system nodes, the number of helper nodes, and the number of failed nodes. Comparing eqs. (4.8) and (4.9), it can be discovered that ConRGCs attain smaller repair bandwidths at both extreme points.

The structure (Zhang et al. 2017, pp. 362–369) of ConRGCs is simpler than that of CooRGCs and can be directly extended from the IA construction of MSR. Meanwhile, ConRGCs are a kind of parameter-adaptive RGCs with relatively lenient requirements for parameters. Furthermore, aside from guaranteeing the reliability of data, DSSs also need to adapt storage parameters in accordance with variations in indicators such as workload and data access frequency. CooRGCs can merely fulfill specific parameters, thus being less practical in terms of parameter adjustment. Nevertheless, Zhang et al. (2017, pp. 362–369) demonstrate that ConRGCs can simply accomplish the expansion from (n, k) to $(n + s, k)$. Specifically, it merely needs to consider the newly added s nodes as the replacement nodes and carry out the repair process. The minimum bandwidth consumed in this process is

$$\sum_{i=1}^{d_s} h_i = \frac{Bs(d_s - s + 1)}{k(d_s - k + 1)}, \tag{4.12}$$

where d_s represents the number of helper nodes, and h_i denotes data transfer bandwidth of the i-th helper node, fulfilling the conditions that $0 < h_i \leq s$, $k \leq d_s \leq n$, and $1 \leq s \leq k$. This enables DSSs to adjust storage parameters more flexibly and thereby makes ConRGC a type of multiple node repair code applicable to distributed heterogeneous systems.

4.2 Optimization Based on Network Topology

Although numerous efficient storage codes currently exist that can independently reduce storage redundancy and optimize repair bandwidth, during the repair process, these codes fail to comprehensively take into account the network topology, thereby leading to the wastage of computing resources and network bandwidth.

Essentially, from the perspective of network topology, there remains a vast space for optimization in node repair within storage coding. This section incorporates the network topology and elaborates on the repair models optimized for single-node and multinode failure repairs.

4.2.1 Repair Tree: Fast Repair for Single Node

Most storage codes typically concentrate merely on the efficiency of the coding algorithm, while neglecting the network topology for repairing. Nevertheless, in reality, the network topology is of paramount importance for the effective operation of storage codes.

The actual storage system is typically deployed on a considerable number of low-cost servers within the network via routers or switches. In this system, $n = k + r$ blocks are distributed across distinct storage nodes. When a fault emerges, the conventional repair procedure involves the replacement node collecting k blocks from other valid servers, computing the corresponding decoding matrix, decoding the original file, and subsequently regenerating the lost data based on the encoding vector corresponding to the failed node. Ultimately, only the repaired data blocks are retained, and irrelevant helper data is discarded. In such circumstances, the overheads of computing resources and network traffic during the repair process are substantial. From the example presented in Figure 4.4, it is observable that for the repair of h_4, the replacement node h'_4 acquires data from h_1, h_2, and h_3, thereby occupying the bandwidth of routers R_3, R_4, and R_6 three times that of the repair data and the bandwidth of R_2 twice that of the repair data.

The hierarchical architecture of the DSS dictates that bandwidth or I/O resources are more valuable at the service layer as they handle a greater number of transactions. This implies that during the repair process, it is highly essential to minimize the associated resource overhead of routers or switches.

Next, a straightforward example is employed to elaborate on the approach of reducing the repair cost. First, logically, the network structure in Figure 4.4 is

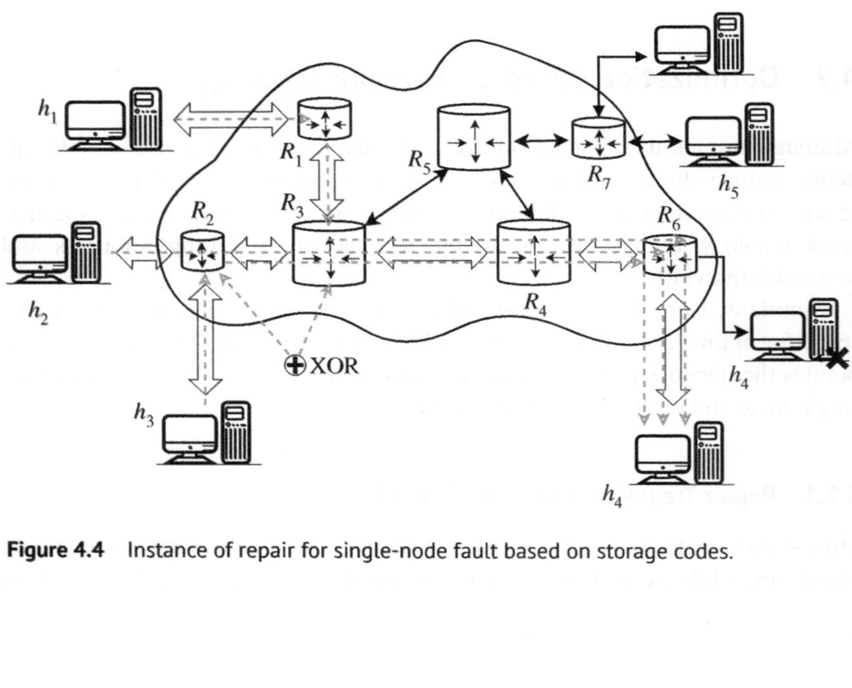

Figure 4.4 Instance of repair for single-node fault based on storage codes.

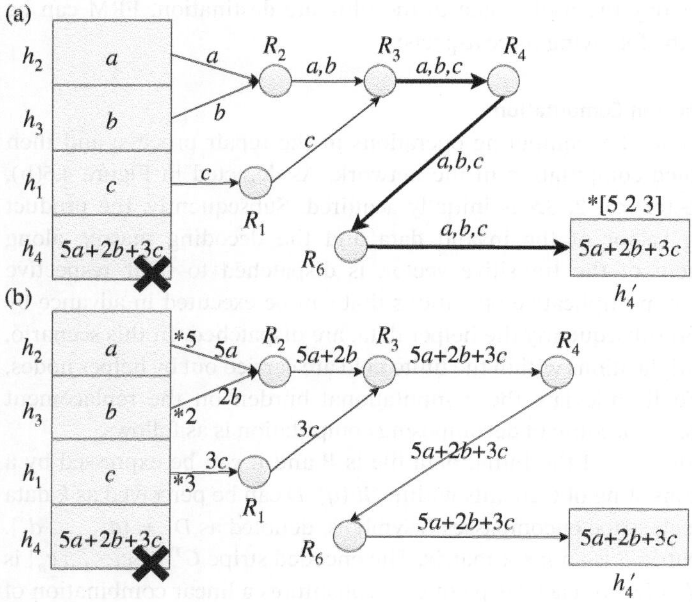

Figure 4.5 Repair information flow graphs (a) and (b).

mapped onto the two information flow graphs (a) and (b) in Figure 4.5. Graph (a) shows that to recover the lost data $\{5a + 2b + 3c\}$ from $\{a, b, c\}$, the traditional routers $\{R_3, R_4, R_6\}$ need to suffer network traffic three times that of the repair data composed of three data blocks $\{a, b, c\}$. However, in the graph (b), after receiving the relevant operation data $\{5a, 2b, 3c\}$ sent by the helper nodes $\{h_2, h_3, h_1\}$, the computational routers $\{R_2, R_3\}$ perform additional operations and then make the network traffic in the links $R_2 - R_3$ and $R_3 - h'_4$ reach the minimum and be the same as the size of the repair data, while the computational consumption of h'_4 also reaches the minimum.

Building upon the notion of the aforementioned examples, Zhang, Li and Li (2016, pp. 1728–1739) put forward a fast repair mechanism (FRM) for single-node faults by integrating the network topology structure into the node repair process. With reference to linear network coding (Li, Yeung and Cai 2003, pp. 371–381), FRM incorporates computational network nodes to mitigate network traffic. The disparity between FRM and linear network coding lies in that network coding conveys sufficient information entropy to the replacement node for decoding the original data without discarding any information, whereas FRM compresses the redundant data through the computation of intermediate nodes and transmits merely the useful data to the ultimate destination. FRM can be categorized into the following three aspects:

4.2.1.1 Decomposing Computation

Decompose the complex computing operations in the repair process, and then perform distributed computation in the network. As depicted in Figure 4.5(b), the transitive vector <5, 2, 3> is initially acquired. Subsequently, the product of the encoding vector of the invalid data and the decoding matrix, along with each element of the transitive vector, is dispatched to their respective helper nodes. The multiplicative operations that can be executed in advance by helper nodes, and subsequently the helper data, are dispatched. In this scenario, the intricate multiplications within the finite field are carried out by helper nodes, which can markedly alleviate the computational burden on the replacement node. The detailed procedure of decomposing computation is as follows:

Assume that the size of the initial data file is B and it can be expressed by a $k * L$ matrix D consisting of elements within $GF(q)$. D can be perceived as k data stripes, where each stripe encompasses L symbols, denoted as $D^T = \{d_1, \dots, d_k\}$. The encoding matrix P is an $n * k$ matrix. The encoded stripe $C^T = \{c_1, \dots, c_n\}$ is derived by $C = P * D$. For each stripe in C, it constitutes a linear combination of the original k data stripes. Typically, P comprises a $k * k$ identity matrix and an $(n - k) * k$ Vandermonde matrix or Cauchy matrix M, and $P^T = \begin{bmatrix} I & M \end{bmatrix}$. Denote the i-th row of P as a k-dimensional vector $\vec{p_i}$, then $\boldsymbol{P}^T = \{\vec{p_1}, \dots, \vec{p_n}\}$. In the stripe c_i, the coefficient f_{ij} of d_j is the j-th element of $\vec{p_i}$, and thus it can be derived that

$$c_i = \vec{p_i} * D = \sum_{j=1}^{k} f_{ij} d_j. \tag{4.13}$$

Suppose c_i is lost. Select any k valid nodes, say $s_1, \dots, s_k$, to acquire the $k * k$ submatrix H from P, where $H^T = \{\vec{p_{s_1}}, \dots, \vec{p_{s_k}}\}$, and compute the inverse matrix of H, H^{-1}. Once the transitive data $C^T = \{c_{s_1}, \dots, c_{s_k}\}$ of the helper nodes is obtained, the original data matrix D is

$$H^{-1} * C = \begin{bmatrix} f_{s_1 1} & f_{s_1 2} & \cdots f_{s_1 k} \\ f_{s_2 1} & f_{s_2 2} & \cdots f_{s_2 k} \\ \vdots & \ddots & \vdots \\ f_{s_k 1} & f_{s_k 2} & \cdots f_{s_k k} \end{bmatrix}^{-1} \begin{bmatrix} c_{s_1} \\ c_{s_2} \\ \vdots \\ c_{s_k} \end{bmatrix}. \tag{4.14}$$

The failed data is restored using D through eq. (4.13). By carefully observing eqs. (4.13) and (4.14), we can first calculate $\vec{p_i} * H^{-1}$ and then the linear combination of C. Thus, the transitive vector can be obtained as

$$\vec{t_i} = p_i * H^{-1} = \langle t_{i1} t_{i2} \dots t_{ik} \rangle. \tag{4.15}$$

Subsequently, the lost data is restored by

$$c_i = \vec{t_i} * C = \sum_{j=1}^{k} t_{ij} c_{s_j}. \tag{4.16}$$

This facilitates the distribution of $t_{ij}c_{s_j}$ among k helper nodes for distributed computation. Zhang, Li and Li (2016, pp. 1728–1739) compared the performance of this method and the Cauchy RS code (Plank and Xu 2006, pp. 173–180). Even though the total number of *XOR* operations is identical in both schemes, the decomposed computation conspicuously enhances the repair speed, and the computational overhead of the replacement node can be negligible.

4.2.1.2 Repair Model

It can be known from (1) that the replacement node will send t_{ij} to the helper node s_j. The s_j calculates $u_{is_j} = t_{ij}c_{s_j}$ and sends the result u_{is_j}. Eventually, the replacement node only needs to calculate the sum of $\{u_{is_j}, \ldots, u_{ks_j}\}$ and restore the lost data. Therefore, the helper nodes serving as the terminal servers share the pressure of the multiplication in the finite field, simplifying the repair process.

Suppose there are computational intermediate nodes. Then the repair bandwidth can be reduced by simple network coding. Computational intermediate nodes have the compute-and-forward function, rather than being limited to the store-and-forward. That is to say, if there are computational intermediate nodes between the helper nodes and the replacement node, and two or more data streams pass through the same computational intermediate node simultaneously, then the *XOR* or addition operations can be performed on these data, and finally the result can be sent to reduce the bandwidth. Therefore, a single repair process can be regarded as an n-to-1 network communication problem, similar to the inverse process of multicast. This repair model can be represented as an information flow graph.

Now consider an information flow graph $G(V, E)$, where the edge set E represents the information propagation path, and the vertex set V is divided into three parts: U, M, and T, denoting the helper nodes set, the computational intermediate nodes set, and the replacement node, respectively. Among them, $V = U \cup M \cup T$, $U = \{u_1, \ldots, u_k\}$, $M = \{m_1, \ldots, m_h\}$, $T = \{t\}$, and $0 \leq h \leq k - 1$. This is because the maximum number of intermediate nodes involved in the computation is $k - 1$ or U is directly connected to T. Hence, G is a tree with T as the root, U as the leaves, and M as the intermediate nodes, which is termed a repair tree. The out-degree and in-degree of node X in graph G, namely, $out(X)$ and $in(X)$, possess the following properties:

$$\forall i \in \{1, \ldots, k\}, \quad out(u_i) = 1, \quad in(u_i) = 0.$$

$$\forall i \in \{1, \ldots, h\}, \quad in(m_i) \geq 2, \quad out(m_i) = 1, \quad in(t) + \sum_{i=1}^{h} in(m_i) = k + h.$$

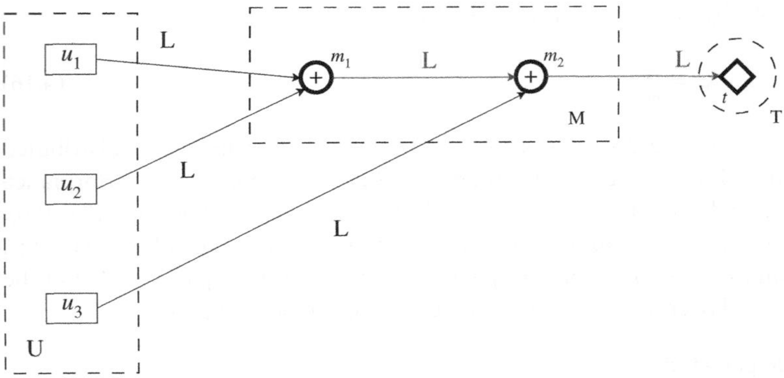

Figure 4.6 Simple repair tree model.

Property (b) suggests that if a node X exists in M and $in(X) = 1$, then X can be absorbed by its neighboring nodes. Only nodes with an in-degree greater than 2 are capable of performing XOR and addition operations. Figure 4.6 represents the abstract model of Figure 4.5(b).

Let the height of the repair tree be $\Gamma(G)$. If $\Gamma(G) > 2$, M can be divided into $\Gamma(G) - 2$ disjoint sets $S_1, \ldots, S_{\Gamma(G)-2}$ to define the flow stages from U to T, where $S_i = \{m_{i_1}, \ldots, m_{i_z}\}$ and $\sum_{i=1}^{\Gamma(G)-2} |S_i| = h$. The in-degree and out-degree of flow stage i are, respectively, in $(S_i) = \sum_{y=1}^{z} in(m_{i_y})$ and $out(S_i) = \sum_{y=1}^{z} out(m_{i_y})$. Let $\delta(S_i)$ be the number of leaf nodes connected to stage S_i. Define $\Phi(S_i)$ as the bandwidth saved at stage S_i. For simplicity, ignore the bandwidth unit and set it as the number of saved flows. Then, compared to the previous stage S_{i-1}, the bandwidth saved at stage S_i is $\Phi(S_i) = in(S_i) - out(S_i) + \Phi(S_{i-1})$. More generally, the saved network bandwidth between stage S_i and stage $S_{i+\Delta}$ is shown in eq. (4.17):

$$\Phi(S_i, S_{i+\Delta}) = in(S_i) - out(S_{i+\Delta}) + \sum_{j=i+1}^{i+\Delta} \delta(S_j). \tag{4.17}$$

In certain extreme circumstances, as depicted in Figure 4.7(a), the minimum saved network bandwidth amounts to 0, where all data is transmitted to the replacement node; as presented in Figure 4.7(b), the maximum bandwidth is $k - 1$, and the repaired data is directly conveyed to the replacement node.

Eq. (4.17) reveals that the bandwidth saved in the lower stage can be allocated to the higher stage. In these two stages, the position of the leaves holds a more significant role than the internal structure. Hence, if the calculation commences at a location further from the replacement node, network bandwidth resources will be conserved on the remaining data path. This is termed the Gauss property

Figure 4.7 Cases of extreme circumstances in repair tree.

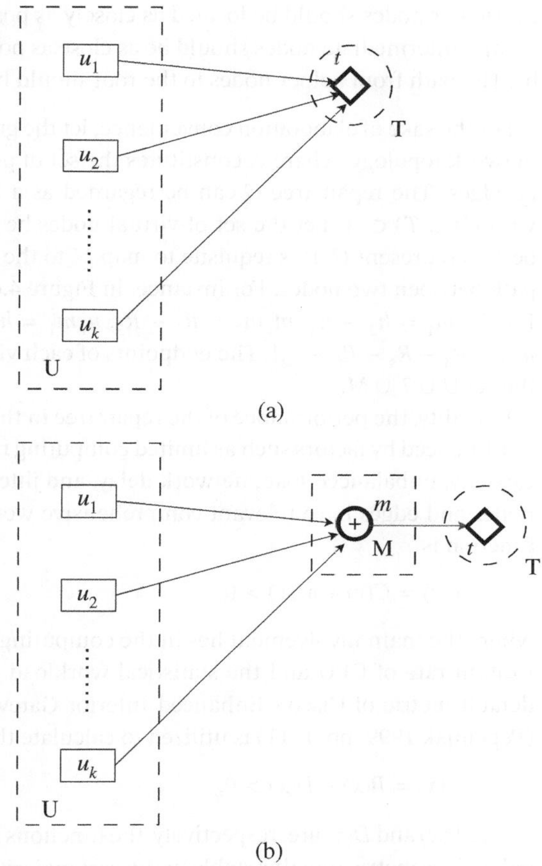

(Kamberaj and Kamberaj 2022, pp. 23–45) of the repair tree. This property can be utilized to generate repair trees from real networks.

4.2.1.3 Construction of Repair Tree

Repair tree depends on the network topology and saves repair traffic through the calculation of computational intermediate nodes, which indicates that it needs to be constructed when the terminal nodes $U \cup T$ are known. When $k \geq 3$, there exist multiple structures under different quantities of intermediate nodes. Even for the same number of intermediate nodes, there are heterogeneous trees. In this case, to construct an explicit repair tree, the following principle is proposed (Zhang, Li and Li 2016, pp. 1728–1739):

a) Helper nodes should be located as closely as possible to the lower flow stages, and intermediate nodes should be as close as possible to the helper nodes.
b) The path from helper nodes to the root should be as short as possible.

For the sake of elaboration convenience, let the graph $\Omega(\Lambda, \Xi)$ be the underlying network topology, where Λ constitutes the set of points and Ξ constitutes the set of edges. The repair tree G can be regarded as a logical graph derived from Ω, with $(U \cup T) \subset A$. Let the set of virtual nodes be M and the set of virtual links be E to represent G. It is requisite to map M to the actual nodes and E to a single path between two nodes. For instance, in Figure 4.6, $M = \{m_1 = R_2, m_2 = R_3\}$ and $\text{E} = \{u_1m_1 = h_2 - R_2, m_1m_2 = R_2 - R_3, u_2m_1 = h_3 - R_2, u_3m_2 = h_1 - R_1 - R_3, m_2t = R_3 - R_4 - R_6 - h_4'\}$. The endpoints of each virtual link must be elements of the set $U \cup T \cup M$.

In reality, the performance of the repair tree in the underlying physical network is influenced by factors such as limited computing resources, restricted bandwidth capacity, unbalanced load, network delay, and jitter. Based on these factors, both nodes and edges have relevant comprehensive weights. For node $v \in \Lambda$, the cost function is

$$\nu(v) = C(v) + M(v) > 0, \tag{4.18}$$

where the main involvement lies in the computing resource $C(v)$, such as the utilization rate of CPU and the statistical workload $M(v)$. For the edge $x \in \Xi$, the default metric of Cisco's Enhanced Interior Gateway Routing Protocol (EIGRP) (Pepelnjak 1999, pp. 1–11) is utilized to calculate the cost, presented as

$$\mu(x) = B(x) + D(x) > 0, \tag{4.19}$$

where $B(x)$ and $D(x)$ are, respectively, the functions associated with bandwidth and delay. This metric remains stable in the vast majority of networks and is applicable to switch-based clusters. For a virtual link $e \in E$, the cost function $\mu(e) = \sum \mu(x_i)$, where x_i represents an edge that constitutes the virtual link e. Hence, given $U \cup T$ in the graph $\Omega(\Lambda, \Xi)$, if the subsequent eq. (4.20) and (4.21) attain the minimum value, the repair tree G is optimal, as follows:

$$\nu(\text{G}) = \sum_{v \in (M \cup U \cup T)} \nu(v), \tag{4.20}$$

$$\mu(\text{G}) = \sum_{e \in \text{E}} \mu(e), \tag{4.21}$$

These two equations imply that the flow from helper nodes to the root is required to pass through the nodes and links with the minimum cost. Evidently, this constitutes a multiobjective optimization problem that is nearly unsolvable. Similar to traditional network issues, Zhang, Li and Li (2016, pp. 1728–1739) consider the cost of nodes as a constant identity and transfer it to the links. Subsequently, only the cost on the edges is taken into account. The cost of link x is defined as

$$w(x) = \mu(x) + \lambda_1 \nu(s^x) + \lambda_2 \nu(t^x), \tag{4.22}$$

where s^x and t^x represent the two terminal nodes of link x, while λ_1 and λ_2 are preset fixed parameters.

The repair tree bears a resemblance to the inverse process of the multicast tree. However, in the multicast tree, the data on each link is a replica of the source information, whereas the data in the repair tree may undergo changes after aggregation at the intermediate nodes. Consequently, the repair tree cannot be straightforwardly constructed by mimicking the multicast. Nevertheless, upon reviewing the multicast tree, Zhang, Li and Li (2016, pp. 1728–1739) discovered that the attributes of the source tree and the shared tree can be utilized for constructing the repair tree. The source tree, also referred to as the shortest-path tree (SPT), is a spanning tree featuring the shortest path from the root to each leaf. Meanwhile, the shared tree has a common root for all multicast groups, known as the rendezvous point. Traffic is forwarded downward from the shared tree and the rendezvous point to reach each receiver.

For the optimal repair tree G, the objective is to identify the minimized $w(G) = \sum_{x \in G} w(x)$, analogous to minimizing the multicast shared tree, which can be considered as the Steiner tree problem. That is to say, given $N = U \cup T$, the aim is to connect all nodes in N via edges with the minimum total cost, such that any two points can be directly connected through edges or interconnected through other points and edges. In fact, Zhang, Li and Li (2016, pp. 1728–1739) utilized the Dijkstra algorithm to successively search for the shortest path, which can provide near-optimal repairs for each $U \cup T$. However, this method focuses only on optimizing the repair of a single failed node and has not yet considered the situation of simultaneous faults in multiple nodes. Moreover, although the Dijkstra algorithm can achieve the shortest path, the complexity still has room for optimization and it does not have the characteristic of adapting to changes in the network situation. In the future, combining with AI to find the optimal repair tree might be a potential research direction.

4.2.2 Tree-Structured Repair Scheme for Multiple Nodes

Network topology exerts a considerable influence on the repair performance of failed nodes in DSS. Qin and Li (2018, pp. 102–109) endeavor to identify the optimal repair cost of a network topology and investigate the influence of diverse network topologies on the repair. Sipos et al. (2018, pp. 1404–1417) put forward a general framework for determining the optimal repair path in a dynamic network topology. You et al. (2014, pp. 325–338) and Xia et al. (2020, pp. 4296–4307) explore special network topologies to enhance the repair efficiency. Nevertheless, the aforementioned studies regarding network topology do not undertake repair optimization for the situation of multiple failed nodes, nor do they propose explicit strategies for multinode repair.

The actual DSS typically consists of a vast number of storage nodes, and multiple nodes frequently fail simultaneously. Frequent and rapid repairs demand a considerable amount of bandwidth resources, thereby influencing the overall performance. Currently, to address this issue, on the one hand, it is requisite to deploy storage codes with substantial parameter values in DSS to fulfill the actual large-scale storage demands; on the other hand, it is necessary to adopt a delay repair strategy to avoid certain unnecessary instantaneous repairs, thereby mitigating the negative impacts brought about by frequent repairs.

Fountain codes (FCs) constitute a category of near-MDS ECs characterized by low computational complexity and rate adaptability (MacKay 2005, pp. 1062–1068). Notably, the longer the codeword, the superior the performance of FCs. Hence, when it is requisite to store large-scale data, FCs can attain more favorable performance than other ECs in enhancing data reliability. Moreover, Luby Transform (LT) codes are a pragmatic type of FCs and are currently extensively employed in data storage (Raouf et al. 2020, p. 101172; Ye et al. 2015, pp. 1–9).

The core concept of delayed repair lies in initiating data repair solely when the number of storage node failures surpasses a threshold, thereby reducing the repair frequency and bandwidth. Currently, Gu et al. (2019, pp. 24179–24191) and Luby et al. (2019, pp. 1–49) have explored the delayed repair for diverse characteristics of DSS, primarily concentrating on determining the appropriate threshold in heterogeneous storage systems to attain the optimal communication overhead during the repair process.

Nevertheless, whether it is the adoption of storage codes applicable to large-scale data or the efficient utilization of delay repair strategy, the exploitation of the network topology of the DSS to optimize the repair process of multiple failed nodes has been overlooked.

Zhou et al. (2021, pp. 21843–21858) integrated the aforementioned diverse studies and proposed an optimal tree-structured repair scheme for multiple failed nodes, hereinafter referred to as tree-structured repair. Tree-structured repair possesses the following characteristics:

1) In large-scale DSS, LT codes with more extensive deployment parameters are utilized to attain the reliability of data storage.
2) For the centralized repair model, the helper data is transmitted to all replacement nodes through the method of network broadcasting.
3) Integrate the delay repair with the network topology structure and introduce a metric named data recovery cost to evaluate the multinode repair

efficiency. The data recovery cost is calculated utilizing the transmitted data and the weight of the network link, and the optimal repair bound is derived with the aim of minimizing the average data recovery cost.

The aforementioned characteristics empower the tree-structure repair to effectively address repair challenges in large-scale data storage with concurrent faults of multiple nodes. Subsequently, the tree-structure repair is elaborated in detail.

4.2.2.1 Preliminaries

In this part, some necessary background knowledge will be introduced, which is the basis of tree-structure repair, including the system model and related definitions.

System Model Zhou et al. (2021, pp. 21843–21858) take into account the network topology among storage nodes to establish a centralized repair model (Ye and Barg 2018, pp. 1639–1656; Zorgui and Wang 2019, pp. 4180–4206), namely, tree-structure repair model. In this model, data reconstruction is accomplished at the leader nodes; that is, the leader node downloads adequate data blocks from the helper nodes and reconstructs the original data file. Subsequently, the leader node transmits the repaired data blocks to each replacement node via broadcasting. Figure 4.8 shows such a simple example. V_{a_0} represents the leader node, V_{n_1}, V_{n_2}, and V_{n_3} represent the replacement nodes, and other nodes represent the helper nodes. Besides, the solid lines represent the selected network links for data transmission.

In this repair model, the leader node is considered the key node, accountable for the reconstruction and allocation of the repaired data blocks; the helper nodes offer adequate helper data for the leader node; the replacement nodes are deemed as the root nodes of the repair model. Under these circumstances, the repair model can be regarded as an n-to-1 model, signifying that n independent data streams

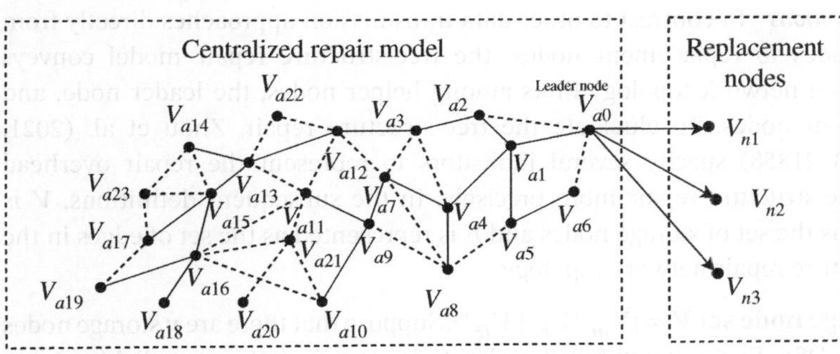

Figure 4.8 Centralized communication model.

from the branches converge at the leader node, and the leader node can eventually transfer the repaired data to the replacement nodes. To enhance the repair performance of the repair model, the following three conditions need to be fulfilled as much as possible:

i) Helper nodes are expected to be located as closely as feasible to the leader node.
ii) The leader node is supposed to be in proximity to both the helper nodes and the replacement nodes.
iii) The overall length of the path from the helper nodes to the replacement nodes should be minimized to the greatest extent possible.

To conduct a more comprehensive analysis of the repair strategy, Zhou et al. (2021, pp. 21843–21858) define a 2D continuous time discrete stochastic process $\{n_a(t), n_f(t)\}$ to signify the system state, where $n_a(t) = \theta, \theta \in \{n - m, \dots, n\}$, representing the quantity of valid nodes at time t; $n_f(t) = \varrho, \varrho \in \{0, 1, 2, \dots, m\}$, indicating the number of failed nodes at time t, and m denoting the number of failed nodes necessary to trigger the repair.

Meanwhile, in the system model, when simulating the storage node faults, it adheres to the Poisson process. The lifetime of the valid nodes in the system can be characterized by an exponential distribution random variable with parameter $\theta\lambda$ to denote the expected survival rate of the nodes. The probability density function (PDF) of the survival time T_θ is

$$f_{T_\theta}(t) = \theta\lambda \cdot e^{-\theta\lambda t}, \quad \theta\lambda \geq 0, \quad t \geq 0. \tag{4.23}$$

Similarly, the node repair time T_ϱ can also be modeled as a random variable of exponential distribution with parameter μ. And the PDF of T_ϱ is

$$f_{T_\varrho}(t) = \mu \cdot e^{-\mu t}, \quad \mu \geq 0, \quad t \geq 0, \tag{4.24}$$

where it is postulated that the repair process is carried out in parallel on different nodes with the identical repair rate μ.

Some Definitions In contrast to other data transmission approaches directly from helper nodes to replacement nodes, the tree-structure repair model conveys data via the network topology links among helper nodes, the leader node, and replacement nodes. To elucidate the tree-structure repair, Zhou et al. (2021, pp. 21843–21858) specify several indicators to represent the repair overhead of the tree-structure repair more precisely. In the subsequent definitions, V is depicted as the set of storage nodes and E is represented as the set of edges in the tree-structure repair network topology.

i) **Storage node set $V = \{V_{a\eta} | V_{n\xi} | V_{f\xi}\}$**: Suppose that there are n storage nodes in the DSS. Excluding m failed nodes, there remain $(n - m)$ available nodes. $V_{a\eta}$ denotes the available nodes, where $\eta = 1, 2, \dots, n - m - 1$. The replacement nodes are indicated by $V_{n\xi}$, and the failed nodes are represented by $V_{f\xi}$, where $\xi = 1, 2, \dots, m$. Node V_{a0} represents the leader node in the tree-structure repair.

ii) **The edge set E between storage nodes is $E = \{(V_{ai}, V_{aj}) | i, j = 0, 1, 2, \dots, n - m - 1\}$:** (V_{ai}, V_{aj}) represents the edge between node V_{ai} and node V_{aj}. Additionally, $(V_{a0}, V_{n\xi})$ represents the edge between the leader node and the replacement nodes, where $\xi = 1, 2, \dots, m$.

iii) **The link weights $W(V_{ai}, V_{aj})$ and $W(V_{a0}, V_{n\xi})$ between storage nodes:** $W(V_{ai}, V_{aj})$ represents the link weight value between available nodes, where $i, j = 0, 1, 2, \dots, n - m - 1$. $W(V_{a0}, V_{n\xi})$ represents the link weight value between the leader node and replacement nodes, where $\xi = 1, 2, \dots, m$. Meanwhile, in this repair model, it is assumed that the network distance between two storage nodes is not always equal, which means that the link weight values are not always the same.

iv) **The data repair cost $c(m)$:** It is characterized as the total of the products of the quantity of data transmitted and the corresponding link weights. This implies that the greater the number of network links through which the data traverses, the more network resources it occupies. Hence, in the tree-structure repair, $c(m)$ can precisely mirror the efficiency of repairing failed nodes.

v) **The average data repair cost $r_c(m)$:** $r_c(m)$ is characterized as the data repair cost per unit time. Given that the system can only commence the repair operation when the number of failed nodes attains the threshold m, this system can be deemed as an independent distributed system with a repair process every T seconds, where T is a random variable signifying the time interval between two repairs.

4.2.2.2 Modeling and Optimization of Tree-Structure Repair

Consistent with the aforementioned, let m denote the number of failed nodes in the DSS, and the number of available nodes is represented as $n - m$. In this section, initially, it is essential to contemplate the network topology of the storage nodes and ascertain the optimal repair threshold m^* to minimize $r_c(m)$.

The tree-structure repair consists of replacement nodes, leader nodes, and helper nodes and employs a centralized communication pattern. According to the given definition above, the tree-structure repair can be represented by $T_{tree} = \{V', E'\}$, where $V' = \{V_{a\eta}, V_{n\xi} | \eta = 0, 1, 2, \dots, n - m - 1, \xi = 1, 2, \dots, m\}$ represents the set of leader nodes, helper nodes, and replacement nodes; $E' = \{(V_{ai}, V_{aj})', (V_{a0}, V_{n\xi})' | i, j = 0, 1, 2, \dots, n - m - 1, \xi = 1, 2, \dots, m\}$ represents the edge set of the tree structure repair model, and E' should satisfy

$$(V_{ai}, V_{aj})' = \begin{cases} 1, & \text{if } (V_{ai}, V_{aj})' \in T_{\text{tree}} \\ 0, & \text{otherwise} \end{cases} \tag{4.25}$$

and

$$\sum_{(V_{ai},V_{aj})'\in E'} ((V_{ai}, V_{aj})') = (1+\varepsilon)k,\ \varepsilon > 0. \tag{4.26}$$

Since large LT codes are a near-MDS code, the total number of nodes accessed for reconstructing the original data must be no less than k. Consequently, $(1+\varepsilon)k$ helper nodes need to be accessed. As a leader node and at least one replacement node are necessary, this indicates that there are at least $(1+\varepsilon)k + 2$ nodes in a tree-structured repair. That is to say, within this centralized communication network, there exists a collection of tree-structure repair models, and the size of this collection is $C_{n-m}^{(1+\varepsilon)k}$. The performances of various repair models differs; thus, an optimal tree-structure repair model exists within this collection. Next, the general tree-structure repair model is analyzed initially.

To restore the lost data, the tree-structure repair model necessitates two procedures. First, the original data file is reconstituted at the leader node through independently downloading α symbols from $(1+\varepsilon)k$ helper nodes. Second, the leader node encodes the original data to acquire the lost blocks and distributes them to the corresponding replacement nodes to accomplish the data repair. Hence, multiplying the link weight by the size of data transmitted, the data repair overhead $c(m)$ during the repair process can be computed as

$$c(m) = \alpha\left[\sum_{(V_{ai},V_{aj})'\in E'} \mathrm{W}(V_{ai}, V_{aj})' + \sum_{\xi=1}^{m} \mathrm{W}(V_{\alpha 0}, V_{n\xi})\right]. \tag{4.27}$$

Furthermore, to ascertain the optimal repair threshold m^*, it is indispensable to contemplate minimizing the average data recovery cost $r_c(m)$, which symbolizes the data repair cost for maintaining the reliability of n storage nodes per unit time.

Calis et al. (2019, pp. 1575–1591) compute $r_c(m)$ by establishing a two-dimensional Markov chain (TDMC) model. This TDMC model characterizes the periodic repair process when storage nodes fail independently. With reference to the preceding statement, the lifetime of each valid node is exponentially distributed with the parameter $\theta\lambda$, and the recovery process of the failed nodes is exponentially distributed with the parameter μ. Based on this TDMC model, $r_c(m)$ is calculated as (Zhou et al. 2021, pp. 21843–21858)

$$r_c(m) = \frac{c(m)}{E[T]}, \tag{4.28}$$

where $E[T]$ represents the average interval time between two consecutive repairs. Regarding T, it complies with

$$T = T_{n,0} + T_{n-1,1} +, \dots, +T_{n-m+1,m-1} + T_{n-m,m}, \tag{4.29}$$

where $T_{\theta,\varrho}$ represents the time in the state $\{\theta, \varrho\}$, and $T_{n-m,m}$ represents the expected time to repair m failed nodes. The random time $T_{\theta,\varrho}$ is exponentially independent and identically distributed with the parameter $\theta\lambda$, while $T_{n-m,m}$ is exponentially distributed with the parameter μ. More precisely, $E[T_{\theta,\varrho}] = \frac{1}{\theta\lambda}$ and $E[T_{n-m,m}] = \frac{1}{\mu}$. Therefore, $E[T]$ is equivalent to the summation of the expectations of independent exponential random variables, as follows:

$$E[T] = \sum_{\theta=n-m+1}^{n} \frac{1}{\theta\lambda} + \frac{1}{\mu} = \frac{H_{n,n-m}}{\lambda} + \frac{1}{\mu}, \tag{4.30}$$

where $H_{n,n-m} = \sum_{\theta=n-m+1}^{n} \frac{1}{\theta}$. Combining eq. (4.28) and eq. (4.30), it can be derived that the average data repair cost $r_c(m)$ of the general tree-structure repair model is presented as

$$r_c(m) = \frac{\lambda\mu\alpha\left[\sum_{(V_{ai},V_{aj})'\in E'} \mathrm{W}(V_{ai}, V_{aj})' + \sum_{\xi=1}^{m} \mathrm{W}(V_{a0}, V_{n\xi})\right]}{\mu H_{n,n-m} + \lambda}. \tag{4.31}$$

Upon obtaining $r_c(m)$, the optimal repair threshold m^* was further derived as

$$m^* = \begin{cases} r = n - k, & \rho \leq \dfrac{\left[\sum_{(V_{ai},V_{aj})'\in E'} \mathrm{W}(V_{ai}, V_{aj})' + \mathrm{W}(V_{a0}, V_{n1})\right] \cdot H_{n-1,k}}{\sum_{\xi=2}^{r} \mathrm{W}(V_{a0}, V_{n\xi})} - \dfrac{1}{n}, \\ 1, & \text{others} \end{cases} \tag{4.32}$$

where $\rho = \lambda/\mu$, and the detailed derivation process can be located (see Appendix A of Zhou et al. 2021, pp. 21843–21858). It can be seen from eq. (4.32) that if the ρ value is low, it indicates that the DSS has a high fault-tolerance performance, and the repair process can be triggered after waiting for multiple failed nodes, as long as the number of faults is within the maximum repair capacity of LT codes. On the other hand, if the ρ value is high, it means that the DSS cannot tolerate multiple node failures within a given time, and the instantaneous repair is more suitable for this situation.

However, in large-scale DSSs, it is expected that network resources are optimally utilized. But establishing m^* only guarantees the validity of the delay repair strategy, and constructing the corresponding tree-structure repair model has $C_{n-m}^{(1+\varepsilon)k}$ helper nodes selection schemes with different data transmission costs. Therefore, further research was conducted, expecting to find the tree-structure repair model with the minimum network resource consumption when m^* was determined. In (Zhou et al. 2021, pp. 21843–21858), the optimal tree-structure repair problem was modeled by using a weighted node graph $G(V, E, W)$ to represent the storage node network structure, where V is the set of storage nodes, E is the set of node edges, and W is the set of edge weights. Subsequently, the optimal tree-structure repair problem can be expressed as

$$\begin{aligned} &\text{Minimize } W_{sum} = \sum_{(V_{ai},V_{aj})' \in E'} \mathrm{W}(V_{ai}, V_{aj})', \\ &\text{Subject to } \sum_{(V_{ai},V_{aj})' \in E'} (V_{ai}, V_{aj})' = (1+\varepsilon)k, \end{aligned} \tag{4.33}$$

where $\varepsilon > 0$, $i, j = 0, 1, 2, \ldots, n - m - 1$.

This is actually an NP problem. To address this problem, a diverse range of algorithms (Zhou et al. 2020, p. 021067) can be employed, encompassing exact algorithms, approximate algorithms, heuristic algorithms, and meta-heuristic algorithms, among others. Zhou et al. (2021, pp. 21843–21858) exploit the concept of Tabu Search (TS) (Lin, Cheng and Tsay 2002, pp. 108–112) to handle this problem and adopt an Improved TS (ITS) algorithm to construct the optimal tree-structure repair model. Compared with the two classical algorithms for resolving the traditional minimum spanning tree problem – Prim algorithm and Kruskal algorithm, despite the fact that the IST algorithm is disadvantaged in terms of computational complexity, it can identify the global optimal solution by comparing multiple optimal repair trees. In contrast, the Prim algorithm and the Kruskal algorithm only generate one optimal repair tree and have a high possibility of falling into a local optimal solution.

Although the tree-structure repair is capable of addressing the circumstance of multifault repair, it still adheres to the concept of delayed repair by aggregating scattered single-node repairs into unified multinode repairs. This imposes a tremendous computational burden on the leader node. Hence, how to distribute the computational pressure constitutes a problem that requires consideration. Additionally, the tree-structure repair takes into account link weights but neglects the heterogeneity of different nodes, leading to a significant disparity between the theoretical performance and practical application.

In reality, optimizing the repair of multiple failed nodes at the network topology level demands the consideration of numerous factors, such as link weights, the geographical distribution of nodes, the computing capabilities of nodes, and the service frequencies of nodes. These factors are complex and interrelated. Currently, an efficient algorithm for quantitatively analyzing these factors and identifying the optimal network topology model is lacking. In the future, perhaps the supercomputing power of AI large models can address the aforementioned challenges.

4.3 Chapter Summary

ECs consume a considerable amount of network bandwidth and disk I/O during the node repair process, significantly influencing the performance of the system. Although diverse erasure coding technologies, such as RGCs and LRCs, have emerged to optimize the node repair performance to the greatest extent possible, there remain numerous challenges in repairing multiple failed nodes, encompassing designing efficient schemes, optimizing transmission paths and computational complexity, etc. This chapter conducts an in-depth exploration of the efficient repair issues and related solutions under multinode failures, mainly elaborating in detail from the perspectives of storage coding and network topology. Generally speaking, regarding the failure repair of large-scale DSSs, a balance still needs to be struck between efficiency and reliability, and more intelligent and efficient solutions should be continuously explored. The combination of efficient and practical storage codes with network topology constitutes a highly promising and potential research direction.

Discussion Questions

1 What is FRC? Briefly explain its construction method and advantages in DSS.
FRC is a coding scheme that combines external MDS codes with an internal repetition structure. The construction of FRC is divided into two steps: first, MDS encoding is applied to the original file to generate redundant blocks, and then each encoded block is replicated multiple times and distributed and stored on different nodes. The advantage of FRC lies in the rapid repair achieved through the internal repetition mechanism. During repair, replicas are directly downloaded from other nodes without complex computations, significantly reducing repair bandwidth and computational overhead. Additionally, FRC supports efficient multinode failure recovery through table-based repair strategies, making them suitable for large-scale DSSs.

2 What are the similarities and differences between HSRCs and PSRCs? Explain their core characteristics respectively.

HSRCs are constructed based on linear polynomials and achieve rapid repair through *XOR* operations in a finite field. Their core feature is that the repair process only depends on partial data blocks and has low computational complexity. PSRCs, on the other hand, are based on projective geometry theory, and the repair process is entirely accomplished through *XOR* operations without the need for polynomial calculations, but they have a higher redundancy. The common point of both is that they support the recovery of failed nodes through partial data, but HSRCs are more efficient in terms of storage, while PSRCs have an advantage in repair speed.

3 How does the repair tree model optimize the repair process of single-node failures? Explain its core idea and function.

The repair tree model introduces computational intermediate nodes to decompose complex operations and execute them at multiple nodes along the network path. The core idea is to compress or perform computations (such as *XOR* operations) on the data passing through the intermediate nodes during the repair process, thereby reducing the amount of data transmitted to the replacement nodes. For instance, intermediate nodes can preprocess multiple data streams and only pass on aggregated results, reducing link bandwidth consumption. This model optimizes the utilization of network resources, reduces repair latency and bandwidth overhead, and is particularly suitable for DSSs with hierarchical network structures.

References

Calis, G., Shivaramaiah, S., Koyluoglu, O.O. and Lazos, L., 2019. Repair strategies for mobile storage systems. IEEE Transactions on Cloud Computing, 9(4), pp. 1575–1591.

Chen, J. and Shum, K.W., 2013, July. Repairing multiple failures in the Suh-Ramchandran regenerating codes. In 2013 IEEE International Symposium on Information Theory (pp. 1441–1445). IEEE.

Designs, B., 2014. Layered, Exact-Repair Regenerating Codes Via Embedded Error Correction and Block Designs. arXiv preprint arXiv:1408.0377 (pp. 1–13).

Dimakis, A.G., Godfrey, P.B., Wu, Y., Wainwright, M.J. and Ramchandran, K., 2010. Network coding for distributed storage systems. IEEE transactions on information theory, 56(9), pp. 4539–4551.

Duminuco, A. and Biersack, E., 2008, September. Hierarchical codes: How to make erasure codes attractive for peer-to-peer storage systems. In 2008 Eighth International Conference on Peer-to-Peer Computing (pp. 89–98). IEEE.

El Rouayheb, S. and Ramchandran, K., 2010, September. Fractional repetition codes for repair in distributed storage systems. In 2010 48th Annual Allerton Conference on Communication, Control, and Computing (Allerton) (pp. 1510–1517). IEEE.

Ernvall, T., 2012. The existence of fractional repetition codes. arXiv e-prints, pp.arXiv-1201.

Gu, S., Li, J., Wang, Y., Wang, N. and Zhang, Q., 2019. DR-MDS: An energy-efficient coding scheme in D2D distributed storage network for the internet of things. IEEE Access, 7, pp. 24179–24191.

Hou, H. and Li, H., 2012, November. Practical self-repairing codes for distributed storage. In 2012 IEEE Asia Pacific Cloud Computing Congress (APCloudCC) (pp. 76–81). IEEE.

Itani, M., Sharafeddine, S. and Elkabbani, I., 2016, June. Practical multiple node failure recovery in distributed storage systems. In 2016 IEEE Symposium on Computers and Communication (ISCC) (pp. 901–907). IEEE

Kamberaj, H. and Kamberaj, H., 2022. Gauss's Law. In: Electromagnetism: With Solved Problems (pp. 23–45). Cham: Springer International Publishing.

Lee, H. and Lee, J., 2017. An outer bound on the storage-bandwidth tradeoff of exact-repair cooperative regenerating codes. IEEE Transactions on Information Theory, 63(11), pp. 7267–7282.

Li H, Huang X, Hou H 2013. Coding, decoding and data repairing method based on homomorphic self-repairing code and storage system thereof: WO. Patent 2013159413A1[P]. 2013-10-13, pp. 1–15.

Li, J. and Li, B., 2014, April. Cooperative repair with minimum-storage regenerating codes for distributed storage. In IEEE INFOCOM 2014-IEEE Conference on Computer Communications (pp. 316–324). IEEE.

Li, Q., Xiang, Q., Wang, Y., et al. 2023. More than capacity: Performance-oriented evolution of pangu in alibaba. In 21st USENIX Conference on File and Storage Technologies (FAST 23) (pp. 331–346).

Li, R., Lin, J. and Lee, P.P., 2013, May. CORE: Augmenting regenerating-coding-based recovery for single and concurrent failures in distributed storage systems. In 2013 IEEE 29th Symposium on Mass Storage Systems and Technologies (MSST) (pp. 1–6). IEEE.

Li, S.Y., Yeung, R.W. and Cai, N., 2003. Linear network coding. IEEE Transactions on Information Theory, 49(2), pp. 371–381.

Lin, W.M., Cheng, F.S. and Tsay, M.T., 2002. An improved tabu search for economic dispatch with multiple minima. IEEE Transactions on power systems, 17(1), pp. 108–112.

Luby, M., Padovani, R., Richardson, T.J., Minder, L. and Aggarwal, P., 2019. Liquid cloud storage. Acm Transactions On Storage, 15(1), pp. 1–49.

MacKay, D.J., 2005. Fountain codes. IEE Proceedings-Communications, 152(6), pp. 1062–1068.

Muralidhar, S., Lloyd, W., Roy, S., et al. 2014. f4: Facebook's warm {BLOB} storage system. In 11th USENIX Symposium on Operating Systems Design and Implementation (OSDI 14) (pp. 383–398).

Oggier, F. and Datta, A., 2011a, April. Self-repairing homomorphic codes for distributed storage systems. In 2011 Proceedings IEEE INFOCOM (pp. 1215–1223). IEEE.

Oggier, F. and Datta, A., 2011b, October. Self-repairing codes for distributed storage – A projective geometric construction. In 2011 IEEE Information Theory Workshop (pp. 30–34). IEEE.

Olmez, O. and Ramamoorthy, A., 2016. Fractional repetition codes with flexible repair from combinatorial designs. IEEE Transactions on Information Theory, 62(4), pp. 1565–1591.

Papailiopoulos, D.S., Luo, J., Dimakis, A.G., Huang, C. and Li, J., 2012, March. Simple regenerating codes: Network coding for cloud storage. In 2012 Proceedings IEEE INFOCOM (pp. 2801–2805). IEEE.

Park, H. and Kim, Y.S., 2016. Construction of fractional repetition codes with variable parameters for distributed storage systems. Entropy, 18(12), 441.

Pepelnjak, I., 1999. EIGRP network design solutions. Cisco press.

Plank, J.S. and Xu, L., 2006, July. Optimizing Cauchy Reed–Solomon codes for fault-tolerant network storage applications. In Fifth IEEE International Symposium on Network Computing and Applications (NCA'06) (pp. 173–180). IEEE.

Porter, A., Silas, S. and Wootters, M., 2018, June. Load-balanced fractional repetition codes. In 2018 IEEE International Symposium on Information Theory (ISIT) (pp. 2072–2076). IEEE.

Qin, S. and Li, Z., 2018, December. Network topology impacts on repair cost in distributed storage system with network coding. In 2018 IEEE International Conference on Electronics and Communication Engineering (ICECE) (pp. 102–109). IEEE.

Raouf, A.H.F., Abouei, J., Jaseemuddin, M. and Uysal, M., 2020. Delivery phase in cache-based wireless networks with modified LT codes. Physical Communication, 42, 101172.

Rashmi, K.V., Shah, N.B., Kumar, P.V. and Ramchandran, K., 2009, September. Explicit construction of optimal exact regenerating codes for distributed storage. In 2009 47th Annual Allerton Conference on Communication, Control, and Computing (Allerton) (pp. 1243–1249). IEEE.

Shum, K.W. and Hu, Y., 2012, July. Functional-repair-by-transfer regenerating codes. In 2012 IEEE International Symposium on Information Theory Proceedings (pp. 1192–1196). IEEE.

Shum, K.W. and Hu, Y., 2013. Cooperative regenerating codes. IEEE Transactions on Information Theory, 59(11), pp. 7229–7258.

Silberstein, N. and Etzion, T., 2015. Optimal fractional repetition codes based on graphs and designs. IEEE Transactions on Information Theory, 61(8), pp. 4164–4180.

Sipos, M., Gahm, J., Venkat, N. and Oran, D., 2018. Network-aware feasible repairs for erasure-coded storage. IEEE/ACM Transactions on Networking, 26(3), pp. 1404–1417.

Sung, C.W. and Gong, X., 2013, July. A ZigZag-decodable code with the MDS property for distributed storage systems. In 2013 IEEE International Symposium on Information Theory (pp. 341–345). IEEE.

Tamo, I., Wang, Z. and Bruck, J., 2011, July. MDS array codes with optimal rebuilding. In 2011 IEEE International Symposium on Information Theory Proceedings (pp. 1240–1244). IEEE.

Tang, C., Yu, K., Veeraraghavan, K., Kaldor, J., et al. 2020. Twine: A unified cluster management system for shared infrastructure. In 14th USENIX Symposium on Operating Systems Design and Implementation (OSDI 20) (pp. 787–803).

Wang, X., Xu, Y., Hu, Y. and Ou, K., 2010, May. MFR: Multi-loss flexible recovery in distributed storage systems. In 2010 IEEE International Conference on Communications (pp. 1–5). IEEE.

Xia, J., Guo, D., Luo, L. and Cheng, G., 2020. Topology-aware data placement strategy for fault-tolerant storage systems. IEEE Systems Journal, 14(3), pp. 4296–4307.

Ye, M. and Barg, A., 2018. Cooperative repair: constructions of optimal MDS codes for all admissible parameters. IEEE Transactions on Information Theory, 65(3), pp. 1639–1656.

Ye, X., Li, J., Chen, W.T. and Tang, F., 2015, May. LT codes based distributed coding for efficient distributed storage in wireless sensor networks. In 2015 IFIP Networking Conference (IFIP Networking) (pp. 1–9). IEEE.

You, P., Peng, Y., Huang, Z. and Wang, C., 2014. Repairing multiple data losses by parallel max-min trees based on regenerating codes in distributed storage systems. In Algorithms and Architectures for Parallel Processing: 14th International Conference, ICA3PP 2014, Dalian, China, August 24–27, 2014. Proceedings, Part II 14 (pp. 325–338). Springer International Publishing.

Zhang, H., Li, H. and Li, S.Y.R., 2016. Repair tree: fast repair for single failure in erasure-coded distributed storage systems. IEEE Transactions on Parallel and Distributed Systems, 28(6), pp. 1728–1739.

Zhang, H., Li, H., Shum, K.W., Hou, H. and Robert Li, S., 2017. Concurrent regenerating codes. IET Communications, 11(3), pp. 362–369.

Zhou, A., Yi, B., Liu, Y. and Luo, L., 2021. An optimal tree-structured repair scheme of multiple failure nodes for distributed storage systems. IEEE Access, 9, pp. 21843–21858.

Zhou, L., Wang, S.T., Choi, S., Pichler, H. and Lukin, M.D., 2020. Quantum approximate optimization algorithm: Performance, mechanism, and implementation on near-term devices. Physical Review X, 10(2), 021067.

Zhu, B. and Li, H., 2015. Adaptive fractional repetition codes for dynamic storage systems. IEEE Communications Letters, 19(12), pp. 2078–2081.

Zhu, B. and Li, H., 2016. Exploring node repair locality in fractional repetition codes. IEEE Communications Letters, 20(12), pp. 2350–2353.

Zhu, B., Shum, K.W. and Li, H., 2019. On the duality and file size hierarchy of fractional repetition codes. The Computer Journal, 62(1), pp. 150–160.

Zhu, B., Li, H. and Li, S.-Y.R., 2017. General fractional repetition codes from combinatorial designs. IEEE Access, 5, pp. 26251–26256.

Zhu, B., Shum, K.W., Li, H. and Hou, H., 2014. General fractional repetition codes for distributed storage systems. IEEE Communications Letters, 18(4), pp. 660–663.

Zorgui, M. and Wang, Z., 2019. Centralized multi-node repair regenerating codes. IEEE Transactions on Information Theory, 65(7), pp. 4180–4206.

5

Distributed Storage Systems

The colossal volume of data has imposed more exacting requirements on storage, encompassing enhancing security, optimizing storage efficiency, reducing cost outlays, and enhancing intelligence levels. The single-machine storage is no longer capable of handling large-scale data, thereby giving rise to distributed storage. DSSs have emerged as effective storage solutions for massive data on account of their remarkable advantages, such as storage capacity, throughput, availability, scalability, and low cost, and have been extensively adopted by most storage vendors. This chapter furnishes a meticulous account of the expeditiously evolving large-scale DSSs in recent years, encompassing Facebook's scalable file storage system, LinkedIn's scalable geographically distributed object storage system, and Alibaba's elastic block storage (EBS) system. It then proceeds to examine the related technologies of key-value storage systems that have emerged over the past decade.

5.1 Background and Introduction

A DSS disperses data among diverse storage nodes to attain high reliability, availability, performance, and scalability. First, distributed storage offers exceptional reliability and availability as data is disseminated and stored in multiple nodes by means of various redundancy strategies, facilitating the system to operate stably even in the event of node failures. Second, distributed storage can heighten data access speed and response time through parallel read and write operations, demonstrating remarkable system performance. Moreover, DSSs are capable of dynamically regulating storage capacity by altering the number of storage nodes to accommodate the requirements of different storage scales. In conclusion, distributed storage contributes to storing and managing data more effectively, which is of paramount importance for any social organization with storage demands. At present, international storage vendors such as Google, Microsoft, and

Distributed Storage in Practice, First Edition. Hui Li, Hanxu Hou, and Hong Tan.

Amazon possess their own large-scale DSSs as their own back-end data storage infrastructures.

1) **WAS:** (Calder et al. 2011, pp. 143–157), a large cloud storage system developed by Microsoft, offers three types of storage: blob, table, and queue. Blob and table are primarily utilized for data storage and access, whereas queue is mainly employed for asynchronous communication among application instances.
2) **GFS:** (Ghemawat, Gobioff and Leung 2003, pp. 29–43) is a distributed file system designed by Google to store its massive amount of data resources internally. It consists of two types of nodes: one is the master node, mainly used to maintain the system's metadata, and the other is the chunk node, mainly used to store data files. Additionally, GFS employs data replication strategies for data reliability. However, taking into account the issue of excessive storage overhead brought about by replication strategies, Colosuss, as the second-generation storage system of GFS, has initiated the use of ECs as a mechanism for ensuring data reliability.
3) **Amazon Simple Storage Service (Amazon S3):** (Daher and Hajjdiab 2018, pp. 85–91) is a large-scale storage system developed by Amazon, which can be regarded as an unlimited network hard disk. It provides reliable, fast, and scalable cloud storage services that support unlimited expansion. Amazon S3 likewise adopts a replication strategy to guarantee data reliability by redundantly storing data across multiple facilities or on multiple devices. It further ensures data durability via fast detection and repair, along with periodic verification mechanisms to validate the integrity of the stored data. Amazon S3 additionally offers enhanced protection for data through version control, enabling the preservation, retrieval, and restoration of different data versions.
4) **OceanStore:** (Kubiatowicz et al. 2000, pp. 190–201) intends to construct a global and permanent data storage system to fulfill the access requirements of billions of users. The system is capable of providing highly available and highly synchronous storage services. Any computer can participate in the infrastructure and obtain economic compensation by offering storage services.
5) **Wuala:** (Mager, Biersack and Michiardi 2012, pp. 237–248) is a global network storage system that is notable for its absence of rigorous constraints on file types, sizes, or traffic, thereby affording users full liberty in file storage. Prior to uploading, files are encrypted locally and subsequently encoded by ECs. The encoded blocks are stored in multiple nodes to uphold the reliability of the files. Furthermore, the system consistently maintains complete encrypted copies of the files, guaranteeing that users can access and retrieve them at any time.

In the domain of distributed storage, storage systems are commonly classified as block storage, object storage, file storage, and key-value storage in accordance with the organization of the stored data.

1) **Block Storage:**
Block storage partitions data into fixed-sized blocks ranging from several KB to several MB and stores them independently to flexibly exploit the storage space. Within this system, each block is assigned a unique identifier, which enables rapid location and access to the data block. In block storage, data is processed in the form of blocks rather than entire data, which can provide more granular control over data access and management. Block storage is typically used in solid-state disk, relational database, cloud storage, etc.
2) **Object Storage:**
Object storage regards the stored data as an object. Multiple objects are placed in a storage bucket, which bears a resemblance to a dictionary, yet lacks the more intricate tree-like structure. Each object encompasses the data itself, a unique identifier, and corresponding metadata. Through the utilization of the unique identifier, one can directly access and obtain the object without the necessity of knowing the object's physical storage path, thereby simplifying the access procedure and enhancing the efficiency of data storage. Metadata is employed to delineate other pertinent information regarding the object, like size, type, creation time, and other custom tags established by the owner. These tags assist in retrieving the object and facilitate on-demand search.
3) **File Storage:**
File storage stores data in the form of files. Each stored file can contain one or more data records or blocks. In a file storage system, each file has a unique identifier, usually the file name, and users primarily access and manipulate files through the file name. File storage typically requires providing a file system abstraction layer to manage file creation, reading, writing, and deletion operations. This type of file management operation through file system interfaces does not require understanding the underlying implementation details of the file storage. Meanwhile, file storage is typically structured hierarchically, such as through directories, for the purpose of organizing and managing files. Directories can encompass files or other directories, thereby forming a tree-like structure. This hierarchical structure facilitates the organization and management of a large number of files and offers enhanced scalability and flexibility. Furthermore, file storage systems usually offer file access control and permission management functionalities to regulate users' access and operation privileges to files. This contributes to safeguarding the security and integrity of files, precluding unauthorized users from accessing and modifying file content.
4) **Key-Value Storage:**
Key-value storage, also known as a key-value database in single-node scenarios, is a storage system that stores, indexes, and retrieves data using

key-value pairs. Unlike traditional relational databases, each record in a key-value storage system consists of only two fields: a key and a value. Keys are globally unique within the key-value database and serve as identifiers for locating records; values are unstructured binary strings whose semantics are generally opaque within the system. Key-value storage has become an essential component of many computer systems and software applications, functioning as a critical element in storage servers, file systems, and large-scale data warehouses. For instance, storage servers can utilize key-value storage to manage mappings between LUN logical offsets and physical space allocations, while file systems can employ it to store directory structures and file metadata.

The fine-grained storage categories are capable of offering targeted solutions for diverse application scenarios, thereby fulfilling various data storage requirements. The subsequent sections present several storage systems in accordance with these storage categories.

5.2 Tectonic: Facebook's Scalable File Storage System

Tectonic (Pan et al. 2021, pp. 217–231) represents Facebook's most recent research and development in distributed file storage, with exabyte-level storage capacity and the ability to meet the performance needs of different tenants, and also optimizes the efficiency of data warehouses and blob storage. Facebook has reaped numerous benefits by adopting Tectonic. The system architecture and core components or functions of Tectonic are expounded in detail in this section.

5.2.1 Overview

Currently, Tectonic furnishes the underlying storage services for approximately 10 large-scale storage facilities, also denominated as tenants, among which some of the storage facilities possess a storage capacity exceeding exabytes, such as data warehouse and blob store. Prior to Tectonic, the underlying storage for tenants was solely offered by a succession of small, dedicated storage systems. For instance, blob store was served by Haystack (Beaver et al. 2010, pp. 1–11) and f4 (Muralidhar et al. 2014, pp. 383–398), while the underlying storage for the data warehouse was constituted by numerous HDFS instances (Karun and Chitharanjan 2013, pp. 132–137). This entailed the necessity for Facebook to develop, manage, and optimize different storage systems independently, augmenting operational costs and consuming a considerable amount of human and material resources.

Tectonic clusters can be effortlessly scaled to exabyte level, facilitating the coverage of an entire data center by a solitary cluster. Simultaneously, the multi-exabyte capacity of Tectonic clusters permits the hosting of multiple large tenants on the same cluster, enabling each tenant to support hundreds of applications. Despite being a multi-exabyte and multi-tenant file storage system, Tectonic is developed, optimized, and managed as a unified system and enables tenants within the cluster to share resources, resembling federation-based storage architectures (Cui, Tso and Jia 2020, pp. 47–53), yet it is more convenient in operation and has superior overall performance.

Tectonic primarily focuses on addressing three high-level challenges: scaling to exabyte level, providing performance isolation between tenants and providing targeted optimizations for specific tenants. An exabyte-level cluster is crucial for simplifying operations and resource sharing, and performance isolation and targeted optimizations can help Tectonic match dedicated storage performance to different tenants.

To effectively scale to exabyte level, Tectonic initially segregates the metadata of files into an independently scalable layer, analogous to Azure Data Lake Store (ADLS) (Ramakrishnan et al. 2017, pp. 51–63). Nevertheless, contrary to ADLS, Tectonic employs hash partitioning for each metadata layer, instead of range partitioning, which effectively precludes the access delay induced by hotspot concentration within the metadata layer. Subsequently, Tectonic integrates a highly scalable data chunk layer with an independently scalable metadata layer, facilitating its scalability to exabyte-level storage capacity.

Tectonic simplifies the management of resources for hundreds of applications by regarding applications with similar traffic patterns and delay requirements within each tenant as a group, thereby enabling Tectonic to manage the resources among dozens of traffic groups instead.

Different tenants possess distinct performance requirements; consequently, Tectonic necessitates optimization for specific tenants to align with dedicated storage performance. These optimizations are enacted by a client-driven microservices architecture that encompasses a copious set of client configurations for governing how tenants interact with Tectonic. For instance, a data warehouse employs write operations based on RS codes to enhance disk I/O and network transfer efficiency when a substantial amount of data is being written. In contrast, blob store utilizes a replicated quorum append protocol to minimize write latency.

5.2.2 Architecture

Clusters are the top-level deployment units in Tectonic. As depicted in Figure 5.1, a Tectonic cluster is capable of covering a data center, enabling it to tolerate host, rack, and power failures while supporting approximately 10 tenants employing the same storage architecture. These tenants, in turn, offer services to hundreds of applications with diverse traffic patterns and performance requirements, such as

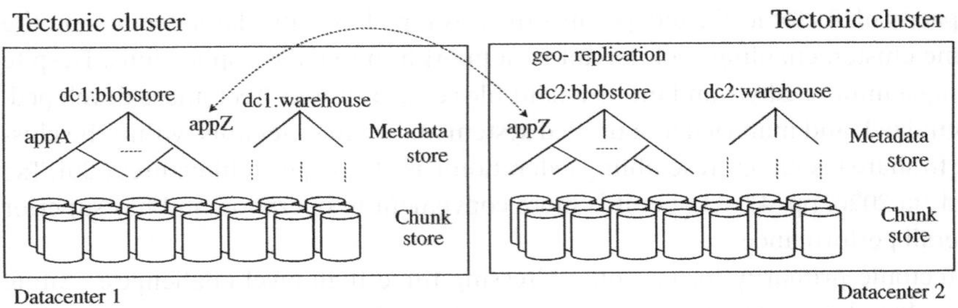

Figure 5.1 Tectonic clusters.

Newsfeed, Search, Ads, and internal services. The metadata layer of the Tectonic cluster supports an arbitrary number and size of namespaces or file system directory hierarchies. Typically, each tenant within the cluster possesses its own namespace, the size of which is solely limited by the size of the cluster and can be constructed with a geographic-level redundancy strategy, as indicated by the blue arrow, to prevent data center failures.

A more detailed architecture of the Tectonic cluster is shown in Figure 5.2. The fundamental component of the Tectonic cluster is the Chunk Store, which constitutes a group of storage nodes employed for storing actual data blocks. Positioned above the Chunk Store is the Metadata Store, which comprises an extensible key-value storage and a series of stateless metadata services on top of the store to establish file system logic. The scalability of this layer empowers Tectonic to store exabytes of data. The Chunk Store and Metadata Store run separate services that handle read and write requests for data and metadata, respectively. These services are coordinated and controlled by the Client Library, which converts the file system API calls made by the client into RPCs to call the services of the Chunk Store

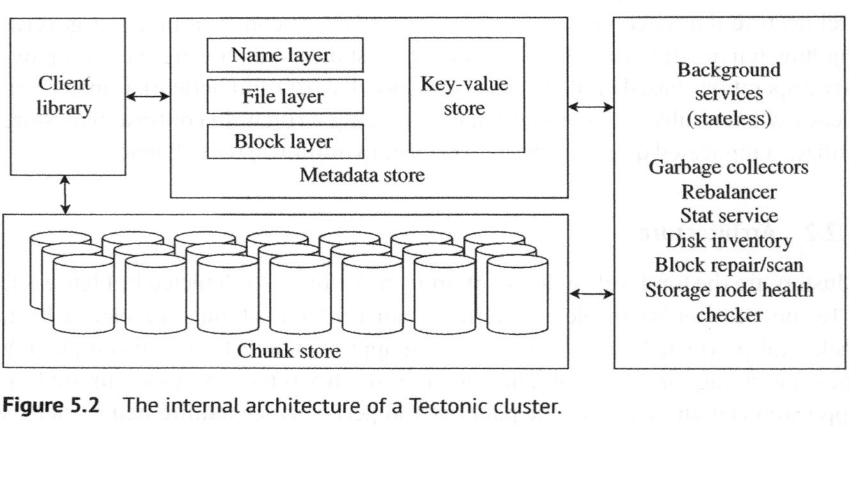

Figure 5.2 The internal architecture of a Tectonic cluster.

and Metadata Store. Finally, each cluster operates stateless background services to continuously ensure that the cluster remains in its optimal and stable state.

5.2.3 Core Components and Functions

As delineated in the system architecture, a Tectonic Cluster necessitates multiple core components to collaborate for attaining high performance.

5.2.3.1 Chunk Store

Tectonic employs Chunk Store for data storage, wherein the fundamental storage unit is referred to as a chunk. Several chunks collectively constitute a block, while multiple blocks together form a Tectonic file. Two key features of the Chunk Store facilitate scalable storage capacity and support multi-tenancy:

a) The flat architecture of the Chunk Store establishes a linear relationship between the number of chunks and the number of storage nodes, thereby enabling the Chunk Store to scale effectively for storing millions of bytes of data.
b) The Chunk Store disregards higher level abstractions such as blocks or files, which are managed and operated by the Client Library and Metadata layer, which simplifies the challenge of delivering optimal performance for multiple tenants within a storage cluster and facilitates the design of tailored operations for reading from and writing to storage nodes that address the specific requirements of individual tenants.

Each storage node runs a local XFS instance (Sung 2018, pp. 497–503) and exposes core APIs to retrieve, place, append to, delete, and scan chunks, while ensuring that the local resources of the storage node are fairly shared among Tectonic tenants. In Facebook's specific design, each storage node is equipped with 36 hard disks dedicated to chunk store, along with a 1-TB SSD for the purpose of storing XFS metadata and caching frequently accessed chunks. Furthermore, a block serves as a logical unit. From the perspective of the upper layers of the system, a block is represented as a byte array; in contrast, within the Chunk Store, a block comprises a collection of multiple chunks. The design of blocks effectively conceals the intricacies of the Chunk Store from higher level system components, thereby simplifying operational complexity.

Tectonic empowers tenants to independently customize their storage capacity, fault tolerance, and performance based on specific requirements in Chunk Store. For instance, a block can be configured for storage using ECs or through direct data replication. Furthermore, chunks within a block must be stored separately across different failure domains, such as distinct racks, to enhance fault tolerance. In the event of data loss due to a failure, background services are capable of repairing damaged or lost blocks to ensure reliability.

5.2.3.2 Metadata Store

The Metadata Store is primarily responsible for storing the directory structure of the file system and the mapping relationship between blocks and chunks. It employs a sharding storage mechanism, implements a fine-grained layered partitioning mapping strategy, and utilizes sealed caching technology to achieve scalability and load balancing.

a) **Sharding Storage:**
Tectonic uses ZippyDB (Cao et al. 2020, pp. 209–223) to store metadata. ZippyDB is a linearized, highly fault-tolerant distributed sharding key-value storage that manages metadata at the shard granularity level. All operations are limited within a shard, and the shard is also the basic unit for maintaining reliability. Each key-value storage node in ZippyDB runs a single-machine key-value storage system RocksDB (Dong et al. 2021, pp. 1–32) to store shard replica and use the Paxos (Lamport 2001, pp. 51–58) protocol to ensure data consistency so that any replica can provide read services, but the services requiring strong consistency are provided by the primary replica. This technology effectively balances node workload, enhances query performance, optimizes latency, and improves the fault tolerance of the Metadata Store.

b) **Layered Partitioning Mapping:**
Tectonic logically organizes metadata into three distinct layers: the Name layer, which maps each directory to its corresponding subdirectories or files; the File layer, which further associates file objects with a list of blocks; and the Block layer, which links each block to a list of disks and chunks while also maintaining a reverse index that correlates disks with their stored blocks. This layered architecture delineates the separation between directory access and specific data retrieval, thereby effectively mitigating operational complexity. Furthermore, the Name layer, File layer, and Block layer are hash-partitioned according to directory IDs, file IDs, and block IDs, respectively. This partitioning strategy effectively mitigates hotspots and balances the load associated with metadata operations. For instance, in the Name layer, although a single directory's list is stored within one shard, it is highly probable that its subdirectory lists reside in different shards due to hash partitioning. Consequently, even when frequently accessing files or subdirectories within the same directory, disk reads will likely occur from different sources—ensuring an even distribution of traffic across shards.

c) **Sealed Cache:**
To enhance query performance, Tectonic facilitates the sealing of various metadata that no longer require modifications. Sealed metadata can be cached on the client side without compromising consistency. However, it is crucial to note that if the sealed object is a directory, there is no recursive effect. Only modifications to the sealed directory itself are restricted, while changes to

its subdirectory contents remain permissible. Furthermore, as chunks may migrate between disks—potentially invalidating the cached sealed block metadata—it becomes essential to verify the validity of the cached sealed block mapping during read operations.

d) **Consistency of Cross-shard Operations:**
As noted in (a), Tectonic's sharding storage does not support consistent transactions; therefore, it offers nonatomic cross-shard operations. For example, in the design of Tectonic, the migration of a directory entails a two-stage process in which the subdirectory *a* within the source directory *c* is relocated to the destination directory *b* on a different shard. Initially, a pointer is established from directory *b* that references *a*, followed by the deletion of *a* from source directory *c*. The moved directory *a* retains a reverse pointer to the source directory *c* to guard against potential failures during migration. Subsequently, cross-directory file movements are executed: a copy of source file is created and then the source file is removed from the source directory. This copying step involves generating a new file object using the underlying blocks of the source file and incorporating it into the new directory, thereby avoiding actual data movement.

5.2.3.3 Client Library

Tectonic employs the Client Library to orchestrate the Chunk Store and Metadata Store services and provides users with a file system abstraction that enables autonomous control over read and write operations. Furthermore, the Client Library executes read and write operations at the granularity of chunks, facilitating highly efficient execution tailored to diverse user needs and preferences. In accordance with user directives, the Client Library can access the Metadata Store for chunk location, update or delete records within the Metadata Store, employ direct replication strategies or erasure coding for writing chunks into the Chunk Store, as well as reading or reconstructing chunks from the Chunk Store. Notably, Tectonic enhances coordination efficiency by deploying a dedicated writer for each file, thus circumventing complex multi-writer serialization requirements; however, it permits tenants to establish their own multi-writer semantics atop Tectonic's foundational infrastructure.

5.2.3.4 Background Services

Background services, primarily responsible for maintaining the consistency of metadata and the reliability and availability of data chunks, can rebalance node data storage, detect errors, and calculate disk usage and other various statistical information after fault repair or expansion. The main background services are listed in Figure 5.2. For example, failed Client Library operations or delayed deletions can result in metadata inconsistency, and each metadata layer's garbage collector is responsible for handling the inconsistent metadata. The rebalancer and repair service need to work together. During hardware failures or storage expansion, the rebalancer identifies the chunks that need to be moved, while the repair service handles the actual data movement by combining the chunk list and the disks-to-blocks inverse mapping for each disk in the system.

5.3 Ambry: LinkedIn's Scalable Geo-distributed Object Storage System

LinkedIn developed Ambry (Noghabi et al. 2016, pp. 253–265) to tackle the storage challenges posed by massive media objects within social networks. Ambry is a highly scalable and geographically distributed large-scale object storage system that facilitates efficient, low-latency data storage and retrieval through techniques such as logical grouping, asynchronous replication, rebalancing, fault detection, caching, etc. The integration of these technologies not only fulfills user requirements for effective upload and access but also guarantees high availability and load balancing, thereby providing a stable and reliable solution for managing vast amounts of data in social networks.

5.3.1 Overview

Over the past decade, social networks have increasingly emerged as the most prevalent communication channels worldwide. Millions of users continuously upload and access vast quantities of media objects, including photos, videos, and documents. These media objects are referred to as blobs; they are typically uploaded once and accessed globally with minimal modification and infrequent deletion. As a prominent global social networking company, LinkedIn must develop a high-performance and scalable storage system capable of efficiently storing and retrieving these read-heavy blobs. However, this faces a series of challenges that need to be addressed.

First, due to the diversity of media types, blob sizes vary significantly, ranging from tens of KBs to several GBs. LinkedIn must efficiently store blobs with such substantial size disparities. Second, both the quantity and access frequency of blobs are experiencing explosive growth. For instance, in 2016, LinkedIn facilitated over 800 million put and get operations daily; this figure nearly doubled in 2017, necessitating the development of a linearly scalable storage system. Third, factors such as user access randomness and system expansion can lead to hotspots that diminish overall throughput. Consequently, it is imperative for the developed storage system to be adaptive and capable of achieving load balancing. Finally, the upload process must be rapid, persistent, and highly available. For example, when a user uploads a blob, even if certain internal infrastructure experiences failure, all friends globally should still have access to view the blob with minimal latency, which necessitates implementing an efficient redundancy mechanism across multiple data centers worldwide to ensure blob reliability while maintaining low access latency.

LinkedIn initially introduced a solution known as Media Server. This solution employed Network Attached Storage (NAS) filters for the storage of raw data and utilized an Oracle database for metadata management. However, Media Server exhibited susceptibility to CPU and I/O spikes when processing substantial volumes of metadata associated with small blobs, and it lacked support for horizontal scaling.

In response to rapid expansion and the anticipated dominance of blobs in future data storage, LinkedIn introduced Ambry in 2016—a large-scale, scalable, geo-distributed object storage system specifically designed for blobs. Ambry utilizes blobs' logical grouping, asynchronous replication, rebalancing mechanism, zero-cost fault detection, and caching technologies to meet the following four objectives:

1) **Low Latency and High Throughput:** The system needs to run on affordable commercial hardware and process a large number of access requests in real time.
2) **Geo-distributed Operation:** The same blob must be distributed across multiple data centers located in different geographic regions to ensure high durability and availability. Furthermore, data can be read from and written to any replica, and when the current data center lacks a stored copy of the blob, proxy requests are redirected to other data centers.
3) **Scalability:** As data volumes continue to increase, the system must be capable of scaling in a cost-effective and efficient manner.
4) **Load Balancing:** A variety of internal and external factors can contribute to the emergence of hotspots, necessitating that the system be capable of adaptive adjustments to maintain an optimal balance as effectively as possible.

5.3.2 Architecture

This subsection aims to present a concise overview of Ambry's overall architecture and features, thereby enabling readers to gain a foundational understanding. Ambry can be distributed across multiple data centers, and its architecture in each data center is shown in Figure 5.3, consisting of three components: frontend layer, data layer, and multiple cluster managers. Each data center functions in a decentralized manner to operate the three components. The frontend layer comprises multiple independent frontend nodes responsible for receiving and transmitting requests; the data layer consists of several independent Datanodes tasked

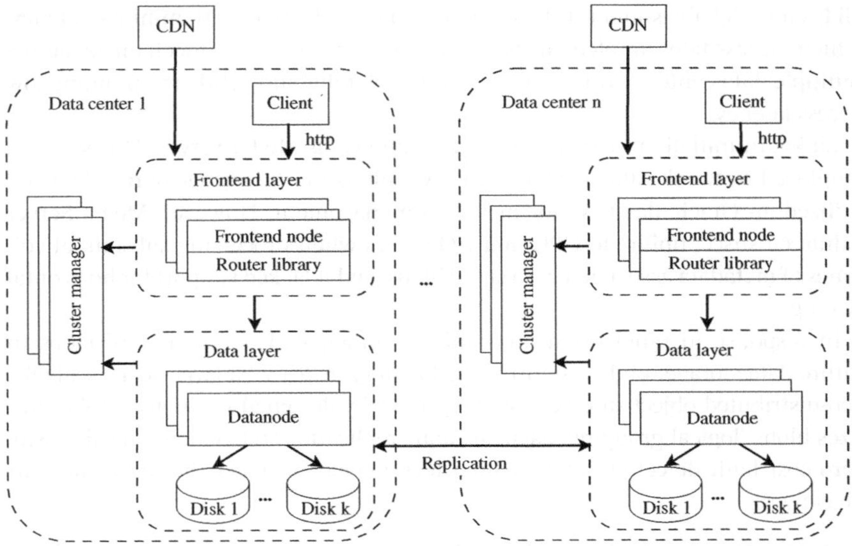

Figure 5.3 Ambry's architecture.

with storing actual data; the cluster managers are accountable for maintaining the cluster state and utilize Zookeeper (Hunt et al. 2010, pp. 5–20) for synchronization.

Ambry does not directly map blobs to physical machines; rather, it randomly organizes blobs into virtual units referred to as partitions, with the specific placement of these blobs on physical machines being managed through separate operations. The decoupling of logical and physical locations facilitates rebalance for data migration and the scalability of storage clusters. The concept of partitions similar to those has been used in other systems, such as Twitter's Blob storage using virtual buckets (Bigian 2012, pp. 1–9) and Petal file system introducing virtual disks (VDs) (Lee and Thekkath 1996, pp. 84–92). However, Ambry employs more efficient load balancing and replica synchronization strategies in comparison to these systems.

Currently, the partition size in Ambry is fixed at 100 GB, which enables it to retain a sufficiently large capacity even after accounting for the storage overhead associated with internal data structures such as indices, logs, and bloom filters. Meanwhile, the fault recovery or reconstruction of a partition is executed in parallel using multiple replicas, allowing a 100 GB partition to be restored within minutes, thereby rendering the impact on the system negligible.

As illustrated in Figure 5.4, a blob is sequentially written to a partition as either a put or delete entry. Both the put and delete entries contain a header that specifies a position offset, along with a blob ID functioning as a unique identifier. The blob

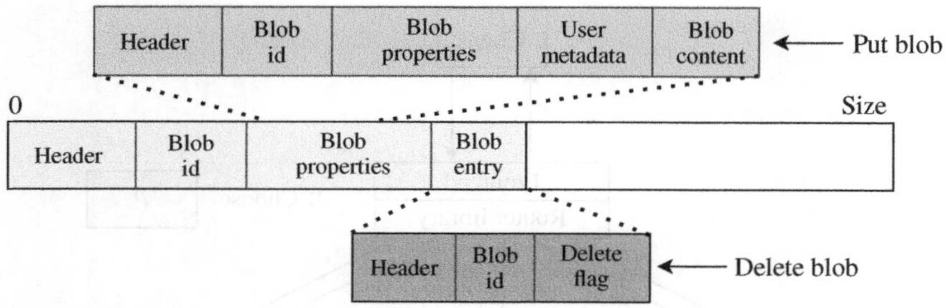

Figure 5.4 Partition and blob layout.

ID comprises the initial 8 bytes representing the partition ID and the subsequent 32 bytes corresponding to the unique ID. While collisions in blob IDs are possible, it necessitates generating an equal unique ID and selecting the same partition for colliding blobs, which occurs at an exceedingly low probability. Additionally, blob ID collisions can be resolved by deferring failed put requests on Datanodes. Furthermore, the put entry encompasses blob properties, user metadata, and blob content. Blob properties detail aspects such as size, time-to-live, creation time, and content type of the blob. User metadata serves as an optional field conveying information about the uploading user. Blob content pertains to the actual data contained within the blob. In contrast, the delete entry is more straightforward and includes solely an additional delete flag for identification purposes.

To enhance the reliability and availability of data, each partition is replicated across multiple Datanodes. Ambry employs a disk space-based greedy algorithm for replica placement, which selects the disk with the maximum unallocated space while simultaneously adhering to the following constraints:

1) A Datanode is not permitted to store multiple replicas of the same partition;
2) The presence of replicas across data centers is essential.

A partition is initially established as a read-write entity, allowing it to perform put, get, and delete operations. Upon reaching its capacity threshold, the partition transitions to a read-only state, thereafter permitting only get and delete operations. The capacity threshold should be maintained at 80–90% of the partition's maximum capacity for two primary reasons. First, once a partition enters a read-only state, its data may not be fully synchronized; thus, it is crucial to reserve space for appending content. Second, deletion requests will still lead to the addition of deleted entries, necessitating further reserved space. By default, deletion requests result in the attachment of a deletion flag to existing blobs and employ compression mechanisms that regularly clean up blobs marked for deletion. Following compression, if sufficient space is freed up, the read-only partition can revert to a read-write state.

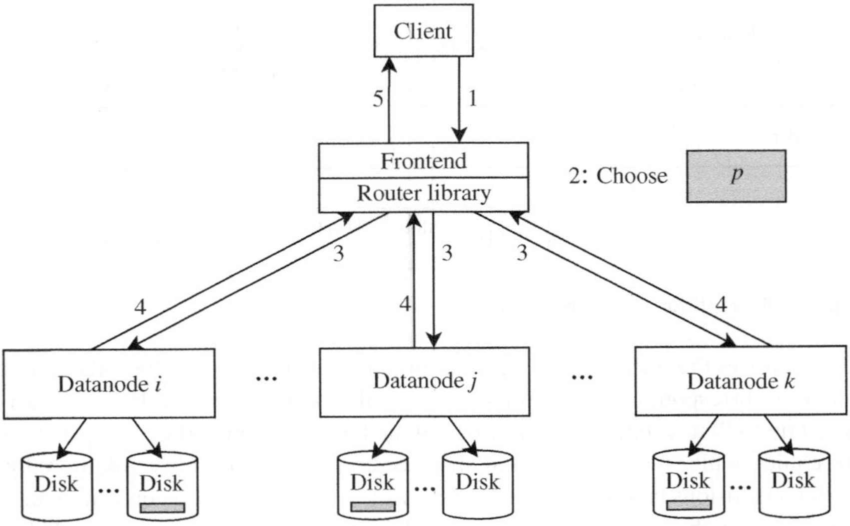

Figure 5.5 Request handling procedure.

Ambry offers a lightweight API that supports three types of requests: put, get, and delete. The request handling procedure is illustrated in Figure 5.5, where the frontend may opt to conduct security checks upon receiving a request. Subsequently, utilizing the Router Library—which encompasses the core logic for operation handling—a partition is selected, and communication with the Datanode responsible for that partition is initiated to facilitate service provision. In a put operation, data balancing necessitates random selection of partitions; conversely, in get or delete operations, the partition is derived from the blob ID.

Additionally, executing put operations on replicas distributed across multiple data centers in a synchronous manner may adversely affect system throughput. To mitigate this issue, Ambry employs asynchronous writes, wherein put operations are executed synchronously only within the local data center. This means that once the put operation is successfully recorded in the data center housing the frontend that receives requests, it is deemed successful. Subsequently, Ambry utilizes a lightweight replication algorithm to propagate the written blobs to other data centers. Furthermore, to ensure read-after-write consistency for a blob prior to its replication across data centers—such as writing data to one data center and subsequently reading it from another—Ambry implements a Proxy Request mechanism. Specifically, if the frontend fails to retrieve the corresponding blob from the local data center, it will forward the request through a proxy to another data center and obtain results from there.

5.3.3 Core Components and Functions

This subsection furnishes a detailed account of Ambry's crucial components, encompassing the Cluster Manager, frontend layer, and data layer, along with the core functions realized through their concerted operation.

5.3.3.1 Cluster Manager

The Cluster Manager is primarily responsible for maintaining the state of the cluster. The local Cluster Manager in each data center uses Zookeeper to keep synchronized with the other data centers. The storage overhead of the Cluster Manager is very small, totaling less than a few MB, and consists of both hardware and logical layout.

a) **Hardware Layout:**
   Ambry functions in a heterogeneous setting, employing diverse hardware and configurations to sustain internal and cross-data center operations. The hardware layout encompasses information regarding the physical structure of the cluster, such as data centers, Datanodes, and disk arrangements. Furthermore, it documents the original capacity and operational status of each disk, including the UP and DOWN states.
b) **Logical Layout:**
   The logical layout sustains the physical location of the replica for each partition, along with its functional state, encompassing read-only and read-write, mainly for choosing the partition for writing new blobs and the Datanode where a given partition resides. To keep partitions up-to-date, the Cluster Manager periodically contacts Datanodes and requests the status of the stored partitions.

5.3.3.2 Frontend Layer

Each data center possesses its own set of frontends. Frontends act as the entry point for user access to the system and are entirely distributed, without the implication of master-slave nodes, thus eliminating the necessity for burdensome synchronization among frontends. This design augments the scalability of frontends, enabling the addition of new frontends without considerable performance degradation; it also heightens the system response rate, signifying that requests can be executed by any frontend; and it boosts the fault tolerance capacity of frontends, indicating that a failed frontend can be rapidly substituted. Frontends have three main responsibilities:

a) **Request Handling:** The key function of frontends lies in employing the Router Library to identify the corresponding Datanode, solicit services from the Datanode, and ultimately return a response to the user.
b) **Security Checking:** Security checks such as virus scanning and authentication can be optionally imposed on the request.

c) **Capturing:** Ambry uses Kafka (Kreps, Narkhede and Rao 2011, pp. 1–7), which has high durability, high throughput, and low overhead, as its change capture system. Frontends can push requests from Ambry to the change capture system for offline analysis, such as analyzing user access preferences and system real-time performance.

The most critical part of a frontend is the Router Library, which contains all the core logic for communication, request handling, and error detection. Specifically, it includes the following four parts:

a) **Routing:**
When a frontend receives requests, it calls the Router Library to identify the appropriate partition. For put requests, a random partition will be chosen; for get or delete requests, the partition ID will be extracted from the blob ID. Subsequently, the Router Library acquires the physical location of the partitions from the Cluster Manager and communicates with the corresponding Datanode until the request is either served or fails.

b) **Chunking:**
When requests pertain to extremely large blobs, such as videos, it may induce load imbalance, obstruct requests for smaller blobs, and thereby give rise to high latency. To mitigate these issues, Ambry partitions a large blob into equal-sized units referred to as chunks. In a put operation, the Router Library initially divides a large blob b into k chunks $\{c_1, c_2, \ldots, c_k\}$. Each chunk is regarded as an individual blob, known as a chunk blob, and undergoes the same placement procedures as a regular put operation. To be capable of retrieving b, the Router Library generates a metadata blob for b, designated as $b_{metadata}$. As depicted in Figure 5.6, $b_{metadata}$ stores the number of chunks and the chunk blob ID in sequential order. Subsequently, the metadata blob is placed within the system as a regular blob, and the blob ID of $b_{metadata}$ is returned to the user for subsequent access.

It is crucial to note that when large blobs are being written, if a write failure takes place prior to the completion of all chunks' writing, the system will eliminate the written chunks and endeavor to reexecute the operation. When a large blob is being read, the Router Library reads the $b_{metadata}$ initially and subsequently extracts the chunk blob ID from it before accessing the stored blob data.

<table>
<tr><td rowspan="2"># Chunks</td><td colspan="2">ChunkId 1</td><td rowspan="2">.....</td><td colspan="2">ChunkId k</td></tr>
<tr><td>PartitionId</td><td>UUID</td><td>PartitionId</td><td>UUID</td></tr>
</table>

Figure 5.6 Metadata blob.

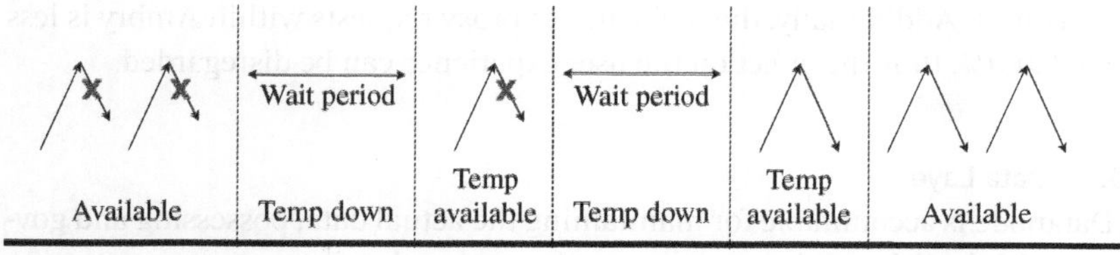

Figure 5.7 Zero-cost fault detection.

Additionally, given that chunks are highly likely to be placed on different Datanodes, this enables independent and parallel queries of large blob chunks. Hence, the Router Library can employ a sliding buffer of size 5 to enhance the efficiency of extracting chunk blobs. Specifically, when a chunk within the buffer is read, the Router Library slides the buffer to the next block and commences reading, while the completed chunk blob is returned to the user.

c) **Zero-Cost Fault Detection:**
In large-scale storage systems, faults are prevalent, encompassing instances such as unresponded requests, connection timeouts, and disk I/O issues. Consequently, Ambry necessitates a fault detection mechanism to identify unavailable Datanodes or disks and evade forwarding requests to them. The Router Library adopts an efficient zero-cost fault detection mechanism that does not entail additional messages like heartbeats or pings.

As depicted in Figure 5.7, the Router Library computes the quantity of consecutive failed requests to a specific Datanode within a predefined check interval and determines whether this number surpasses the MAX_FAIL threshold, which is set at 2. If the MAX_FAIL threshold is exceeded, the Datanode will be marked as temporarily down and remain in such a state for a duration, referred to as the wait period. In this state, all incomplete requests for that Datanode will eventually time out, and new requests initiated by the user will be distributed to the valid Datanodes providing the service. Once the wait period has elapsed, the Datanode is marked as temporarily available. When the Datanode is in the temporarily available state, if the first request sent to it fails, it will reenter the temporarily down phase. Otherwise, it will be marked as available for normal operation and repeat the aforementioned operation at the next check interval.

d) **Proxy Requests:**
As stated in the previous subsection, Ambry employs Proxy Requests to attain greater availability and read-after-write consistency in remote data centers. When a blob has not been replicated locally or the local copy malfunctions, requests for that blob are re-routed to other data centers for providing service, which is known as Proxy Requests. The core logic of Proxy Requests is furnished by the Router Library, rendering it transparent to the user initiating

the request. Additionally, the incidence of proxy requests within Ambry is less than 0.001%, thus the effect on the user experience can be disregarded.

5.3.3.3 Data Layer

The Datanode is accountable for maintaining the actual data, possessing and governing multiple disks, and responding to the read-and-write requests concerning the partitions placed on its disks. Among these, the put or delete operation is essentially handled by appending writes to the partition file, whereas the get operation might consume more time due to querying the specific location of the blob. To minimize the request latency, Ambry adopts a series of optimization techniques in Datanodes.

a) **Partition Index:**
To locate a blob within a partition with smaller latency, each Datanode sustains a lightweight in-memory index for each partition. As depicted in Figure 5.8, the index is sorted by blob ID and maps it to the starting offset of the blob within the partition. The index is updated in real time whenever blobs are inserted or deleted. Analogous to the Sorted String Table (Chang et al. 2008, pp. 1–26), Ambry restricts its size by segmenting the index and storing older segments on the disk and maintains a bloom filter (Mitzenmacher 2001, pp. 144–150) for each disk segment. Additionally, the index retains flags indicating whether a blob has been deleted and, optionally, its expiration time (TTL). During a get

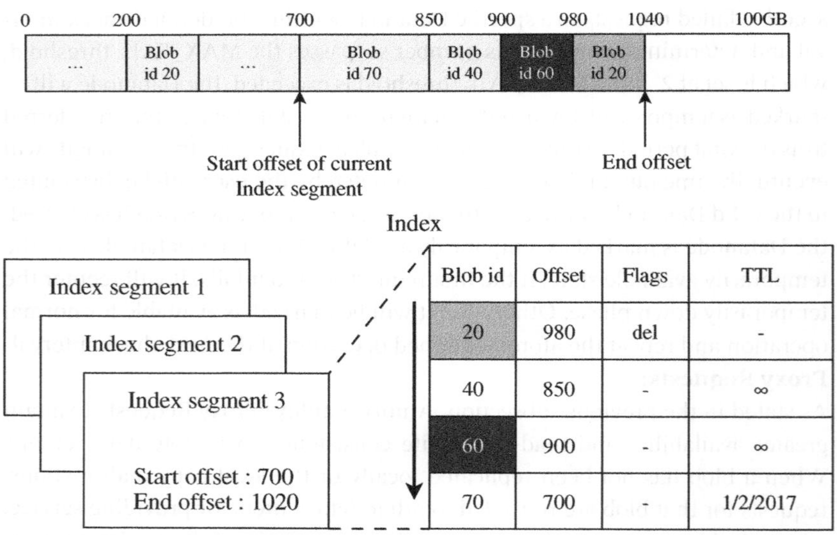

Figure 5.8 Index structure of partition index.

operation, if the blob has expired or has been deleted, an error message will be returned rather than the actual data being read. In the event of a Datanode failure, the entire index can be reconstructed from the partition. The offset of a blob is determined in reverse chronological order, specifically from the most recently created index segment to the earliest one. This ensures that during the retrieval of a blob, deleted entries are encountered prior to those that have been put, thereby guaranteeing that deleted blobs remain inaccessible.

b) **Exploiting OS Cache:**
Ambry limits RAM utilization across its components and leverages the operating system's cache to read the majority of data from RAM. The most recently written data, encompassing both real and index data, is automatically cached by the OS without incurring additional overhead. This approach facilitates substantial memory access, thereby significantly enhancing performance. Furthermore, to mitigate lookup delays for disk segments, Ambry maintains a bloom filter in memory for each index segment that contains the corresponding Blob IDs. Employing a bloom filter enables Ambry to efficiently exclude some of the blobs that are not present within the segment.

c) **Batched Writes and Zero-Copy Gets:**
Ambry consolidates consecutive write operations within the same partition during a refresh cycle and periodically flushes this batch of write operations to disk. Consequently, for a series of sequential write operations, at most only one disk seek is necessary. Furthermore, since Datanodes do not perform any computations on the data during get operations, Ambry employs a zero-copy (Stancevic 2003, p. 3) mechanism when reading blobs, allowing the kernel to directly transfer data from the disk to the network buffer without involving the application layer.

5.3.3.4 Load Balancing

Skewed workloads and cluster expansion can lead to load imbalance, thereby impacting system throughput. Ambry effectively achieves load balancing in both static nonscalable and dynamic scalable clusters, resulting in equitable disk access.

a) **Static Cluster:**
In a nonscalable cluster, partitioning large blobs into smaller chunks and randomly distributing put operations across partitions can facilitate load balancing. Furthermore, employing larger partitions in conjunction with Content Delivery Networks (CDNs) to manage hot data can significantly mitigate the occurrence of hotspots.

b) **Dynamic Cluster:**
In practice, read-write partitions handle all write traffic and the majority of read traffic. Given that partitions expand in a semibalanced manner, the

number of read-write partitions emerges as a significant contributor to load imbalance. Following cluster expansion, new Datanodes exclusively contain read-write partitions, whereas older Datanodes predominantly consist of read-only partitions, resulting in considerable system imbalance. To mitigate this issue, Ambry implements a rebalancing approach that restores the cluster to a semi-balanced state with minimal data movement.

Ambry defines the ideal load balancing state as a triplet (*idealRW*, *idealRO*, *idealUsed*), which signifies the optimal number of read-write partitions, the optimal number of read-only partitions, and the desired disk utilization rate for each disk. This ideal state is determined by dividing both the total counts of read-write and read-only partitions in the cluster and the total utilized disk space by the number of disks. If a disk exhibits more or fewer read-write or read-only partitions, or deviates from the expected disk usage compared to this ideal state, it is classified as being above or below that state.

The rebalancing strategy employs a two-stage method to transfer partitions from disks that exceed the ideal state to those that fall below it, aiming to achieve this optimal configuration. Specifically, Ambry relocates all partitions exceeding the ideal state into the partitionPool, ensuring that by the conclusion of this stage, no disk remains above the ideal state. During this process, Ambry initially moves read-write partitions in accordance with *idealRW* and subsequently addresses read-only partitions based on both *idealRO* and *idealUsed*. In relocating read-write partitions, Ambry typically selects those with smaller capacity; conversely, for read-only partitions, selection is performed randomly. Following this stage, Ambry allocates partitions from the partitionPool to disks below the ideal state—beginning with read-write partitions before proceeding to only-read ones. This allocation utilizes a random round-robin method: Ambry identifies all disks underperforming relative to the ideal state, sorts them accordingly, and distributes partitions in a circular manner until the partitionPool is depleted. It is important to note that for efficiency purposes, this allocation primarily involves modifications to metadata; actual data movement will occur subsequently. Ambry has adopted a seamless movement strategy: first create a new copy on the target disk, then use a replication protocol to synchronize the new copy with the old copy on the source disk, and finally delete the old copy.

5.3.3.5 Replication

All replicas of a partition may experience data synchronization loss due to write failures or the partial writing of data across data centers. To rectify inconsistencies among replicas, Ambry employs an asynchronous replication algorithm that periodically synchronizes these replicas. This algorithm is entirely decentralized, allowing each replica to function as a primary replica independently and synchronize with other replicas in a fully peer-to-peer manner. Furthermore, the algorithm utilizes an asynchronous two-stage replication protocol and adopts a pull-based approach, wherein each replica autonomously requests missing blobs from its peers.

In the first stage, the replica queries for missing blobs by requesting the blob IDs of all blobs written since the last synchronization and subsequently filters out those that are locally absent. In the second stage, replicas issue requests for these missing blobs to recover lost data. To facilitate rapid identification of the most recently written blobs, each replica maintains an auxiliary data structure called journal. The journal serves as a cache for the most recently written blobs, organized by offset.

Figure 5.9 shows an example of two replicas r_1 and r_2 and a two-stage synchronization process in which r_1 synchronizes with r_2. In the first phase, r_1 requests all the most recently added blobs in r_2 after the latestOffset 600. The log r_2 then returns a list of blob IDs $B = \{55, 40, 70, 90\}$. r_1 filters out the missing blobs based on B. In the second phase, r_1 requests missing blobs and appends the accepted blobs to the end of the replica, updating the journal, index, and latestOffset. Additionally, to improve the system's efficiency and scalability, the replication algorithm employs a number of further optimizations. First, Ambry uses separate thread pools for inter-datacenter and intra-datacenter replication within the data center. Second, Ambry implements batch processing requests for replicas of the same partition between two Datanodes, as well as batch transfers of replicas across data centers; finally, Ambry prioritizes stale replicas for faster synchronization.

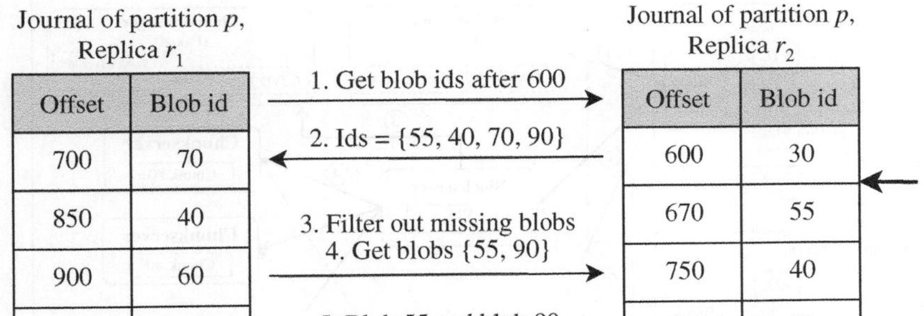

Figure 5.9 A two-stage synchronization process.

5.4 Evolution of Alibaba's Cloud Block Storage

As a fundamental component of Alibaba's cloud computing services, EBS spans multiple global regions and is distinguished by its high performance, exceptional reliability, scalability, and a range of additional advantages. Through continuous technological advancements and iterative development processes, EBS has enabled flexible storage management and rapid data transfer and access, effectively meeting users' demands for utilization of storage resources. This section outlines the developmental trajectory of EBS (Zhang et al. 2024, pp. 277–291).

5.4.1 Elastic Block Storage I

In the first generation of EBS I in Alibaba, there are two notable design features: in-place updates from VDs to physical disks and exclusive management of VDs. Specifically, EBS I directly maps the VDs in a virtual machine (VM) to a series of 64 MB Ext4 files on the back-end storage server. Additionally, EBS I uses a set of stateless BlockServers to manage VDs, with each VDS being exclusively handled by a single BlockServer.

Figure 5.10 provides a high-level architecture of EBS I, and it mainly consists of a compute cluster and a storage cluster. A compute cluster consists of multiple compute servers, each of which runs a BlockClient. It can host multiple VMs. A VM can mount one or more VDs. Users can access VDs as regular block devices and forward I/O requests to the storage cluster through the BlockClient. The storage cluster uses a separate set of dedicated servers for storage and management.

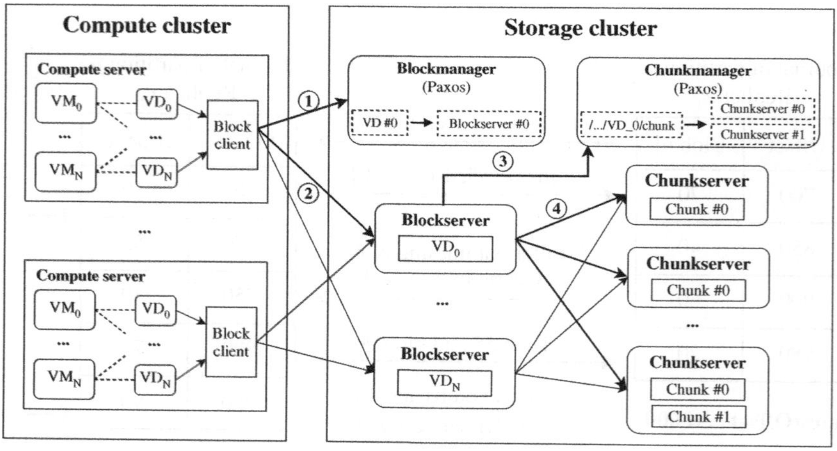

Figure 5.10 System architecture of EBS I.

Specifically, each storage cluster consists of a BlockManager, a ChunkManager, BlockServers, ChunkServers, and Chunks. The BlockManager is a three-node set supported by Paxos, primarily responsible for maintaining the metadata of VDs, such as capacity and snapshot versions. BlockServers are responsible for handling multiple I/O requests to VDs. Chunk is another data abstraction introduced by EBS I, where the logical block address (LBA) space of each VD is divided into a series of 64 MB chunks. Similarly, ChunkManager is a three-node set supported by Paxos for managing chunk metadata. ChunkServer stores 64 MB chunks as 64 MB Ext4 files, also known as DataFile, and performs in-place updates on the chunk where the write request was executed.

EBS I has two main types of networks: a frontend network used to connect the computing cluster to the storage cluster, and a backend network used to connect the BlockServers to the ChunkServers within the storage cluster. Both networks use the Clos topology and rely on a 10-Gbps network with a kernel TCP/IP stack. When a VM sends a new write request to one of its VDs, the BlockClient first contacts the BlockManager to locate the BlockServer that corresponds to the request. Then, the BlockClient forwards the write request to the corresponding BlockServer. The BlockServer then requests the ChunkManager to determine the ChunkServer and complete the data write. Additionally, BlockClient can establish a mapping from VDs to BlockServers, while BlockServers can cache a mapping from Chunks to ChunkServers to improve the efficiency of the entire communication.

EBS I attains remarkable flexibility in deployment, scalability, and evolution by segregating compute and storage into distinct clusters and interconnecting them via data center networks. Nevertheless, as EBS I constituted the initial step taken by Alibaba toward constructing a compute storage decomposed architecture, its constraints also emerged conspicuously, specifically that direct virtualization gave rise to severe space amplification and performance bottlenecks. For instance, with the aim of reducing storage overhead, Alibaba intends to employ data compression. However, compression will randomly modify the size of the data, thereby disrupting the direct mapping of in-place updates; concurrently, the performance of a VD will be restricted by its BlockServer, which might be influenced by hotspot issues under burst workloads.

5.4.2 Elastic Block Storage II

In reaction to the deficiencies of EBS I, Alibaba engineered the second-generation EBS (EBS II), the most notable alteration of which is that it no longer directly undertakes data persistent storage. Instead, it relies on a DSS named Pangu (Li et al. 2023, pp. 331–346) to furnish append-only file semantics and a distributed lock service based on a tailored Raft protocol for data storage.

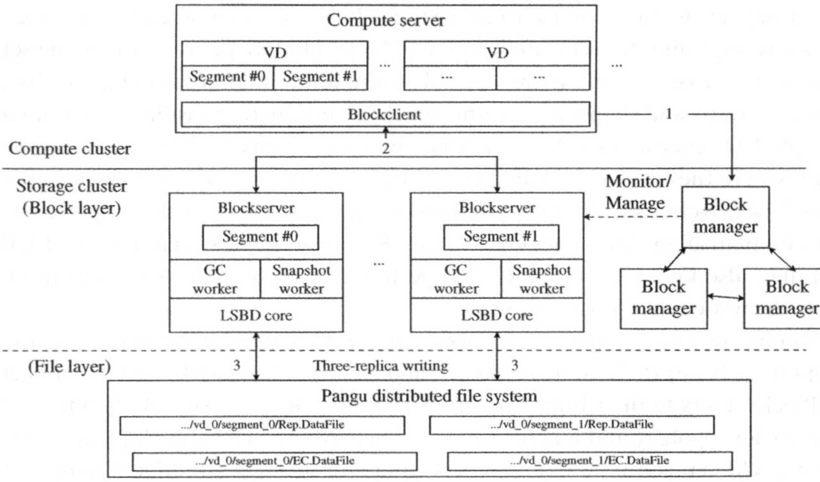

Figure 5.11 Overall architecture of EBS II.

Figure 5.11 presents the system architecture of EBS II. Herein, BlockServers, which achieve efficient data compression during garbage collection (GC) in the background, are structured in a log-based manner (Rosenblum and Ousterhout 1992, pp. 26–52) and are accountable for converting a write request from VDs into an append-only write to the Pangu system. Additionally, EBS II subdivides each VD into smaller segments, approximately 32 GB each. This shifts the mapping between VDs and BlockServers from the VD level to the segment level, modifying the granularity of failover from VDs to segments and thereby reducing the cost of failover. Furthermore, the BlockManager can directly utilize the lock service offered by the Pangu system without the necessity of employing the Paxos algorithm again.

Upon EBS II receiving an operation request for VDs, BlockClient shall initially retrieve the address of the corresponding segment from the BlockManager and subsequently forward the I/O request to the corresponding BlockServer. Next, the BlockServer employs a log-structured block device (LSBD) to transform I/O requests into APIs of the Pangu storage system and then invokes the embedded Pangu client for reading and writing data. It is notable that EBS II still upholds the architecture of computing storage separation. BlockServers and Pangu's ChunkServers might be situated on the same physical server, but they are independent processes logically and rely on the back-end network for data transmission.

EBS II employs a segmentation strategy to attain two distinct levels of parallelism, thereby facilitating the reduction of the frequency of hotspot accessing in

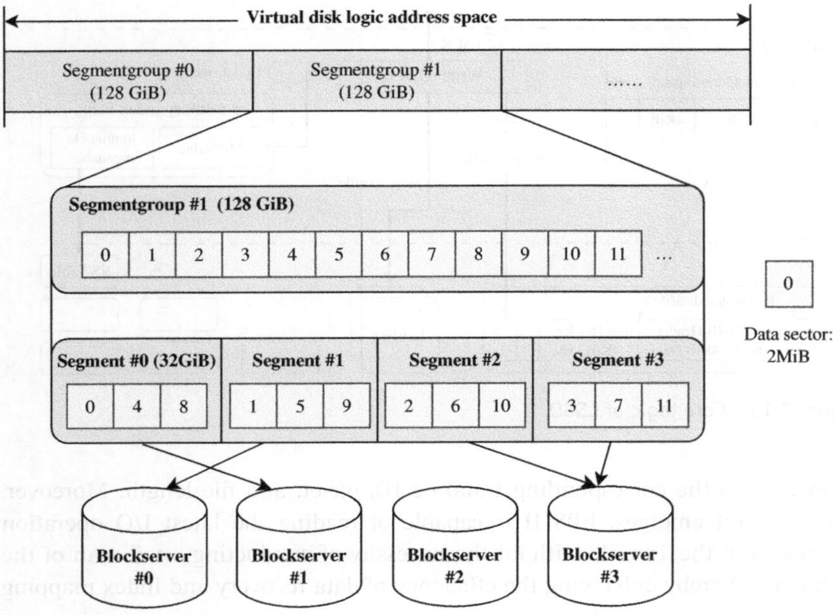

Figure 5.12 Disk segmentation design in EBS II.

VDs. As depicted in Figure 5.12, EBS II partitions the LBA of a VD into several 128GB SegmentGroups, within which each SegmentGroup encompasses four 32 GB segments. The BlockServer operates at the granularity of segments. EBS II arranges SegmentGroup into a succession of data sectors and allocates adjacent sectors to different segments in a round-robin manner to accomplish parallel disk access. Furthermore, EBS II correlates one segment with multiple data files of the Pangu systems, also referred to as DataFiles, to support parallel write operations.

EBS II also developed an LSBD core to optimize the process of locating from LBA to DataFile and the efficiency of fault recovery. As shown in Figure 5.13, when a user initiates some write operations, the execution flow of LSBD core proceeds as follows:

1) Persist user data as 64 B metadata and 4 KB data blocks and write them to the end of the corresponding DataFile;
2) Send an ACK response to the user;
3) Record the operation in the Transaction File (TxnFile);
4) Update the index mapping in memory.

Specifically, the index mapping is essentially a log-structured merge tree (LSM-tree), which accelerates the locating process through storing a mapping

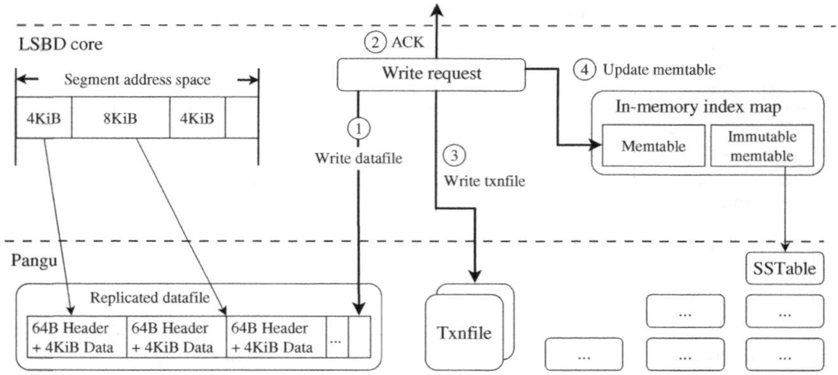

Figure 5.13 Core logic of LSBD.

from LBA to the corresponding DataFile ID, offset, and file length. Moreover, when a fault emerges, EBS II is capable of reading the latest I/O operation records from the TxnFile without the necessity of conducting a tail scan of the DataFiles, thereby enhancing the efficiency of data recovery and index mapping reconstruction.

When the outdated data in the DataFiles reaches a certain threshold, EBS II is capable of optimizing storage efficiency through performing GC. Specifically, EBS II operates at the granularity of DataFiles, gathering valid data from the dirtiest DataFiles within the same extent and combining them into new DataFiles. Subsequently, it updates the TxnFile and memory index to modify the mapping of LBA and DataFiles, thereby attaining the goal of GC. Additionally, coding techniques can be utilized during the GC process to further decrease storage overhead, such as employing ECs to code cold data and redundant copies.

Additionally, EBS II has many small optimizations compared to EBS I. For example, the metadata of VDs is stored in a persistent key-value storage to avoid data loss and prolonged repair time; EBS II replaces the kernel TCP with Luna (Zhu et al. 2023, pp. 673–687) to improve front-end network performance and uses RDMA network to improve back-end network performance (Gao et al. 2021, pp. 519–553).

5.4.3 Elastic Block Storage III

In 2019, Alibaba further upgraded EBS II, giving birth to EBS III. Compared with EBS II, the overall architecture and core functions of EBS III have not undergone significant changes. The main optimization is concentrated on I/O operations, hardware acceleration, and front-end and back-end network performance.

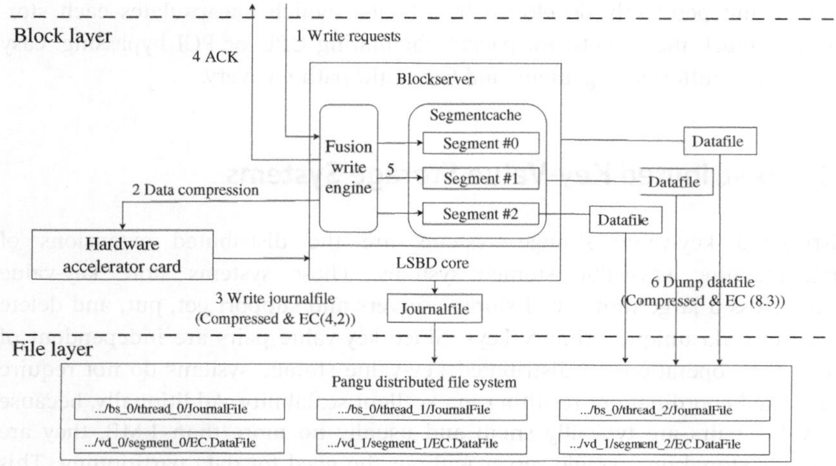

Figure 5.14 The architecture of EBS III.

As depicted in Figure 5.14, EBS III employs the fusion write engine (FWE) to accumulate write operation requests from diverse VDs and various segments, consolidates these accumulated write operation requests into a solitary DataBlock, and subsequently transmits them to the FPGA-based hardware accelerator for data compression. Precisely, FWE awaits until the aggregate amount of requested data attains a specific threshold prior to forming a DataBlock, while the FPGA is a bespoke hardware accelerator tailor-made by Alibaba specifically for expediting compression and decompression operations within EBS III. Subsequently, EBS III will perpetuate the DataBlocks encoded with EC(4, 2) as JournalFiles and deposit them in the Pangu system for fault tolerance. Once the JournalFiles are stored, EBS III dispatches a message to the VDs signifying that the I/O request has been accomplished, which significantly enhances the system's response speed and throughput.

In the subsequent background operation, EBS III first copies the uncompressed write data and stores them separately in the corresponding SegmentCache within the BlockServer. Finally, when the data in a SegmentCache reaches a certain threshold, EBS III compresses the data via the host CPU with EC(8, 3) and appends it to the corresponding DataFiles, and updates the TxnFile and memory index. For read requests, EBS III first queries the corresponding SegmentCache in the BlockServer to retrieve the latest data. If no data is found, EBS III will further read the index mapping in memory and perform a similar query process as EBS II.

Furthermore, in contrast to EBS II, the front-end and back-end networks of EBS III adopt Solar (Miao et al. 2022, pp. 753–766), a UDP-based transmission protocol independently developed by Alibaba, which encapsulates each storage data block into a network packet, facilitating CPU or PCI bypassing, easy receive-side buffer management, and fast multi-path recovery.

5.5 Distributed Key-Value Storage Systems

Distributed key-value storage systems are the distributed extensions of single-machine key-value storage systems. These systems store key-value pairs across a large number of storage servers and support get, put, and delete operations via unique primary keys. Since key-value pairs are independent of each other, operations in distributed key-value storage systems do not require distributed coordination, resulting in excellent scalability. Additionally, because key-value pairs are typically small and usually no more than 1 MB, they are generally stored on a single server without the need for data partitioning. This ensures that a single key-value operation involves only one server, thereby guaranteeing low-latency operation.

The application scenarios of distributed key-value storage systems are extensive, making them ideal for back-end storage in large-scale applications such as e-commerce platforms and social media networks. For example, Amazon employs Dynamo (DeCandia et al. 2007, pp. 205–220) to store data for its online shopping platform. Moreover, these systems can support other distributed storage solutions, such as distributed file systems that leverage key-value stores to manage file metadata.

This section focuses on key technologies employed in distributed key-value storage systems, including storage engines, data layout, distributed replicas, and secondary index.

5.5.1 Storage Engines

Storage engines are additional structures derived from the main data, used to record the location information of key-value pairs on storage devices without altering the data content. Storage engines directly affect the access efficiency of key-value data and play a crucial role in key-value storage systems. This subsection will focus on introducing three common storage engines: hash table, B+ tree, and LSM-tree.

5.5.1.1 Hash Table

Hash table is a data structure that directly maps keys to storage locations. It uses a hash function to convert input keys into hash values, which are integers used to determine the storage locations. Each storage location is referred to as a bucket and can hold one or more records. Due to the simplicity of locating key-value pairs, hash tables offer very fast lookup speeds.

To achieve higher space utilization and get operation performance, an ideal hash function should exhibit both uniformity and randomness. Uniformity ensures that keys are evenly distributed across all buckets, while randomness guarantees that the hash function does not depend on the specific distribution of keys and does not require any particular relationships between keys.

Because each bucket has limited storage space, newly inserted keys may be mapped to full buckets, resulting in hash collisions. Different hash tables employ distinct strategies to handle these collisions. For example, in chained hashing, each bucket maintains a singly linked list to store multiple key-value pairs. In probing-based hashing, the system attempts to insert the record into alternative buckets associated with the current bucket. Chained hashing falls under closed addressing, while probing-based hashing belongs to open addressing. Closed addressing allows multiple key-value pairs to be stored in the same bucket, but this can reduce the efficiency of get operations. Open addressing is more suitable for workloads dominated by get and put operations, but it is less appropriate for scenarios involving deletion operations, as keys may be scattered across multiple buckets, complicating the deletion process.

Dynamic hashing enables hash tables to dynamically expand and contract in response to changes in data volume, thereby adapting to the needs of data growth or reduction. It does not require users to pre-estimate the maximum space needed for the hash table, thus achieving higher space utilization and avoiding performance degradation caused by putting and deleting.

Extendable hashing (Fagin et al. 1979, pp. 315–344) is a well-known dynamic hashing technique that adapts to changes in database size through the dynamic splitting and merging of buckets. Compared to the traditional method of locking the entire hash table and doubling its space, extendable hashing only expands individual buckets as needed. This technique results in a smaller impact on concurrent read/write operations and reduces performance jitter.

An extendable hash table consists of two components: the directory and buckets. During a get operation, the hash value of the key is first calculated, and this hash value is used as an index to locate the corresponding directory entry in the directory. The bucket pointed to by the directory entry is the one that corresponds to the key. Each directory entry points to only one bucket, but a single bucket may be referenced by multiple directory entries. Whenever a record to be inserted maps to a full bucket, the system allocates a new bucket and migrates approximately half of the keys from the full bucket to the new bucket. Simultaneously, the directory and directory entries are updated accordingly. When deleting a record, the system locates the corresponding bucket in a manner similar to a get operation and then deletes the matching record from the bucket. If the load on the bucket becomes low after deletion, the system may merge less full buckets when necessary.

5.5.1.2 B+ Tree

The B+ tree is a balanced multiway tree composed of root nodes, internal nodes, and leaf nodes. It can be considered a variant of the B tree optimized for block storage devices, with the primary goal of reducing the number of I/O operations during search processes. To minimize I/O operations, it is essential to reduce the tree's depth as much as possible, necessitating a high fan-out coefficient for tree nodes. Consequently, the B+ tree stores all values exclusively in the leaf nodes, while internal nodes only store keys and pointers to child nodes. This design saves space for storing more keys and child node pointers. Additionally, unlike the B tree, the B+ tree maintains sibling pointers between leaf nodes, which significantly accelerates range queries.

As shown in Figure 5.15, the internal nodes of a B+ tree contain *n* keys (K_1, ..., K_n) and $n+1$ pointers $(P_0, \ldots, P_n)$ to child nodes. These *n* keys partition the key space managed by the current node into $n+1$ segments, each assigned to one of its $n+1$ child nodes. The keys and pointers within the node are stored in sorted order, such that for any $i<j$, $K_i < K_j$, and all keys in the child node pointed to by P_i are less than all keys in the child node pointed to by P_j. This ordering ensures the sequential nature of records in the B+ tree.

For leaf nodes, the first $n-1$ pointers reference the storage locations of $n-1$ key-value pairs, and the last pointer P_n points to the next adjacent sibling node. Consequently, P_n links all leaf nodes together in a linked list structure, facilitating efficient range queries. From another perspective, the nonleaf nodes of a B+ tree can be viewed as multilevel sparse indexes that support the organization of leaf nodes.

When getting *key*1 in a B+ tree, the search process begins at the root node and recursively traverses from the current node to the appropriate child node until a leaf node is reached. Consequently, the query cost in a B+ tree is directly proportional to the height of the tree. If the key is located in a leaf node, the query succeeds; otherwise, the query fails, indicating that *key*1 does not exist in the tree.

The process of range query in a B+ tree is similar to that of point query. When querying records within the range of K_1 to K_n, first find the key that is not less than K_1 and then visit the subsequent keys one by one along the sibling pointers until a key greater than K_n is encountered. Due to the maintenance of sibling

n	P_0	K_1	P_1	K_2	P_2	...	K_n	Pn

Figure 5.15 An internal node of B+ tree.

pointers among the leaf nodes of the B+ tree, the cost of its range query operation is relatively low.

When inserting or updating key-value pairs in a B+ tree, the system attempts to update the leaf nodes. This process may cause the size of a leaf node to exceed its maximum allowed capacity. To address this issue, the B+ tree performs a node split, dividing the overflowing leaf node into two half-filled leaf nodes. After the split, pointers to the new leaf node are inserted into the parent node to maintain the consistency of the tree structure. If the parent node overflows as a result, it may trigger a cascading update, leading to modifications in multiple nodes.

Theoretically, the depth of a B+ tree storing N records does not exceed $\left\lceil \log_{\lceil \frac{n}{2} \rceil}(N) \right\rceil$. In practical applications, a query on a B+ tree usually only requires a few I/O operations to complete. The node size of a B+ tree is generally set to the block size of the storage device, typically 4 KB. Assuming the key length is 12 bytes and the pointer size is 8 bytes, a node can store more than 200 keys and pointers. Even if a B+ tree stores one million key-value pairs, a single search only needs to access $\lceil log_{200}1000000 \rceil = 3$ nodes. Since the root node is usually kept in memory for a long time, the above example actually only requires two disk I/O operations.

5.5.1.3 LSM-Tree

The long structured-merge tree (LSM-tree), a storage engine commonly used in key-value stores, was first introduced in the late 1990s. It became widely recognized about ten years later for its outstanding performance in systems like BigTable and LevelDB (Wang et al. 2017, pp. 421–428).

In the LSM-tree, a core storage component called the Sorted String Table (SSTable) is employed to house a designated number of key-value pairs, organized based on their keys. SSTables are arranged in a layered hierarchy, where most levels consist of sequentially ordered SSTables with nonoverlapping key ranges. The quantity of SSTables increases substantially at lower levels compared to their adjacent higher levels, forming a hierarchical, tree-like structure. When the number of SSTables at a particular level surpasses a predefined threshold, a merge sort operation is triggered to consolidate the selected SSTables into a lower level. During a get operation, the LSM-tree performs a binary search starting from the highest level and progressing downward until it either finds the desired key-value pair or reaches a "Not Found" status.

LSM-tree-based key-value storage systems, like LevelDB, typically comprise both memory and disk components. As shown in Figure 5.16, the MemTable and immutable MemTable reside in memory, whereas key-value pairs are persistently stored on disk as SSTables, which are logically organized into multiple levels. Except for level 0, all key-value pairs in the other levels are sorted to ensure that SSTables within each level have nonoverlapping key ranges.

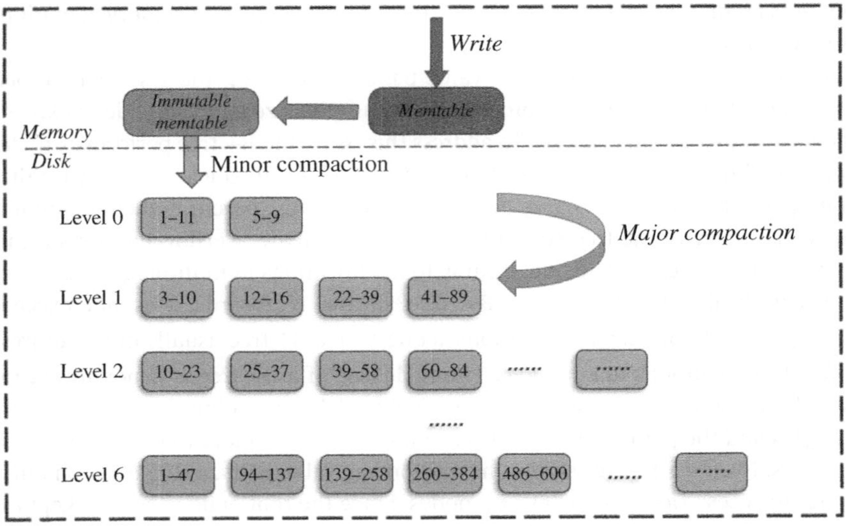

Figure 5.16 Key-value storage structure based on LSM-tree.

Put operations initially occur in the MemTable. When the MemTable reaches its full capacity, it becomes an immutable MemTable, preventing any further modifications. This immutable MemTable is then converted into a persistent SSTable and added to level 0 via a process referred to as minor compaction.

SSTables in level 0 are directly flushed from the immutable table in memory, which can result in overlapping key ranges among different SSTables. When the total size of level 0 exceeds a predefined threshold, a major compaction process is initiated to merge these SSTables into level 1. During major compaction, a merge sort combines SSTables from level 0 with those in level 1 that share overlapping key ranges. The sorted key-value pairs are then written back into level 1 as new SSTables. Similarly, if the size of level 1 or any subsequent levels surpasses their respective thresholds, major compaction will be triggered to compact selected SSTables into their adjacent lower levels.

Get operations in this system are relatively simple. To retrieve key-value pairs, the process begins with an in-memory search, followed by sequential disk access starting from level 0 down to the lowest level. Since SSTables in level 0 may have overlapping key ranges, all SSTables at this level must be searched. For other levels, however, only one SSTable needs to be examined due to their nonoverlapping structure. Within each SSTable, a binary search is conducted to locate the desired key-value pair. As data volumes continue to expand, the latency caused by binary search operations becomes more pronounced, highlighting the need for a more efficient indexing mechanism to enhance read performance.

The HL-LSM (Wang et al. 2024, pp. 71–76), proposed by the authors of this book, integrates machine learning into the LSM-tree to develop a learned index (Kraska et al. 2018, pp. 489–504), which replaces the conventional block index. This learned index enables the retrieval of values associated with specific keys by directly predicting the location of the corresponding key-value pairs. When successful, this approach achieves read operations in time complexity $O(1)$; even when predictions are not entirely accurate, it significantly reduces unnecessary comparisons compared to binary search. To be specific, HL-LSM introduces a single-pass learned index based on prefix search (Higuchi et al. 2021, pp. 45–48), allowing get operations on SSTables within a specified error margin. By traversing the training data only once, this method not only enhances get performance but also minimizes training time, making it well suited for managing frequently updated SSTables.

5.5.2 Data Layout

When an update operation occurs, there are typically two update methods. One is to directly write the new value to the original storage location, known as in-place update; the other is to write the new value to a new location, referred to as out-of-place update. For out-of-place updates, this subsection will introduce a widely used data layout form, namely, log-structured layout.

1) **In-place Update:**

   Atomic write refers to a write operation on a storage device that either succeeds completely or does not occur at all and will not be left in a partially completed state. Most storage devices support a specific atomic write granularity and ensure that this guarantee remains valid even in the event of device failure or system crash. Assuming the block size of the storage device is 4 KB, storage devices typically provide an atomic write guarantee for aligned block granularities. Therefore, the atomic write of the storage device can be leveraged to achieve in-place update of data.

   When using hash tables, records are typically stored in separately allocated blocks, whereas with B+ trees, records are stored in leaf nodes whose size matches the block size of the storage device. If a record is updated and the block or leaf node can still accommodate the updated data, an in-place update can be performed.

   In-place update offers two advantages. First, the storage location of the record remains unchanged, eliminating the need for an index structure update. Second, in-place update does not generate invalid blocks, thereby avoiding the overhead of GC. However, in-place update also has limitations. If a record is too large and spans multiple blocks, or if a single block cannot accommodate the updated data, in-place update cannot be performed; otherwise, a system crash during the update process may result in data inconsistency. Additionally, if the update operation involves multiple blocks, such as node splitting in a B+ tree, in-place updates are also not feasible.

2) **Log-Structured Layout:**
In the log-structured layout, all put, update, and delete operations are sequentially written to the persistent storage device as log records. To support read operations, this data layout typically works in conjunction with an index structure. The index structure points to valid and up-to-date log entries, while the remaining unindexed log entries are considered invalid.

In a key-value storage system, log entries corresponding to overwritten or deleted keys become invalid data but continue to occupy storage space. To address this issue, the log-structured data layout periodically executes a GC algorithm to reclaim space occupied by these invalid log entries. A typical GC algorithm involves traversing the storage index, copying all valid log entries to new contiguous storage locations, and updating the index to reflect these new positions. Once the copying is complete, the original log space can be fully reclaimed.

The log-structured layout offers significant advantages. All write operations are performed as sequential writes, which are highly efficient for most storage devices, particularly disk-based systems. Due to its out-of-place update feature, data modifications retain a copy of the original data, enhancing both concurrent read and crash recovery efficiency. However, this layout incurs additional overhead from GC.

5.5.3 Distributed Replication

Distributed key-value storage systems provide high availability and reliability by adopting distributed replication technologies. For instance, Dynamo uses the quorum-based replication (Lin, Chiu and Cho 2002, pp. 1442–1447), while RAMCloud (Ousterhout et al. 2015, pp. 1–55) employs the primary backup replication (Lamport, Malkhi and Zhou 2009, pp. 312–313). This subsection provides a simple introduction to the distributed replication based on consensus protocols.

As illustrated in Figure 5.17, in the distributed replication based on consensus protocols, each replica comprises a command log and a state machine. The command log records user requests, such as key-value pair updates, while the state machine executes these commands sequentially. If the command logs of all replicas are identical, their state machines will remain synchronized. Consensus protocols ensure that the contents of the command logs across different replicas are consistent. Common consensus protocols include Paxos and Raft (Ongaro and

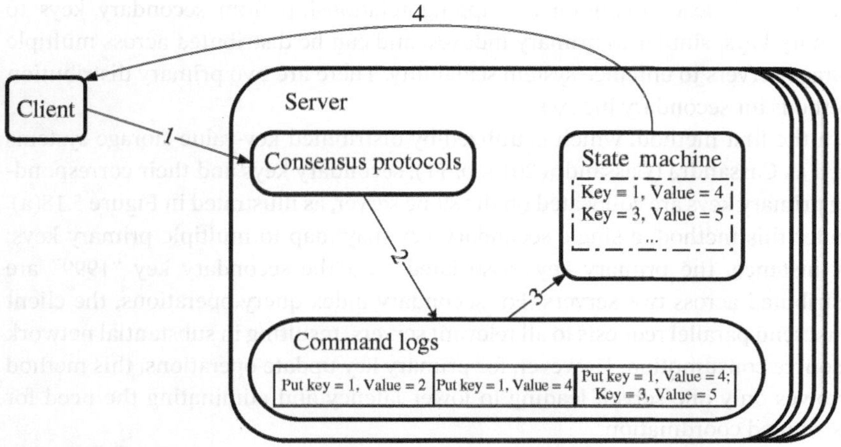

Figure 5.17 The distributed replication based on consensus protocols.

Ousterhout 2015, p. 2022). Next, a brief overview of the Raft protocol's execution process is provided.

In the Raft protocol, each replica server can assume one of three roles: Leader, Follower, or Candidate. The Leader is responsible for coordinating the replication process of the command log. Clients send requests to the Leader, which appends these requests to its local command log and broadcasts them to all Followers. Upon receiving the requests, Followers write them to the corresponding positions in their own command logs. Once the Leader receives acknowledgment from a majority of Followers, it confirms that the request has been successfully committed, applies the request to the state machine, and replies to the client. If a Follower detects Leader failure through a timeout mechanism, it transitions to a Candidate and attempts to initiate an election to become the new Leader. The Raft protocol divides time into incrementally numbered periods called terms, ensuring, through a specific election mechanism, that there is only one Leader per term. Even in cases of network partitions leading to multiple Leaders (i.e., different terms existing simultaneously), the Raft protocol guarantees that no log entry will be committed with differing contents across replicas.

Distributed replication based on a consensus protocol ensures the consistency of log records of different storage nodes and significantly improves the efficiency of concurrent read operations.

5.5.4 Distributed Secondary Indexes

Distributed key-value storage systems support access to key-value pairs from secondary keys through secondary indexes (Barcucci and Pinzani 1990, pp. 32–38).

Secondary indexes maintain a mapping relationship from secondary keys to primary keys, similar to primary indexes, and can be distributed across multiple storage servers to enhance system scalability. There are two primary distribution methods for secondary indexes.

In the first method, which is utilized by distributed key-value storage systems such as Cassandra (Cassandra 2014, p. 11), secondary keys and their corresponding primary keys are co-located on the same server, as illustrated in Figure 5.18(a). Under this method, a single secondary key may map to multiple primary keys; for instance, the primary keys associated with the secondary key "1999" are distributed across two servers. For secondary index query operations, the client must send parallel requests to all relevant servers, resulting in substantial network resource consumption. However, for primary key update operations, this method involves only one server, leading to lower latency and eliminating the need for distributed coordination.

In the second method, adopted by DSSs such as RAMCloud, secondary indexes are distributed across multiple servers based on the secondary keys, as illustrated in Figure 5.18(b). Under this method, a secondary index query operation requires two network interactions: first, querying the server where the corresponding secondary index resides to obtain the list of primary keys; then, querying the server where the corresponding primary index resides based on these primary keys to retrieve the target key-value pair. For primary index update operations, multiple network interactions are required: first, send a request to server A (where the primary index resides) to query and obtain the old secondary key; then, A sends the data to the server hosting the new secondary key's secondary index to create a new secondary index entry; subsequently, A writes the new key-value pair to the primary index; finally, A sends a request to the server hosting the old secondary key's secondary index to delete the old secondary index entry.

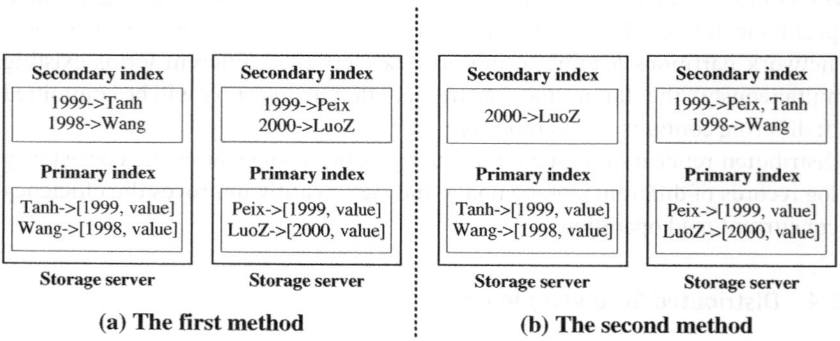

Figure 5.18 Two distribution methods for the secondary index.

5.6 Chapter Summary

DSSs have manifested distinctive advantages in addressing large-scale data storage challenges. Confronted with the exponential escalation of data, DSSs have emerged as the new favorites in the industry, owing to their superior performance and flexibility. In this chapter, we undertake an in-depth exploration of several large-scale DSSs and their key technologies. These case studies not only expose the potent potential of distributed storage technology in practical applications but also furnish valuable insights and precious lessons, which are of paramount importance for guiding the design and optimization of future storage systems.

Discussion Questions

1 What are the core differences between block storage, object storage, and file storage in DSSs? Explain their respective applicable scenarios.

Block storage divides data into fixed-size blocks, each with a unique identifier, supporting high-performance and low-latency fine-grained operations, and is suitable for database and virtualization scenarios. Object storage regards data as objects containing metadata and unique identifiers, simplifying the access process, and is suitable for massive unstructured data (such as multimedia storage). File storage organizes data in a hierarchical structure of files and directories, providing a file system interface, and is suitable for the management of user-generated files (such as documents and images).

2 How does Tectonic achieve EB-Level scalability through architectural design? What are the key strategies of its metadata management and data storage layer?

Tectonic separates metadata from real data storage: the metadata layer uses a hash-partitioned key-value store (such as ZippyDB) to avoid hotspots and support independent scaling; the data layer (Chunk Store) achieves linear capacity expansion through a flattened storage structure. Chunk Store ignores high-level abstractions (such as files) and directly manages data blocks, supporting multi-tenant resource sharing; Metadata Store achieves load balancing through sharding storage and hierarchical mapping (name layer, file layer, block layer), uses the Paxos protocol to ensure consistency, and reduces query overhead through cache sealing technology.

3 How does Ambry achieve high availability and data reliability?

Ambry encrypts files and then uses ECs to generate encoded blocks, which are distributed and stored in multiple geographical locations to ensure data persistence and cross-regional disaster recovery. The system always retains a complete encrypted copy, allowing users to access and restore data at any time.

It protects data integrity through a version control mechanism, regularly verifies the stored content, and uses fast detection and repair functions to handle node failures. It is suitable for global, high-concurrency unstructured data storage scenarios.

4 How does Alibaba Cloud's EBS system optimize storage performance and network efficiency? Illustrate its key technologies with examples.

Alibaba cloud block storage employs RS codes combined with the LZ4 compression algorithm to reduce network traffic. For instance, when writing data, using EC(4, 2) encoding reduces the network traffic amplification ratio from 4*x* to 2.25*x*. To address the high cost of writing small files, a batch processing mechanism is adopted to reduce resource consumption. Intel ISA-L is introduced to accelerate the encoding and decoding process, reducing the computational delay by 2.5–3 times compared to Jerasure. It also supports dynamic redundancy strategies (such as erasure coding or replication), allowing tenants to flexibly adapt between storage capacity, fault tolerance, and performance.

References

Barcucci, E. and Pinzani, R., 1990. Optimal selection of secondary indexes. IEEE Transactions on Software Engineering, 16(1), pp. 32–38.

Beaver, D., Kumar, S., Li, H.C., Sobel, J. and Vajgel, P., 2010. Finding a needle in haystack: Facebook's photo storage. In 9th USENIX Symposium on Operating Systems Design and Implementation (OSDI 10) (pp. 1–11).

Bigian, A., 2012. Blobstore: Twitter's in-house photo storage system. Twitters in-house photo storage system (pp. 1–9).

Calder, B., Wang, J., Ogus, A., Nilakantan, N., Skjolsvold, A., McKelvie, S., Xu, Y., Srivastav, S., Wu, J., Simitci, H. and Haridas, J., 2011. Windows azure storage: a highly available cloud storage service with strong consistency. In Proceedings of the Twenty-Third ACM Symposium on Operating Systems Principles (pp. 143–157).

Cao, Z., Dong, S., Vemuri, S. and Du, D.H., 2020. Characterizing, modeling, and benchmarking {Rocks DB}{Key-Value} workloads at facebook. In 18th USENIX Conference on File and Storage Technologies (FAST 20) (pp. 209–223).

Cassandra, A., 2014. Apache cassandra. http://planetcassandra.org/what-is-apache-cassandra 13, p. 11.

Chang, F., Dean, J., Ghemawat, S., et al., 2008. Bigtable: A distributed storage system for structured data. ACM Transactions on Computer Systems (TOCS), 26(2), pp. 1–26.

Cui, L., Tso, F.P. and Jia, W., 2020. Federated service chaining: Architecture and challenges. IEEE Communications Magazine, 58(3), pp. 47–53.

Daher, Z. and Hajjdiab, H., 2018. Cloud storage comparative analysis amazon simple storage vs. Microsoft azure blob storage. International Journal of Machine Learning and Computing, 8(1), pp. 85–91.

DeCandia, G., Hastorun, D., Jampani, M., et al., 2007. Dynamo: Amazon's highly available key-value store. ACM SIGOPS operating systems review, 41(6), pp. 205–220.

Dong, S., Kryczka, A., Jin, Y. and Stumm, M., 2021. Rocksdb: Evolution of development priorities in a Key-value Storage serving large-scale applications. ACM Transactions on Storage (TOS), 17(4), pp. 1–32.

Fagin, R., Nievergelt, J., Pippenger, N. and Strong, H.R., 1979. Extendible hashing—a fast access method for dynamic files. ACM Transactions on Database Systems (TODS), 4(3), pp. 315–344.

Gao, Y., Li, Q., Tang, L., Xi, Y., Zhang, P., Peng, W., Li, B., Wu, Y., Liu, S., Yan, L. and Feng, F., 2021. When cloud storage meets {RDMA}. In 18th USENIX Symposium on Networked Systems Design and Implementation (NSDI 21) (pp. 519–533).

Ghemawat, S., Gobioff, H. and Leung, S.T., 2003. The Google file system. In Proceedings of the nineteenth ACM symposium on Operating systems principles (pp. 29–43).

Higuchi, S., Takemasa, J., Koizumi, Y., Tagami, A. and Hasegawa, T., 2021. Feasibility of longest prefix matching using learned index structures. ACM SIGMETRICS Performance Evaluation Review, 48(4), pp. 45–48.

Hunt, P., Konar, M., Junqueira, F.P. and Reed, B., 2010. {ZooKeeper}: Wait-free coordination for internet-scale systems. In 2010 USENIX Annual Technical Conference (USENIX ATC 10) (pp. 5–20).

Karun, A.K. and Chitharanjan, K., 2013. A review on hadoop—HDFS infrastructure extensions. In 2013 IEEE conference on information & communication technologies (pp. 132–137). IEEE.

Kraska, T., Beutel, A., Chi, E.H., Dean, J. and Polyzotis, N., 2018. The case for learned index structures. In Proceedings of the 2018 international conference on management of data (pp. 489–504).

Kreps, J., Narkhede, N. and Rao, J., 2011. Kafka: A distributed messaging system for log processing. In Proceedings of the NetDB (Vol. 11, No. 2011, pp. 1–7).

Kubiatowicz, J., Bindel, D., Chen, Y., et al., 2000. Oceanstore: An architecture for global-scale persistent storage. ACM SIGOPS Operating Systems Review, 34(5), pp. 190–201.

Lamport, L., 2001. Paxos made simple. ACM SIGACT News (Distributed Computing Column) 32, 4 (Whole Number 121, December 2001), pp. 51–58.

Lamport, L., Malkhi, D. and Zhou, L., 2009. Vertical paxos and primary-backup replication. In Proceedings of the 28th ACM symposium on Principles of distributed computing (pp. 312–313).

Lee, E.K. and Thekkath, C.A., 1996. Petal: Distributed virtual disks. In Proceedings of the seventh international conference on Architectural support for programming languages and operating systems (pp. 84–92).

Li, Q., Xiang, Q., Wang, Y., Song, H., Wen, R., Yao, W., Dong, Y., Zhao, S., Huang, S., Zhu, Z. and Wang, H., 2023. More than capacity: Performance-oriented evolution of pangu in alibaba. In 21st USENIX Conference on File and Storage Technologies (FAST 23) (pp. 331–346).

Lin, C.M., Chiu, G.M. and Cho, C.H., 2002. A new quorum-based scheme for managing replicated data in distributed systems. IEEE Transactions on Computers, 51(12), pp. 1442–1447.

Mager, T., Biersack, E. and Michiardi, P., 2012. A measurement study of the Wuala on-line storage service. In 2012 IEEE 12th International Conference on Peer-to-Peer Computing (P2P) (pp. 237–248). IEEE.

Miao, R., Zhu, L., Ma, S., Qian, K., Zhuang, S., Li, B., Cheng, S., Gao, J., Zhuang, Y., Zhang, P. and Liu, R., 2022. From luna to solar: the evolutions of the compute-to-storage networks in alibaba cloud. In Proceedings of the ACM SIGCOMM 2022 Conference (pp. 753–766).

Mitzenmacher, M., 2001. Compressed bloom filters. In Proceedings of the twentieth annual ACM symposium on Principles of distributed computing (pp. 144–150).

Muralidhar, S., Lloyd, W., Roy, S., Hill, C., Lin, E., Liu, W., Pan, S., Shankar, S., Sivakumar, V., Tang, L. and Kumar, S., 2014. f4: Facebook's warm {BLOB} storage system. In 11th USENIX Symposium on Operating Systems Design and Implementation (OSDI 14) (pp. 383–398).

Noghabi, S.A., Subramanian, S., Narayanan, P., Narayanan, S., Holla, G., Zadeh, M., Li, T., Gupta, I. and Campbell, R.H., 2016. Ambry: Linkedin's scalable geo-distributed object store. In Proceedings of the 2016 International Conference on Management of Data (pp. 253–265).

Ongaro, D. and Ousterhout, J., 2015. The raft consensus algorithm. Lecture Notes CS, 190, p. 2022.

Ousterhout, J., Gopalan, A., Gupta, A., et al., 2015. The RAMCloud storage system. ACM Transactions on Computer Systems (TOCS), 33(3), pp. 1–55.

Pan, S., Stavrinos, T., Zhang, Y., Sikaria, A., Zakharov, P., Sharma, A., Shuey, M., Wareing, R., Gangapuram, M., Cao, G. and Preseau, C., 2021. Facebook's tectonic filesystem: Efficiency from exascale. In 19th USENIX Conference on File and Storage Technologies (FAST 21) (pp. 217–231).

Ramakrishnan, R., Sridharan, B., Douceur, J.R., Kasturi, P., Krishnamachari-Sampath, B., Krishnamoorthy, K., Li, P., Manu, M., Michaylov, S., Ramos, R. and Sharman, N., 2017. Azure data lake store: a hyperscale distributed file service for big data analytics. In Proceedings of the 2017 ACM International Conference on Management of Data (pp. 51–63).

Rosenblum, M. and Ousterhout, J.K., 1992. The design and implementation of a log-structured file system. ACM Transactions on Computer Systems (TOCS), 10(1), pp. 26–52.

Stancevic, D., 2003. Zero copy I: user-mode perspective. Linux Journal, 2003(105), p.3.

Sung, K., 2018. Analysis of Linux System changes by adoption XFS File System. Journal of Digital Contents Society, 19(3), pp. 497–503.

Wang, L., Ding, G., Zhao, Y., Wu, D. and He, C., 2017. Optimization of LevelDB by separating key and value. In 2017 18th International Conference on Parallel and Distributed Computing, Applications and Technologies (PDCAT) (pp. 421–428). IEEE.

Wang, X., Li, H., Tan, H., Wang, X., Lu, P. and Wang, H., 2024 HIndex-FLSM: Fragmented log-structured merge trees integrated with heat and index. In 2024 3rd International Joint Conference on Information and Communication Engineering (JCICE) (pp. 71–76). IEEE.

Zhang, W., Xu, E., Wang, Q., Zhang, X., Gu, Y., Lu, Z., Ouyang, T., Dai, G., Peng, W., Xu, Z. and Zhang, S., 2024. What's the story in {EBS} Glory: Evolutions and lessons in building cloud block store. In 22nd USENIX Conference on File and Storage Technologies (FAST 24) (pp. 277–291).

Zhu, L., Shen, Y., Xu, E., Shi, B., Fu, T., Ma, S., Chen, S., Wang, Z., Wu, H., Liao, X. and Yang, Z., 2023. Deploying user-space {TCP} at cloud scale with {LUNA}. In 2023 USENIX Annual Technical Conference (USENIX ATC 23) (pp. 673–687).

6

Integrating Blockchain in Distributed Storage Systems

This chapter highlights a series of studies that integrate blockchain technology into DSSs. Initially, in Section 6.1, we discuss the evolution and key technologies of blockchain. Subsequently, in Section 6.2, we explore decentralized storage systems (DDSs) based on blockchain. Finally, in Section 6.3, we focus on the endogenously secure mimic distributed storage and its logging system based on the Parallel Proof of Vote (PPoV) consensus algorithm.

6.1 Fundamentals of Blockchain

Blockchain is one of the most revolutionary emerging technologies in recent years. By employing decentralization, it ensures the transparency, security, and immutability of data, thereby transforming traditional mechanisms of transaction and trust. With its broad application in fields such as supply chain management and digital finance, blockchain has demonstrated significant potential and value.

6.1.1 Introduction to Blockchain

The onset of the 2008 financial crisis, precipitated by the collapse of Lehman Brothers, sent shockwaves worldwide from the United States. In response, global governments and central banks deployed extraordinary fiscal and monetary measures, including bailouts for financial giants rocked by their own errors. This led to increased doubt about the reliability of conventional financial systems.

That October, a paper by the enigmatic Satoshi Nakamoto proposed Bitcoin (Nakamoto 2008, pp. 1–11), a decentralized electronic cash system eliminating the need for trusted intermediaries, and introduced blockchain technology. By November, the Bitcoin protocol's first version was made public, and the following January, the genesis block was mined, launching Bitcoin.

Distributed Storage in Practice, First Edition. Hui Li, Hanxu Hou, and Hong Tan.

Bitcoin's launch marked the beginning of a new era for blockchain-based systems. As the cornerstone of Bitcoin, blockchain is seen as a transformative force across industries such as finance, logistics, media, advanced manufacturing, social services, education, and job markets.

A blockchain, essentially, is a peer-to-peer network system that facilitates the creation of an unchangeable, verifiable, and traceable chain of data blocks. This structure operates under clear and reliable protocols designed to manage transactions effectively. The technology is underpinned by a secure, collectively maintained distributed ledger that resists alteration. Within this framework, cryptographic principles, not external trust, safeguard the ledger's integrity as network nodes validate new data and transactions. The ledger comprehensively captures all transactions in a sequential chain of blocks. The blockchain stands out for its decentralization, immutability, and trustlessness.

1) **Decentralization:** Blockchain employs a decentralized, peer-to-peer network architecture where nodes operate with equal status, and there is no central administrative node overseeing the system. This structure contrasts with the traditional client/server model, which relies on a central server for data management. In a blockchain's peer-to-peer setup, nodes assume dual roles, functioning as both servers and clients, and they facilitate information exchange among users without the need for central servers. This approach emphasizes the distributed nature of blockchain, distributing responsibilities across the network.
2) **Immutability:** The blockchain's data architecture is based on a chained data structure, reinforced with robust mathematical encryption methods, which makes it highly secure against tampering and forgery. Once data is validated and added to the blockchain, it cannot be altered or counterfeited without causing a cascading failure in the verification process. This mechanism safeguards the completeness, authenticity, and security of the entire blockchain system.
3) **Trustlessness:** Advanced cryptographic techniques and an extensive authentication framework allow parties in a transaction to transact with trust without revealing their identities or relying on a third party for trust assurance. This enables secure and confidential transactions even in anonymous settings. Within the network, every node can serve as a "supervisor," protecting the privacy of individuals involved in the transaction data.

6.1.2 Key Technologies

In the following, we delve into some key technologies within blockchain systems, which form the foundation for building and maintaining these systems, including smart contracts and consensus mechanisms.

6.1.2.1 Smart Contracts

The idea of smart contracts was initially put forth by Nick Szabo in 1994, envisioning them as digitally encoded protocols (Szabo 1994, pp. 1–10). The Ethereum platform was a trailblazer in integrating smart contracts into blockchain, offering a decentralized, Turing-complete environment for developers to build applications and launch tokens tailored to their specifications (Buterin 2013, pp. 1–2). Within Ethereum's ecosystem, smart contracts are stored as data and code at a unique address, becoming operational under predefined conditions. They facilitate trustworthy, traceable, and irreversible transactions without the need for intermediaries.

In the realm of network management, the multi-identifier system (MIS) serves as the management layer for a future network called multi-identifier network (MIN). It utilizes an EVM-based identifier management contract that enhances regulatory capabilities and provides adaptable identifiers. MIS also supports a variety of identifier types in its data layer, such as content, service, IP addresses, and hyperbolic Coordinate. At the consensus layer, MIS employs the PPoV mechanism to sustain a consistent global state, which includes transaction and contract states (Wang et al. 2023, pp. 150–157).

Smart contracts offer a level of reliability that can surpass that of traditional, paper-based agreements. Traditional contracts rely on the good faith of parties to perform their parts, whereas smart contracts leverage the blockchain's inherent trustlessness to automate the execution of agreements. Fully governed by code, smart contracts operate autonomously once deployed, following preset conditions without manual intervention. They are decentralized, eliminating the need for trust in central authorities, and achieve network-wide consensus and functionality across blockchain nodes.

6.1.2.2 Consensus Mechanisms

Consensus mechanisms are essential to blockchain technology, functioning as algorithms that facilitate agreement among various nodes in a decentralized manner. They enable blockchain networks to maintain consistent data across all honest nodes without relying on a central authority. These mechanisms address the distributed consensus challenge, drawing inspiration from the Byzantine Generals Problem, which has been a cornerstone for research in this field.

The Byzantine Generals Problem, introduced by Leslie Lamport in 1982 (Lamport, Shostak, and Pease 1982, pp. 203–226), illustrates the difficulty of achieving consensus in the presence of potential traitors. In the scenario, multiple generals, each commanding their own division, must agree on a common strategy to attack or retreat, with the requirement that more than half must agree to attack for success. However, the threat of traitors manipulating or blocking messages complicates the agreement on a unified plan. Lamport's research showed that to ensure a unified decision against f traitors, at least $3f + 1$ loyal generals are necessary.

Blockchain systems, being open networks, are susceptible to Byzantine nodes—those that act maliciously. Consensus mechanisms tackle Byzantine faults in two primary ways: voting-based approaches, like Practical Byzantine Fault Tolerance (PBFT) (Castro and Liskov 1999, pp. 173–186), which maintain consensus despite a certain number of malicious nodes; and proof-based approaches, such as Proof of Work (PoW) (Nakamoto 2008), which increase the cost for malicious behavior to reduce its incidence. The following discussion will explore common consensus mechanisms that utilize voting, proof, or a combination of both.

Voting-based Consensus In voting-based consensus models, every node has equal say in the decision-making process, voting on the validation of transactions or blocks, with the majority vote determining the outcome. The PBFT algorithm is a prime example of such a consensus mechanism.

Within the PBFT framework, nodes are designated to three roles: clients who submit transaction requests, a primary node responsible for creating blocks from these transactions and initiating the consensus process for each round, and replica nodes that engage in the consensus process alongside the primary. The primary and replica nodes rotate through a cycle known as a view, where the primary takes the lead in one round, and the others act as replicas. The primary node is determined by the formula $p = v \, mod \, |R|$, with v being the view number, p the primary node identifier, and $|R|$ the total number of replicas.

The PBFT consensus procedure is divided into three phases: pre-prepare, prepare, and commit. The pre-prepare and prepare stages are crucial for ordering transactions within a view, ensuring they are processed in a sequential manner by all nodes. Using a network with four replicas labeled $i = 0, 1, 2, 3$ as an example, replica 0 acts as the primary node. Here, N denotes the total number of replicas, and f signifies the number of faulty or Byzantine nodes. In an ideal scenario with no abnormal nodes ($f = 0$), the consensus process is illustrated in Figure 6.1.

Step 1: A client sends a request message m to each replica node. The primary node, node 0 in the current view, assigns the request a sequence number n and sends a pre-prepare message $\langle\langle PRE - PREPARE, v, n, D(m)\rangle, m\rangle$, to all replicas. Here, v is the current view number, and D denotes the digest of the message content.

Step 2: Upon receiving the pre-prepare message, replica node i checks for any conflicts with existing messages having the same sequence number n and view number v, but a different abstract D. If the sequence number n is valid for the current view v, node i accepts the request m from the primary and broadcasts a prepare message $\langle PREPARE, v, n, D(m)\rangle$. It also logs the pre-prepare and prepare

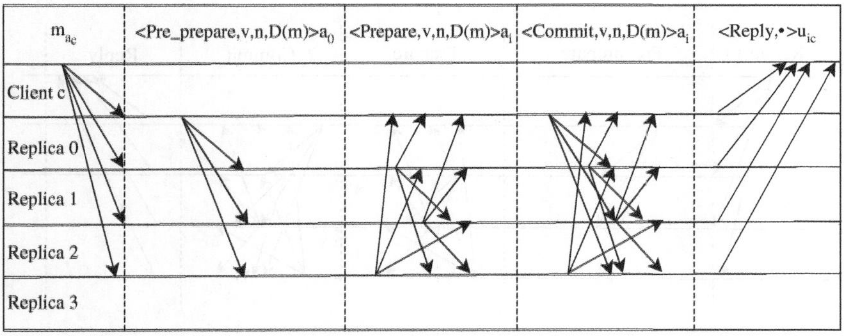

Figure 6.1 Message passing diagram of PBFT. (**N = 4, f = 0**).

messages. Node i is said to be in a pre-prepared state for request m once it sends either the pre-prepare or prepare message.

Step 3: Node i transitions to a prepared state for request m after receiving at least $2f + 1$ pre-prepare or prepare messages from different nodes, including itself, within an allotted time frame. This signifies that a quorum of nodes has acknowledged the request's validity.

Step 4: Node i sends a commit message $\langle COMMIT, v, n\rangle$ to signal to other nodes that request n under view v has been prepared locally. Node i considers request m to be committed once it receives at least $2f + 1$ commit messages from different nodes, including its own, indicating a majority consensus on the request's preparation.

Step 5: Node i executes the requests in order of their sequence number n and then communicates the outcome back to the client. The client considers the consensus round successful upon receiving matching messages from $f + 1$ nodes, confirming the request has been processed.

For the PBFT algorithm to function correctly, the total number of nodes N must meet the condition $N \geq 3f + 1$, ensuring the system can tolerate up to f faulty nodes. As depicted in Figure 6.2, the consensus process remains intact even if node 3 fails. It demonstrates that with $N = 4$, the PBFT consensus can accommodate a single faulty replica, thus ensuring the network's healthy and legitimate operation.

The PBFT consensus algorithm facilitates a tokenless and high-throughput operation within blockchain systems, typically achieving consensus within a short delay of about 2–5 seconds. However, PBFT has a communication complexity of $O(n^2)$, meaning that the required communication effort increases quadratically with the number of nodes in the network. In terms of fault tolerance, PBFT is designed to manage up to one-third of the nodes that are Byzantine fault tolerant. If one-third or more of the nodes act maliciously and partition the network,

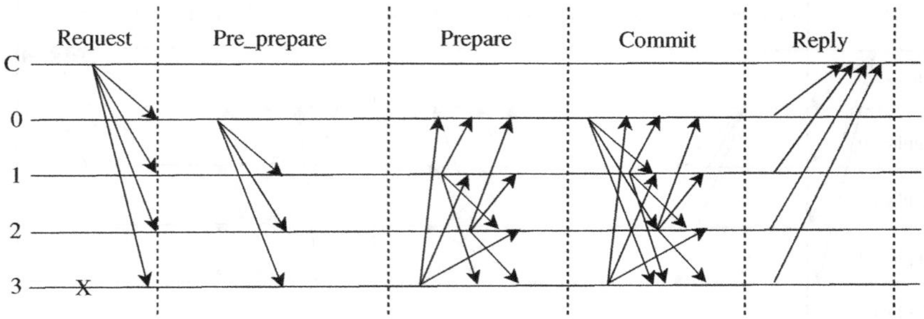

Figure 6.2 PBFT consensus process (**$N = 4, f = 1$**).

creating a scenario where a fork in the blockchain could occur, such an attack would be detectable through cryptographic evidence left behind.

Proof-based Consensus The essence of proof-based consensus algorithms is to elevate the costs associated with malicious activities, thereby reducing the probability of such behavior. The PoW consensus algorithm exemplifies this by demanding that nodes solve a cryptographic puzzle with a difficulty level that adjusts dynamically. The node that successfully uncovers the solution first earns the right to mine a new block.

Upon discovering a valid hash, a node proposes a block and disseminates it across the network. Any bookkeeping nodes that have not yet solved their own puzzle upon receiving this message cease their attempts and verify the legitimacy of the proposed block. If the block is deemed valid, they append it to their blockchain and proceed to tackle the next puzzle. Due to the nature of hash functions, nodes must on average make numerous attempts to find a solution. The difficulty of the puzzles is adjusted every 2016 blocks to maintain an average block addition interval of 10 minutes.

In some competitive scenarios, certain nodes may solve the puzzle before they receive a valid block from the network. Driven by the rewards for block generation, these nodes may still opt to broadcast their own blocks. This can lead to the creation of multiple conflicting blocks when other nodes receive them. In such cases, nodes prioritize the first block they receive and ignore subsequent conflicting ones, which can result in forks. To resolve these forks, nodes are permitted to continue block generation on different forks until one becomes the longest chain. Essentially, in the event of a fork, all nodes adhere to the rule of following the longest main chain, as depicted in Figure 6.3.

PoW consensus mechanism is lauded for its straightforward logic and several notable benefits. It simplifies the consensus process, requiring no additional

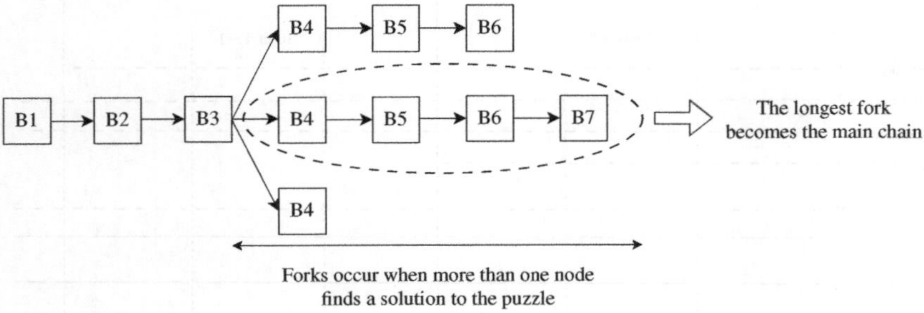

Figure 6.3 Forking issue in PoW consensus.

messaging between nodes, and its security features make it economically unfeasible for adversaries to undermine the network. Above all, PoW excels in promoting complete decentralization, allowing nodes to join and leave freely.

However, PoW is not without its flaws. It is often criticized for its low efficiency and the potential for delays, which can result in frequent forks that affect the finality of transactions. Moreover, the computational process of block generation consumes considerable resources, leading to substantial energy expenditure. As a result, Bitcoin, which utilizes PoW, has garnered the majority of the world's computational power, leaving other PoW-based blockchains to struggle for the necessary computational resources to maintain their security. This concentration of power poses a challenge to the ideal of decentralization that PoW aims to support.

Consensus Integrating Proof and Voting The performance limitations of proof- and voting-based consensus algorithms stem from computational demands and communication overhead, respectively. Each algorithm thus has its own strengths in scalability and efficiency. The PoV consensus algorithm, designed for permissioned blockchains, amalgamates the benefits of both approaches, offering high partition tolerance and reduced communication complexity (Li et al. 2017, pp. 466–473).

PoV consensus algorithm innovatively segments the responsibilities of nodes within a blockchain network into two distinct roles: bookkeeping and voting. Nodes with bookkeeping rights, known as bookkeepers, are authorized to form new blocks, while those with voting rights, referred to as voters, validate these transactions. A node can hold either role or both, and nodes without these roles have read-only access but can become active participants by applying to be bookkeeper candidates and competing in elections.

The block generation process in PoV involves a collaborative effort between bookkeepers and voters, as outlined in Figure 6.4. A block is made up of a header

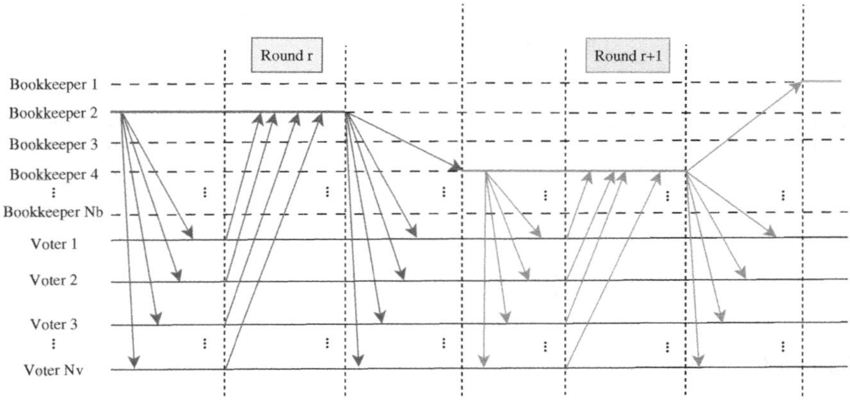

Figure 6.4 PoV consensus flowchart. (The color rendition of this image is available on the book's landing page on wiley.com).

and a set number of transactions. During a consensus round, the duty bookkeeper selects transactions from the pool to form a preblock, which is missing certain elements such as a timestamp, voter confirmations, and the identity of the next duty bookkeeper. The duty bookkeeper then circulates this preblock to voters for review. Voters validate the preblock by checking its header and transactions, and if they approve, they sign the header, signifying their consent. Once the duty bookkeeper has collected affirmative votes from over half of the voters, the preblock is transformed into an official block and distributed across the network. This process ensures that the blockchain's growth is both consensus-driven and efficient.

The PoV consensus algorithm distinguishes itself from PoW and PoS by not relying on computational power, which leads to quicker block generation times and higher transaction per second (TPS) rates. In terms of partition tolerance, the PoV consensus can operate continuously without forks, provided that over half of the voters and at least one honest bookkeeper are functioning correctly. Compared to PBFT, PoV significantly reduces communication complexity to $O(N_v)$, a stark contrast to PBFT's $O\left(N_{all}^2\right)$, which scales with the total number of nodes.

Unlike many consensus algorithms where only one bookkeeper generates blocks per round, leaving others idle and thus operating sequentially, PoV allows for more efficient use of network resources. However, there is still potential to enhance the performance of blockchain consensus mechanisms, especially when compared to the data throughput capabilities of traditional distributed systems.

To address the performance limitations inherent in sequential consensus processes, the PPoV consensus algorithm has been introduced. PPoV refines the data structure and consensus procedure of PoV, enabling multiple bookkeepers to generate blocks in parallel, which increases the system's throughput.

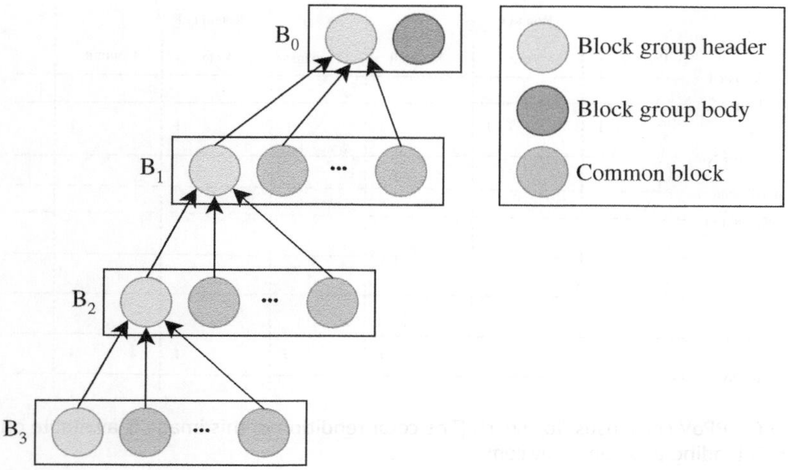

Figure 6.5 PPoV block dependency relationship. (The color rendition of this image is available on the book's landing page on wiley.com).

In the PPoV framework, data is organized into block groups, each consisting of a block group header and body. The header contains the group's height and voting results, while the body includes only blocks that have passed the voting stage. Each block within a group contains the hash of the previous block group, a Merkle root, the generator's public key, timestamp, and a set of transactions. Since blocks within a group are independent, an unbalanced tree structure, as shown in Figure 6.5, can be used to represent the dependencies among blocks in PPoV. This structure allows for a more flexible and efficient consensus process, optimizing the blockchain's ability to handle a higher volume of transactions.

The PPoV consensus model defines the entire process of producing a block group as a single consensus round. With each bookkeeper capable of generating a block within one round, PPoV introduces an additional consensus role: the aggregation right. Nodes granted this right, known as aggregators, are tasked with collecting and consolidating votes.

The PPoV consensus process is outlined in Figure 6.6 and consists of the following steps for each round:

Step 1: Prepare phase. Each bookkeeper autonomously creates a block and releases it into the network. Nodes on the blockchain collect these blocks, with a transaction allocation mechanism ensuring that each bookkeeper's transaction pool is unique, leading to distinct blocks from each bookkeeper.

Step 2: Vote phase. After collecting blocks from various bookkeepers, voters cast individual votes for each block and compile a comprehensive voting message

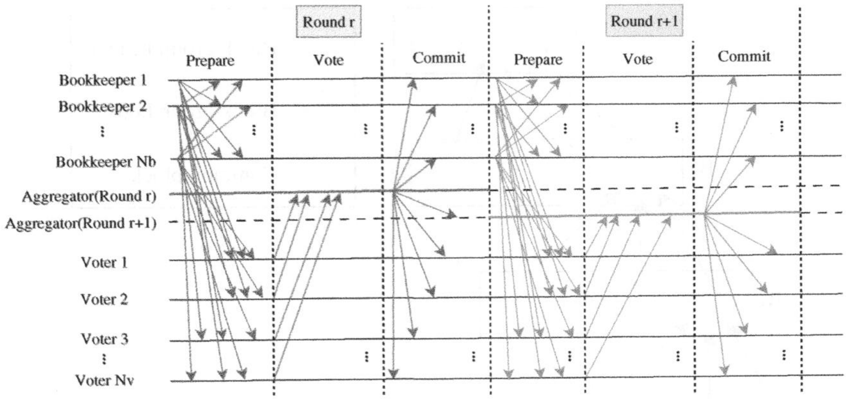

Figure 6.6 PPoV consensus flowchart. (The color rendition of this image is available on the book's landing page on wiley.com).

to send to the aggregator. This message includes the hash of each block, a vote indicating support or opposition (represented as $-1, 0, 1$), and relevant signature data.

Step 3.1: Commit phase. The aggregator consistently awaits incoming voting messages and tallies the votes. Once the count of affirmative or negative votes for any block exceeds two-thirds of the total voters, the aggregator includes these results and their corresponding voting messages in the block group header. The aggregator then generates a random number, known as the aggregator number for the next round, and includes it in the block group header before broadcasting it.

Step 3.2: Upon receiving all blocks from bookkeepers and the block group header from the aggregator, nodes locally compile these into a block group and store it in the database. Nodes then execute the transactions within the valid blocks of the block group. In addition to executing transactions, nodes update parameters such as the start time for the next consensus round, the next aggregator number, and the current consensus height according to the information in the block group header. This sequence ensures an efficient and democratic consensus process, optimizing the blockchain's ability to process transactions in a decentralized manner.

The PPoV consensus protocol significantly amplifies the blockchain's capacity for concurrent storage, functioning as an append-only database. PPoV maintains security and scalability, with a peak throughput exceeding 280,000 TPS. When compared to HotStuff, a consensus algorithm known for its efficiency, PPoV delivers a similar level of throughput but with a transaction confirmation latency that is only half of that experienced with HotStuff. In performance and functionality evaluations conducted by the China Academy of Information and Communications Technology, the PPoV-based blockchain platform reliably achieved a single-chain TPS of over 30,000 with perfect accuracy, demonstrating its robustness in high-throughput scenarios.

6.2 Blockchain-based Decentralized Storage

The explosive growth of global data volumes has made data storage an increasingly important issue. The continuously increasing demand for data storage is driving the rapid development of the entire storage market. Traditional centralized cloud storage has also revealed some problems, such as the risk of single-node failures, privacy and security risks, and high costs. To address these issues, decentralized storage systems based on blockchain technology have emerged. Representative decentralized storage systems based on blockchain, such as IPFS, Sia, and Storj, provide users with safer, more reliable, and flexible data storage solutions through innovative technical architectures and security mechanisms.

In this storage model, data is stored across multiple nodes in the network instead of being concentrated on centralized servers controlled by a single entity. Each node contains a complete copy of the data, and blockchain technology is used to verify and record data access and transactions, ensuring the integrity and security of the data. Decentralized storage emphasizes the sharing and distribution of data, making it more transparent, resistant to attacks, and traceable, while reducing the risk of data loss or tampering. The emergence of this storage model has promoted the innovation of data management methods and has also opened up a new frontier for data security and privacy protection, opening a new route for data storage and management in the digital age.

6.2.1 InterPlanetary File System

The InterPlanetary File System (IPFS) is a peer-to-peer distributed file system (Trautwein et al. 2022, pp. 739–752), which adopts distributed hash tables (DHTs), self-propagating block exchange, self-validating namespaces, etc., thereby offering functions like permanent data preservation, version control, and content-addressed addressing. Additionally, it has the characteristic of high throughput, saving nearly 60% of network bandwidth. Filecoin is a blockchain project built on top of the IPFS protocol, with built-in economic incentives and cryptography to ensure that files can be stored reliably over a long period. Users need to pay fees to store files on Filecoin storage nodes. Storage nodes are computers responsible for storing files, and they can earn token rewards by providing storage space.

The relationship between Filecoin and IPFS can be understood as IPFS providing the underlying infrastructure for file storage and distribution, while Filecoin is the incentive layer built on top of the IPFS architecture (Guidi, Michienzi and Ricci 2022, pp. 13–18). Filecoin utilizes the distributed storage capabilities of the IPFS network, encrypts and stores file fragments on nodes within the IPFS network, and encourages nodes to provide reliable storage space through economic incentives. This combination allows Filecoin to achieve a more secure and reliable decentralized storage solution, providing a mutually beneficial mechanism for both storage providers and users.

6.2.1.1 System Architecture

The IPFS protocol is divided into a set of subprotocols responsible for different functions, including the identity layer, network layer, routing layer, exchange layer, object layer, file layer, and naming layer, comprising seven subprotocols (Benet 2014). As shown in Figure 6.7, these subprotocols do not exist independently but are integrated with each other, leveraging their respective characteristics to jointly construct the IPFS protocol stack. This integration enables IPFS to provide a more comprehensive and efficient distributed file system functionality, offering users powerful decentralized storage and distribution capabilities.

a) **Identities:** Identities comprise protocols for verifying and managing node identities, ensuring that nodes within the network are trustworthy. Nodes are identified through NodeID, which is a cryptographic hash created using the Kademlia algorithm.
b) **Network:** Built on the Libp2p protocol, the network layer is a versatile peer-to-peer network protocol stack that offers secure, reliable, and flexible

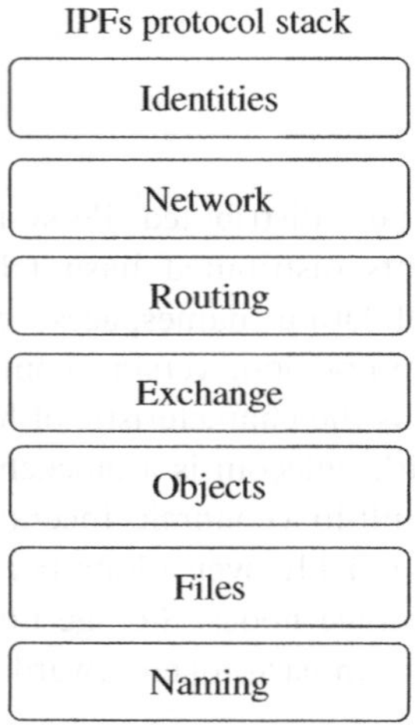

Figure 6.7 The IPFS protocol stack.

communication mechanisms between nodes. It supports a variety of transport protocols and encryption methods, enhancing the flexibility and security of communications between nodes.

c) **Routing:** Routing layer maintains information to locate specific peers and objects. Responds to both local and remote queries. Defaults to a DHT, but is swappable. Utilizes a DHT, storing data in nodes across the network in the form of <Key, Value> pairs. The Key is the hash value obtained after hashing the file, and the Value is the IP address where the file is stored. Through DHT, IPFS nodes can quickly locate data based on the hash value of the content, facilitating efficient data transfer.

d) **Exchange:** Exchange layer is responsible for managing data transfer and exchange between nodes. The IPFS protocol is inspired by BitTorrent, distributing data through the exchange of data blocks between peer nodes. To encourage data block sharing between nodes, IPFS has innovated upon BitTorrent by introducing a system that includes credit and policy mechanisms, resulting in a new data exchange protocol called BitSwap. Under the BitSwap protocol, sending data to other nodes increases a node's credit, while receiving data decreases it. This means that if a node continues to share data, the probability of other nodes sending data to it increases; conversely, if a node only receives data without sharing, the likelihood of other nodes sending it data decreases, potentially to the point of being ignored by other nodes.

e) **Objects:** Objects refer to the data objects stored on the IPFS network. These data objects can include files, directories, JSON data, etc., and each object has a unique hash identifier. IPFS uses the Merkle DAG data structure to represent and manage data within the object layer. Merkle DAG is a directed acyclic graph where each node is identified by the hash value of its data block, and nodes are linked by hash values to form a complete data structure.

f) **Files:** Files pertain to the part of IPFS that is used for storing and managing files. IPFS operates on files, allowing users to add, retrieve, and share files. IPFS uses content addressing to locate and access files, with each file having a unique hash identifier determined by its content. This means that the address of a file is generated based on its content, not its storage location.

g) **Naming:** Naming refers to the mechanism for assigning readable and memorable names to content. IPFS's naming layer primarily consists of IPNS (InterPlanetary Name System). Through IPNS, users can create a naming record and update it to point to the hash value of IPFS content, enabling the naming and dynamic publication of content.

6.2.1.2 Core Functions

Content Addressing IPFS utilizes content addressing to precisely locate and access data, where the unique identifier of the data is the hash value of the data content itself, rather than using file paths or names as in traditional location-based file systems. Typically, in IPFS, the SHA-256 algorithm is used to hash each file, generating a unique hash value, also known as a content identifier (CID) or content ID.

When users upload a file to an IPFS node, they receive a unique hash value calculated based on the file's content. Due to the properties of hash algorithms, files with the same content will always generate the same hash value, ensuring the uniqueness of the file. This means that no matter which node in the IPFS network the file is stored on, as long as the file's hash value is known, the file can be accurately located and retrieved. This mechanism eliminates the naming conflicts in traditional file systems.

Furthermore, since the hash value is calculated based on the content, if the file content changes, the hash value will also change. Therefore, IPFS can ensure data integrity by verifying the hash value, preventing data from being tampered with during transmission or storage.

IPFS also optimizes storage space by establishing hash deduplication, achieving persistent preservation of data. In IPFS, the same data content is de-duplicated across the network, reducing storage costs. Since data blocks with the same content have the same hash value, duplicate data can be easily removed, saving storage space. This ingenious design allows IPFS to manage and store data efficiently while ensuring the security and reliability of the data.

Version Control IPFS provides a sustainable way to store data on the Internet and offers the functionality to trace back to historical versions of data. IPFS combines the popular version control system Git with the powerful Merkle DAG object model to capture changes to the file system tree in a distributed-friendly manner. With IPFS, users can easily compare differences between different versions, recover previous versions, or view the status of files at specific points in time. This flexible history version management function gives users more control, helping them better manage and protect their data.

InterPlanetary Name System IPNS allows users to use a mutable, memorable name to point to the latest version of some content. Even if the content changes, users can access the latest version of the content through the same name. By updating the IPNS records, users can point to new IPFS content CIDs, achieving content updates and publishing. This mechanism allows users to easily manage dynamic content and ensures that users can access the latest version of the data.

6.2.1.3 Application Prospects

IPFS is suitable for storing large-scale data and provides users with secure, efficient, and reliable storage solutions. It is ideal for scientific data, medical images, digital assets, and other types of data that require long-term preservation and secure storage. For instance, IPFS is widely used for storing and sharing digital assets such as cryptocurrency wallets and nonfungible tokens (NFTs), ensuring the integrity and accessibility of the data.

Building upon IPFS, Filecoin introduces economic incentives through a token economy model. Storage providers can rent out their storage space to data holders and receive token rewards based on the storage space and duration provided. Filecoin utilizes proof mechanisms such as Proof of Replication (PoRep) and Proof of Spacetime (PoSt) to verify that storage providers have stored the data as agreed, ensuring the security and reliability of the data (Würsten and Cachin 2022). As one of the largest decentralized storage providers, Filecoin holds a significant market share, and its growth is essentially parallel to the expansion of the entire industry.

6.2.2 DDSs: Sia and Storj

Cloud storage services like Dropbox and Google Cloud have revolutionized the way we store and share large files online. The massive amount of data requires distributed systems for storage indexing. Existing centralized cloud services also employ distributed schemes, such as Spanner and TiDB. These entities can revoke access to accounts at any time, share their files with government agencies, or even delete files without cause. These storage models lead to unclear ownership of data assets and effectively allow large Internet companies like Amazon and Google to monopolize data. Therefore, being distributed does not necessarily mean being decentralized, but being decentralized definitely involves distribution.

The storage field is inherently suitable for decentralized applications for the following reasons: Firstly, it addresses issues of user data privacy and ownership. Files stored on decentralized file services are not influenced by any centralized authority, such as government agencies that might wish to control and audit content. It also prevents private companies from taking actions like auditing services or sharing files with law enforcement. Unlike centralized storage architectures, existing decentralized solutions divide data into small chunks, store them encrypted across various nodes globally, and create multiple copies of the data, enhancing the recovery capability against data loss. Next, we introduce decentralized cloud storage systems with Sia and Storj as examples.

6.2.2.1 Sia

Simple decentralized storage (Sia) is a blockchain-based decentralized cloud storage platform proposed in 2014, aiming to compete with existing storage solutions in both peer-to-peer and enterprise-level domains. Unlike renting storage space from a centralized provider, participants in Sia rent storage space from each other.

Sia itself only stores the storage contracts formed between parties, defining the terms of their agreements. By entering into contracts, storage providers agree to store the customer's data and regularly submit proofs of their ongoing storage until the contract expires. Each storage proof is specific to a particular file contract. Since these proofs are publicly verifiable and visible on the blockchain, network consensus can be used to automatically enforce storage contracts. Initially, Sia will be implemented as a blockchain-based Altcoin. Future plans include supporting a two-way peg with Bitcoin, as detailed in "Enabling Blockchain Innovations with Pegged Sidechains" (Vorick and Champine 2014).

System Architecture As shown in Figure 6.8, Sia adopts a system architecture similar to Bitcoin, which from bottom to top consists of the storage layer, data layer, network layer, consensus layer, Remote Procedure Call (RPC) layer, and application layer.

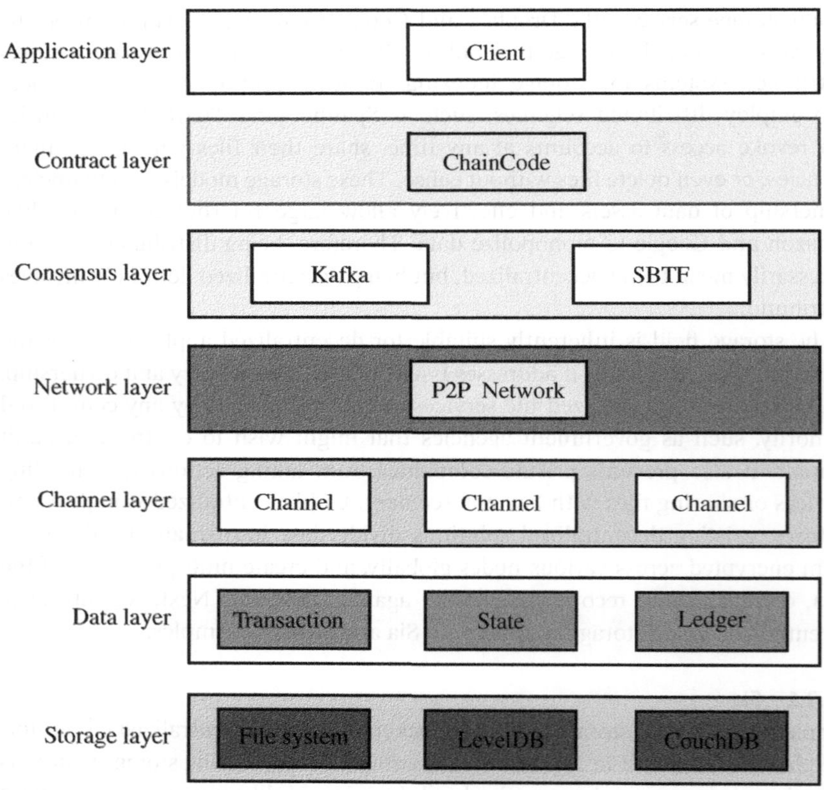

Figure 6.8 Sia system architecture.

i) **Storage layer:** Responsible for the persistence and management of data, ensuring the security and availability of the blockchain and related information.
ii) **Data layer:** Responsible for storing and managing all transaction and block information.
iii) **Network layer:** Responsible for the dissemination and communication of information between nodes.
iv) **Consensus layer:** The mechanism that ensures all nodes in the network reach a consensus, ensuring the validity of transactions and the security of the blockchain.
v) **RPC layer:** An interface that allows external applications to interact with Sia nodes.
vi) **Application layer:** The interface through which users directly interact with the Bitcoin network.

Sia differs from Bitcoin primarily in the way transactions are conducted. Bitcoin uses a scripting system to support various types of transactions, such as pay-to-public-key-hash (P2PKH) and pay-to-script-hash (P2SH). In contrast, Sia opts for an M-of-N multi-signature scheme for all transactions, completely abandoning the scripting system, which reduces complexity and attack surfaces. Sia's transactions include the following fields:

i) **Version:** The version number of the Sia protocol
ii) **Arbitrary data:** Each transaction has an arbitrary data field that can be used for any type of information. If this arbitrary data is signed by a node in the transaction, the node will be required to store that arbitrary data. These arbitrary data provide a decentralized way for hosts and clients to self-organize; they can be used to advertise available space or seek hosts for files, or to create decentralized file trackers.
iii) **Miner fee:** The reward given to miners
iv) **Inputs/outputs:** Incoming funds/outgoing funds
v) **File contract:** Agreements between storage providers and users, where users agree to pay storage providers for holding files, and storage providers agree to hold files for users for a certain period of time. The core of a file contract is the Merkle root hash of the file. To construct this hash, the file is split into fixed-size segments and hashed into a Merkle tree. The root hash, along with the file size, can be used to verify storage proofs.
vi) **Storage proof:** Proof that a storage provider has stored a particular file. Each storage proof is specific to a file contract. Storage proofs do not require any inputs or outputs; they only need a contract ID and proof data.

vii) **Signatures:** Each input in the transaction must be signed. The cryptographic signature itself is paired with an input ID, a time lock, and a set of flags indicating which parts of the transaction have been signed. The input ID indicates the input to which the signature is being applied.

Core Functions

Host Protections Contracts need to be agreed upon between storage providers and clients, allowing providers to reject unfavorable terms or illegal files. Providers can also refuse to sign contracts before the entire file upload is completed. Contract terms offer some flexibility to storage providers. They can advertise themselves as minimally reliable providers to attract clients with low prices and agree to minimal penalties for lost files, or they can advertise themselves as highly reliable providers, charge higher prices, and agree to severe penalties for lost files. Additionally, hosts are vulnerable to denial-of-service attacks, which could prevent them from submitting storage proofs or transferring files. Protecting themselves from such attacks is the responsibility of the hosts.

Client Protections Clients can use ECs, such as regenerating codes, to prevent hosts from going offline. These codes typically operate by splitting files into n blocks so that the file can be recovered from any m blocks of all blocks, where the values of n and m vary depending on the specific EC and redundancy rate. Each block is then encrypted and stored on multiple hosts. This ensures high file availability for clients even in situations of low network reliability. For an extreme example, if only 10 blocks are needed to recover the file and there are 100 blocks in total, the client is effectively relying on the 10 most reliable hosts rather than the average reliability. Availability can also be improved by re-hosting file blocks that are offline. Moreover, clients can reduce latency by downloading from the 10 nearest hosts or increase download speed by downloading from the 10 fastest hosts. These downloads can be carried out in parallel to maximize available bandwidth.

Uptime Incentives Storage proofs do not include mechanisms to enforce continuous uptime, nor do they require hosts to transfer files upon client request. Therefore, there might be concerns that hosts could hold clients' files hostage, demanding high fees for downloads. However, this attack can be mitigated by using ECs. This strategy allows clients to ignore uncooperative hosts and interact only with cooperative ones. Thus, power shifts from the hosts to the clients, turning "download fees" into "upload incentives."

In this scenario, clients offer rewards for file retrieval, and hosts must compete to provide the best quality of service (QoS). Clients can request files at any time, which incentivizes hosts to maximize their uptime to collect as many rewards as possible. Clients can also incentivize higher throughput and lower latency by offering relatively larger rewards. Clients can even perform random "checks," rewarding hosts simply for being online, even if they do not want to download anything. Online incentives are not part of the Sia protocol but rely entirely on client behavior.

Payments for downloads are expected to be conducted through existing micropayment channels. Micropayment channels allow clients to make multiple consecutive small payments with minimal delay and blockchain burden. Hosts can transmit a small part of the file and continue the transmission upon receiving a small payment. Using many consecutive payments minimizes the risk of being cheated for both parties. The amount of micropayments is small enough and fast enough to allow payments every few seconds without significantly affecting throughput.

Basic Reputation System Clients need a reliable method to select quality hosts. Simply analyzing a host's history is insufficient, as these records can be spoofed. Hosts can form contracts with themselves repeatedly, promising to store large "fake" files, such as files containing only zeros. In this case, obtaining storage proofs becomes very easy, while no actual data is being stored.

To mitigate this Sybil attack, clients can require hosts declaring in the arbitrary data field to have a certain number of coins locked for a period of time. For example, if 10 coins are time locked for 14 days, it can be said that the host has created a lock valued at 140 coin-days. By prioritizing hosts that have created high-value locks, clients can reduce the risk of Sybil attacks, as creating valuable locks is not a simple task.

Each client can freely choose their own equation for picking hosts and consider various factors, including price, locked value, provided storage capacity, and the penalties the host is willing to pay for lost files. Additionally, more complex systems, such as those using manual reviews or other metrics, can be implemented in a more centralized environment.

Application Prospects Sia is a variant of the Bitcoin protocol, designed to achieve decentralized file storage through encrypted contracts. These contracts can be used to enforce storage agreements between users and hosts. Once an agreement to store a file is reached, the host must periodically submit storage proofs to the network. Regardless of the user's actions, the host will automatically receive payment for storing the file.

Siafunds, a type of token within the Sia network, is the primary source of revenue for Nebulous Inc., the company responsible for the release and maintenance of Sia. Siafunds generate income based on the actual usage of the network, rather than through premining. This makes the revenue directly related to the network's activity, reducing the impact of malicious entities manipulating the network's currency market, thus providing a more stable economic model. Miners can also receive a portion of block subsidies from Siafunds, increasing their sources of income. In the long term, Siafunds will support two-way pegging with various currencies, providing an effective economic incentive mechanism for the Sia network and promoting the development of decentralized storage services.

6.2.2.2 Storj

Storj is a decentralized cloud storage platform based on blockchain technology (Li et al. 2023, pp. 1–10), designed to provide a secure, scalable, and cost-effective file storage solution. By splitting and encrypting users' files and storing them across multiple nodes globally, Storj not only enhances data security and privacy protection but also avoids the risk of single-node failures. Users can earn token rewards by providing storage space, promoting network participation and resource utilization, making data storage more flexible and efficient.

System Architecture As shown in Figure 6.9, the Storj network differs from other decentralized storage networks as it not only includes users and storage nodes but also introduces satellites as a third role. The three form an interdependent yet independently functioning relationship, achieving an efficient, secure, and reliable decentralized storage solution.

i) **Clients:** Users or applications that upload and download data within the network.

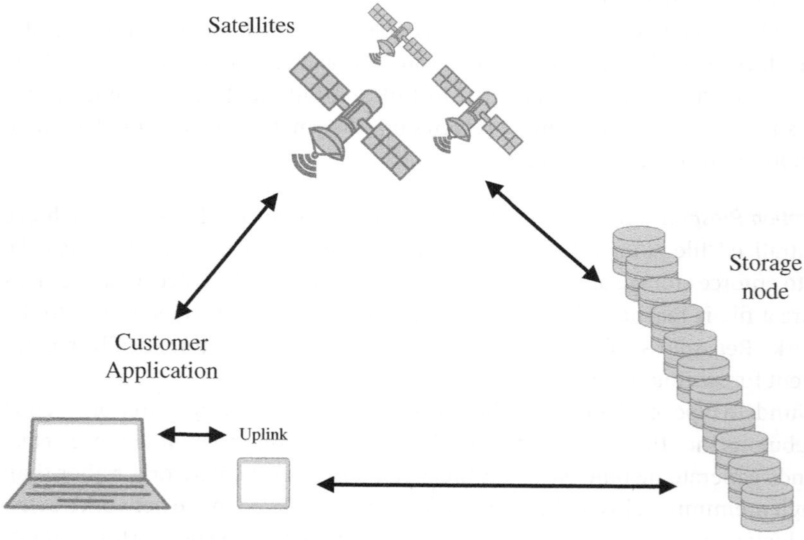

Figure 6.9 Storj system architecture.

ii) **Storage nodes:** Allow users to store data and earn rewards for storage and bandwidth.
iii) **Uplink nodes:** Interact on behalf of clients with other nodes. These nodes use the libuplink library, which provides the necessary functions for direct interaction with storage nodes and satellite nodes, to complete data storage and retrieval functions. These nodes do not need to stay online like the other two types and are relatively lightweight.
iv) **Satellite nodes:** Responsible for connecting users with storage nodes and acting as coordinators within the network. They manage storage node address information, object metadata; maintain storage node reputation, aggregate billing data, pay storage nodes, perform audits and repairs, and manage authorization and user accounts. Users have accounts on specific satellite nodes and trust them; any user can run their own satellite node. To avoid operational complexity, Storj recommends that users create accounts on satellite nodes hosted by trusted third parties, such as Storj Labs, friends, groups, or companies. Note that these satellite nodes are not satellites in space but a role within the distributed system.

Core Function

Data Recovery For all storage devices, node failure is inevitable. Hard drives will eventually fail after wearing down, and the servers providing network access to these drives will also encounter problems. Network links may be disrupted, power failures can occasionally cause serious damage, and storage media will become unreliable over time. Therefore, data must be stored with sufficient redundancy to recover from single-node failures. More importantly, no data should remain in one location indefinitely. In such an environment, the system must consider issues such as data repair and the replacement of lost redundancy.

Storj's redundancy strategy aims to store data in a way that ensures high-probability access to the data even when any number of individual nodes are offline. To ensure high durability of data, that is, the ability to access data even when failures occur, the Storj network uses RS codes (Storj Labs I 2018). Erasure coding is typically described by two parameters, k and n. If original data is encoded with EC (k, n), a total of n coding blocks are generated, and only any k of these blocks are needed to recover the original data. If the size of the data block is s bytes, then each block is approximately s/k bytes in size. In this way, Storj can recover the original data from the remaining any k valid blocks, repair the lost blocks, and store them on new storage nodes.

Data Auditing In a network with untrusted nodes, verifying the accuracy of the data returned by these nodes and whether their behavior conforms to expectations is crucial for ensuring the normal operation of the system. Auditing is a method of confirming the stability of nodes. Auditors, such as satellite nodes, will send challenges to storage nodes and expect valid responses. The challenge here is a request to the storage node to prove that it has the expected data.

In the Storj storage system, a fundamental assumption is that most storage nodes behave honestly, and the incentive mechanism ensures that most data is stored faithfully. As long as this assumption holds, RS code can detect and correct errors through mechanisms such as the Berlekamp-Welch error correction algorithm. Storj uses erasure coding on small stripes, reading a stripe as a challenge at a time, and then verifying the response of coding blocks. This allows Storj to conduct arbitrary audits without pregenerated challenges. During an audit, we first select a stripe and request all responsible storage nodes to provide the coding blocks for that stripe. Then, we run the Berlekamp-Welch algorithm [39, 73] on all coding blocks. When enough storage nodes return the correct information, the system can easily identify any errors or missing responses.

Reputation Management In a decentralized network, reputation indicators are a key part of promoting cooperation between nodes, ensuring that malicious actors in the network are excluded, thereby improving security, reliability, and durability. The reputation of storage nodes can be divided into four subsystems. The first subsystem is the PoW identity system, which requires storage node providers to provide short-term proof of their investment in time, equity, or resources. The second subsystem is the initial audit process, where satellite nodes will select a small number of unaudited storage nodes to join the target node list each time a file is uploaded. When a storage node successfully stores enough data and continues for a period (at least one payment cycle), the satellite node will begin to include that storage node in the general upload node selection. At the same time, it will send a signed message to the node stating that the audit process is complete and the storage node can now enter the routing tables of other nodes. The third subsystem is the filtering system, which prevents bad storage nodes from participating. Disqualified behaviors include too many audit failures; failure to return data at a reasonable speed; and too many normal operation time check failures. Finally, the fourth subsystem is the preference system. After filtering out unqualified storage nodes, the remaining statistics during the audit are used to prioritize the selection of better storage nodes during uploads. These statistics include performance characteristics such as throughput and latency, reliability and uptime history, geographic location, etc.

Application Prospects In the future, Storj plans to enhance its prospects as a decentralized storage platform through various innovations, including optimizations for popular file and content distribution, the ability for satellite nodes to pause access when necessary to increase file redundancy, and improvements to the user experience for metadata. By building a platformized approach to satellite nodes, Storj aims to completely eliminate centralized control over metadata. The advantages lie in emphasizing QoS and security privacy, avoiding Byzantine distributed consensus to improve efficiency, and deeply considering the details of redundancy and durability design. Additionally, by introducing an auditing and reputation system, Storj injects a positive and beneficial impact on the overall economic ecosystem, making its prospects in the field of decentralized storage even broader.

6.3 DSS Based on Blockchain and Mimic Security

In the context of the urgent need to solve storage security issues today, this section starts from the original intention of the design of a mimic distributed secure storage system and discusses in detail the design and implementation of the endogenously secure mimic distributed object storage system, analyzing how the system ensures the security and reliability of data. Finally, our focus lies on exploring the application of blockchain in the storage field through a blockchain logging system based on the PPoV consensus algorithm and further exploring the application of blockchain in the field of storage.

6.3.1 Background and Introduction

The ascent of blockchain technology has demonstrated significant benefits for the establishment of decentralized networks. It offers all nodes within a trustless network a tamper-resistant, unified view of transaction logs, allowing each node to independently access, and verify the entire record of global transactions. As a result, various storage domains, including cloud storage systems, DSSs, and databases, are increasingly integrating blockchain technology to enhance security (Sharma, Jindal, and Borah 2021, p. 102970; Hong et al. 2023, pp. 1685–1698; Lai, Liu, and Lo 2023, pp. 1–28; Ge et al. 2022, pp. 1092–1104). By integrating with blockchain, DSSs can achieve decentralized management of transactions and data, ensuring the security of metadata and the consistency and reliability of application data.

Despite these advancements, challenges such as double-spending, selfish mining, and 51% attacks remain, posing threats to the integrity of the blockchain ledger. Looking ahead, the development of distributed storage technologies integrated with blockchain should aim to create a decentralized, inherently secure storage ecosystem. This will require research into consensus algorithms that minimize communication costs and maximize robustness, as well as the exploration of decentralized identity management, key management, and access control technologies. These innovations will be crucial for ensuring data immutability and transparent processes.

Mimic defense (MD) (Zheng et al. 2022, pp. 422–435), as a type of adaptive defense based on endogenous mechanisms, was introduced into cyberspace by Professor Jiangxing Wu from the Chinese Academy of Engineering (Wu 2022, p. 156301). This method has proven effective in addressing cybersecurity challenges in cyberspace, especially when facing significant threats such as unknown vulnerabilities, backdoors, viruses, and trojans. It overcomes several limitations of traditional security methods in dealing with uncertain threats.

Currently, prototypes and products of routers, Web servers, and DSSs with MD attributes have been successively launched, accompanied by rigorous testing. The findings demonstrate that MD technology indeed reduces the probability of unknown vulnerabilities and backdoor exposure, and can greatly improve system security.

Traditional DSSs can alleviate the pressure brought by the growing amount of massive data. However, they still face significant security challenges. Introducing MD mechanisms into storage systems provides a dynamic and adaptive security solution. The mimic distributed object storage system, which leverages blockchain technology and MD principles, is characterized by its decentralized structure and inherent security features. It also incorporates a proprietary blockchain logging system designed for tamper-proof operation.

6.3.2 Mimic Distributed Secure Storage System

Against the backdrop of an urgent need to address storage security issues, the concept of endogenously secure mimic DSSs has been proposed for the first time and is continuously being developed and perfected. The following will describe the design and implementation of the mimic distributed secure storage system from three aspects: system principles, system architecture, core functions, as well as analyze how the system ensures the security and reliability of data.

6.3.2.1 System Principle

Drawing on the principles of MD and erasure coding (EC) technology, the object storage architecture typically encompasses three main components: the client, the object storage device, and the metadata server. The client offers users a straightforward and user-friendly platform for storage services, interacting with both the metadata servers and the object storage devices. The metadata server manages the storage and handling of object metadata, offering services such as object location and access control permissions to clients. The object storage device, the central element, manages persistent objects and provides an interface for clients to access data for reading and writing operations.

The mimic distributed object storage model incorporates multiple ECs, dynamic random transformations, and employs various redundancies along with active

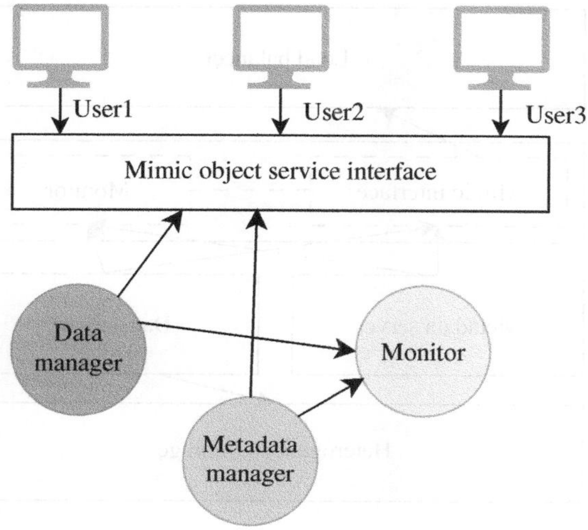

Figure 6.10 Mimic distributed object storage model.

defense mechanisms. These features enhance data storage redundancy and increase the unpredictability of data storage, enabling the system to counter attacks and bolster overall security.

In practical system design, data management and metadata management are often decoupled, with a monitoring component integrated into the system. This allows for dynamic configuration of both data management nodes and metadata management nodes. The system provides users with a mimic object service interface that facilitates redundancy and heterogeneity. The system model is illustrated in Figure 6.10.

The distributed object storage system infused with mimic features boasts several key attributes:

a) **Redundancy:** The system employs a dual approach to data redundancy, utilizing ECs for object data to enhance hardware utilization and data reliability, and multiple copies for object metadata.
b) **Heterogeneity:** The system introduces diversity at both the software and hardware levels. Different ECs are used for data coding at the software level, while data nodes and metadata nodes operate on a variety of hardware devices with distinct architectures, operating systems, and versions, increasing the system's heterogeneity and safeguarding against targeted exploits.
c) **Dynamic configuration:** The system's dynamic MD is primarily executed by a monitor module, which oversees data and metadata nodes. It updates their states based on detected attacker activity, proactively takes nodes offline when necessary, and initiates data migration. Once a node is safely offline, it must be repaired by an administrator to mitigate security threats. Secure nodes can be

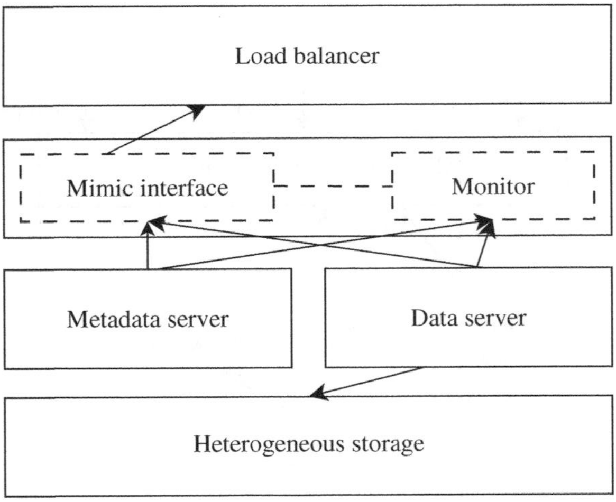

Figure 6.11 Architecture of the mimic distributed object storage system.

brought online at any time to join the operational system. Furthermore, when ECs are used for data encoding, the system dynamically adjusts the parameters to increase uncertainty and strengthen security.

d) **Low storage cost:** The system leverages multiple ECs as its redundancy and heterogeneity strategy, which is more space-efficient and fault-tolerant compared to multicopy strategies. It requires less memory, offers higher fault tolerance, and has a smaller repair bandwidth. Files are encoded with ECs and stored in parity chunks, enabling granular data deduplication and further enhancing space utilization.
e) **Tamper-proof logs:** Log data is immutably stored in a blockchain, ensuring its integrity and preventing unauthorized alterations. The system can develop strategies based on log audits, further enhancing its security performance.

6.3.2.2 System Architecture

The architecture of the mimic distributed object storage system, as depicted in Figure 6.11, is primarily divided into three components: the mimic interface service module, the metadata service module, and the data service module. Each service module comprises multiple service nodes, which support horizontal scaling, effectively addressing the issue of data capacity. Both the metadata service module and the data service module operate transparently to users.

Mimic Interface Service The nodes within the mimic interface service module operate in one of three states: executor, monitor, and candidate, with all states designed to support deployment across multiple nodes. The executor node offers Representational State Transfer Hypertext Transfer Protocol Secure (RESTful HTTPS) interface services and handles client requests that are routed by the load balancer. The monitor node is tasked with overseeing the status of metadata and data service nodes, detecting any security breaches or data loss. Each monitor is assigned a unique set of data nodes and is responsible for tracking the status of both its own nodes and those managed by other monitors. The system dynamically adjusts the monitor topology as new monitors join or existing ones leave.

Each monitor must have at least one candidate node to ensure business continuity in the event of monitor unavailability. A candidate node can step in as a new monitor, ensuring uninterrupted service delivery and maintaining high availability.

The mimic interface service module maintains awareness of data and metadata nodes through heartbeat signals. It uses consistent hashing to locate and route data and metadata through two separate hash rings. Data exchanges between the mimic interface service, metadata service, and data service are secured via the HTTPS protocol. This approach ensures secure and efficient communication across the system.

Metadata Service The metadata service module plays an essential role in handling the metadata associated with data objects, including details such as creation timestamps, permission settings, and EC metadata. This module is composed of multiple independent metadata service instances, each functioning as a standalone program, and is designed to support horizontal scaling.

Metadata is stored within an Elasticsearch cluster, which the metadata service utilizes to manage structured metadata efficiently. The metadata service and the Elasticsearch cluster operate autonomously, ensuring flexibility and redundancy. The service provides a RESTful HTTPS interface for secure communications and also regularly sends heartbeat signals to announce its operational status to other nodes in the system, thereby maintaining a robust and dynamic node registry.

Data Service The data service module is integral to the storage of data within the system. It consists of multiple data services designed for horizontal scalability, with each service operating as an independent program. This flexibility allows the module to integrate with various storage clusters, including IPFS and Ceph's File System (CephFS), ensuring a diverse and interchangeable storage infrastructure.

Within the mimic distributed object storage system, the data service manages the storage of data objects on the local file system. Rather than storing the entire object, it saves the data blocks resulting from erasure coding. Each block, post-erasure coding, becomes the fundamental unit within the data service for data storage. The metadata service, in turn, stores the location information for each of these blocks.

The data service offers a RESTful HTTPS interface for secure data transactions. Furthermore, each data service instance transmits heartbeat signals to other nodes, thereby continuously signaling its operational status and presence within the network. This mechanism contributes to the overall health monitoring and fault tolerance of the system.

6.3.2.3 Core Functions

Data Positioning In distributed systems, consistent hashing (Karger et al. 1997, pp. 654–663) addresses the challenges of data distribution and routing in dynamic network topologies. By employing consistent hashing, systems can streamline operations related to locating and accessing data.

The mimic distributed object storage system utilizes two hash rings to manage data and metadata. When an object is uploaded, the system encodes it, and all resulting blocks are stored in the data nodes. Concurrently, the object's metadata is stored in the metadata nodes, with three copies made for redundancy.

During an object upload request from a client, the load balancer module routes the request to the interface service module for processing by an executor. The system dynamically selects three ECs, encodes the uploaded object, and stores the coding blocks in the corresponding data nodes as directed by the data location algorithm. The object's metadata is then stored in the relevant metadata nodes, again with three copies. Finally, the outcome of the object upload request is communicated back to the client. The object upload process is further detailed in Figure 6.12.

Data positioning in the system is bifurcated into handling data and metadata separately: (1) **Data.** The system stores both the parity blocks resulting from ECs and the original data blocks in the data nodes. Each block goes through a series of operations for storage. Initially, the system computes the hash value for each block. Then, it identifies the data node with the smallest hash value that is larger than the computed block hash. Finally, the block is stored on the designated data node. (2) **Metadata.** The system stores the metadata across three metadata nodes. During this process, the system generates a hash value based on the object ID and maps it onto the hash ring using a pseudo-random algorithm. Subsequently, three metadata nodes are selected on the hash circle for storing the relevant metadata information.

Upon receiving an object download request, the load balancer module routes the request to the interface service module for processing by an executor. The system first calculates the hash value from the object ID, maps this hash value onto the metadata hash ring through a pseudo-random algorithm, and retrieves the metadata information from the first metadata node. Afterward, it extracts the hash values of all parity chunks using the metadata information and maps these onto the hash ring. The target nodes are chosen as the smallest data nodes greater

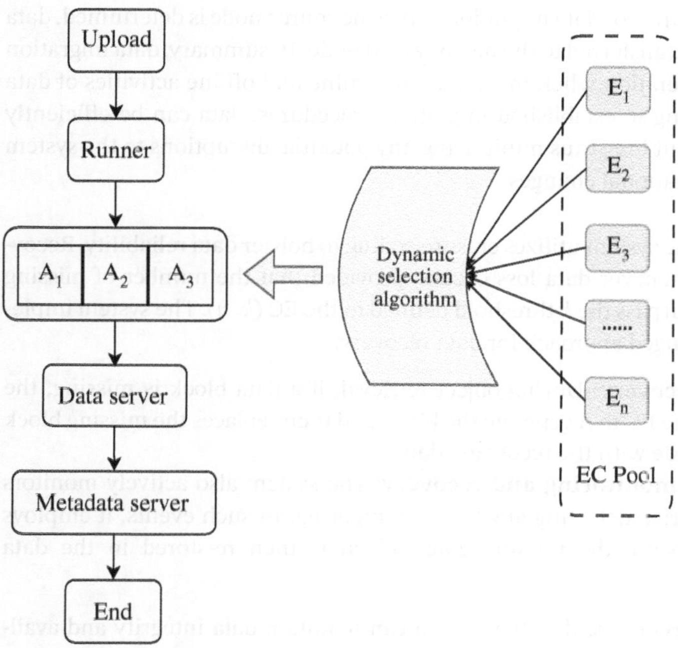

Figure 6.12 The process of uploading an object in the mimic distributed object storage system.

than each respective hash value to obtain the parity chunk information. The object information is then decoded using the corresponding EC and parameter information. Finally, the decoded object is returned to the client, applying multivalue judgment principles.

Data Migration Data migration is a crucial process that occurs during the online and offline activities of data nodes to ensure the integrity and continuity of the system. In scenarios where a data node goes offline, migration is necessary due to repeated security breaches that diminish the node's reliability or because the node becomes non-operational due to hardware failures or other issues. The migration process from the offline node must be managed carefully to prevent any data loss. This involves identifying the next data node in the clockwise direction on the hash ring and transferring all data from the current node to this designated successor node. Conversely, in online scenarios, data migration is triggered by the addition of a new data node to the system. This process involves positioning the new node on the hash ring and then reallocating some of the data from an existing node to the new one. The starting point for this operation is the placement of the new node on the ring, and the first node encountered moving clockwise from this point is selected as the source for data migration. Once the source node is determined, data from this node is transferred to the newly added node. In summary, data migration is an essential operation when managing the online and offline activities of data nodes. By adhering to established migration procedures, data can be efficiently transferred without loss, thus minimizing any potential disruptions to the system during these operational changes.

Data Recovery The system utilizes erasure coding to bolster data reliability. Recovery is feasible whenever data loss occurs, provided that the number of missing blocks does not surpass the k threshold defined in the EC (k, n). The system implements a dual-pronged approach for data recovery:

i) **Real-time recovery:** During object retrieval, if a data block is missing, the system uses the EC to regenerate the block and then replaces the missing block in the data node with the recovered data.
ii) **Continuous monitoring and recovery:** The system also actively monitors for data integrity, detecting any loss or tampering. In such events, it employs the EC to restore the missing data, which is then re-stored in the data node.

These strategies ensure that the system can maintain data integrity and availability, even in instances of data loss or node failure.

6.3.3 Logging System Based on Consortium Blockchain

Blockchain, as a rapidly developing distributed ledger technology, features decentralization, data immutability, and trustlessness. In the mimic storage system, logs are used to record system anomalies and state changes. All operations in the mimic system are written to the log system in the form of logs. Logs must be permanently saved and cannot be tampered with, ensuring that all state changes are traceable and documented. However, mimic storage faces issues such as logs being easily attacked and records being easily tampered with. Therefore, the mimic storage system uses blockchain technology to record logs. Records in the blockchain are tamper-proof, and logs written to the blockchain are permanently saved. To further improve the scalability of the blockchain system, this system employs the PPoV consensus algorithm, enabling the blockchain system to support multiple bookkeeping nodes to generate blocks simultaneously.

6.3.3.1 System Architecture

The blockchain server network is central to the mimic storage logging system, where nodes interact to form a decentralized network that offers a log storage service accessible to external entities. PPoV consensus protocol is utilized to

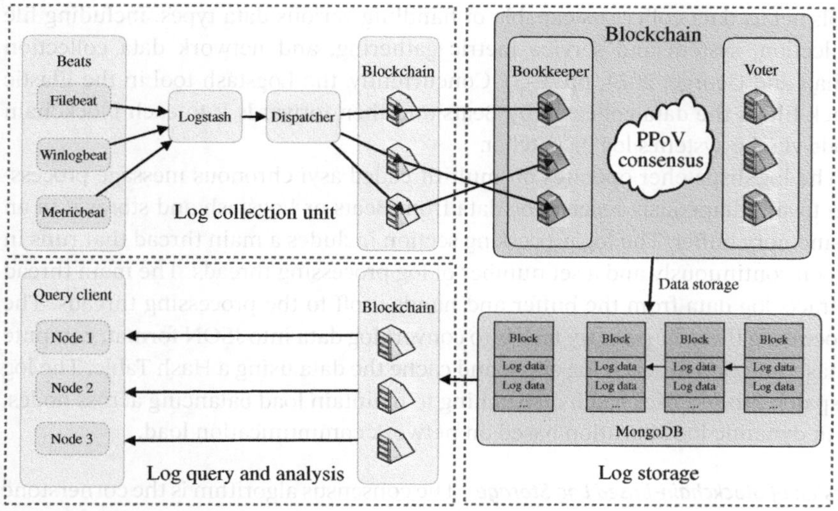

Figure 6.13 The architecture of the blockchain-based logging system.

boost the efficiency, scalability, and security of this blockchain-driven logging system.

As shown in Figure 6.13, the integrated blockchain logging system architecture consists of a log collection unit, a log storage unit, and a log query and analysis unit. The mimic DSS includes various log sources such as I/O agents, a range of heterogeneous executors, and clustered configuration management modules. The log collection unit's role is to collect log data from these modules, discard any invalid logs, standardize the log formats, and then randomly select server nodes for the dissemination of log data. The log query and analysis unit is designed to extract log entries from the blockchain, enabling queries based on criteria like blockchain height, block logs, time frames, and error codes.

6.3.3.2 Core Function

The core functions of the consortium blockchain-based mimic storage logging system can be divided into two principal areas: log collection and dispatch, and log storage. The former pertains to the aggregation and organization of log data, while the latter involves various components that handle block communication, synchronization, and the storage of logs. The specifics are as follows:

Log Collection and Dispatch The log collection unit is tasked with collecting log data. This system employs an open-source log collection tool along with a custom-developed log dispatcher. Within the Elastic application stack, the Beats tools act as data collectors capable of handling various data types, including file collection, system and service metric gathering, and network data collection (Shaji and George, 2024, pp. 1–5). Concurrently, the Logstash tool in the Elastic stack filters the data collected by Beats and then forwards it to each blockchain node via the system's log dispatcher.

The log dispatcher operates on multithreaded asynchronous message processing to simultaneously receive log data from Beats or Logstash and stores it in an in-memory buffer. The log processing section includes a main thread that runs in a loop continuously and a set number of log processing threads. The main thread extracts log data from the buffer and hands it off to the processing threads. The processing threads' primary task is to convert log data into JSON format, compute a hash function for each log entry, and cache the data using a Hash Table. The log dispatch process uses batch dispatching to maintain load balancing across nodes, with dynamic log allocation based on network communication load.

Design of Blockchain-based Log Storage The consensus algorithm is the cornerstone of the blockchain, relying on various elements such as network and database modules for its operation. These foundational components together form the infrastructure of the logging system's blockchain, as shown in Figure 6.14.

A detailed introduction to each module is as follows:

i) **Network module:** The network module is a crucial element of the blockchain, serving as the backbone of all communication within the system. It facilitates two primary methods for sending messages: one method sends messages directly to a specific node using its IP address and port, while the other method disseminates messages across the entire network to every node. This dual approach ensures both targeted and widespread communication as needed.
ii) **Database module:** Built on MongoDB, this module is tasked with storing block data and provides an interface for general data queries, ensuring efficient data retrieval and management.
iii) **Account management module:** This module oversees the on-chain records of various accounts, including those of voters, candidates, and bookkeepers, ensuring the integrity and proper management of user accounts within the system.
iv) **Message management module:** It establishes a standardized message format and offers methods for creating different types of messages, streamlining communication within the blockchain network.
v) **Key management module:** Responsible for key management functions, this module handles random key generation, loading of existing keys, data signing and verification, and data hashing, providing a secure foundation for transactions and data integrity.

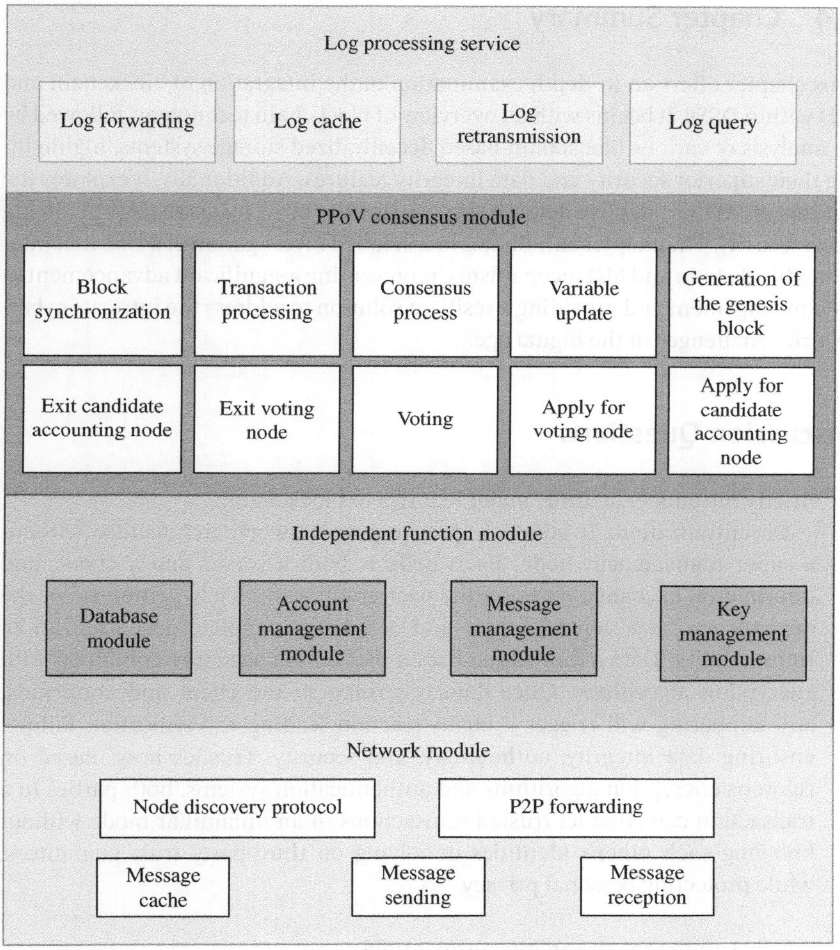

Figure 6.14 Functional modules of the blockchain-based logging system.

vi) **PPoV consensus module:** Implementing the PPoV consensus algorithm, this module includes auxiliary functions for block synchronization, genesis block creation, and the generation of ordinary blocks, catering to the specific needs of the application.

vii) **Log processing service module:** Based on the PPoV blockchain implementation, this service Module provides comprehensive log reception, processing, and query services, enhancing the system's ability to manage and retrieve log data efficiently.

6.4 Chapter Summary

This chapter offers an in-depth examination of the integration of blockchain and MD within DSSs. It begins with an overview of blockchain technology, followed by an analysis of various blockchain-based decentralized storage systems, highlighting their superior security and data integrity features. Additionally, it explores the concept of MD, an adaptive defense strategy that has proven effective in enhancing cybersecurity. The chapter culminates in a detailed investigation of a DSS that integrates blockchain and MD mechanisms, representing a significant advancement in data management and providing a resilient solution to address the intricate cybersecurity challenges in the digital age.

Discussion Questions

1 Briefly introduce the three major features of blockchain.

Decentralization: It adopts a peer-to-peer network architecture without a super management node. Each node is both a server and a client, and information exchange relies on the user group, completely getting rid of the dependence on a central server and achieving complete decentralization. Immutability: Data organization uses a blockchain structure combined with encryption algorithms. Once data is written to the chain and confirmed, any tampering will trigger a chain reaction leading to verification failure, ensuring data integrity, authenticity, and security. Trustlessness: Based on rigorous encryption algorithms and authentication systems, both parties in a transaction can conduct trusted transactions in an unfamiliar mode without knowing each other's identities or relying on third-party trust guarantees, while protecting personal privacy.

2 Briefly summarize the architecture of IPFS.

The IPFS protocol is composed of seven subprotocols: identity layer, network layer, routing layer, exchange layer, object layer, file layer, and naming layer, which together form the protocol stack. The identity layer verifies the identity of nodes; the network layer implements secure communication based on the Libp2p protocol; the routing layer uses DHT to store data; the exchange layer realizes data exchange through the BitSwap protocol; the object layer manages data using Merkle DAG; the file layer operates on a file-by-file basis; and the naming layer implements content naming through IPNS. This architecture enables IPFS to have efficient distributed storage and distribution capabilities, providing users with a powerful decentralized storage solution that meets the data storage and access needs of different scenarios.

3 Briefly introduce the core functions of the blockchain-based mimic storage log system.

Log collection and Dispatch: Open-source log collection tools are combined with self-developed Log Dispatchers. Beats collects data, Logstash filters and processes it, and Log Dispatcher handles concurrent log data reception in multithreaded asynchronous mode, converts it into JSON format and caches it, and dynamically allocates the number of logs based on network load to distribute them to blockchain nodes. Blockchain log storage system design: The blockchain architecture includes a network module, a database module, an account management module, a message management module, a key management module, a PPoV consensus module, and a log processing service. The network module supports two message sending methods; the database module stores block data based on MongoDB; the account management module maintains the list of accounts on the chain; the message management module defines a unified message format; the key management module provides key management functions; the PPoV consensus module implements the consensus algorithm and related functions; and the log processing service provides log reception, processing, and query services.

References

Benet J. 2014. Ipfs-content addressed, versioned, p2p file system. arXiv preprint arXiv:1407.3561.

Buterin V. Ethereum white paper. GitHub repository, 2013.

Castro, M. and Liskov, B., 1999. Practical byzantine fault tolerance. OsDI., 99(1999), pp. 173–186.

Ge, Z., Loghin, D., Ooi, B.C., Ruan, P. and Wang, T., 2022. Hybrid blockchain database systems: design and performance. Proceedings of the VLDB Endowment, 15(5), pp. 1092–1104.

Guidi B, Michienzi A, Ricci L. 2022. Evaluating the decentralisation of filecoin. Proceedings of the 3rd International Workshop on Distributed Infrastructure for the Common Good. (pp. 13–18).

Hong, Z., Guo, S., Zhou, E., et al., 2023. GriDB: Scaling Blockchain Database via Sharding and Off-Chain Cross-Shard Mechanism. Proceedings of the VLDB Endowment, 16(7), pp. 1685–1698.

Karger D, Lehman E, Leighton T, et al. 1997, May. Relieving hot spots on the World Wide Web. Proceedings of the 29th Annual ACM Symposium on the Theory of Computing. (pp. 654–663).

Lai, Z., Liu, C. and Lo, E., 2023. When Private Blockchain Meets Deterministic Database. Proceedings of the ACM on Management of Data, 1(1), pp. 1–28.

Lamport, L., Shostak, R. and Pease, M., 1982. The Byzantine Generals Problem. ACM Transactions on Programming Languages and Systems, 4(3), pp. 382–401.

Li K, Li H, Hou H, et al. 2017, Proof of vote: a high-performance consensus protocol based on vote mechanism & consortium blockchain. In 2017 IEEE 19th International Conference on High Performance Computing and Communications; IEEE 15th International Conference on Smart City; IEEE 3rd International Conference on Data Science and Systems (HPCC/SmartCity/DSS) IEEE, (pp. 466–473).

Li H, Mi X, Dou Y, et al. 2023. An empirical study of storj dcs: ecosystem, performance, and security IEEE/ACM 31st International Symposium on Quality of Service (IWQoS). IEEE, 2023: (pp. 1–10).

Nakamoto, S., 2008. Bitcoin: a peer-to-peer electronic cash system. Decentralized business review, 5(2).

Shaji A S, George M M. 2024. Elastic stack: a comprehensive overview. In 2024 IEEE Recent Advances in Intelligent Computational Systems (RAICS) (pp. 1–5).

Sharma, P., Jindal, R. and Borah, M.D., 2021. Blockchain-based decentralized architecture for cloud storage system. Journal of Information Security and Applications, 62, 102970.

Storj Labs I. 2018. Storj: A decentralized cloud storage network framework.

Szabo N. 1994, Smart contracts[J]. Unpublished manuscript.

Trautwein D, Raman A, Tyson G, et al. 2022. Design and evaluation of IPFS: a storage layer for the decentralized web. Proceedings of the ACM SIGCOMM 2022 Conference. (pp. 739–752).

Vorick, D, Champine, L. 2014. Sia: Simple decentralized storage[J]. Retrieved May, 8: 2018.

Wang H, Li H, Wang Z, et al. 2023. Optimizing read performance in lightweight blockchain with cooperative storage scheme. In 2023 Fifth International Conference on Blockchain Computing and Applications (BCCA). IEEE, (pp. 150–157).

Wu, J., 2022. Development paradigms of cyberspace endogenous safety and security. Science China Information Sciences, 65(5), 156301.

Würsten, M, Cachin, C. 2022. Filecoin consensus.

Zheng, Y., Li, Z., Xu, X. and Zhao, Q., 2022. Dynamic defenses in cyber security: Techniques, methods and challenges. Digital Communications and Networks, 8(4), pp. 422–435.

7
Quantum Bit, Q-Computers, and Q-Networks

As quantum computing progresses rapidly, we are stepping into a new era shaped by the fundamentals of quantum mechanics. This cutting-edge computing model brings unparalleled computational capabilities and speed. Additionally, communication theories and technologies rooted in quantum computing provide more secure and efficient means of transmitting information, addressing the limitations and weaknesses of traditional communication systems. This chapter explores the core principles of quantum computing, quantum memory, quantum transmission, and quantum networks, examining the transformative impact quantum technology will have on the world.

7.1 Fundamental Principles of Quantum Computing

Everything in the quantum world originates from the fundamental principles of quantum physics, including phenomena such as quantum superposition and quantum entanglement. This section provides the basic definitions and an introduction to the quantum world, with a particular focus on quantum information. It explores what makes quantum information unique and how it differs from classical information.

7.1.1 The Concept and Properties of Quantum Bits

Classical Newtonian mechanics posits that the universe consists of isolated objects that interact with one another through forces. Newtonian mechanics describes the motion of objects as deterministic, with objects occupying definite positions in space and time, and their motion following well-defined trajectories. From a philosophical perspective, the worldview based on classical Newtonian mechanics leads to an important conclusion: the future of objects is entirely predictable. Although the interactions between objects in complex systems may be difficult to

Distributed Storage in Practice, First Edition. Hui Li, Hanxu Hou, and Hong Tan.

fully compute and determine, once the initial states and all interactions are known, the outcomes are predictable.

The renowned French mathematician Pierre-Simon Laplace proposed that, since Newton's equations can predict the trajectories of all objects, the future states of everything in existence can be fully determined. He imagined a supreme intelligence capable of calculating the future states of the entire universe, including all aspects of human society's development. This hypothetical entity is often referred to as "Laplace's Demon." However, the advent of quantum mechanics gradually challenged and ultimately undermined the notion of "Laplace's Demon."

In physics, if a thing has an indivisible fundamental unit, it is considered "quantized," and this smallest unit is referred to as a "quantum." The renowned Heisenberg Uncertainty Principle states that the position and momentum of a quantum particle cannot be simultaneously measured with arbitrary precision. Accepting this principle necessitates abandoning the notion of a particle being fully localized, meaning that the concept of a particle existing deterministically at a specific point in space-time does not hold. Consequently, the description of existence in Newtonian mechanics fundamentally differs from that in quantum mechanics—it is a distinction between locality and nonlocality. The nonlocality is intrinsically related to the essence of quantum existence (Han et al. 2021, pp. 74–116).

Understanding the nature of quantum phenomena is often illustrated by the thought experiment known as Schrödinger's Cat: a cat inside a box exists in a superposition of being both alive and dead, and only when the box is opened and observed does the cat transition into a definite state of either being alive or dead. The experiments conducted by Otto Stern and Walther Gerlach on the spin of silver atoms provide a more scientific means of elucidating the concept behind Schrödinger's Cat.

According to the classical planetary model of the atom, a silver atom has an unpaired electron in its outermost shell, producing a small magnetic field as it spins, behaving like a tiny magnet. Stern and Gerlach designed an experimental apparatus, as shown in Figure 7.1, containing a uniform magnetic field. As silver atoms pass through this magnetic field, they experience deflection due to the electron's spin.

According to classical physics, the degree of deflection of the silver atoms depends on the orientation of the atom's magnetic moment, which in turn depends on the direction of the electron's spin. In vertical measurements, only the rotation within the 2D plane is considered. If the magnetic axis is completely horizontal, the silver atoms will not deflect; conversely, if the magnetic axis is completely vertical, the silver atoms will experience maximal deflection. The direction of the spin's north or south pole indicates the direction of the electron's spin, with the upward vertical direction defined as the 0° direction. As shown in

Figure 7.1 Stern-Gerlach experimental apparatus.

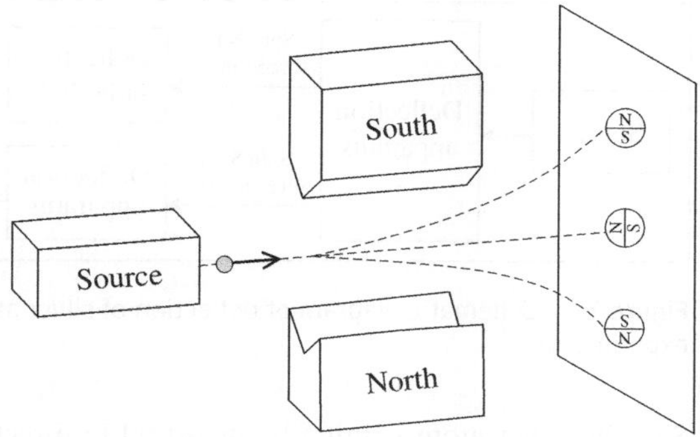

Figure 7.2 Direction of electron spin and its representation.

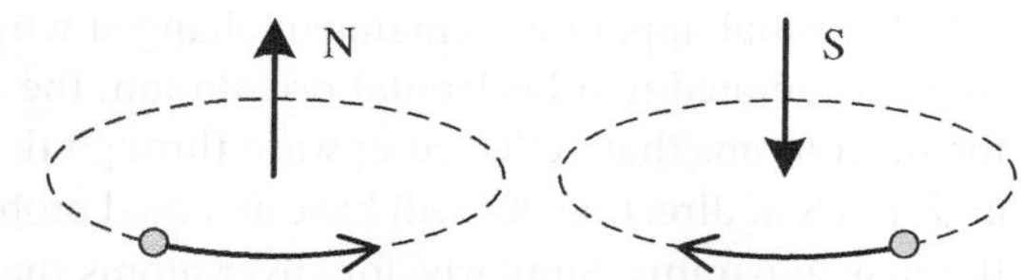

(a) Spin N in direction 0° (b) Spin S in direction 0°

Figure 7.3 Schematic diagram of the deflection of silver atoms in the Stern-Gerlach experiment.

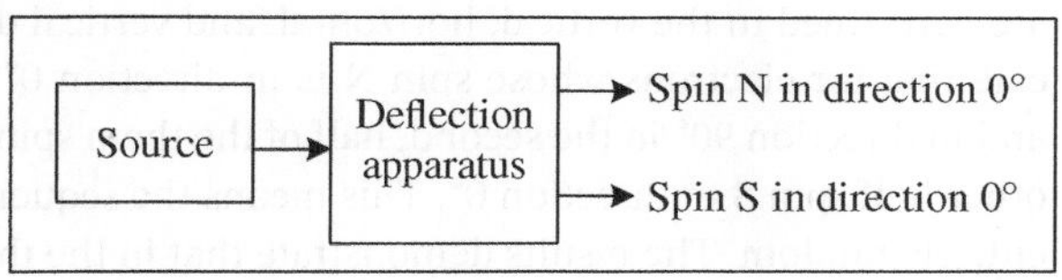

Figure 7.2, these correspond to the spin north (N) in the direction 0° and spin south (S) in the direction 0°.

From the perspective of classical physics, when a large number of atoms are emitted through this apparatus, one would expect to see a continuous line extending from the top to the bottom of the screen. However, the experimental results revealed only two points at the top and bottom of the screen. This indicates that all the silver atoms were divided into two beams, each behaving like vertically aligned bar magnets. All electrons had their spin either N in direction 0° or S in direction 0°, with their magnetic axes oriented solely in the vertical direction, as illustrated in Figure 7.3.

In further extension experiments, two additional apparatuses were placed behind the original apparatus, one for capturing atoms deflected upward in the first apparatus, and the other for capturing atoms deflected downward. As shown in Figure 7.4, after repeating the same experiment, if the spin N of a silver atom is measured in direction 0° in the first experiment, the spin N of the same silver atom will still be in direction 0° in the second measurement. Similarly, if the spin

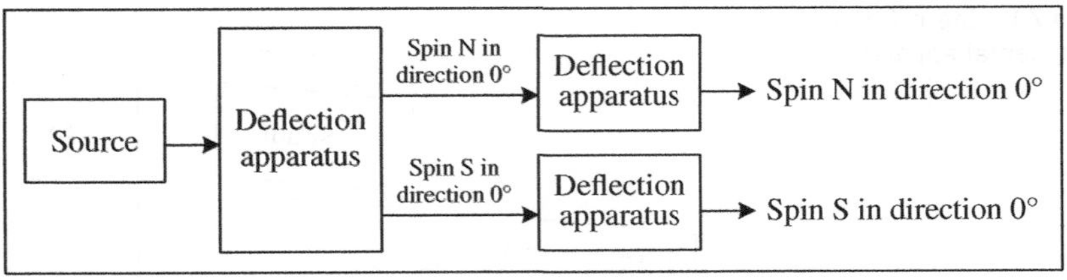

Figure 7.4 Schematic diagram of deflection of silver atoms in repeated Stern-Gerlach experiments.

S of the silver atom is initially measured in direction 0°, the spin S of the same silver atom will remain in direction 0° in the second measurement.

If the initial apparatus remains unchanged while the two subsequent apparatuses are rotated to a horizontal orientation, the following results are observed: for silver atoms that deflected upward through the initial apparatus, their spin N and spin S in direction 90° will have an equal probability when they pass through the new apparatus. Similarly, for silver atoms that initially deflected downward, the probabilities of their spin N and spin S in direction 90° are also equal.

In the experiment shown in Figure 7.5, where three consecutive measurements are performed in the vertical, horizontal, and vertical directions, the results indicate that for electrons whose spin N is in direction 0° in the first measurement and in direction 90° in the second, half of the them spin N in direction 0°, and the other half spin S in direction 0°. This means the sequence of spin N and spin S is entirely random. The results demonstrate that in the third vertical measurement, the electron's spin direction is independent of its spin direction in the first vertical measurement.

The aforementioned experiment demonstrated numerous phenomena that classical mechanics could not explain, making it a landmark in the history of quantum mechanics. However, it faced a significant limitation. Due to the constraints of experimental technology at the time, the particle source could only emit a large number of particles simultaneously, rather than a single particle at a time. As a

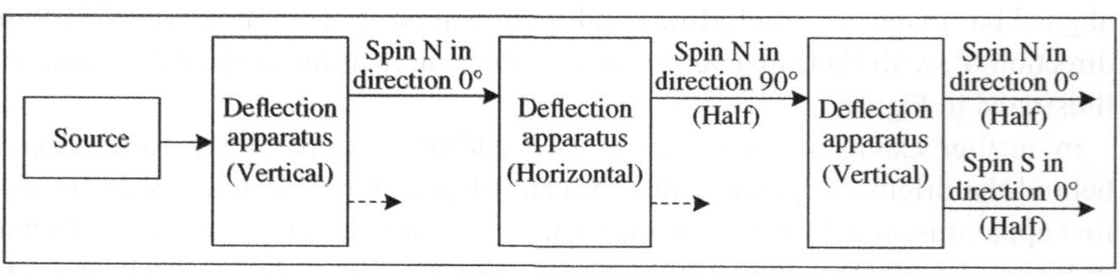

Figure 7.5 Schematic diagram of deflection of silver atoms in three consecutive Stern-Gerlach experiments.

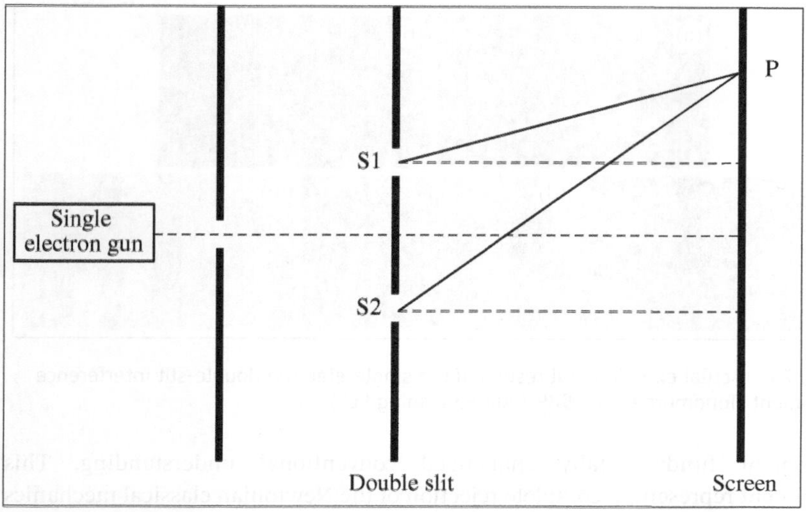

Figure 7.6 Schematic diagram of the single-electron double-slit interference experiment.

result, the experimental outcomes were merely statistical, and many interfering factors during the process could not be eliminated. This considerably weakened the experiment's effectiveness in revealing and verifying the principles of quantum mechanics.

In the 1980s, Japanese researcher Tonomura successfully developed a device capable of emitting individual particles—a single-electron gun. Using this device, Tonomura and his collaborators conducted what is widely regarded as the first true single-electron double-slit interference experiment (Tonomura et al. 1989, pp. 117–120). A schematic of the experiment is shown in Figure 7.6. On the far left is the single-electron gun, while S1 and S2 represent two slits. Electrons emitted from the gun pass through the two slits and strike a screen on the far right, forming a bright spot P. This process is repeated, with only one electron emitted at a time, eventually producing many bright spots on the screen.

According to classical Newtonian mechanics, each electron would pass through one of the slits, and the screen would display two bright regions corresponding to the slits. However, the actual experimental results, as shown in Figure 7.7, revealed an interference pattern. Interference refers to the phenomenon where two or more waves overlap in space and combine to form a new wave pattern. This result indicated that each single electron emitted during the experiment passed through both slits simultaneously.

If the Stern-Gerlach experiment revealed some fascinating phenomena of the quantum world without fully overturning existing theories, then Tonomura's

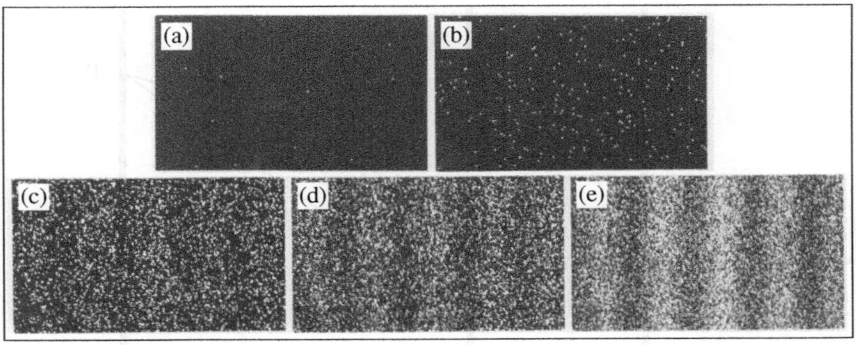

Figure 7.7 Actual experimental results of the single-electron double-slit interference experiment (Tonomura et al. 1989 / AIP Publishing LLC).

experiment fundamentally challenged conventional understanding. This experiment represents a complete rejection of the Newtonian classical mechanics in quantum world and a refutation of the notion that the future behavior of all atoms can be entirely predicted and determined. By extension, it also marks the ultimate denial of the concept of Laplace's Demon, which posits the ability to predict humanity's future. This serves as a watershed moment in the shift from the realist perspective of Newtonian mechanics to the nonlocal holistic realist view of quantum mechanics.

Since the 1980s, the intersection of quantum mechanics and information science has given rise to a new research field—quantum information. Corresponding to the "First Quantum Revolution" marked by the birth of quantum mechanics, the emergence of quantum information is referred to as the "Second Quantum Revolution." The primary driving force behind this revolution is the improvement in our ability to manipulate individual quantum particles (Yuan 2022, pp. 19–21). In the early stages of quantum mechanics, researchers observed and controlled the collective behavior of large ensembles of particles rather than individual particles. Tonomura and collaborators successfully developed the single-electron gun, achieving control over individual particles. This milestone can be considered a pivotal moment. From this point onward, it became increasingly clear that the most fundamental unit of the existence of information is the quantum, and information itself is a fundamental property of the quantum.

This chapter focuses not on quantum mechanics but on quantum information, which arises from the integration of quantum mechanics and information science. From the perspective of information science, the three most significant properties of quantum mechanics are superposition, measurement, and entanglement. These concepts are briefly introduced using the mathematical representation of qubits.

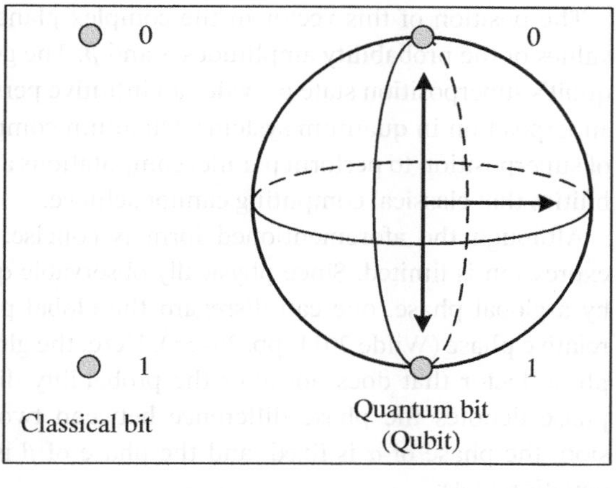

Figure 7.8 Comparison of classical bits and qubits (Swan, Santos, Witte 2020 / World Scientific Publishing Company).

In quantum computing, qubits differ greatly from classical bits. While classical bits can only represent either a 0 or 1, qubits can exist in a superposition of both states at the same time, as shown in Figure 7.8. This superposition allows quantum computing to harness a potential far beyond that of classical computing, enabling it to process a greater amount of information simultaneously.

In quantum information, qubit states are commonly represented using Dirac notation, which incorporates vertical bars and angle brackets. An arbitrary superposition state of a qubit can be expressed as follows:

$$|\psi\rangle = \alpha|0\rangle + \beta|1\rangle, \tag{7.1}$$

where α and β are complex numbers known as probability amplitudes. The states $|0\rangle$ and $|1\rangle$ are the basis states of the qubit, forming an orthogonal basis in a 2D complex vector space. The state of the qubit $|\psi\rangle$ is a unit vector within this 2D vector space. The squared magnitudes of the probability amplitudes $|\alpha|^2$ and $|\beta|^2$ represent the probabilities of measuring the qubit in the basis states $|0\rangle$ and $|1\rangle$, respectively. Since the sum of measurement probabilities must equal 1, it follows that $|\alpha|^2 + |\beta|^2 = 1$. To better describe the qubit's superposition state, the basis states can be represented as vectors:

$$|0\rangle = \begin{bmatrix} 1 \\ 0 \end{bmatrix}, \ |1\rangle = \begin{bmatrix} 0 \\ 1 \end{bmatrix}. \tag{7.2}$$

Thus, the superposition state of the qubit can be expressed as

$$|\psi\rangle = \alpha|0\rangle + \beta|1\rangle = \begin{bmatrix} \alpha \\ \beta \end{bmatrix}, \tag{7.3}$$

showing that the qubit's state is a vector in a 2D complex vector space. Given that the state $|\psi\rangle$ is a unit vector satisfying $|\alpha|^2 + |\beta|^2 = 1$, it can geometrically be represented as a unit vector pointing to a specific point in the complex plane.

The position of this vector in the complex plane corresponds to the complex values of the probability amplitudes α and β. The geometric interpretation of the qubit's superposition state provides an intuitive perspective on the nature of state superposition in quantum systems. Quantum computing leverages this property of superposition to perform parallel computations and process information, capabilities that classical computing cannot achieve.

Although the aforementioned form is concise, its capacity for information expression is limited. Since physically observable quantum states are unaffected by a global phase, one can disregard the global phase and focus solely on the relative phase (Wilde 2011, pp. 39–55). Here, the global phase refers to a common phase factor that does not alter the probability distribution, while the relative phase denotes the phase difference between two coefficients. In this expression, the phase of α is fixed, and the phase of β is considered, as illustrated in equation (7.4):

$$|\psi\rangle = \alpha|0\rangle + e^{i\varphi}\beta|1\rangle, \tag{7.4}$$

where α, β, and φ are all real numbers. Since $|\alpha|^2 + |\beta|^2 = 1$, one can substitute using trigonometric functions, replacing α and β with a single variable θ. Therefore, an alternative expression for equation (7.4) is

$$|\psi\rangle = cos\frac{\theta}{2}|0\rangle + e^{i\varphi}sin\frac{\theta}{2}|1\rangle, \tag{7.5}$$

where $cos\frac{\theta}{2}$ and $sin\frac{\theta}{2}$ are the trigonometric transformations of α and β, respectively:

$$\alpha = cos\frac{\theta}{2}, \quad \beta = sin\frac{\theta}{2}\,. \tag{7.6}$$

In equation (7.5), φ and θ can be used to define a point on the surface of a 3D unit sphere, as illustrated in Figure 7.9. This sphere is referred to as the Bloch sphere, which essentially maps the 2D complex vector space onto a 3D real vector space, providing a more intuitive visual representation of qubit behavior and properties. However, for higher dimensional vector spaces, such visual representations remain significantly limited, making simple generalization challenging.

When dealing with multiple qubits, their states are typically described using the tensor product. For instance, for two qubits, we can use the standard orthonormal bases $(|a_0\rangle, |a_1\rangle)$ and $(|b_0\rangle, |b_1\rangle)$. The first qubit can be described as $|v\rangle = c_0\,|a_0\rangle + c_1\,|\,a_1\rangle$, while the second qubit can be described as $|w\rangle = d_0|b_0\rangle + d_1|b_1\rangle$. The tensor product between the two states is denoted as $|v\rangle \otimes |\,w\rangle$, where the symbol $\otimes$ may be omitted, allowing the expression to be simplified to $|v\rangle\,|w\rangle$ or $|vw\rangle$. Upon expansion, this can be represented as follows:

$$|vw\rangle = c_0d_0|a_0b_0\rangle + c_0d_1\,|a_0b_1\rangle + c_1d_0|a_1b_0\rangle + c_1d_1\,|a_1b_1\rangle. \tag{7.7}$$

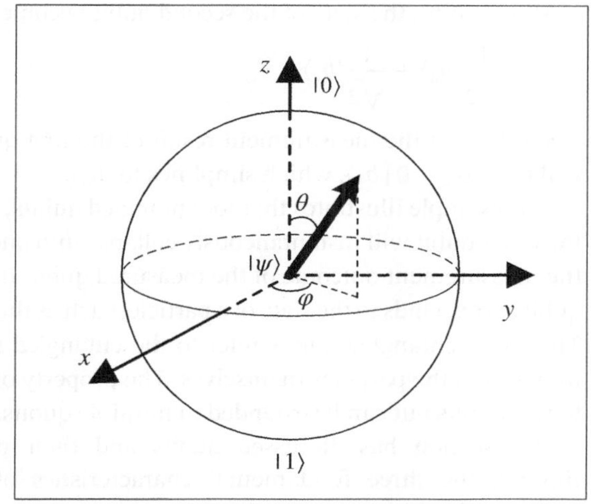

Figure 7.9 Schematic of the Bloch sphere.

For brevity, we can replace the probability amplitudes with letters as follows:

$$r = c_0 d_0, \quad s = c_0 d_1, \quad t = c_1 d_0, \quad u = c_1 d_1. \tag{7.8}$$

Substituting these into equation (7.7) yields the following form:

$$r|a_0\rangle|b_0\rangle + s|a_0\rangle|b_1\rangle + t|a_1\rangle|b_0\rangle + u|a_1\rangle|b_1\rangle. \tag{7.9}$$

As previously stated, the sum of the probabilities for all possible outcomes must equal 1, satisfying $r^2 + s^2 + t^2 + u^2 = 1$. Since the two qubits in equation (7.10) are independent of each other, meaning they are nonentangled, we have $ru = st$. Conversely, for entangled qubits, if $ru \neq st$, the two qubits are considered to be entangled (Bernhardt, 2019). For example, consider the following two qubits:

$$\frac{1}{2}|a_0\rangle|b_0\rangle + \frac{1}{2}|a_0\rangle|b_1\rangle + \frac{1}{\sqrt{2}}|a_1\rangle|b_0\rangle + 0|a_1\rangle|b_1\rangle. \tag{7.11}$$

Assuming we measure the first qubit and rewrite the tensor product as:

$$\frac{1}{\sqrt{2}}|a_0\rangle\left(\frac{1}{\sqrt{2}}|b_0\rangle + \frac{1}{\sqrt{2}}|b_1\rangle\right) + \frac{1}{\sqrt{2}}|a_1\rangle(1|b_0\rangle + 0|b_1\rangle). \tag{7.12}$$

From equation (7.12), it can be inferred that if the first qubit is measured first, it has equal probabilities of being $|a_0\rangle$ or $|a_1\rangle$. Assuming the measurement result of the first qubit is $|a_0\rangle$, the tensor product transforms into the following nonentangled state:

$$|a_0\rangle\left(\frac{1}{\sqrt{2}}|b_0\rangle + \frac{1}{\sqrt{2}}|b_1\rangle\right). \tag{7.13}$$

At this point, the state of the second qubit becomes

$$\frac{1}{\sqrt{2}}|b_0\rangle + \frac{1}{\sqrt{2}}|b_1\rangle. \tag{7.14}$$

Similarly, if the measurement result of the first qubit is $|a_1\rangle$, the second qubit will be $1 \mid b_0\rangle + 0 \mid b_1\rangle$, which simplifies to $|b_0\rangle$.

This example illustrates that for entangled qubits, when one qubit is measured, the other qubit will instantaneously collapse into one of two states, depending on the measurement outcome of the measured qubit. It is important to note that the qubit corresponds to the state of a particle, such as the spin direction of an electron. Therefore, entangled qubits refer to the entangled state vectors of the particles, rather than the particles themselves. The property of entanglement is not limited to two qubits but can be extended to multiple qubits.

This section has discussed qubits and their mathematical representation through the three fundamental characteristics of quantum mechanics. The concept of qubits can be realized in various physical systems, such as the spin of electrons, the polarization of photons, the quantum states of superconducting circuits, the states of ions in ion traps, and certain internal energy levels of atoms.

7.1.2 Quantum Gates and Quantum Circuits

After gaining a deeper understanding of qubits and their mathematical representation, the next step is to explore how to manipulate these qubits. This leads to the concept of quantum gates, which are essential tools for performing operations and control of qubits.

In classical computing, logical operations such as AND, OR, and NOT are commonly used. These operations can be viewed as functions. For example, the AND operation is a function that takes two inputs and returns a single output, while the NOT operation takes one input and returns one output. Mathematically, if a function takes a set of Boolean values (0 or 1) as input and returns a Boolean value as output, it is referred to as a Boolean function. Using Boolean functions, we successfully represent logical operations algebraically.

In 1913, American logician Henry M. Sheffer published a paper demonstrating that any Boolean function can be represented using combinations of the AND and NOT operations. He referred to this property as functional completeness. Functional completeness means that a set of logical operations can be combined to represent all possible Boolean functions. Thus, the combination of AND and NOT operations is functionally complete.

The functional completeness of Boolean functions and the AND-NOT operations naturally led to the idea that if a machine could be designed to perform the AND-NOT operation, it could implement any Boolean function. This concept was

Table 7.1 Truth table of the classical CNOT gate.

Input		Output	
x	y	x	$x \oplus y$
0	0	0	0
0	1	0	1
1	0	1	1
1	1	1	0

confirmed by the renowned scholar Claude Shannon, the founder of information theory. Shannon demonstrated that all Boolean function operations could be realized using electrical switches. This principle forms one of the foundational ideas of modern computer circuit design. The circuit components designed to perform specific logical operations based on different input combinations are called gates, such as AND gates, OR gates, and NOT gates. Connecting gates together forms circuits. Since the AND-NOT operations are functionally complete, the AND-NOT gate is considered a universal gate, capable of implementing any Boolean function independently. This enables fundamental computer functionalities such as computation and storage.

Following the definition of classical gates, a quantum gate can similarly be defined as a function that computes outputs based on inputs, but in this case, the inputs and outputs are qubits. To illustrate the differences between classical and quantum gates, we can take the Controlled-NOT (CNOT) gate as an example. A classical CNOT gate has two inputs and two outputs, and its behavior is defined as shown in Table 7.1, where x represents the control bit.

The inputs and outputs of a quantum gate are qubits. Therefore, qubits replace classical bits in the representation, with $|0\rangle$ substituting for 0 and $|1\rangle$ substituting for 1. This results in a quantum CNOT gate, as defined in Table 7.2.

By representing the inputs and outputs in a simplified form, the functional expression of a quantum CNOT gate can be written as: $CNOT(r\,|\,00\rangle + s\,|\,01\rangle + t\,|\,10\rangle + u\,|\,11\rangle\,) = r\,|\,00\rangle + s\,|\,01\rangle + t\,|\,11\rangle + u\,|\,10\rangle$. This indicates that the quantum CNOT gate swaps the probability amplitudes of $|10\rangle$ and $|11\rangle$.

A single-qubit state, $|0\rangle$ or $|1\rangle$, corresponds to a 2D vector, while two-qubit states, $|00\rangle$, $|01\rangle$, $|10\rangle$, and $|11\rangle$, correspond to 4D vectors. Together, these vectors form an ordered orthogonal basis. The CNOT gate implements the substitution of this ordered orthogonal basis, which can be accomplished by an orthogonal matrix, and thus the CNOT gate corresponds to an orthogonal matrix. Denoting

Table 7.2 Truth table of the quantum CNOT gate.

Input		Output	
x	y	x	$x \oplus y$
$\lvert 0\rangle$	$\lvert 0\rangle$	$\lvert 0\rangle$	$\lvert 0\rangle$
$\lvert 0\rangle$	$\lvert 1\rangle$	$\lvert 0\rangle$	$\lvert 1\rangle$
$\lvert 1\rangle$	$\lvert 0\rangle$	$\lvert 1\rangle$	$\lvert 1\rangle$
$\lvert 1\rangle$	$\lvert 1\rangle$	$\lvert 1\rangle$	$\lvert 0\rangle$

this matrix as *CNOT*, we can express it as follows:

$$CNOT \cdot \begin{bmatrix} r \\ s \\ t \\ u \end{bmatrix} = \begin{bmatrix} r \\ s \\ u \\ t \end{bmatrix}. \tag{7.15}$$

It can be concluded through calculation:

$$CNOT = \begin{bmatrix} 1 & 0 & 0 & 0 \\ 0 & 1 & 0 & 0 \\ 0 & 0 & 0 & 1 \\ 0 & 0 & 1 & 0 \end{bmatrix}. \tag{7.16}$$

Based on the example of the CNOT gate, it is evident that both quantum gates and classical gates can be regarded as functions that transform inputs into outputs. The functions corresponding to quantum gates can be described using orthogonal matrices. Furthermore, each quantum gate corresponds uniquely to an orthogonal matrix. Since the number of orthogonal matrices in any dimension is infinite, the types of quantum gates are also infinite. This implies that, in theory, quantum gates and their corresponding matrices can be designed and computed as needed.

Common quantum gates that act on a single qubit include the gate I, gate Z, gate X, gate Y, and Hadamard gate. The first four of these gates are named after the scholar Wolfgang Pauli and are collectively referred to as the Pauli transformations.

1) Gate I: Gate I corresponds to the identity matrix $\begin{bmatrix} 1 & 0 \\ 0 & 1 \end{bmatrix}$, which does not alter the state of the qubit.
2) Gate Z: Gate Z corresponds to the matrix $\begin{bmatrix} 1 & 0 \\ 0 & -1 \end{bmatrix}$, which leaves the probability amplitudes of $\lvert 0\rangle$ unchanged and only modifying the sign of the probability amplitude for $\lvert 1\rangle$.

3) Gate X: Gate X corresponds to the matrix $\begin{bmatrix} 0 & 1 \\ 1 & 0 \end{bmatrix}$, which causes the exchange of probability amplitudes of $|0\rangle$ and $|1\rangle$.
4) Gate Y: Gate Y corresponds to the matrix $\begin{bmatrix} 0 & -i \\ i & 0 \end{bmatrix}$, which not only exchanges probability amplitudes of $|0\rangle$ and $|1\rangle$ but also applies a rotation in 3D space.
5) Hadamard gate: Hadamard gate corresponds to the matrix $\frac{1}{\sqrt{2}}\begin{bmatrix} 1 & 1 \\ 1 & -1 \end{bmatrix}$, which converts standard basis vectors into superposition state and operates solely on a single qubit. For example,

$$H(|0\rangle) = \frac{1}{\sqrt{2}}\begin{bmatrix} 1 & 1 \\ 1 & -1 \end{bmatrix}\begin{bmatrix} 1 \\ 0 \end{bmatrix} = \frac{1}{\sqrt{2}}\begin{bmatrix} 1 \\ 1 \end{bmatrix} = \frac{1}{\sqrt{2}}(|0\rangle + |1\rangle), \tag{7.17}$$

$$H(|1\rangle) = \frac{1}{\sqrt{2}}\begin{bmatrix} 1 & 1 \\ 1 & -1 \end{bmatrix}\begin{bmatrix} 0 \\ 1 \end{bmatrix} = \frac{1}{\sqrt{2}}\begin{bmatrix} 1 \\ -1 \end{bmatrix} = \frac{1}{\sqrt{2}}(|0\rangle - |1\rangle). \tag{7.18}$$

For quantum gates that act on two qubits, in addition to the previously mentioned CNOT gate, there are also gates such as the Swap gate. The Swap gate is used to exchange the tensor product order of two qubits. Its mathematical expression is given by: $Swap(|\psi_1\rangle \otimes |\psi_2\rangle) = |\psi_2\rangle \otimes |\psi_1\rangle$. The Swap gate operates on two qubits and thus corresponds to a 4×4 orthogonal matrix, denoted as *Swap*. Let $|\psi_1\rangle = a_1|0\rangle + b_1|1\rangle$ and $|\psi_2\rangle = a_2|0\rangle + b_2|1\rangle$. Substituting these expressions, the formula can be expanded as: $Swap(a_1a_2|00\rangle + a_1b_2|01\rangle + b_1a_2|10\rangle + b_1b_2|11\rangle) = a_2a_1|00\rangle + b_2a_1|10\rangle + a_2b_1|01\rangle + b_2b_1|11\rangle$. This formula can also be expressed in vector form as

$$Swap \cdot \begin{bmatrix} a_1a_2 \\ a_1b_2 \\ b_1a_2 \\ b_1b_2 \end{bmatrix} = \begin{bmatrix} a_2a_1 \\ a_2b_1 \\ b_2a_1 \\ b_2b_1 \end{bmatrix}. \tag{7.19}$$

Through calculation, it can be concluded that the matrix corresponding to the Swap gate is

$$Swap = \begin{bmatrix} 1 & 0 & 0 & 0 \\ 0 & 0 & 1 & 0 \\ 0 & 1 & 0 & 0 \\ 0 & 0 & 0 & 1 \end{bmatrix}. \tag{7.20}$$

The Hadamard gate, CNOT gate, and Swap gate are commonly used in quantum algorithm and transmission, and their diagrams are shown in Figures 7.10–7.12.

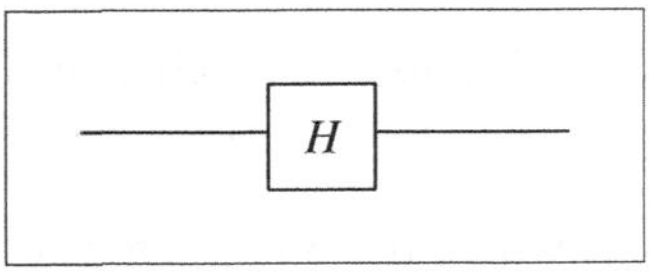

Figure 7.10 The Hadamard gate.

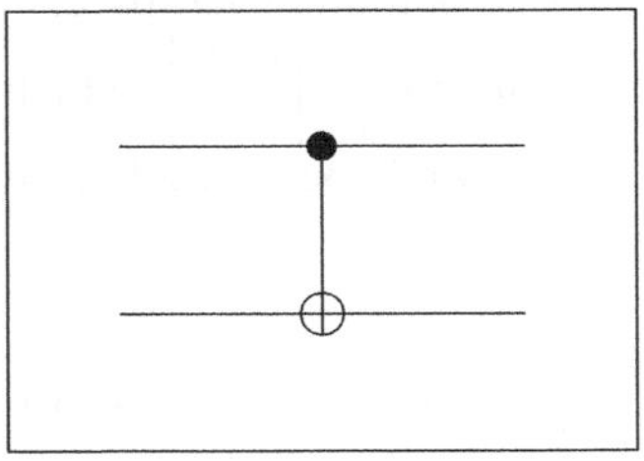

Figure 7.11 The CNOT gate.

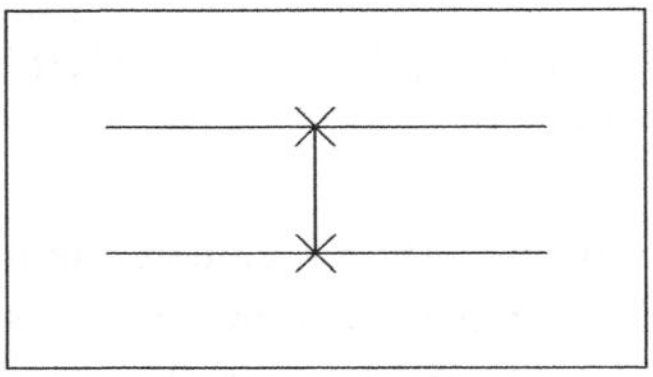

Figure 7.12 The Swap gate.

Quantum gate operations have the following special properties:

1) The number of quantum gates is infinite: In classical functions, when the input is n bits, there are only 2^n possible Boolean functions, which equals the number of classical gates. In contrast, quantum gates correspond to orthogonal matrices. Since the number of orthogonal matrices in any given dimension is infinite, the number of quantum gates is also infinite.
2) There is no universal quantum gate: Using only a finite number of gates and connecting them in a finite way leads to a finite number of circuits. Therefore, it is impossible to simulate an infinite number of quantum gates using a finite number of circuits. In other words, a universal quantum gate does not exist.
3) Quantum gates are linear and reversible: Since quantum gates correspond to orthogonal matrices, matrix operations satisfy linearity, and orthogonal matrices are always invertible, quantum gates are inherently linear and reversible. If the inverse of an orthogonal matrix equals itself, then applying the corresponding quantum gate twice in succession will return the qubits to their initial state.
4) No cloning gate exists: Classical gates can perform duplication operations for any information, but quantum gates cannot. There is no quantum gate capable of duplicating arbitrary qubits. In the context of the quantum world, the term "cloning" is commonly used to describe such duplication operations.

Figure 7.13 A hypothetical quantum cloning gate.

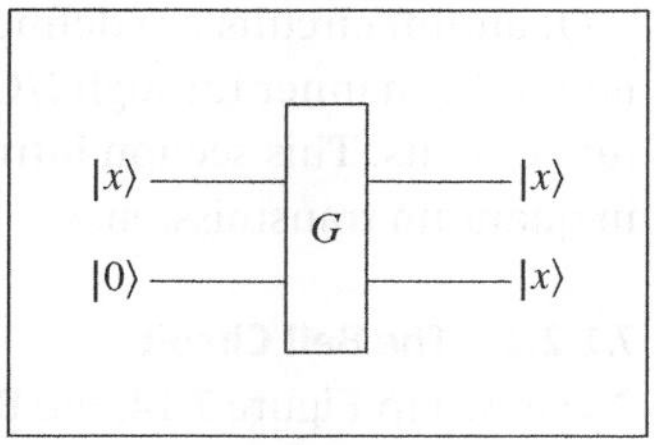

As shown in Figure 7.13, for a hypothetical quantum cloning gate, $|0\rangle$ is an auxiliary qubit and $|x\rangle$ is the qubit that needs to be cloned. The proposition that a qubit can be cloned is equivalent to the existence of the G gate. Therefore, we can use proof by contradiction to disprove this. Assuming the G gate exists, we can logically follow this premise to obtain a contradictory result. The detailed proof is as follows:

Assuming G gate exists, based on its cloning properties, the following conclusions can be drawn:

$$G(|00\rangle) = |00\rangle; \text{(conclusion a)}$$

$$G(|10\rangle) = |11\rangle; \text{(conclusion b)}$$

$$G\left(\left(\frac{1}{\sqrt{2}}(|0\rangle + |1\rangle)\right)|0\rangle\right) = \left(\frac{1}{\sqrt{2}}(|0\rangle + |1\rangle)\right)\left(\frac{1}{\sqrt{2}}(|0\rangle + |1\rangle)\right)$$
$$= \frac{1}{2}(|00\rangle + |01\rangle + |10\rangle + |11\rangle). \text{ (conclusion c)}$$

Since the G gate is linear, combining conclusions a) and b), it can be inferred that

$$G\left(\frac{1}{\sqrt{2}}|00\rangle + \frac{1}{\sqrt{2}}|10\rangle\right) = \frac{1}{\sqrt{2}}|00\rangle + \frac{1}{\sqrt{2}}|11\rangle. \tag{7.21}$$

Considering conclusion c), the following contradictions exist:

$$\frac{1}{\sqrt{2}}|00\rangle + \frac{1}{\sqrt{2}}|11\rangle \neq \frac{1}{2}(|00\rangle + |01\rangle + |10\rangle + |11\rangle). \tag{7.22}$$

Therefore, there is no quantum gate that can clone any specific qubit. The above proof selects $|0\rangle$ as the auxiliary bit; however, no matter what state is chosen as the auxiliary qubit, the same method of proof can be used to disprove it. This conclusion is known as the no-cloning theorem, which is fundamental to many quantum technologies and provides a theoretical guarantee for the security of quantum communication. It is important to note that the no-cloning theorem states that an unknown quantum state cannot be copied or cloned. However, if the quantum state is known, it can be directly prepared, with the preparation process replacing the cloning operation.

Quantum circuits are defined as specific sets of quantum gates connected in a noncyclic manner through I/O lines. In theory, there are countless types of quantum circuits. This section introduces three quantum circuits that are widely used in quantum transmission.

7.1.2.1 The Bell Circuit

As shown in Figure 7.14, the Bell circuit is the combination of the Hadamard gate and the CNOT gate.

Considering a qubit pair $|00\rangle$ that passes through a Hadamard gate, the first qubit $|0\rangle$ becomes $\frac{1}{\sqrt{2}}(|0\rangle + |1\rangle)$ and the qubit pair becomes $\frac{1}{\sqrt{2}}(|00\rangle + |10\rangle)$. When they subsequently pass through the CNOT gate, they transform into $\frac{1}{\sqrt{2}}(|00\rangle + |11\rangle)$.

Similarly, the corresponding outputs for the other three pairs of standard bases can also be computed, with each input in the circuit corresponding to a specific output. The Bell circuit is used to prepare entangled states. As shown in Table 7.3, all the inputs are nonentangled, while the output states are entangled. Since the inputs form a standard orthonormal basis in R^4, the outputs also constitute a standard orthonormal basis. The basis that includes these four entangled states is called the Bell basis, and these states are referred to as Bell states, also known as EPR states or EPR pairs, named after the scholars Bell and Einstein, Podolsky, and Rosen, who were the first to highlight the properties of these states.

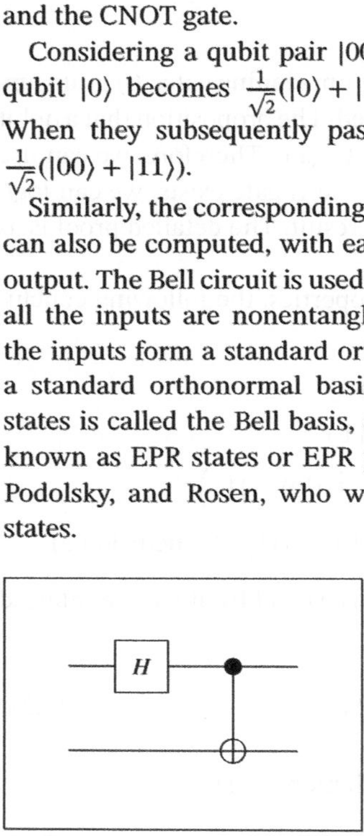

Figure 7.14 The Bell circuit.

Table 7.3 Truth table for the Bell circuit.

Input	Output
$\|00\rangle$	$\frac{1}{\sqrt{2}}(\|00\rangle + \|11\rangle)$
$\|01\rangle$	$\frac{1}{\sqrt{2}}(\|01\rangle + \|10\rangle)$
$\|10\rangle$	$\frac{1}{\sqrt{2}}(\|00\rangle - \|11\rangle)$
$\|11\rangle$	$\frac{1}{\sqrt{2}}(\|01\rangle - \|10\rangle)$

7.1.2.2 Reverse Bell Circuit

Since both Hadamard gate and CNOT gate support reconstructing outputs to inputs, as shown in Figure 7.15, a reverse Bell circuit can be defined, which takes the Bell state as input and outputs the standard basis. The output truth value table is shown in Table 7.4.

7.1.2.3 Greenberger–Horne–Zeilinger (GHZ) Circuit

The GHZ state is a type of multipartite entangled state involving at least three qubits, named after Greenberger, Horne, and Zeilinger. A GHZ state with N qubits can be defined as

$$|GHZ\rangle = \frac{1}{\sqrt{2}}(|000\cdots 0\rangle + |111\cdots 1\rangle) = \frac{1}{\sqrt{2}}(|0\rangle^{\otimes N} + |1\rangle^{\otimes N}), \tag{7.23}$$

where $|0\rangle^{\otimes N}$ represents the state where all N qubits are in the $|0\rangle$ state, and $|1\rangle^{\otimes N}$ represents the state where all N qubits are in the $|1\rangle$ state. In other words, the GHZ state has a special property: after measurement, the results for all qubits will be the same. Figure 7.16 illustrates a three-qubit GHZ circuit. The GHZ state plays an important role in various quantum algorithms.

Quantum algorithms typically exhibit significant advantages in execution speed over classical algorithms, primarily due to the superposition property of quantum states. By placing the input state in a superposition of multiple possible states and processing these superposed states in parallel, quantum algorithms can efficiently

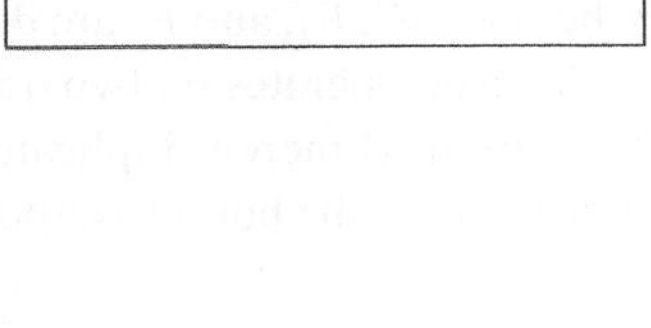

Figure 7.15 The reverse Bell circuit.

Table 7.4 Truth table for the reverse Bell circuit.

Input	Output
$\frac{1}{\sqrt{2}}(\|00\rangle + \|11\rangle)$	$\|00\rangle$
$\frac{1}{\sqrt{2}}(\|01\rangle + \|10\rangle)$	$\|01\rangle$
$\frac{1}{\sqrt{2}}(\|00\rangle - \|11\rangle)$	$\|10\rangle$
$\frac{1}{\sqrt{2}}(\|01\rangle - \|10\rangle)$	$\|11\rangle$

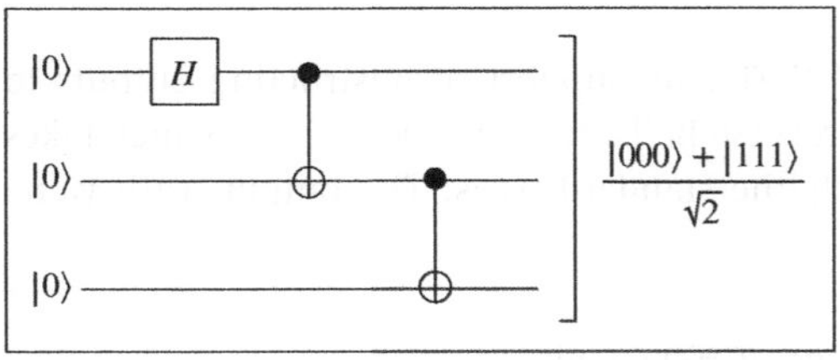

Figure 7.16 A GHZ circuit consisting of three qubits.

perform computational tasks. Famous quantum algorithms include the Deutsch algorithm, Shor's algorithm, Grover's algorithm, and others.

One of the pioneers in quantum computing, David Deutsch, published a seminal paper in 1985 (Deutsch 1985, pp. 97–117), which introduced the concepts of quantum Turing machines and quantum computation. This paper also presented the first example demonstrating that quantum algorithms can outperform classical algorithms—the Deutsch algorithm. This algorithm involves an important concept known as query complexity. Query complexity describes the number of times an algorithm needs to query a function when solving a specific problem, where this function is often referred to as an oracle.

Deutsch's algorithm addresses a function with inputs and outputs of either 0 or 1, resulting in four possible functions: f_0, f_1, f_2, and f_3, where $f_0(0) = f_0(1) = 0$; $f_1(0) = 0, f_1(1) = 1; f_2(0) = 1, f_2(1) = 0; f_3(0) = f_3(1) = 1$. Here f_0 and f_3 are constant functions because their outputs are the same for all inputs. f_1 and f_2 are balanced functions because half of their outputs are 0 and the other half are 1. Deutsch posed the question: given a randomly chosen function among f_0, f_1, f_2, and f_3, how many queries to the oracle are necessary to determine whether the function is constant or balanced?

In classical computing, to answer this question, one would need to evaluate the function for both 0 and 1 inputs, requiring a minimum of two queries. However, with quantum gates and quantum circuits, fewer queries are needed. As shown in Figure 7.17, corresponding gates can be constructed for these four functions, where F_0, F_1, F_2, and F_3 are defined.

The gate operates on two qubits, producing outputs for both qubits, where the top output $|x\rangle$ merely duplicates the original input information. However, the specific result of the bottom output $|y \oplus f_i(x)\rangle$ depends on the bottom input $|y\rangle$, being

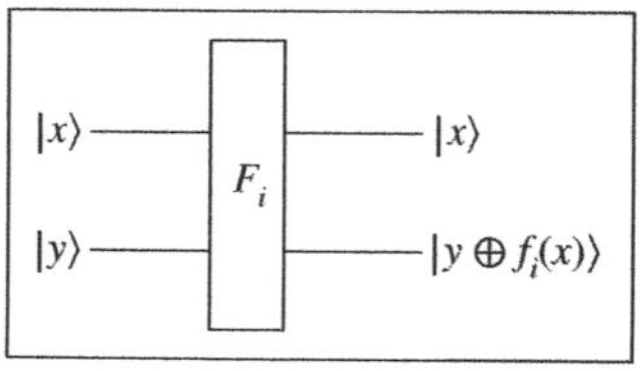

Figure 7.17 The quantum gates corresponding to the four functions.

Figure 7.18 The circuit of the Deutsch algorithm.

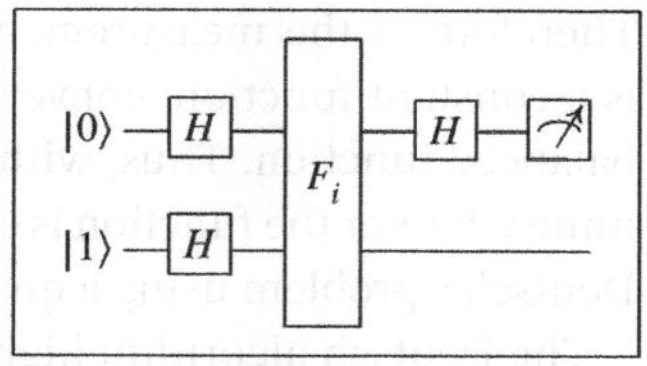

either the value of the top input function or its negation. As depicted in Figure 7.18, through the combination of multiple quantum gates, the corresponding circuit for the Deutsch algorithm is designed. The symbol at the right end of the top wire in the circuit diagram represents a measurement of that qubit.

Assuming the inputs are $|0\rangle \otimes |1\rangle$, the following state is obtained after passing through the Hadamard gate:

$$\frac{1}{2}(|00\rangle - |01\rangle + |10\rangle - |11\rangle). \tag{7.25}$$

After passing through the F_i gate, the following state is obtained:

$$\frac{1}{2}(|0\rangle \otimes |f_i(0)\rangle - |0\rangle \otimes |1 \oplus f_i(0)\rangle + |1\rangle \otimes |f_i(1)\rangle - |1\rangle \otimes |1 \oplus f_i(1)\rangle). \tag{7.26}$$

Since $|f_i(0)\rangle - |1 \oplus f_i(0)\rangle$ is equal to either $|0\rangle - |1\rangle$ or $|1\rangle - |0\rangle$, equations (7.27) and (7.28) are obtained.

$$|f_i(0)\rangle - |1 \oplus f_i(0)\rangle = (-1)^{f_i(0)}(|0\rangle - |1\rangle), \tag{7.27}$$

$$|f_i(1)\rangle - |1 \oplus f_i(1)\rangle = (-1)^{f_i(1)}(|0\rangle - |1\rangle). \tag{7.28}$$

Therefore, the quantum states passing through the F_i gate can be rewritten as

$$\frac{1}{\sqrt{2}}\left((-1)^{f_i(0)}|0\rangle + (-1)^{f_i(1)}|1\rangle\right) \otimes \frac{1}{\sqrt{2}}(|0\rangle - |1\rangle). \tag{7.29}$$

That is, the two qubits are nonentangled, and the top qubit has the following state:

$$\frac{1}{\sqrt{2}}\left((-1)^{f_i(0)}|0\rangle + (-1)^{f_i(1)}|1\rangle\right). \tag{7.30}$$

Based on this, each possible state can be determined. Then, the qubits are passed through the Hadamard gate and measured, resulting in four possible outcomes.

If $i = 0$, the qubit is $|0\rangle$.
If $i = 1$, the qubit is $|1\rangle$.
If $i = 2$, the qubit is $-|1\rangle$.
If $i = 3$, the qubit is $-|0\rangle$.

When the qubit is measured in the standard basis, if i equals 0 or 3, the measurement outcome will be 0; conversely, if i equals 1 or 2, the outcome will be 1.

Therefore, if the measurement yields 0, it can be determined that the function is a constant function; conversely, if the measurement yields 1, the function is a balanced function. Thus, with just one query to the oracle, it is possible to determine whether the function is constant or balanced, improving the speed of solving Deutsch's problem using a quantum algorithm.

The Deutsch algorithm highlights the distinct advantages of quantum computing over classical approaches, serving as a foundational concept in quantum theory and a precursor to more in-depth studies in the field. However, its practical applications are relatively narrow. In contrast, Shor's algorithm offers much greater potential for real-world use in quantum computing (Shor 1994, pp. 124–134). Its primary function is to factor large integers into prime components—a task that, on classical computers, requires exponential time, but can be executed in polynomial time on quantum machines. This capability positions Shor's algorithm as a game-changer in areas like cryptography, secure communication, and data encryption.

Quantum algorithms represent a cutting-edge area of quantum computing, and the potential of quantum computing becomes particularly significant when addressing large-scale data and complex problems. Machine learning, a field that requires the handling of vast amounts of data and intricate issues, has led to the

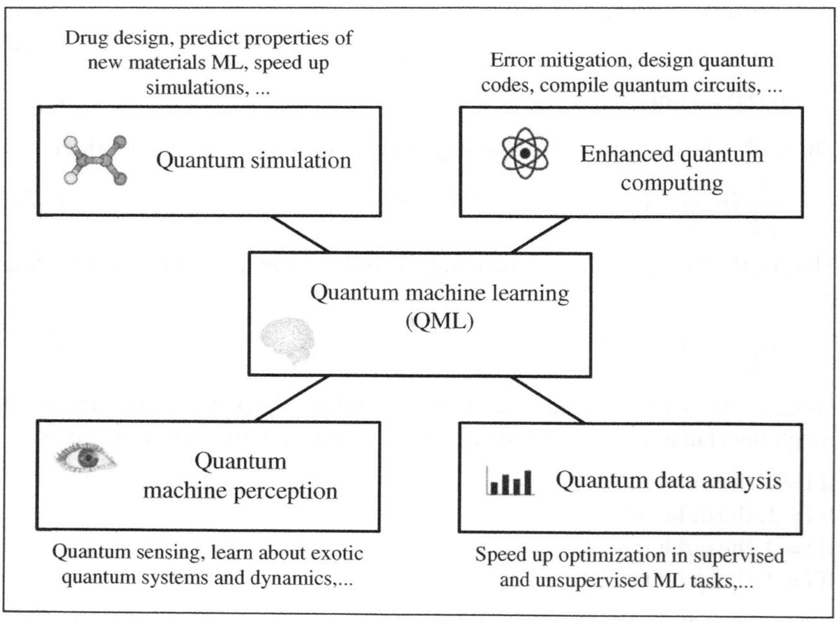

Figure 7.19 Applications of QML (Cerezo et al. 2022 / Spinger Nature).

emergence of a new research discipline by combining machine learning theory with quantum computing, known as quantum machine learning (QML). QML is expected to play a crucial role in various fields, offering new possibilities for solving problems that traditional computers struggle to handle, as illustrated in Figure 7.19.

7.2 Quantum Memory and Quantum Computer

In reference to classical computing methods, quantum computing requires the use of quantum computers and quantum memory devices, with quantum memory serving as a crucial component of quantum computers. However, in current quantum computing experiments, qubits are typically used directly rather than obtaining quantum information from quantum memory. This is primarily because the existing technology for quantum computers remains in its nascent stages, with most experiments not yet necessitating the long-term storage of quantum information. Consequently, quantum computers and quantum memory represent two relatively independent research fields, unlike the inclusive relationship between classical computers and memory. However, to realize a large-scale, fault-tolerant quantum computer in the future, it is essential to integrate quantum memory with quantum computing technology and embed it within quantum computers. This section will introduce the fundamental principles, classifications, and current developments of quantum memory devices and quantum computers.

7.2.1 Quantum Memory

Quantum memory is a device used for storing quantum information, analogous to the memory in classical computers, but it stores qubits rather than classical bits. In the field of quantum information, photons are regarded as excellent carriers of information due to their high propagation speed, strong resistance to interference, and large information capacity.

The origins of quantum storage devices can be traced back to experiments involving slow light, which investigate the interaction between light and matter by altering the speed of light in a medium. In a vacuum, the speed of light is a constant value c relative to any inertial reference frame, approximately 3×10^8 m/s. However, in certain special media, the propagation speed of light can be significantly lower than this value, primarily due to the dispersive effects of the medium. As a light pulse travels through a medium, the phase relationships among its frequency components gradually change, resulting in alterations to the pulse shape, known as the slow light phenomenon.

In addition to dispersion, the medium can absorb light pulses. If a light pulse is absorbed and converted into a coherent state of atoms, this coherent state can be retransformed into a light pulse after a certain period, thereby achieving the storage and retrieval of light pulses. The earliest optical storage devices were designed for storing classical light pulses. Subsequently, researchers attempted to store individual photons carrying quantum information, which represented the prototype of quantum memory.

Since then, a plethora of experimental and theoretical studies on quantum memory have emerged, with the main schemes including electromagnetically induced transparency quantum memory, Duan-Lukin-Cirac-Zoller (DLCZ) memory scheme, Faraday interaction, reversible inhomogeneous broadening, and atomic frequency combs. The core of these schemes involves the interaction between light and matter, as well as the evolution and recovery of interference or phase relationships of internal states within the matter. A brief introduction to these concepts follows.

7.2.1.1 Electromagnetically Induced Transparency Quantum Memory

Electromagnetically Induced Transparency (EIT) is a phenomenon associated with quantum physics, referring to the ability to propagate light through a medium that would normally absorb it, without loss, through the application of external control fields. This phenomenon is based on two distinct optical fields: a strong control field and a weak probe field. When only the weak probe field interacts with the medium, it is typically absorbed. However, when the strong control field is simultaneously applied, it alters the atomic quantum states within the medium, significantly reducing absorption of the probe field within a specific frequency range. More specifically, EIT relies on a three-level atomic system, which consists of a ground state, an excited state, and an intermediate state. The control light couples the ground and intermediate states, while the probe light interacts with the intermediate state and excited state. When both fields interact with the three-level system, quantum interference effects can suppress the absorption of the probe field, rendering the medium transparent within that frequency range.

EIT quantum storage (Chanelière et al. 2005, pp. 833–836) is a method that utilizes this phenomenon to store optical information, encompassing the processes of photon pulse storage and retrieval. Initially, a single photon pulse is incident alongside the control light field into the medium. Through the EIT effect, the photon pulse is slowed and ultimately stopped, with its phase information stored in the long-lived metastable state of the atomic system. When the retrieval of the photon pulse is necessary, the control light field is reactivated, converting the phase information in the atomic system back into a photon pulse, thus facilitating the reading of quantum information.

EIT quantum storage possesses numerous advantages, such as extended storage times suitable for medium- to long-distance quantum communication, high fidelity that effectively preserves the coherence of the stored information, and strong controllability that enables precise management of the photon storage and retrieval processes. Consequently, it is widely regarded as a crucial component for future quantum information processing and quantum communication systems. However, this technology also faces several challenges, such as environmental noise potentially affecting the stability of the EIT effect, leading to reduced storage efficiency. Furthermore, implementing EIT quantum storage requires high-precision control of both the control and probe light fields, placing significant demands on experimental setups and operational techniques.

7.2.1.2 DLCZ Memory Scheme

The DLCZ memory scheme (Duan et al. 2001, pp. 413–418), proposed by L. M. Duan, M. D. Lukin, J. I. Cirac, and P. Zoller in 2001, is primarily employed for long-distance quantum communication and quantum networking. The core of this scheme lies in establishing entanglement between two spatially separated atomic ensembles. An atomic ensemble is a system consisting of a large collection of atoms that interact and collectively respond to optical excitation, leading to the establishment of a coherent, collective quantum state.

The setup for the DLCZ scheme is illustrated in Figure 7.20, where two atomic ensembles, L and R, are irradiated by weak laser pulses. Upon receiving the

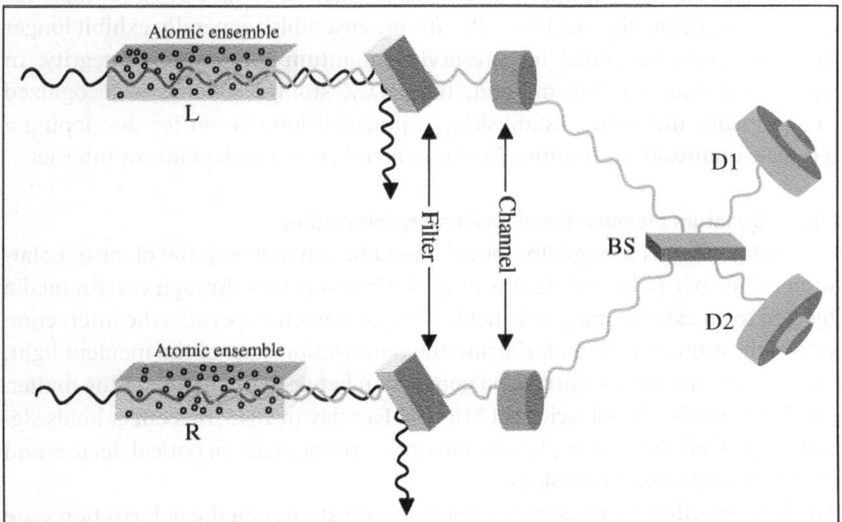

Figure 7.20 Principle of entanglement establishment between two atomic ensembles in the DLCZ scheme.

laser pulse, each atomic ensemble has the potential to emit a signal photon. However, because the likelihood of photon emission is low, usually only one atomic ensemble successfully emits a photon. The emitted signal photon first passes through filters, which eliminate unwanted frequencies or modes, ensuring that the transmitted photon is the desired signal photon. The filtered photon then enters a fiber optic channel, leading to a beam splitter. The beam splitter is a critical component of the entire setup, as it randomly divides the incoming photon into two paths directed toward two photon detectors, D1 and D2, effectively erasing the path information of the photon. If a detector registers a photon, the inability to discern which atomic ensemble emitted it introduces uncertainty, resulting in the generation of quantum entanglement between the two atomic ensembles.

By entangling multiple atomic ensembles through this exchange process, further distances in quantum communication can be achieved. This quantum entanglement, realized through photon detection, allows the collective excited states of the two atomic ensembles to be utilized as quantum memories. Upon confirmation of the entangled state, these collective excited states can store quantum information. When required, specific operations can convert these collective excited states back into new photons, effectively transferring the quantum information from the original signal photon.

The DLCZ scheme offers the advantage of not requiring precise control over individual atoms, instead leveraging the collective behavior of the atomic ensemble. This approach considerably reduces experimental complexity and improves the scheme's practicality. Additionally, atomic ensembles generally exhibit longer coherence times, beneficial for preserving quantum information integrity. In quantum information transmission, the DLCZ storage scheme is recognized as a significant milestone, establishing a practical foundation for developing a large-scale quantum communication system and even a real quantum Internet.

7.2.1.3 Quantum Memory Based on Faraday Interaction

The Faraday effect is a magneto-optical phenomenon in which the plane of polarization of linearly polarized light is rotated when it passes through certain media subjected to an external magnetic field. This phenomenon permits the interaction between the atoms in the material and the polarization state of the incident light, thus enabling quantum information conversion between the light and the matter. First discovered by British scientist Michael Faraday in 1845, this effect holds significant application value in physics and optics, particularly in optical devices and quantum information technology.

The Faraday effect enables interaction between atoms and the polarization state of light, facilitating quantum information conversion between light and matter, and thus can be applied to quantum memory (Julsgaard et al. 2004, pp. 482–486).

In this scheme, an external magnetic field is applied to control the atomic states within the material, modifying their interaction with light. As the incoming light enters the material under the influence of the magnetic field, its polarization state undergoes rotation due to the Faraday effect, resulting in a new polarization state. This new polarization state can be read out again to form an output light pulse, which reflects the interaction process between the atoms in the material and light.

Precise control over the parameters of the external magnetic field and the atomic states in the material is important during the storage and retrieval processes. In the storage phase, the direction and intensity of the magnetic field are fine-tuned to optimize the Faraday rotation effect. In the retrieval phase, the conditions of the magnetic field are modified so that the atoms in the material can reemit the previously stored polarization state of the light.

The strength of this quantum memory scheme is its ability to operate at room temperature without requiring highly condensed atomic states, making it particularly practical for certain specific applications. Additionally, the rapid response of the magnetic field adjustments and the Faraday effect make this scheme suitable for high-frequency information storage and retrieval. However, due to material and environmental limitations, its implementation is currently more feasible under laboratory conditions, while facing numerous technical and cost challenges for large-scale applications.

7.2.1.4 Atomic Frequency Comb Quantum Memory

The Atomic Frequency Comb (AFC) quantum memory scheme (Afzelius et al. 2009, p. 052329) is a quantum storage technology based on specific energy level structures in solid-state materials. In the AFC quantum memory scheme, the absorption spectrum of the material is preconditioned by laser pulses to form a periodic frequency structure resembling a comb, which is known as an atomic frequency comb. Each frequency component represents the resonant absorption capability of different ions for photons of a particular frequency, meaning that only light of specific frequencies is absorbed, while light of other frequencies passes through the medium without absorption.

As shown in Figure 7.21, when an optical pulse interacts with such a specialized frequency comb structure, it is absorbed by each of the comb teeth. Subsequently, after a specific time delay, the optical pulse is reemitted. This time delay is closely related to the characteristics of the frequency comb, particularly determined by the spacing between adjacent teeth. By carefully designing the spacing and shape of the frequency comb, efficient storage and on-demand retrieval of optical pulses can be realized. With precise optimization, the AFC scheme can provide high storage efficiency. More importantly, due to the periodic structure of the frequency comb, AFC can simultaneously store multiple frequency or temporal modes of optical

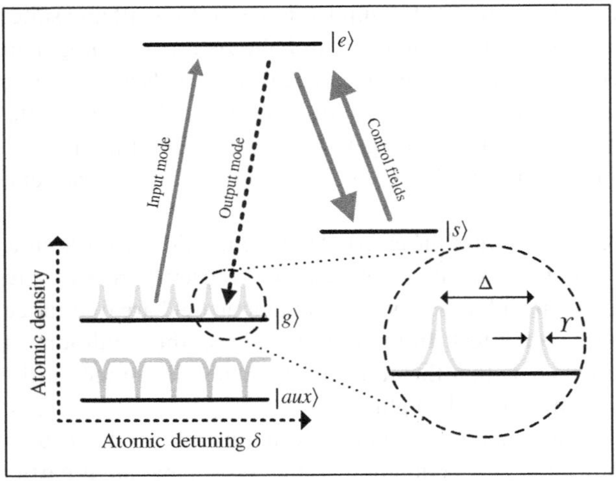

Figure 7.21 Schematic of AFC quantum memory principle.

pulses, facilitating multimode quantum storage. Currently, AFC is mainly applied to rare-earth-ion-doped solid-state crystals, as these crystals possess energy level structures suitable for constructing the desired frequency combs, thereby meeting the requirements for quantum information storage.

Over recent years, the development of quantum storage technology has made remarkable progress, evolving from single-photon-level storage to the realization of multiplexed quantum memories, and from solid-state implementations to hybrid quantum systems. The current advances in quantum memory show significant potential for integration into quantum communication and computing networks. However, challenges persist, particularly in achieving scalability, high fidelity, extended coherence time, and compatibility with other quantum systems. To address these challenges, ongoing efforts are focused on both optimizing existing quantum storage platforms and investigating emerging hybrid solutions. Such advances are crucial for driving the quantum storage field toward practical applications, marking an essential step in the evolution of quantum information technology.

7.2.2 Quantum Computer

Similar to classical computers, quantum computers are also designed to address computational problems, with both input data and output results consisting of classical data. The key distinction lies in the method of data processing. Quantum computers first initialize the data into quantum states, which are then input into quantum circuits for manipulation. The resulting output, referred to as the

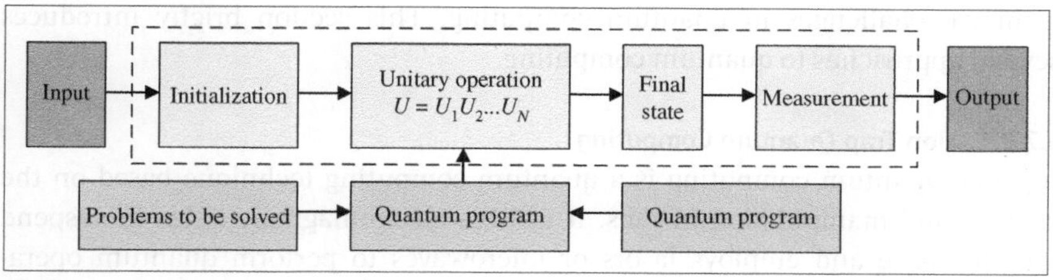

Figure 7.22 The fundamental principles of a quantum computer.

final state, can be measured to obtain the final result. The design of operations within the quantum circuit is termed a quantum program, which is contingent upon the specific problem to be solved and the corresponding quantum algorithm. Figure 7.22 illustrates the fundamental principles of a quantum computer.

The development of quantum computers can be divided into three stages. The first stage involves experimental quantum computing prototypes, which represent the initial phase of quantum computers, focusing on constructing small-scale quantum systems to verify fundamental quantum principles and operations. Quantum computers in this stage primarily emphasize feasibility verification for research purposes rather than performing practical computational tasks. These prototypes are typically small in scale, with a limited number of qubits, and are significantly affected by noise, thus offering no advantages over classical computers.

The second stage is characterized by demonstrating the superiority of quantum computers, often referred to as the quantum supremacy stage. In this phase, quantum computers successfully outperform the most advanced classical computers on certain specific tasks. It is important to note that these tasks are meticulously designed, exhibiting exponential or super-exponential time complexity on classical computers, while requiring polynomial time on quantum computers. However, their practical utility may be limited. Currently, the most advanced quantum computers are in this second stage.

The third stage refers to universal quantum computers, which are fully functional and possess robust computational capabilities. This stage represents the ultimate goal of quantum computer development. The emergence of universal quantum computers will signify humanity's true entry into the era of quantum computing, leading to widespread applications across various fields and fundamentally transforming current computational paradigms. Universal quantum computers must meet at least two criteria: the number of qubits should reach tens of thousands to millions, and they must employ practical error-correcting fault-tolerant techniques.

Similar to quantum storage, quantum computing has multiple technical paths that, although implemented in different ways, all aim to solve the core technical challenges in quantum computing. This section briefly introduces several approaches to quantum computing.

7.2.2.1 Ion Trap Quantum Computing

Ion trap quantum computing is a quantum computing technique based on the capture and manipulation of ions. It utilizes electromagnetic fields to suspend ions in space and employs lasers or microwaves to perform quantum operations. In this approach, each ion represents a qubit, with common ions such as ytterbium, calcium, and beryllium, all of which possess suitable energy level structures for quantum operations. The electronic transitions between the energy levels of the ions are used to denote the binary states of qubits, 0 and 1. Precise laser pulses control the quantum states of the ions, enabling quantum gate operations, while the readout of quantum states is also achieved through laser interactions.

In the ion trap, laser interactions with the ions facilitate single-qubit operations. However, multi-qubit operations necessitate the introduction of additional methods, such as mode coupling. Once trapped, ions form a lattice structure, interacting with each other through Coulomb forces. The collective motion of these ions can be harnessed to enable multi-qubit coupling, which also requires specific laser pulses. This coupling allows for the implementation of logic gate operations among multiple ions.

Ion trap technology offers several unique advantages. First, it enables precise control over ions, resulting in highly accurate quantum gate operations. Additionally, since the ions are captured in a vacuum environment, they are less susceptible to interference from the external environment, allowing for relatively long coherence times essential for handling complex quantum computations. However, this approach also encounters challenges. As more ions are added to the system, maintaining control over each ion's quantum state becomes increasingly complex, which can lead to errors and thus limit the scalability of quantum computing. Moreover, ion trap quantum gate operations are slower compared to some alternative technologies.

Ion trap quantum computing has undergone decades of research. In the early stages of quantum computing research, Dave Wineland's team (Monroe et al. 1997, p.R2489) built the first CNOT gate using ion traps, an achievement that earned him the Nobel Prize in Physics in 2012. Currently, multiple companies and research teams, including IonQ and Honeywell, are actively developing and optimizing ion trap quantum computing technology. In 2022, Thomas Monz's team (Postler et al. 2022, pp. 675–680) in Austria implemented a set of operations suitable for universal computation on two logical qubits using a 16-ion trap quantum computer, achieving the first demonstration of universal computation on fault-tolerant qubits.

7.2.2.2 Superconducting Quantum Computing

Superconducting quantum computing leverages the microscopic quantum properties inherent in superconducting circuits, with a critical component being the Josephson junction. A Josephson junction is a structure formed by two superconducting films separated by a layer of insulator or nonsuperconducting metal. This junction enables superconducting qubits to perform high-precision quantum operations and measurements. By applying precisely controlled microwave pulses, the phase difference across the Josephson junction can be altered, facilitating quantum gate operations. During the readout of qubit states, changes in the current–voltage characteristics of the Josephson junction can be detected and measured.

Furthermore, the high coherence and low noise characteristics of the Josephson junction are crucial to superconducting quantum computing. The coherence time of qubits is vital for the performance of quantum computations. The Josephson junction, due to its intrinsic quantum properties, can provide long coherence times in low-temperature environments. These features also allow superconducting quantum computing to utilize Josephson junctions for quantum error correction and fault-tolerant computations.

Compared to other technological approaches, the most significant advantages of superconducting quantum computing are its integrability and operation speed. Leveraging these advantages, researchers can integrate a large number of superconducting qubits on a relatively small chip while providing high qubit operation speed, which facilitates the execution of quantum algorithms requiring complex operations. The disadvantage of superconducting quantum computing is its stringent environmental requirements; factors such as temperature, thermal noise, and microwave radiation can significantly affect its performance.

Currently, superconducting quantum computing is one of the most prominent technological pathways, marked by rapid breakthroughs and leading achievements. Numerous companies have made significant contributions to this field, with Google and IBM being key players. In 2019, Google published a landmark paper in *Nature*, reporting that their superconducting quantum computer, Sycamore, demonstrated quantum supremacy by achieving a sampling instance of a quantum circuit with 53 qubits in 200 seconds (Arute et al. 2019, pp. 505–510). In 2023, IBM announced the release of the first quantum computing processor, Condor, with over 1000 qubits, comprising 1121 qubits (Gambetta, 2023). The company also introduced a comprehensive research roadmap aimed at achieving practical quantum computing within the next decade.

7.2.2.3 Photonic Quantum Computing

The various properties of photons, such as polarization, orbital angular momentum, and spatiotemporal modes, can all be used for the storage, transmission, and processing of qubits. Implementing photonic quantum computing requires specific photonic quantum logic gates, which are typically based on linear optical elements such as beam splitters, phase modulators, and polarization rotators. However, a purely linear optical system cannot implement all necessary quantum logic gates, so a universal photonic computing model also requires the incorporation of nonlinear optical devices and nonlinear optical effects to achieve universal quantum operations.

Photonic quantum computing is currently one of the most advanced technological approaches. Compared to superconducting quantum computing, it has less stringent environmental requirements, particularly avoiding the need for complex cooling systems. Additionally, since photons are widely used in quantum information transmission, photonic quantum computing is likely to achieve better compatibility with other technologies in the future. The main challenge of photonic quantum computing is related to efficiency, including preparation efficiency, computational efficiency, and measurement efficiency.

China is a leading country in the field of photonic quantum computing. In 2020, a research group headed by Jian-Wei Pan and Chao-Yang Lu from the University of Science and Technology of China successfully developed a photonic quantum computing prototype featuring 76 photons (Zhong et al. 2020, pp. 1460–1463), which was named "Jiuzhang." This quantum computer achieved quantum supremacy. In October 2023, the team built a new quantum computing prototype called "Jiuzhang 3.0," capable of manipulating 255 photons (Deng et al. 2023, p. 150601).

7.2.2.4 Neutral Atom Quantum Computing

A neutral atom refers to an atom with zero net charge, meaning the number of electrons equals the number of protons, resulting in no overall electric charge. Commonly used neutral atoms are alkali metal atoms, such as rubidium (Rb) or cesium (Cs). These atoms have simple and easily controllable electronic structures, making them well suited to serve as qubits. This approach achieves basic quantum computing operations through laser cooling of neutral atoms, optical trapping, precise laser pulse manipulation, and fluorescence imaging for readout.

The advantages of neutral atom quantum computing stem from the inherent properties of neutral atoms, including their natural characteristics and charge neutrality. The natural properties of neutral atoms provide inherent standardization and repeatability for the quantum system, while the charge neutrality offers excellent scalability. Neutral atoms can be tightly arranged into arrays, with focused laser beams setting their spacing at a micrometer scale. These atomic arrays can be extended to contain thousands or even millions of qubits without significantly increasing the overall spatial footprint of the system. Moreover, the closed outer electron shell of alkali metal atoms makes them less sensitive to environmental perturbations, which helps reduce decoherence effects. However, similar to other technological approaches, neutral atom quantum computing still faces unresolved challenges in areas such as experimental environments and operational efficiency.

In recent years, neutral atom quantum computing has achieved numerous breakthroughs. For example, in 2022, the team led by Hannes Bernien created a dual-element neutral atom array consisting of rubidium and cesium atoms, realizing the first neutral atom system composed of 512 qubits (Singh et al. 2022, p. 011040). Atom Computing has announced plans to launch a second-generation neutral atom quantum computer. The company has already created an array of 1,225 atomic sites in its quantum computing platform, with 1,180 qubits currently filled (Atom Computing, 2023).

The quantum computing technologies discussed in this section represent some of the most developed or longest-researched methodologies. However, beyond these methods, many other quantum computing pathways are continually advancing toward the goal of universal quantum computation. In the upcoming quantum era, it is highly probable that various approaches will coexist, with the selection of technology being determined by specific application needs, technological maturity, and economic feasibility. Regardless of the chosen method, the primary focus will continue to be on enhancing the quality and scalability of qubits, as well as developing robust fault-tolerant error correction techniques. There is no doubt that the evolution of quantum computing will significantly influence the progress and transformation of numerous fields of scientific research in the future.

7.3 Quantum Secure Transmission

The overarching goal of information transmission has always been the secure sending, transfer, and reception of information. Traditional information security typically employs encryption and decryption methods: the communicating parties establish one or more keys based on an agreed-upon protocol, with the sender using the key for encrypting and transmitting the original information to the recipient. Upon receiving the encrypted message, the recipient uses the corresponding key to decrypt it, thereby recovering the original information. The security of this encrypted communication hinges on the key; thus, the security of the key ensures the security of the information. However, classical keys cannot guarantee absolute security, as symmetric keys are susceptible to eavesdropping during transmission, while asymmetric keys can be compromised by quantum computing.

On the one hand, quantum technology poses a threat to classical key systems; on the other hand, it can be employed to generate absolutely secure keys. Quantum key distribution (QKD) is a type of key generation protocol that utilizes the quantum no-cloning theorem to successfully ensure the security of keys, with this security being mathematically proven as absolute security (Lo and Chau, 1999, pp. 2050–2056).

Moreover, quantum technology not only serves as a means to ensure information security under classical transmission methods but can also be utilized for information transmission itself. Superdense coding and quantum teleportation exemplify this. Superdense coding is a quantum communication technique that allows the transmission of two classical bits of information using a single qubit and shared entanglement. Quantum teleportation is a process that transfers a quantum state from one location to another using shared quantum entanglement, without physically transmitting the quantum state's carrier.

7.3.1 Quantum Key Distribution

The keys generated by QKD are symmetric keys, analogous to classical symmetric keys. The encrypted communication process using quantum keys is illustrated in Figure 7.23: first, a quantum key is generated and exchanged based on the agreed QKD protocol, and then communication occurs using this quantum key over a classical channel.

There are various implementations of QKD, among which the most renowned is the BB84 protocol proposed by Bennett and Brassard in 1984 (Bennett and Brassard 2014, pp. 7–11). This was the first QKD protocol in history, and its concise and efficient approach laid the foundation for the development of quantum encryption technologies, providing significant inspiration and insights for many subsequent protocols.

The BB84 protocol utilizes two ordered standard orthogonal bases, the vertical linear polarization basis V and the diagonal linear polarization basis H:

$$V : \begin{bmatrix}1\\0\end{bmatrix}\begin{bmatrix}0\\1\end{bmatrix}, \quad H : \begin{bmatrix}\frac{1}{\sqrt{2}}\\ \frac{-1}{\sqrt{2}}\end{bmatrix}\begin{bmatrix}\frac{1}{\sqrt{2}}\\ \frac{1}{\sqrt{2}}\end{bmatrix}. \tag{7.31}$$

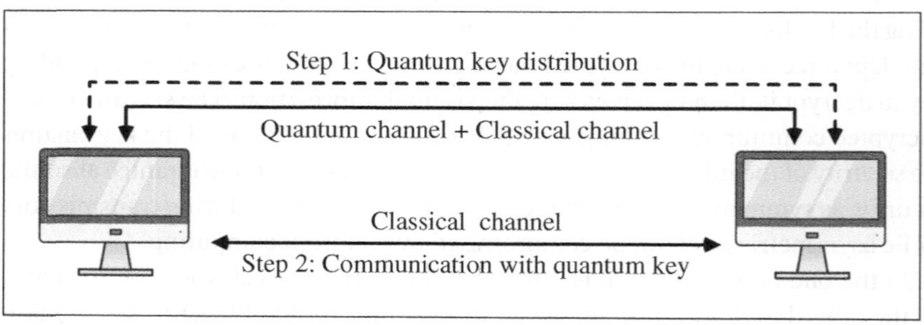

Figure 7.23 Communication process utilizing QKD.

In this ordered basis, the first vector corresponds to the classical bit 0, while the second vector corresponds to the classical bit 1.

To illustrate this protocol, consider the following scenario: Alice wishes to send a ciphertext to Bob, and they decide to use the BB84 protocol to generate a quantum key. In this process, Eve attempts to intercept the key to gain access to the encrypted information.

First, Alice selects a string of classical bits. For convenience, let us assume that the length of this string is $8n$. For each bit, Alice randomly and uniformly selects one from the two bases, V and H. Then she sends each qubit through the quantum channel to Bob and records which basis was used for each qubit. Consequently, she obtains a string of length $8n$ consisting of V and H.

Bob similarly randomly and uniformly selects from the two bases, then measures the qubits sent by Alice using the chosen basis, also recording which basis he selected. After the measurement is completed, he possesses two strings of length $8n$: one consisting of the measured bits (0s and 1s) and the other comprising his selected V and H.

Once the qubit transmission concludes, they will communicate over a classical channel, which may be susceptible to eavesdropping. They will compare their chosen bases over this classical channel. If their choices are entirely random, there is a 50% probability that they will select the same basis for a given qubit. The BB84 protocol stipulates that if they select the same basis, the bit is retained; if they select different bases, the bit is discarded. The final outcome is an approximately $4n$-bit long binary string.

If no eavesdropping occurs, the remaining binary string can be used as the key. If eavesdropping is a possibility, it can be detected. For Eve to intercept the key, she must eavesdrop on both the quantum channel and the classical channel. In the quantum channel, to avoid detection, Eve must measure the qubits sent by Alice and then resend the same qubits to Bob. However, due to the no-cloning theorem, Eve cannot directly clone the qubits; she must measure them before resending.

Eve's measurement also requires her to select a basis. Regardless of her strategy, there is only a 1/4 probability that she selects a basis identical to those chosen by both Alice and Bob. In other words, if Alice and Bob select the same basis, there is a 50% chance that Eve also chooses the same basis. In the remaining 50% of incorrect selections, Eve has a 50% chance of obtaining the wrong bit, meaning that approximately n of the bits sent by Eve to Bob are erroneous.

The final step involves Alice and Bob comparing half of the bits obtained when they chose the same basis, which is approximately $2n$ bits. If this subset of bits matches, it verifies that Eve did not eavesdrop on their communication, allowing them to use the remaining $2n$ bits as the key. The bits involved in the comparison cannot be used as the key due to their transmission over an insecure channel. If approximately n of the compared $2n$ bits differ, it indicates that Eve has been eavesdropping, prompting them to seek alternative methods to ensure communication security.

In addition to BB84, there are various QKD protocols, such as the E91 protocol (Ekert, 1991, p. 661) and the BBM92 protocol (Bennett, Brassard and Mermin, 1992, p. 557), many of which are improvements and developments of the BB84 protocol, incorporating new features. As quantum technology continues to advance, new QKD protocols will emerge to address the limitations and challenges of current protocols. Researchers are committed to enhancing the security, reliability, and practicality of QKD systems, promoting the widespread application of QKD in real-world scenarios. Whether in long-distance communication, satellite communication, or cybersecurity, QKD will play a crucial role in ensuring the security of data transmission, bringing revolutionary changes to the field of information security.

7.3.2 Superdense Coding

Superdense coding (Bennett and Wiesner, 1992, p. 2881) is a quantum communication protocol that enables the sender to convey two classical bits of information by sending only one qubit. This process leverages the unique properties of quantum entanglement, significantly enhancing the efficiency of information transmission compared to classical communication methods.

Alice and Bob aim to communicate using superdense coding. Initially, they need to share a pair of entangled qubits:

$$\frac{1}{\sqrt{2}}|00\rangle + \frac{1}{\sqrt{2}}|11\rangle. \tag{7.32}$$

Suppose Alice wants to send two classical bits of information to Bob, which could be one of 00, 01, 10, or 11. First, Alice will perform different operations depending on the information she wants to send. These operations involve the use of quantum gates to transform the entangled quantum state into the corresponding Bell state. For example, if Alice intends to send 00, she will not perform any operation. If Alice wants to send 01, she will apply an X gate, which transforms her $|0\rangle$ into $|1\rangle$ and $|1\rangle$ into $|0\rangle$. The state of the two qubits will then change to

$$\frac{1}{\sqrt{2}}|10\rangle + \frac{1}{\sqrt{2}}|01\rangle. \tag{7.33}$$

To send the classical bit 10 or 11, Alice would apply a Z gate or a Y gate, respectively. The correspondence between the information Alice wishes to send and the operations she performs on the qubit is illustrated in Table 7.5, which aligns perfectly with the truth table of the Bell circuit. After making the necessary transformations, Alice transmits the qubit to Bob, who then processes the two qubits using the inverse Bell circuit to convert them into an unentangled state. By measuring

Table 7.5 Information to be transmitted and the state of entangled qubits.

Information Alice wishes to transmit	State of entangled qubits
00	$\frac{1}{\sqrt{2}}(\|00\rangle + \|11\rangle)$
01	$\frac{1}{\sqrt{2}}(\|01\rangle + \|10\rangle)$
10	$\frac{1}{\sqrt{2}}(\|00\rangle - \|11\rangle)$
11	$\frac{1}{\sqrt{2}}(\|01\rangle - \|10\rangle)$

the unentangled quantum state, Bob can retrieve the original information that Alice intended to transmit. This process transmits only one qubit while successfully conveying the information of two classical bits.

Superdense coding leverages Bell circuits and inverse Bell circuits to achieve information transmission that far exceeds the efficiency of classical communication. It is one of the key technologies for realizing quantum communication and quantum networks. As quantum technology advances, superdense coding will play an increasingly important role in efficient and secure information transmission.

7.3.3 Quantum Teleportation

Quantum teleportation (Bouwmeester et al. 1997, pp. 575–579) is a quantum information transmission technology that allows the transfer of the information of a quantum state from one location to another without the need for the actual transmission of a physical carrier. This process also exploits the unique properties of quantum entanglement.

The initial setup for quantum teleportation is analogous to that of superdense coding, where Alice and Bob share a pair of entangled qubits, denoted as A and B, respectively. In addition to this, Alice possesses another qubit C, represented as $|\psi\rangle = a\,|\,0\rangle + b\,|\,1\rangle$, although Alice is unaware of the values of the probability amplitudes a and b. Initially, the state of the three qubits can be expressed as

$$(a|0\rangle + b|1\rangle) \otimes \left(\frac{1}{\sqrt{2}}|00\rangle + \frac{1}{\sqrt{2}}|11\rangle \right). \tag{7.34}$$

At the conclusion of the process, Alice and Bob transform the state of qubit B into $a\,|\,0\rangle + b\,|\,1\rangle$ without transmitting $|\psi\rangle$ itself. Clearly, Bob's qubit B has transitioned from its initial entangled state to a nonentangled state. This transformation requires Alice to perform operations on her qubits A and C. To differentiate the three qubits, equation (7.34) can be rewritten as follows:

$$\frac{a}{\sqrt{2}}|00\rangle \otimes |0\rangle + \frac{a}{\sqrt{2}}|01\rangle \otimes |1\rangle + \frac{b}{\sqrt{2}}|10\rangle \otimes |0\rangle + \frac{b}{\sqrt{2}}|11\rangle \otimes |1\rangle. \quad (7.35)$$

Initially, the two qubits A and C controlled by Alice are input into the inverse Bell circuit, which consists of two steps. The first step involves applying a CNOT gate to the two qubits:

$$\frac{a}{\sqrt{2}}|00\rangle \otimes |0\rangle + \frac{a}{\sqrt{2}}|01\rangle \otimes |1\rangle + \frac{b}{\sqrt{2}}|11\rangle \otimes |0\rangle + \frac{b}{\sqrt{2}}|10\rangle \otimes |1\rangle. \quad (7.36)$$

The second step consists of applying a Hadamard gate to qubit C. After simplification, the state of the three qubits becomes

$$\begin{aligned}&\frac{1}{2}|00\rangle \otimes (a|0\rangle + b|1\rangle) + \frac{1}{2}|01\rangle \otimes (a|1\rangle + b|0\rangle)\\&+ \frac{1}{2}|10\rangle \otimes (a|0\rangle - b|1\rangle) + \frac{1}{2}|11\rangle \otimes (a|1\rangle - b|0\rangle).\end{aligned} \quad (7.37)$$

After inputting into the inverse Bell circuit, Alice will measure her two qubits in the standard basis. She will obtain one of the states $|00\rangle$, $|01\rangle$, $|10\rangle$, or $|11\rangle$, each with a probability of 1/4. Each result will cause Bob's qubit B to transition to the corresponding state. For instance, if Alice measures $|01\rangle$, then Bob's qubit B will transition to the state $a\,|\,1\rangle + b\,|\,0\rangle$.

Alice then sends her measurement result to Bob, informing him of the state of his qubit. The information from these two bits can be transmitted using a classical channel. Finally, based on the state of his qubit, Bob applies the corresponding quantum gate to successfully transform it into $a\,|\,0\rangle + b\,|\,1\rangle$.

There are two noteworthy issues in the process of quantum teleportation. The first is the cloning of qubits. At any moment during the process, only one qubit exists in the state $a\,|\,0\rangle + b\,|\,1\rangle$; thus, the process does not violate the no-cloning theorem. The second issue is the speed of information transmission. Upon Alice measuring the two qubits, Bob's qubit immediately collapses into one of the four possible states. However, Bob does not acquire any information at this stage, as he must wait for Alice to transmit two classical bits. Only after receiving this classical information can Bob apply quantum gates to proceed with further operations. Thus, the transfer of information from Alice to Bob does not occur instantaneously.

Quantum teleportation and superdense coding can be viewed as complementary processes. In superdense coding, Alice communicates two classical bits of information to Bob by sending just a single qubit. In contrast, quantum teleportation involves Alice transmitting the state of one qubit to Bob by sending two classical bits. Additionally, in superdense coding, Alice encodes information using corresponding quantum gates, while Bob decodes it with an inverse Bell circuit.

In quantum teleportation, Alice encodes using the inverse Bell circuit, and Bob decodes the qubit state using the corresponding quantum gates. This symmetry highlights the inverse relationship between the two protocols.

Experimental research on QKD, superdense coding, and quantum teleportation has long been a focal point in the study of quantum transmission. Since the first quantum teleportation experiment, significant progress has been made in this field. In 1997, the Austrian team led by Zeilinger successfully conducted the world's first quantum teleportation experiment (Bouwmeester et al. 1997, pp. 575–579), marking a major breakthrough in the area. In 2012, Pan Jianwei's team achieved quantum teleportation over a distance of over 100 km along with QKD in the Qinghai Lake region (Yin et al. 2012, pp. 185–188), further advancing the practical implementation of quantum communication. By 2017, China's "Micius" quantum satellite successfully realized quantum teleportation from space to Earth, demonstrating the immense potential of quantum technologies in satellite communication (Lu et al. 2022, p. 035001). In 2022, the Hermans team successfully implemented quantum teleportation between nonadjacent nodes in a three-node network, pushing forward the development of quantum networks (Liu et al. 2023, p. 210801). In 2023, Pan Jianwei's team achieved twin-field QKD over a distance of more than 1,000 kilometers through optical fiber (Hermans et al. 2022, pp. 663–668), marking yet another significant leap in long-distance quantum communication technologies.

7.3.4 Quantum Error Correction Codes

For information composed of classical bits, if certain bits are influenced by environmental factors and flip from 0 to 1, or from 1 to 0, the information may be lost or corrupted. However, the high reliability of modern classical computers means that such errors are infrequent, and established error correction schemes can safeguard data storage and transmission.

In contrast to classical bits, qubits are more susceptible to environmental noise, and due to the unique properties of qubits, the potential error rates are significantly higher than those of classical bits, with a wider variety of possible error types. This leads to an essential difference between qubits and classical bits, making it inappropriate to directly apply classical error correction methods to quantum systems. A straightforward example is the classical repetition error correction code. For a single bit of information, it can be repeated three times as: $0 \rightarrow 000$, $1 \rightarrow 111$. During decoding, the majority rule is employed to deduce the result, which can be verified through parity checks. For instance, if the measurement yields 010, the decoding result should be 0. However, in quantum systems, the no-cloning theorem prevents the direct repetition of unknown qubits during the encoding process. Furthermore, due to the nature of measurement collapse,

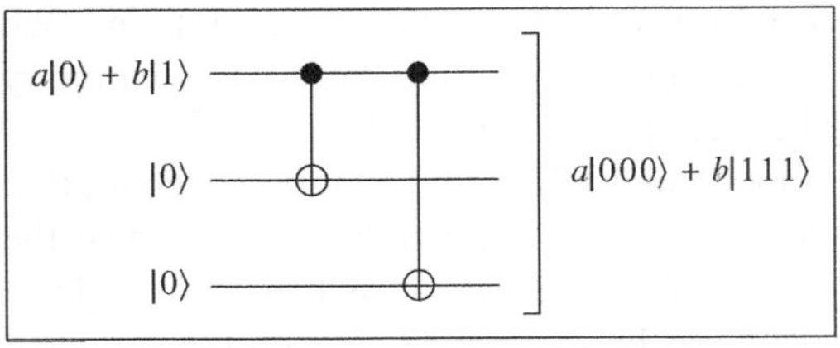

Figure 7.24 Quantum circuit for the encoding process of the repetition code.

decoding measurements can lead to the loss of information contained within the qubits. Therefore, a quantum error correction code specifically designed for quantum systems is required.

While classical error correction codes cannot be directly employed, quantum error correction codes can still draw inspiration from classical approaches. For instance, considering a repetition code, if we wish to encode a qubit $|\psi\rangle = a\,|\,0\rangle + b\,|\,1\rangle$, two CNOT gates can be utilized to perform this operation, as illustrated in Figure 7.24. The decoding process cannot directly measure the quantum state $|\psi'\rangle = a\,|\,000\rangle + b\,|\,111\rangle$, as this would result in information loss. Instead, the solution involves adding two additional qubits and employing the quantum circuit depicted in Figure 7.25. It is important to note that the newly added qubits are not entangled with the original qubits.

Assuming the final quantum state is $a\,|\,c_1c_2c_3\rangle + b\,|\,d_1d_2d_3\rangle$. For simplicity, we first focus on the top four wires in Figure 7.25, which have the quantum state $a\,|\,c_0c_1c_2\rangle\,|\,0\rangle + b\,|\,d_0d_1d_2\rangle\,|\,0\rangle$. The two CNOT gates on the fourth wire perform parity checks on the first two digits. The four qubits on the right side of the circuit can yield two scenarios:

1) If $c_0 \oplus c_1 = d_0 \oplus d_1 = 0$, their quantum state will be $a|c_0c_1c_2\rangle|0\rangle + b|d_0d_1d_2\rangle|0\rangle = (a|c_0c_1c_2\rangle + b|d_0d_1d_2\rangle)|0\rangle$.
2) If $c_0 \oplus c_1 = d_0 \oplus d_1 = 1$, their quantum state will be $a|c_0c_1c_2\rangle|1\rangle + b|d_0d_1d_2\rangle|1\rangle = (a|c_0c_1c_2\rangle + b|d_0d_1d_2\rangle)|1\rangle$.

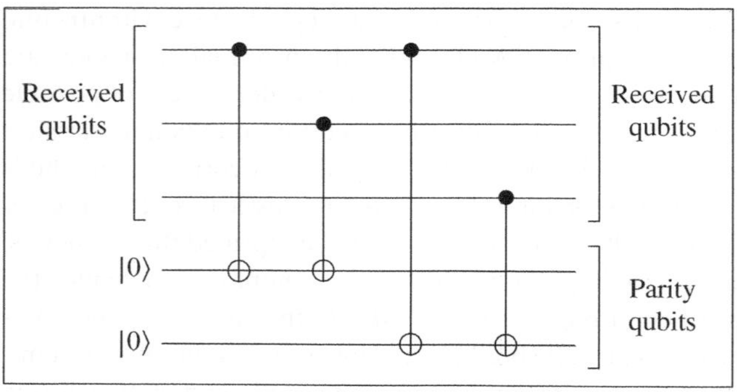

Figure 7.25 Quantum circuit for the decoding process of the repetition code.

In both cases, the fourth qubit does not become entangled with the first three qubits.

Similarly, for the fifth qubit, if $c_0 \oplus c_2 = d_0 \oplus d_2 = 0$, it will be $|0\rangle$, and if $c_0 \oplus c_2 = d_0 \oplus d_2 = 1$, it will be $|1\rangle$.

The fifth qubit also does not become entangled with the first three. Therefore, by measuring the last two qubits, one can ascertain the states of the first three qubits and identify which bits need modification. This measurement process does not affect the first three qubits due to the absence of entanglement quantum states, necessitating modifications or redesigns of classical methods. A simple example of the aforementioned quantum error correction code illustrates that the core concept of quantum error correction is to utilize redundancy coding and error-correcting codes to distribute the information of a logical qubit across multiple physical qubits, which aligns with classical error correction principles. However, unlike classical error correction, quantum error correction needs to deal with the superposition and entanglement characteristics of quantum states, which makes the classical method cannot be directly used, and needs to be modified or redesigned. The first quantum error correction code capable of correcting errors in quantum computing was proposed by mathematician Peter Shor in 1995 (Shor, 1995, p.R2493). Its fundamental idea is to encode the information of one logical qubit into multiple physical qubits. Following this, research on quantum error correction codes rapidly progressed, as depicted in Figure 7.26, which illustrates the development of quantum error correction codes. Nevertheless, due to the complexity, irreversibility, and environmental noise affecting quantum error correction encoding, experiments faced challenges that led to increasing errors. It was not until 2023 that Ni et al. demonstrated a breakthrough in achieving a positive correlation between the scale of error correction coding and performance metrics such as coherence time and error rates (Ni et al., 2023, pp. 56–60), proving that increasing the scale of error correction codes can reduce error rates and validating the practical feasibility of quantum error correction.

Although the experimental breakthrough in quantum error correction surpassing the breakeven point is a significant milestone, the existing technical solutions still face considerable gaps in error correction efficiency, fault tolerance thresholds,

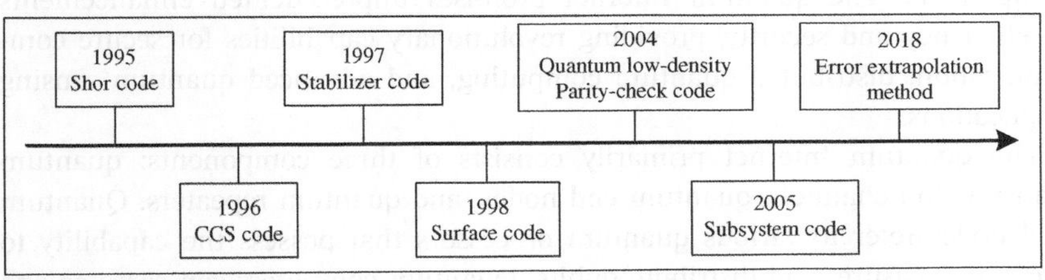

Figure 7.26 Development of quantum error correction codes.

and metrics such as the fidelity of quantum computing hardware's logic gates and the number of coherently controllable qubits. The practical implementation of quantum error correction has become a key focus within the global quantum computing community, and further advancements and achievements are expected in the future.

7.4 Quantum Computer Networks

In the technological wave of the 21st century, quantum technology is poised to play a significant role. Among all quantum technologies, quantum computing is undoubtedly one of the most important innovations. However, while individual quantum computers have already surpassed current classical computers, their true potential is realized when they are interconnected. This network of interconnected quantum computers will usher in an unprecedented era, significantly transforming how information is processed, problems are solved, and the unknown is explored. In this era, efficient and secure information transmission and processing will profoundly impact developments across various fields.

7.4.1 Quantum Internet

Reflecting on the technological advancements of the past century, many revolutionary technologies have transformed the world, with the Internet being one of them. Its emergence altered the way information is transmitted, connecting the globe into a vast network. In the modern era of quantum technology advancements, a new revolution is quietly unfolding: the quantum information network, also known as the quantum Internet, which is shown in Figure 7.27.

The quantum Internet is a novel network that relies on both quantum and classical technologies for information transmission and processing. As illustrated in Figure 7.27, the future quantum Internet will not serve as a replacement for the classical Internet but will instead be built upon it to create a quantum network. However, the term "quantum Internet" typically refers specifically to its quantum components. The quantum Internet promises unprecedented enhancements in efficiency and security, providing revolutionary capabilities for secure communication, distributed quantum computing, and advanced quantum sensing applications.

The quantum Internet primarily consists of three components: quantum transmission channels, quantum end nodes, and quantum repeaters. Quantum end nodes refer to various quantum processors that possess the capability to prepare, measure, and distribute qubits. Quantum computers can serve as one type of quantum end node. Quantum transmission channels are responsible for

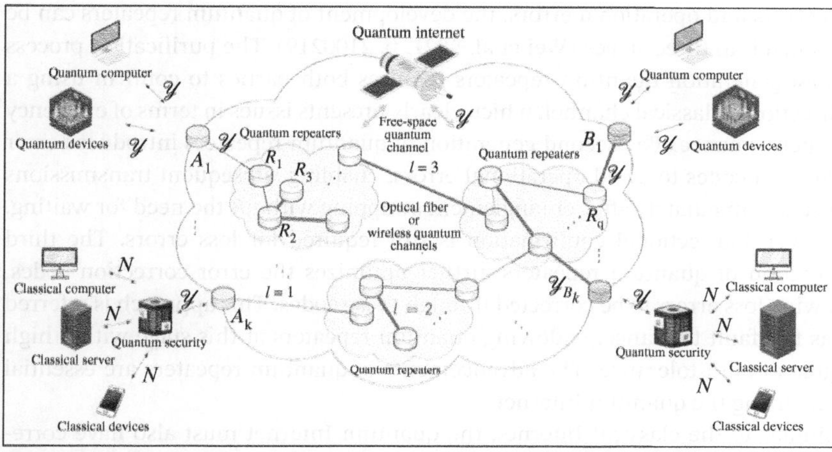

Figure 7.27 Schematic diagram of the quantum Internet (Adapted from Gyongyosi and Imre 2022).

connecting different quantum endpoints and primarily include two forms: fiber optic channels and free-space channels. Fiber optic channels offer advantages in stability and cost, while free-space channels provide longer transmission distances and greater flexibility. The transmission distance of a single quantum channel is limited, necessitating the use of quantum repeaters to extend this distance. Since current quantum transmission largely relies on entanglement, the essence of a quantum repeater is to extend the range of entanglement.

Quantum repeaters have two core functions: entanglement swapping and entanglement purification. Entanglement swapping refers to the process of extending the entanglement distance through quantum repeaters. Entanglement purification, also known as entanglement distillation, involves error correction during the transmission process, whereby high-quality entangled states are generated from lower quality entangled states, ensuring the accuracy of the communication process. Consequently, the transmission process involving quantum repeaters can be broadly divided into three parts. The first part is establishing entanglement between adjacent nodes, which include both end nodes and repeaters. The second part is entanglement swapping, which ultimately establishes entanglement between communication nodes. The third part is entanglement purification, which should be noted occurs throughout the entire entanglement swapping process, not solely after the final entanglement is established.

The entanglement swapping process may encounter two types of errors: loss errors resulting from transmission loss and operational errors arising from internal operations of the repeater. Based on the different approaches to handling loss errors and operational errors, the development of quantum repeaters can be classified into three stages (Wei et al. 2021, p. 2100219). The purification process of first-generation quantum repeaters requires both parties to confirm using a bidirectional classical channel, which clearly presents issues in terms of efficiency and performance. The second generation of quantum repeaters introduces error correction codes to avoid operational errors, enabling subsequent transmissions to occur immediately after entanglement swapping without the need for waiting. However, bidirectional confirmation is still required for loss errors. The third generation of quantum repeaters further optimizes the error correction codes, allowing loss errors to be corrected through these codes. This approach is referred to as full fault tolerance, endowing quantum repeaters at this stage with a high degree of fault tolerance. The advancements of quantum repeaters are essential for realizing the quantum Internet.

Similar to the classical Internet, the quantum Internet must also have corresponding network architectures and protocols. Due to the distinctions between classical and quantum transmission, it is unreasonable to directly apply existing network frameworks to the quantum Internet. However, classical network architectures can provide inspiration for building the quantum Internet. Wehner et al. based their proposal on the TCP/IP model a layered model for quantum networks (Dahlberg et al. 2019, pp. 159–173), as illustrated in Table 7.6. This model divides the network into five layers: physical layer, link layer, network layer, transport layer, and application layer. Each layer has its corresponding protocols and functions, with a primary focus on the physical and link layers.

The physical layer is responsible for attempting to generate entanglement during clearly defined time slots, with devices attempting to generate entanglement at a given moment referred to as automated nodes. The term "attempt" is used because the physical layer does not actually determine whether entanglement is generated; it relies on a specific protocol to coordinate the automated nodes, known as the Midpoint Heralding Protocol (MHP). The MHP stipulates that the physical layer must poll the link layer to determine whether entanglement generation is

Table 7.6 Layered model of the quantum Internet.

Layer	Function
Application	—
Transport	Qubit transmission
Network	Long-distance entanglement
Link	Robust entanglement generation
Physical	Attempt entanglement generation

required. Upon receiving a confirmation signal, it triggers an activation signal, and the physical layer provides results through specific heralding signals.

The link layer is based on the Quantum Entanglement Generation Protocol (QEGP). The QEGP requires the link layer to receive entanglement requests from higher layers, which should include node information, the number of entangled pairs, minimum fidelity, and other essential details. Based on the entanglement information, the link layer issues corresponding instructions to the lower layer. The QEGP can evaluate the entanglement generated at the lower layer based on the request information and can also schedule entanglement requests. This protocol ensures that the link layer can generate robust entanglement that meets the specified requirements. In addition to entanglement generation, the link layer can request the physical layer to perform other operations, such as initialization or measurement of qubits.

The configurations of the network layer, link layer, and application layer are less detailed. The network layer handles the creation of long-distance entanglement by leveraging the link layer's capabilities, often through entanglement swapping. Additionally, it incorporates an entanglement manager to monitor entanglement resources across the network. The transport layer is tasked with transmitting qubits in response to requests from the application layer, utilizing techniques like quantum teleportation.

The five-layer network architecture proposed by Wehner et al. is a bold vision for the future quantum Internet, and there are many similar designs. Figure 7.28

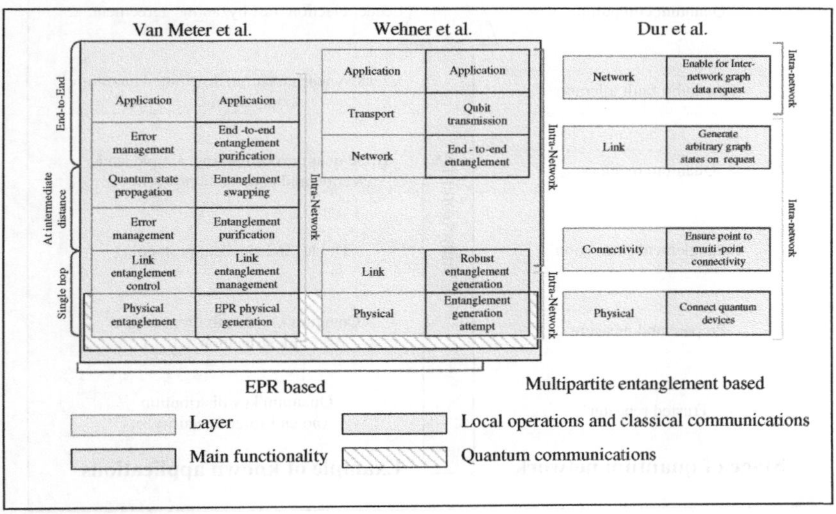

Figure 7.28 Three models of quantum Internet (Illiano, J., Caleffi, M., Manzalini, A. and Cacciapuoti, A.S., 2022 / Elsevier).

presents the three most comprehensive and well-founded quantum Internet architecture designs. These designs all draw inspiration from classical network models, each with its own focus, and all have areas that require improvement in terms of layer separation, functional allocation, and protocol design.

Although the quantum Internet holds immense potential, it is important to acknowledge that its current development is still in its infancy. Therefore, it is essential to create a detailed plan for the future development of the quantum Internet. The team led by Stephanie Wehner published an article in *Science* outlining a developmental blueprint for the quantum Internet (Wehner, Elkouss, and Hanson 2018, p. eaam9288). They categorized the development of the quantum Internet into six stages, as shown in Figure 7.29. It is evident that the development of the quantum Internet is a progressive process, where each stage builds upon the previous one by adding new functionalities. Moreover, a stage can only be considered achieved when all functionalities from the previous and current stages are accessible to all terminal nodes within the network.

The first stage is referred to as the trusted repeater network. This is a transitional phase that significantly differs from the subsequent stages, as it does not support end-to-end qubit transmission. This phase requires at least two

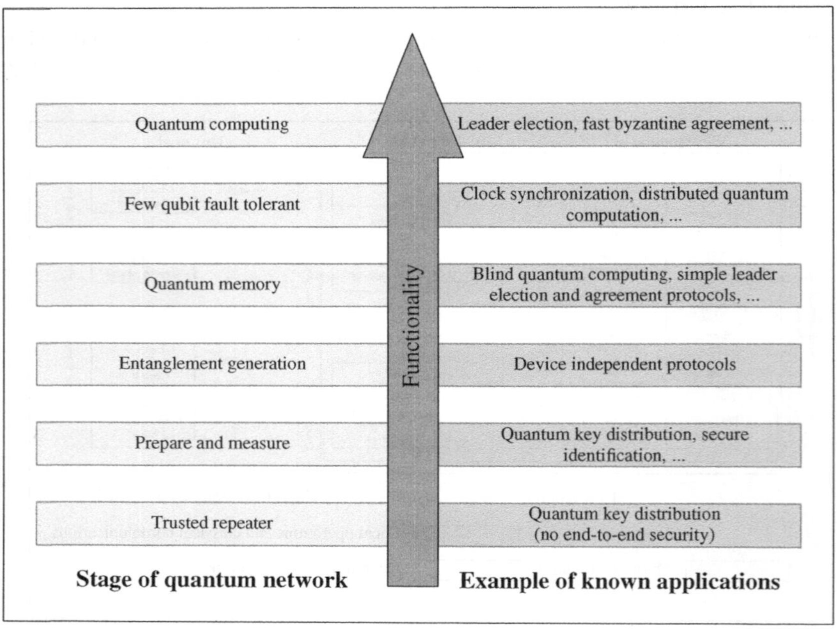

Figure 7.29 Six stages of quantum Internet development and their corresponding applications.

end nodes and a series of short-distance links connecting nearby relay nodes, where the connections between these relay nodes rely on QKD to exchange encryption keys. Through these paired keys, the end nodes can generate their own keys, provided that all intermediate nodes are trusted. The Trusted Relay Network can be viewed as a stepping stone toward the quantum Internet, laying the foundational technologies and development directions for future quantum networks. For instance, these trust-based relay devices are likely to evolve into true quantum repeaters in the future.

The second stage, referred to as the prepare and measure network, represents the initial stage where end-to-end QKD functionality is achieved, signifying a major step forward in the evolution of the quantum Internet. At this stage, two end nodes can directly conduct QKD without the need to trust any intermediate relay nodes or devices. In addition to QKD, this stage also supports an important function: preparation and measurement. The sender can prepare and send complex quantum states to different nodes in the network, which can then be measured by the receiving nodes. Notably, the preparation and measurement processes allow for post-selection, meaning that if unforeseen events occur during quantum communication or measurement, the system can choose to disregard these events afterward and only process the successful outcomes. For example, if a qubit is transmitted between nodes and the receiving node fails to detect it, the receiving node can opt to ignore these undetected events and assume that the qubits have been lost. This implies that this stage cannot deterministically transmit arbitrary unknown states of qubits, as the latter requires each transmission to succeed without any post-selection. This limitation fundamentally distinguishes this stage from higher-level quantum communication phases.

The third stage is referred to as the entanglement distribution network. In this stage, deterministic or heralded quantum entanglement can be established end-to-end. Determinism here means that the success rate of entanglement generation approaches 100%, thus eliminating the need to provide a success signal for the entanglement process. In contrast, heralded quantum entanglement requires a signal during the generation process to indicate the successful creation of entanglement. This stage begins to incorporate more advanced capabilities, such as multipartite entanglement generation and quantum memory at the end nodes. However, these capabilities are not prerequisites for entering this stage; rather, they represent preliminary developments for more advanced stages and lay the foundation for future quantum protocols.

The fourth stage is the quantum memory network. In this stage, quantum end nodes are equipped with practical local quantum storage capabilities and general local control functions. The novel capabilities of this stage are primarily enabled by advancements in quantum memory, quantum computing, and improvements in quantum fault-tolerant error correction. These capabilities allow the network to support more complex quantum protocols, such as consensus protocols in distributed systems. It is important to note that, although the network possesses fault-tolerant error correction capabilities, this stage does not impose strict requirements on the precision of qubit operations, and the network has not yet reached a fully fault-tolerant level.

The fifth stage is the few-qubit fault-tolerant network. This stage focuses on achieving fault tolerance in local qubit operations and storage. Building upon the developments of the previous stage, this stage realizes truly practical fault-tolerant error correction techniques. With the fault-tolerant capabilities of local storage and operations, many more complex and multi-round protocols will emerge at this stage. Despite these advanced capabilities, the number of qubits remains relatively small, necessitating further development in subsequent stages.

The final stage is the quantum computing network. In this ultimate stage, quantum computers will be able to freely and arbitrarily exchange quantum information, forming a highly powerful computational network through their collaboration. This network will possess the capability to tackle complex tasks that are beyond the reach of classical computers. Thus, in this stage, quantum technology truly provides us with a new ability: the means to solve computational problems that cannot be efficiently addressed by classical machines. Each quantum computer in this stage will be considered a supernode within the network, capable not only of executing advanced local quantum algorithms but also of sharing, exchanging, and integrating information with other quantum computers to perform larger scale collaborative tasks. This stage will have sufficient capability to support new algorithms, new communication protocols, and new security standards. The quantum Internet at this stage marks not only a significant technological leap but also the potential for groundbreaking innovations in various frontier scientific, engineering, and commercial applications.

The six stages described above are classified based on functional implementation and technical requirements. Alternatively, the quantum Internet can also be divided into three stages—quantum encryption network, quantum memory network, and quantum computing network—according to the anticipated application scenarios. These classification methods represent current projections for the future development of quantum technologies, but they may have certain limitations. Nevertheless, it is clear that the quantum Internet is still in its early stages, and research in this area remains in an open exploration phase. Key technologies for the quantum Internet, such as quantum storage, quantum repeaters, and quantum measurement, are still undergoing theoretical and experimental exploration. While some performance indicators are steadily improving, there remains a significant gap between current progress and practical implementation.

In response to the development and opportunities of the quantum Internet, governments across different countries are actively advancing quantum technology, investing substantial funds and research resources. In 2018, the European Union launched the "Quantum Flagship" initiative, aiming to invest over one billion euros in quantum technology research by 2028. In 2023, the European Quantum Internet Alliance initiated a "Seven-Year Plan," allocating twenty-four million euros to develop Europe's first large-scale quantum Internet. The United States also places significant emphasis on the development of the quantum Internet, publishing the "U.S. Quantum Internet Strategy" in 2020 and making large-scale investments in this field. In 2023 alone, the U.S. allocated eight hundred fifty million dollars for quantum Internet research. China has also dedicated substantial human and material resources to related research and holds a leading position in many key technologies. Given these research efforts, there is reason to believe that the quantum Internet will gradually enter the daily lives of ordinary people in the near future.

7.4.2 Quantum Multi-identifier Network Architecture with Quantum Identifier

The realization of a quantum Internet in the short term remains unlikely, but applying quantum technologies to the current classical Internet is feasible. This integration not only enhances the security of today's networks but also provides insights and experiences for the future development of a fully operational quantum Internet. Currently, various network architectures exist globally, and the multi-identifier network (MIN) is one such emerging architecture (Li and Yang, 2021). In the MIN network, the types of identifiers are diverse and can be continuously expanded. Therefore, quantum identifiers can be introduced into the MIN architecture, creating a Q-MIN that supports quantum identifiers (Li et al. 2023). This approach enhances the competitiveness of MINs in the quantum era, representing explorations and experiments in future quantum network communications.

Since the MIN is a system built on classical communication methods, and there are fundamental differences between the physical implementations of classical and quantum communication, the Q-MIN requires the construction of a hybrid network that integrates classical and quantum networks. This means that both classical and quantum communication hardware will need to be used simultaneously, along with the provision of corresponding software support to ensure the interoperability of the two network technologies. Specifically, the following hardware and software conditions are necessary:

Hardware Condition 1: Classical communication hardware devices that support the MIN

Software Condition 1: Software systems for MIN, including the multi-identifier system (MIS) the software systems for the multi-identifier router (MIR)

Hardware Condition 2: Hardware devices that support the preparation, distribution, and measurement of qubits

Software Condition 2: A software system capable of managing and controlling the hardware devices specified in Hardware Condition 1

In addition to the four independent requirements mentioned above, the quantum and classical systems must also be able to collaborate with each other and meet normal communication requirements. This collaboration necessitates the integration of classical hardware and software with quantum hardware and software. Therefore, in the Q-MIN, the MIR becomes the quantum multi-identifier router (Q-MIR), which supports quantum identifiers, and the MIS becomes the quantum multi-identifier system (Q-MIS), also designed to support quantum identifiers.

Based on the above description, the Q-MIN supports progressive deployment on the existing MIN, ensuring that quantum communication and classical communication within the MIN do not interfere with each other. A deployment example is shown in Figure 7.30.

As shown in Figure 7.31, the classical MIN utilizes a TLV encoding scheme for MIN packets. This scheme offers significant extensibility and flexibility, allowing

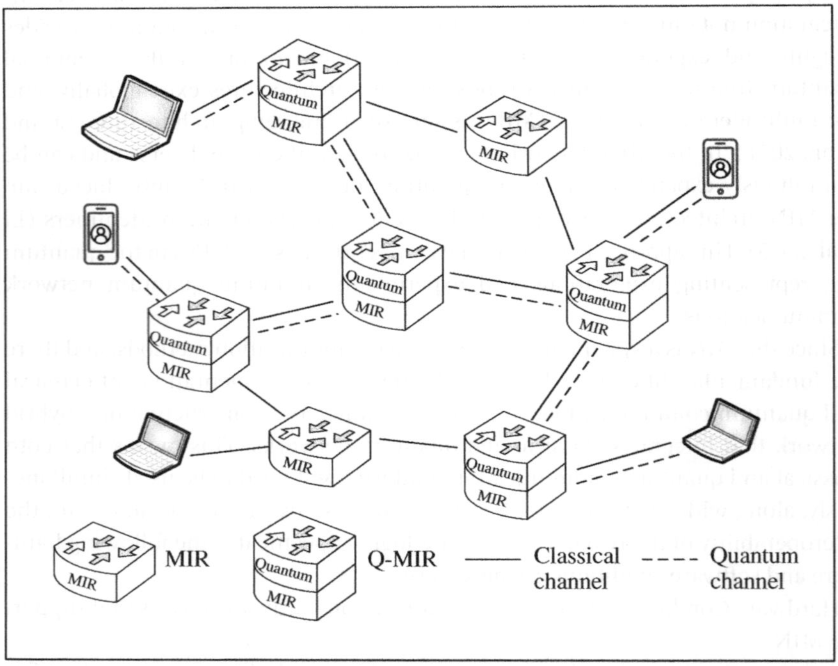

Figure 7.30 Example of overlapping deployment of classical MIN and Q-MIN.

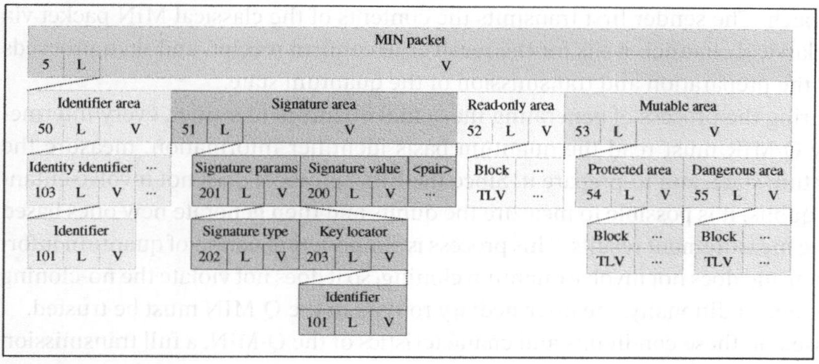

Figure 7.31 General format of MIN packet.

for the addition or removal of content as needed. Different TLV blocks can also be combined to form more comprehensive information expressions. The Q-MIN adopts this scheme and introduces improvements in two key areas: the identifier area and the signature area.

The identifier area contains multiple network identifiers, with the Type and Length of each identifier determined based on actual requirements. In the Q-MIN, the modification to the identifier area includes the addition of a new identifier type, namely the quantum identifier. The signature area contains one or more digital signatures, typically involving signatures for the identifier area and the read-only area. Each signature includes two TLV blocks: the metadata for the signature and the signature result. Since the identifier area varies, the Q-MIN also differs in the signature area. Q-MIN signs both the identifier area and the read-only area separately, then combines all the signature TLV blocks to form the signature area of the Q-MIN packet. The aforementioned improvements to the identifier and signature areas align with the basic principles of the MIN regarding the registration of new identifiers and the store-and-forward mechanism of routers, and they can be correctly read, recognized, and processed by Q-MIS and Q-MIR.

The concept of a quantum identifier currently lacks a formal definition. In this section, we provide an example of a quantum identifier based on the BB84 protocol. The BB84 protocol leverages quantum measurement collapse and the no-cloning theorem to ensure the security of key generation. Q-MIN uses this security feature to designate the quantum key generated by the protocol as a quantum identifier. Additionally, since communication is required between both parties before the quantum key is generated, the quantum basis sequence is used as a temporary identifier prior to the creation of the actual quantum identifier.

Given the potential communication time delay between the two channels, the transmission of classical and quantum information follows a "stop-and-wait" approach. The sender first transmits the contents of the classical MIN packet via the classical channel, waits for the receiver to confirm receipt, and then proceeds with the preparation and transmission of the quantum state.

During the process of generating the actual quantum identifier, every intermediary Q-MIR must read the quantum basis identifier information, measure the quantum state, and re-prepare it. Since the BB84 protocol does not involve entangled qubits, it is possible to measure the qubits and then generate new ones based on the measurement results. This process is simply a replication of quantum information and does not involve quantum cloning, so it does not violate the no-cloning theorem. Additionally, the intermediary routers in the Q-MIN must be trusted.

Based on these conditions and characteristics of the Q-MIN, a full transmission process is illustrated in Figure 7.32.

Step 1 (Optional): The newly added user requests their quantum identifier information from Q-MIS, including the quantum basis identifier and quantum identifier.

Step 2: The sender packages the information to be sent and adds the randomly generated quantum basis sequence as a quantum basis identifier to the Identifier area in the MIN packet. The sender should also sign the quantum basis identifier and the contents of the read-only field. The intermediary router Q-MIR will re-sign the modified identifier area and add these signatures to the signature area of the MIN packet. The final MIN packet is then sent to the receiver.

Step 3: Upon receiving the MIN packet, the receiver will verify the signatures and other relevant information. Based on the Type field in the identifier section, the receiver will also recognize that the MIN packet requires the complete quantum identifier, but the corresponding qubits have not yet been transmitted. The receiver will then send a request to the sender, stating "MIN packet received, please provide quantum state information."

Step 4: The sender utilizes its quantum identifier and the stored quantum basis sequence to prepare the corresponding quantum state and transmits it to the receiver.

Step 5: The receiver decodes the actual information of the quantum identifier based on the quantum basis data in the received MIN packet. Next:

Step 5.1: Verify whether the original sender's public key is available.

Step 5.1.1: If the public key is not available, the current receiver requests Q-MIS to download the identity and public key information of the original sender.

Step 5.1.1.1: If the retrieval is successful, proceed to step 5.2.

Step 5.1.1.2: If the retrieval fails, proceed to step 5.3.

Step 5.1.2: If the public key is available, proceed to step 5.2.

Step 5.2: Use the available public key to verify the signature. If the signature verification is successful, proceed to step 6. If the verification fails, proceed to step 5.3.

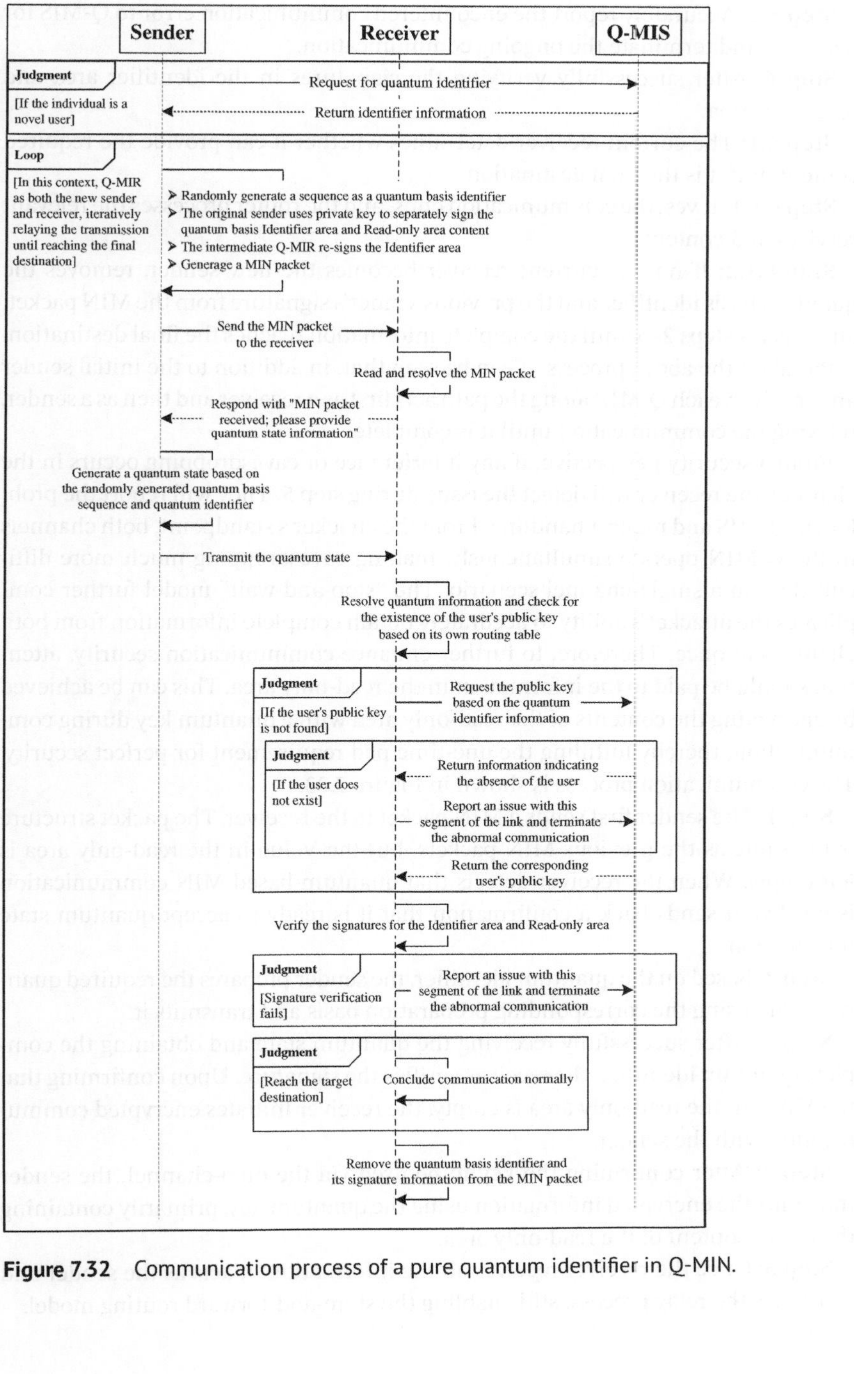

Figure 7.32 Communication process of a pure quantum identifier in Q-MIN.

Step 5.3: Accurately report the encountered communication error to Q-MIS for handling and terminate the ongoing communication.

Step 6: After successfully verifying the signatures in the identifier area and read-only area:

Step 6.1: The current receiver determines whether it can provide the required content or if it is the final destination.

Step 6.1.1: If yes, the communication ends, and the router processes the relevant services and content.

Step 6.1.2: If no, the current receiver becomes the new sender, removes the quantum basis identifier and the previous sender's signature from the MIN packet, and repeats steps 2–6 until the complete information reaches the final destination.

Based on the above process, it can be seen that, in addition to the initial sender and receiver, each Q-MIR along the path acts first as a receiver and then as a sender, relaying the communication until it is complete.

From a security perspective, if any interference or eavesdropping occurs in the channel, the receiver will detect the issue during step 5. They will report the problem to Q-MIS and request handling. From the attacker's standpoint, both channels in the Q-MIN operate simultaneously, making eavesdropping much more difficult than in a single-channel scenario. The "stop-and-wait" model further complicates the attacker's ability to accurately obtain complete information from both channels at once. Therefore, to further enhance communication security, attention should be paid to the information in the read-only area. This can be achieved by encrypting the contents of the read-only area with a quantum key during communication, thereby fulfilling the one-time pad requirement for perfect security. The communication process is shown in Figure 7.33.

Step 1: The sender first sends a MIN packet to the receiver. The packet structure is the same as the previous MIN packets, but the Value in the read-only area is left empty. When the receiver detects that quantum-based MIN communication is needed, it sends back a confirmation that it is ready to accept quantum state information.

Step 2: Based on the quantum identifier, the sender prepares the required quantum state using the corresponding preparation basis and transmits it.

Step 3: After successfully receiving the quantum state and obtaining the complete quantum identifier, the receiver verifies the signature. Upon confirming that the Value in the read-only area is empty, the receiver initiates encrypted communication with the sender.

Step 4: After confirming the key to be used via the dual-channel, the sender transmits the encrypted information using the quantum key, primarily containing the entire content of the read-only area.

Step 5: Once the receiver receives all the information, it acts as the sender and continues the relay process, still enabling the store-and-forward routing model.

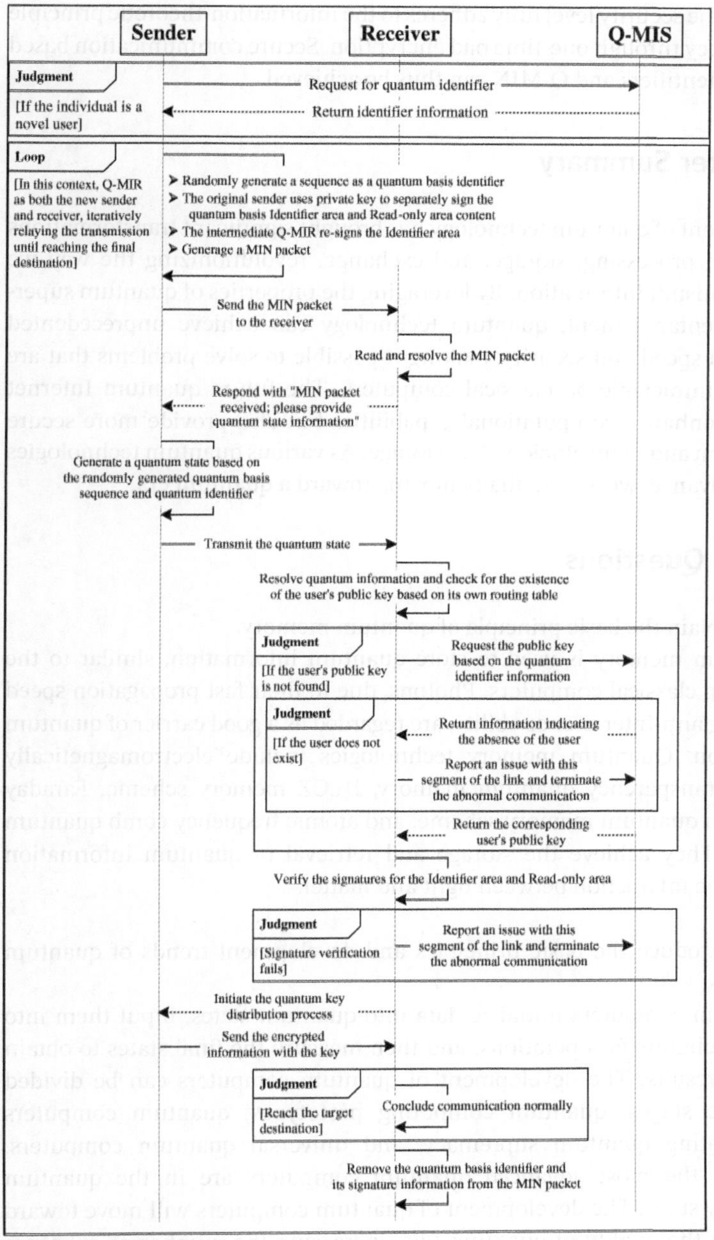

Figure 7.33 Communication of a quantum identifier in Q-MIN with one-time pad.

In this way, the security level fully adheres to the information-theoretic principle of perfect secrecy through one-time pad encryption. Secure communication based on quantum identifiers and Q-MIN can thus be achieved.

7.5 Chapter Summary

The development of quantum technology has brought significant transformations to information processing, storage, and exchange, revolutionizing the way we handle and transmit information. By leveraging the properties of quantum superposition and entanglement, quantum technology can achieve unprecedented computational speed and security, making it possible to solve problems that are inefficient or intractable on classical computers. The future quantum Internet will not only enhance computational capabilities but also provide more secure communication and more efficient data storage. As various quantum technologies continue to advance, we are gradually moving toward a quantum era.

Discussion Questions

1 Briefly explain the basic principle of quantum memory.

Quantum memory is used to store quantum information, similar to the memory in classical computers. Photons, due to their fast propagation speed and strong anti-interference ability, are regarded as a good carrier of quantum information. Quantum memory technologies include electromagnetically induced transparency quantum memory, DLCZ memory scheme, Faraday interaction quantum memory scheme, and atomic frequency comb quantum memory. They achieve the storage and retrieval of quantum information through the interaction between light and matter.

2 Briefly introduce the basic principles and development trends of quantum computers.

Quantum computers initialize data into quantum states, input them into quantum circuits for operations, and then measure the final states to obtain the final results. The development of quantum computers can be divided into three stages: quantum computing prototypes, quantum computers demonstrating quantum supremacy, and universal quantum computers. Currently, the most advanced quantum computers are in the quantum supremacy stage. The development of quantum computers will move toward improving the quality of quantum bits, increasing the number of quantum bits, and developing effective error correction and fault-tolerance strategies. In the future, quantum computers will play a significant role in scientific research, cryptography, AI, and other fields, completely transforming the existing computing paradigm.

3 **Briefly summarize the principle and significance of quantum teleportation.**

Quantum teleportation is a quantum information transmission technology that enables the transfer of the information of a quantum state from one location to another without the actual physical transmission of the carrier. Alice and Bob share a pair of entangled qubits. Alice performs operations on the qubit to be transmitted and the shared entangled qubit, and then sends the measurement results to Bob through a classical channel. Bob then operates on his qubit based on the measurement results, thereby achieving the transmission of the quantum state. Quantum teleportation is of great significance in fields such as quantum communication and quantum computing. It can realize the remote transmission of quantum bits and provide support for the construction of distributed quantum computing and quantum networks. In addition, quantum teleportation can also be applied in areas such as quantum encryption, enhancing the security of communication.

References

Afzelius, M., Simon, C., De Riedmatten, H. and Gisin, N., 2009. Multimode quantum memory based on atomic frequency combs. Physical Review A, 79(5), 052329.

Arute, F., Arya, K., Babbush, R., et al., 2019. Quantum supremacy using a pro-grammable superconducting processor. Nature, 574(7779), pp. 505–510.

Atom computing, Quantum startup atom computing first to exceed 1,000 qubits. 2023. https://atom-computing.com/quantum-startup-atom-computing-first-to-exceed-1000-qubits/

Bennett, C.H. and Brassard, G., 2014. Quantum cryptography: Public key distribution and coin tossing. Theoretical Computer Science, 560, pp. 7–11.

Bennett, C.H. and Wiesner, S.J., 1992. Communication via one-and two-particle operators on Einstein-Podolsky-Rosen states. Physical Review Letters, 69(20), p. 2881.

Bennett, C.H., Brassard, G. and Mermin, N.D., 1992. Quantum cryptography without Bell's theorem. Physical Review Letters, 68(5), p. 557.

Bernhardt, C., 2019. Quantum computing for everyone. Mit Press.

Bouwmeester, D., Pan, J.W., Mattle, K., et al., 1997. Experimental quantum teleportation. Nature, 390(6660), pp. 575–579.

Cerezo, M., Verdon, G., Huang, H.Y., Cincio, L. and Coles, P.J., 2022. Challenges and opportunities in quantum machine learning. Nature Computational Science, 2(9), pp. 567–576.

Chanelière, T., Matsukevich, D.N., Jenkins, S.D., et al., 2005. Storage and retrieval of single photons transmitted between remote quantum memories. Nature, 438(7069), pp. 833–836.

Dahlberg, A., Skrzypczyk, M., Coopmans, T., Wubben, L., Rozpędek, F., Pompili, M., Stolk, A., Pawełczak, P., Knegjens, R., de Oliveira Filho, J. and Hanson, R., 2019. A link layer protocol for quantum networks. In Proceedings of the ACM special interest group on data communication (pp. 159–173).

Deng, Y.H., Gu, Y.C., Liu, H.L., et al., 2023. Gaussian boson sampling with pseudo-photon-number resolving detectors and quantum computational advantage. Physical Review Letters, 150601.

Deutsch, D., 1985. Quantum theory, the Church–Turing principle and the universal quantum computer. Proceedings of the Royal Society of London A. Mathematical and Physical Sciences, 400(1818), pp. 97–117.

Duan, L.M., Lukin, M.D., Cirac, J.I. and Zoller, P., 2001. Long-distance quantum communication with atomic ensembles and linear optics. Nature, 414(6862), pp. 413–418.

Ekert, A.K., 1991. Quantum cryptography based on Bell's theorem. Physical Review Letters, 67(6), p. 661.

Gambetta, J., 2023. The hardware and software for the era of quantum utility is here.

Gyongyosi, L. and Imre, S., 2022. Advances in the quantum Internet. Communications of the ACM, 65(8), pp. 52–63.

Han, F., He, M., Zhang, X.C. and Bao, S., 2021. Blockchain and the Wealth of Nations: Future Wealth Based on Global Credit Algorithm Consensus. China Machine Press.

Hermans, S.L.N., Pompili, M., Beukers, H.K.C., et al., 2022. Qubit teleportation between non-neighbouring nodes in a quantum network. Nature, 605(7911), pp. 663–668.

Illiano, J., Caleffi, M., Manzalini, A. and Cacciapuoti, A.S., 2022. Quantum Internet protocol stack: A comprehensive survey. Computer Networks, 213, 109092.

Julsgaard, B., Sherson, J., Cirac, J.I., Fiurášek, J. and Polzik, E.S., 2004. Experimental demonstration of quantum memory for light. Nature, 432(7016), pp. 482–486.

Li, H. and Yang, X., 2021. Co-governed Sovereignty Network: Legal Basis and Its Prototype & Applications with MIN Architecture. Springer Nature.

Li, H., Meng, X.Z., Lin, L.H., Wang, F., Yao, Y., Wang, X.P., Wang, B., Zhang, H.Y., Hou, H.X., Ma, H.J. and Zhang Z., 2023. A High-Security Communication System with Quantum Identifier Routing and Addressing in the Network Layer. Chinese Patent No. CN116527248A.

Liu, Y., Zhang, W.J., Jiang, C., et al., 2023. Experimental twin-field quantum key distribution over 1000 km fiber distance. Physical Review Letters, 130(21), 210801.

Lo, H.K. and Chau, H.F., 1999. Unconditional security of quantum key distribution over arbitrarily long distances. Science, 283(5410), pp. 2050–2056.

Lu, C.Y., Cao, Y., Peng, C.Z. and Pan, J.W., 2022. Micius quantum experiments in space. Reviews of Modern Physics, 94(3), 035001.

Monroe, C., Leibfried, D., King, B., et al., 1997. Simplified quantum logic with trapped ions. Physical Review A, 55(4), p. R2489.

Ni, Z., Li, S., Deng, X., et al., 2023. Beating the break-even point with a discrete-variable-encoded logical qubit. Nature, 616(7955), pp. 56–60.

Postler, L., Heußen, S., Pogorelov, I., et al., 2022. Demonstration of fault-tolerant universal quantum gate operations. Nature, 605(7911), pp. 675–680.

Shor, P.W., 1994. Algorithms for quantum computation: discrete logarithms and factoring. In Proceedings 35th annual symposium on foundations of computer science (pp. 124–134). IEEE.

Shor, P.W., 1995. Scheme for reducing decoherence in quantum computer memory. Physical Review A, 52(4), p. R2493.

Singh, A., Dev, K., Siljak, H., Joshi, H.D. and Magarini, M., 2021. Quantum Internet - applications, functionalities, enabling technologies, challenges, and research directions. IEEE Communications Surveys & Tutorials, 23(4), pp. 2218–2247.

Singh, K., Anand, S., Pocklington, A., Kemp, J.T. and Bernien, H., 2022. Dual-element, two-dimensional atom array with continuous-mode operation. Physical Review X, 12(1), 011040.

Swan, M., Dos Santos, R.P. and Witte, F., 2020. Quantum computing: physics, blockchains, and deep learning smart networks. World Scientific, pp. 29–40.

Tonomura, A., Endo, J., Matsuda, T., Kawasaki, T. and Ezawa, H., 1989. Demonstration of single-electron buildup of an interference pattern. American Journal of Physics, 57(2), pp. 117–120.

Wehner, S., Elkouss, D. and Hanson, R., 2018. Quantum Internet: A vision for the road ahead. Science, 362(6412), eaam9288.

Wei, S.H., Jing, B., Zhang, X.Y., et al., 2022. Towards real-world quantum networks: a review. Laser & Photonics Reviews, 16(3), p. 2100219.

Wilde, M.M., 2011. From classical to quantum Shannon theory. arXiv preprint arXiv:1106.1445, pp. 39–55.

Yin, J., Ren, J.G., Lu, H., et al., 2012. Quantum teleportation and entanglement distribution over 100-kilometre free-space channels. Nature, 488(7410), pp. 185–188.

Yuan, L.F., 2022. A Brief Introduction to Quantum Information for Everyone to Understand the New Scientific Revolution. University of Science and Technology of China Press.

Zhong, H.S., Wang, H., Deng, Y.H., et al., 2020. Quantum computational advantage using photons. Science, 370(6523), pp. 1460–1463.

Index

Distributed Storage in Practice, First Edition. Hui Li, Hanxu Hou, and Hong Tan.

b

c

Printed and bound by CPI Group (UK) Ltd, Croydon, CR0 4YY

17/09/2026

14964234-0004